Stirling Castle, late 1930s.
(Courtesy of A&SH Regimental Museum)

MOON OVER MALAYA

A Tale of Argylls and Marines

Jonathan Moffatt and Audrey Holmes McCormick

COOMBE PUBLISHING

1999

Contents

INTRODUCTION III

ACKNOWLEDGEMENTS IV

ABBREVIATIONS VII

CHAPTER ONE THE SOLDIERS I

CHAPTER TWO THE BATTLES IN THE NORTH –
DECEMBER 1941 43

CHAPTER THREE SLIM RIVER DISASTER – JANUARY 7th 1942 78

CHAPTER FOUR RETREAT, REORGANISATION AND ESCAPE 97

CHAPTER FIVE THE PLYMOUTH ARGYLLS: THE BATTLE FOR SINGAPORE
FEBRUARY 8th–15th 1942 109

CHAPTER SIX "INTREPID AGAINST ALL ADVERSITY" –
JAPANESE CAPTIVITY 143

CHAPTER SEVEN HOMEWARD BOUND AND AFTER 189

ILLUSTRATIONS *between pages* 77-78; 108-109; 143; 203-204

SONG MOON OVER MALAYA *at the end of first plate section (77-78)*

ROLL OF HONOUR 2ND ARGYLL AND SUTHERLAND HIGHLANDERS 204
PLYMOUTH ARGYLL ROYAL MARINES 219

WREATH LAYING 221

BIBLIOGRAPHY 222

INDEX 224

INTRODUCTION

'I expected terrible forfeits in the East, but all this would be merely a passing phase… there was no more doubt about the end,' wrote Winston Churchill in his History of the Second World War of the news of the Japanese attack on Pearl Harbour and the entry of the USA into the war.

This was more than 'a passing phase' in the lives of the men of the 2nd Argyll and Sutherland Highlanders and Plymouth Argyll Royal Marines in Malaya and Singapore. This is the first time so many of them have spoken so plainly about their fighting experiences in the Malayan Campaign.

A Royal Marine told us that he was looking into things he had preferred to forget. Now he found he wanted to know more: he wanted to understand what had happened all those years ago. An Argyll said, 'If you start remembering how people suffered, it is as if it was yesterday.'

Now they did wish to talk about their experiences.

ACKNOWLEDGEMENTS

We are particularly indebted to the following for their help:

Brigadier A.D.R.G. (David) Wilson CBE, for his advice and lively recollections of the events following the Slim River disaster; Lt Colonel Alastair Scott Elliot, Regimental Secretary A&SH, Stirling Castle; Mrs Rena McRobbie and also the Museum Staff, particularly the Assistant Curator Roderick Mackenzie and Archie Wilson; Lt Colonel John Lauder of the West of Scotland Argyll Association for all generously giving a good deal of time to assist our enquiries. Also the Rev.Dr.Ernest Gordon, Major Derrick Montgomery-Campbell, Major Eric Moss, Major Ian Stonor MBE, the Rev. Hartley Beattie, Captain Kenneth I. McLeod, Captain Jimmy McLean and the late Captain Richard Webber; Jockie Bell, Albert 'Civvy' Cameron, John Carter, Duncan Ferguson, John Hunter, Joe Lonsdale, Alex McDougall, Finlay McLachlan, Fred Murray, Stan Roberts, Bob Ramsay, William 'Hooky' Walker, the late Tom Wardrope, all 2nd Argylls in Malaya, with the late Major James 'Doc' Doherty MBE, former Battalion Quartermaster, for his encouraging words. Also Henry Steuart Fothringham OBE of Grantully, Malky Waugh, Dick Lee, Sandy McDougall, B.D. 'Bob' McCutcheon of Stirling, and Alex Bean with strong Argyll connections. And Mrs Rose Denny (RSM McTavish's daughter); Mrs. Kathy Russell and Mrs. Peggy Thomson (widows of Joe Russell and Billy Thomson); Peter Carruthers (son of the late Alec Carruthers 2 A&SH) Julie Buchanan of Callander, with the music of 'Moon over Malaya' and her sister Moira; Paul Gibbs Pancheri of the Straits Settlement Volunteer Force (SSVF); the Rev. Geoffrey Mowat, Malay Civil Service and Federated Malay States Volunteer Force (FMSVF); Professor Emeritus J.B. Mackie OBE of New Zealand and Ernest A. Barron, both FMSVF officers; Alex Mackenzie, a Volunteer Sapper in Malaya; John Hedley (Johore Volunteer Engineers/1st Mysore Infantry), and the late K.J. Archer, FMS Armoured Car Regiment. Also Dr. Ian MacNicol of Appin Historical Society, Argyll; Jack McPherson (son of the late J.W. McPherson DSM RM); M.G. Little (Archivist RM Museum, Southsea); David Tan of Singapore; Plymouth Argyll Royal Marines Terry Brooks, Peter Dunstan, Maurice Edwards, Charles Miller, Tom Webber, Jack Wren and Peers Crompton; former Malayan Police officers Douglas Weir (also 2 A&SH) and Colin Woolhouse; Chye Kooi Loong, Malaysian military historian; Peter Bruton, Alexandra Hospital historian; former FEPOWs Arthur Lane, 1st Manchesters; Les Dennison, RASC; Arthur Titherington, Royal Signals; John Wyatt, East Surreys; Walter Green, RAF Singapore; Alex Richards RM; Len Chandler RM, Captain Derek Oakley MBE RM and Major A.M. Fradgley MBE RE – all of whom corresponded with us in varying degrees.

Thanks to the Imperial War Museum and also to many of those above mentioned, for photographs of the Argylls in Malaya and of the Prince of Wales Royal Marines; to Singapore National Archives and National Library; the Commonwealth War Graves Commission; the Public Records Office; Maps courtesy of Thomas Nelson & Sons Limited. Originaly in Brigadier Stewart's 1947 *History of A & SH in Malaya*; the Paisley Daily Express; Erskine Hospital; to our designer, Tom Bee and to our respective partners for their great assistance and patience given to us in this project.

Audrey Holmes McCormick was born in Singapore and was evacuated in 1941. She has been a professional journalist, TV researcher and producer, and made BBC TV's documentary *The Kilt in Warfare*. She has family links in the Argylls, and lived in Stirling. She is currently researching the Volunteer Forces of Malaya and the Straits Settlements, now Malaysia and Singapore.

Jonathan Moffatt studied at Warwick University and has taught History in the U.K and at a leading Singapore school. He is a member of the Royal Marines Historical Society and writes for their journal Sheet Anchor.

Published in 1999 by Coombe Publishing
Fax: (UK) 01203 545 013
Designed by Tom Bee
Printed by Bell & Bain, Glasgow
Cover photographs courtesy of the Imperial War Museum.
Main Image: Captain Tam Slessor on his motorbike with Lanchester Armoured Car.
Inset Image: March past on the Mersing march. Ian Stewart (right), Captain Beckett (left),
RSM Munnoch (centre).

© 1999 Jonathan Moffatt/Audrey Holmes McCormick

MOON OVER MALAYA

A Tale of Argylls and Marines

ABBREVIATIONS

ADC	Aide-de-camp (an officer assisting a senior officer)
AIF	Australian Imperial Forces
CO	Commanding Officer (as of a battalion)
2 i/c	Second in Command
CB	Confined to Barracks
Cpl	Corporal
C.Sgt	Colour Sergeant
CSM	Company Sergeant Major
Don-R	Dispatch Rider
FEPOW	Far East Prisoner of War
FMSVF	Federated Malay States Volunteer Force
GSO	General Staff Officer (variously numbered according to function e.g. GSO2
HMS	His/Her Majesty's Ship
HMAS	His/Her Majesty's Australian Ship
IAMS	Indian Army Medical Service
INA	Indian National Army
JVE	Johore Volunteer Engineers
L.Cpl	Lance Corporal
Lt	Lieutenant
2nd Lt	Second Lieutenant
Lt Colonel	Lieutenant Colonel
L.Sgt	Lance Sergeant
MCS	Malayan Civil Service
MO	Medical Officer
MP	Military Police
MPAJA	Malayan People's Anti-Japanese Army
MT	Motor Transport
NCO	Non-Commissioned Officer
OC	Officer Commanding (as of a Company)
ORs	Other Ranks
POW	Prisoner of War
PSM	Platoon Sergeant Major
PWD	Public Works Department
QMS	Quartermaster Sergeant
RA	Royal Artillery
RAMC	Royal Army Medical Corps
RAPWI	Rehabilitation of Allied Prisoners of War and Internees organisation
RE	Royal Engineers
RM	Royal Marines
RQMS	Regimental Quartermaster Sergeant
RSM	Regimental Sergeant Major
Sgt	Sergeant
SSVF	Straits Settlement Volunteer Force

CHAPTER ONE

THE SOLDIERS

They were a Highland Regiment, first raised in the glens of Sutherland, and embodied at Inverness 200 years ago. But when the Second World War arrived their ranks contained many of the sons of Scotland's industrial belt, and 'Geordie' boys from Newcastle and County Durham. Their fierce reputation in battle was forged in the 1850s at Balaclava in the Crimea and at the Relief of Lucknow in the Indian Mutiny. They arrived in Singapore from India in 1939 and it was in Malaya that a Highland Laird called Ian Stewart created an effective jungle fighting force from a tough bunch of streetwise young men, many of them from broken homes, drawing them together in absolute loyalty. This was the 93rd Sutherland Highlanders, which duly became the 2nd Battalion of the Argyll and Sutherland Highlanders, still referred to as 'the Old 93rd'.

IAN MCALISTER STEWART, 13th Laird of Achnacone and a member of Clan Appin, was no ordinary soldier. He came from an old Scottish Highland military family. His ancestors had fought against the English at the battles of Flodden in 1513 and Culloden in 1746. Two sons of the 6th Laird, Alexander and Duncan Stewart, were killed at Culloden. One ancestor had served with Admiral Nelson at the great sea victory of Copenhagen and another had been killed fighting the French in the Peninsular War.

The family home since the 1540s, a small but attractive residence, is still situated at Achnacone, just south of Appin village, about halfway up the coast of Argyll between Connel Ferry and Ballachulish. In the house is a jacket that once belonged to Bonnie Prince Charlie.

Clan Appin, like most Highland clans, was divided into five parts: Stewart of Appin (the Chief), Stewart of Ardshiel, Stewart of Invernahyle, Stewart of Fasnacloich and Stewart of Achnacone (in Gaelic this means 'a very narrow place'). The title was hereditary and the Chiefs were known as Lairds or Tacksmen.

Ian Stewart was born at Sirur, India on October 17th 1895, the third son of Alexander Stewart, a medical officer serving with the Poona Horse. Alexander, also born in India, was a keen Rugby player who captained the Edinburgh University team and twice played for Scotland against England. He also captained the Poona Horse polo team. In 1880 he served in the campaign in Afghanistan and was at the siege of Kandahar.

Alexander Stewart was twice married: his first wife Harriet died in childbirth and a few years later he married Ian's mother, Annie. Alexander retired from the Indian Medical Service in 1897 with the rank of Lt Colonel and returned to the family estate at Achnacone where he spent much of his retirement researching, writing the family history, and involving himself in the affairs of the local community. He was also a Commissioner of Income Tax for Argyll. The family was strict Episcopalian and Ian was a teetotaller.

Educated at a British public school, Cheltenham, and at Sandhurst Military Academy, Ian Stewart in 1913 became the youngest officer in the British Army, joining the 2nd Argyll and Sutherland Highlanders at Fort George in northeast Scotland. In August 1914, as an eighteen-year-old platoon commander, he was the first British officer to land on French soil and the first to be mentioned in dispatches. As his subsequent career was to show, Ian Stewart did not lack a sense of history.

Leading a charge on a German position in the First World War battle of Le Cattier, claymore in hand, he suffered the indignity of tripping over his sword scabbard and being turned over by a distressed platoon sergeant, shaking his head with the words: "Poor wee laddie!"

There is a story that when a fellow officer lost all his equipment, Ian Stewart made a gesture more romantic than practical: he gave him his own revolver but retained the sword.

In the retreat from Mons in 1914, Stewart and his men were cut off from the battalion. Showing the same determination and initiative that was to characterise his later career, he hi-jacked a train and returned his men safely to friendly territory. He may well have witnessed the famous Christmas 1914 football match with the Germans in no-man's land for he had a photo at his home in Achnacone of these German footballers.

Badly wounded in 1915 he was awarded the Military Cross and, in 1917, a Bar to his MC. There was a further mention in dispatches. He had been so badly wounded that he was told he would never again serve in the Infantry. On his recovery, Stewart was sent to the newly formed Tank Corps as a staff captain to Major-General J.F.C. 'Boney' Fuller. In 1917, Stewart participated in the highly successful tank attack at Cambrai by Brigadier Hugh Elles' First Tank Brigade where he observed the vulnerability of infantry to attack from well co-ordinated armoured vehicles.

Ian's elder brother Alexander Dugald distinguished himself serving with the Gordon Highlanders. During the retreat from Mons he saved the life of his commanding officer and was recommended for the Victoria Cross but because of the controversial surrender of the Gordons the award did not materialise and he received an MC instead. Released by the Germans in 1918, Captain Alexander Stewart was killed in a road accident while serving with the Gordon Highlanders in Dublin. This family tragedy put Ian Stewart in line for the title of Laird of Achnacone, which he was to inherit on the death of his father in February 1945.

Between the wars Ian Stewart served with the Argylls in the West Indies, Peking, Hong Kong, Shanghai and India. In 1925 he commanded B Company on the Isle of Wight. His health in the years after the First World War was uncertain; he was on the Sick List, then retired on half-pay and at one stage he came close to discharge on medical grounds. The battalion moved to the West Indies in 1926, was ordered to China in 1929, then on to Hong Kong.

In Shanghai in 1932 as part of the International Force that guarded the International Settlement the then Captain Stewart had his first successful encounter with the Japanese. At that time the Japanese Navy was making an abortive attempt to take Shanghai. Stewart captured a whole truckload of Japanese marines that had entered the Shanghai international zone.

In Hong Kong he owned and rode a racehorse 'Mistake the Second' that became something of a legend. Although well over six feet tall, Stewart was extremely thin and by this time very fit. He proved a successful jockey.[1]

Ian Stewart refused a place at Staff College; he never had a high opinion of staff officers and later in life would write asides on his letters "Not bad for a chap who didn't go to Staff College."[2]

He was commanding officer at the Regimental Headquarters, Stirling Castle from 1934 to 1937. Here he earned a reputation for his consideration for the Jocks, introducing such comforts as a hot water system and a cup of tea after lunch. Cups or rather mugs of tea were later to play no small part in Ian Stewart's jungle training programme in Malaya.

In 1937, before his departure for India to join the 2nd battalion, Ian Stewart married Ursula Morley-Fletcher, the niece and secretary of the Duchess of Atholl. Ursula was English and came from a Christian Scientist family who lived in Surrey. Ian and Ursula's first daughter, Marigold Almond, born in London, died in infancy at Trimulgherry, India of gastro-enteritis. A second daughter, Cherry Linnhe, was to be born in Singapore General Hospital in June 1940.

The 2nd Argylls had come to India from China in 1934 and was based at Rawalpindi. In 1937 the Fakir of Ipi incited the Pathans of Waziristan to attack the British and started distance raiding. The Argylls were sent to Coronation Camp in North Waziristan on the North-West Frontier and thus saw action against fierce Pathan warriors on the desert plains of the Deccan. A most inhospitable place to fight.

In 1937 twenty year old Pte Tom Wardrope arriving after a voyage from Southampton was met at Rawalpindi railway station by the orderly sergeant and marched to the barracks. Two weeks later he was on active service in Waziristan where the sun was so hot that eggs could be fried on the rocks and scorpions and dysentery were as feared as the Pathans.[3]

In the European war scare of September 1938 the battalion, now based at Secunderabad, was ordered to prepare for departure to Malaya. They were already entraining at Madras when news came through of the Munich Conference and British Prime Minister Neville Chamberlain's "Peace for our time" deal with Germany's dictator Adolph Hitler. Their move was halted. The following year the Argylls, having been converted to a mechanised machine-gun battalion, returned to their former status as a rifle battalion and with war now clearly imminent prepared to depart from Trimulgherry Fort, near Secunderabad in southern India, for Malaya. However, many, including half the officers and more than half of the Sergeants and Warrant Officers, were to return to the UK either before departure to Singapore or soon after arrival, their time with the battalion having expired.

Most of those coming to Malaya were mature, unmarried soldiers aged 25 and over with several years of service behind them. A few like Ptes 'Civvy' Cameron and his friend James Ramsay were in Boy Service. Civvy was born in Dundee and went to primary school in Grandtully, Perthshire before getting a job as an egg tester on the Dunnach estate while his elder sister worked in service in the 'big house' on the estate. Following the death of his father, 15 year old Civvy joined the Argylls in January 1938 in Oban, Argyllshire. He was sent to Stirling Castle and later joined the 1st Argylls at Aldershot. Boy soldiers received an education as well as drill and military training. They got lower pay than other Privates and had a choice of being a drummer or piper. Civvy chose to be a drummer. After a year with the 1st Battalion he was sent to India to join the 2nd Argylls and celebrated his sixteenth birthday in Bombay docks. At eighteen he went into Man Service.[4]

Boy Ramsay "a big strapping red haired fellow" was even younger when his mother brought him up to Stirling Castle and he joined the Argylls – fourteen years old, coming to Malaya aged eighteen. He was later to die in Changi POW camp's Roberts Hospital.

The battalion formed part of 12th Indian Infantry Brigade, formerly known as the Secunderabad Light Infantry Brigade, based at Secunderabad in the independent southern Indian State of Hyderabad. Most of the 2nd Argylls arrived at Singapore on the SS Egra, which departed Madras on August 3rd 1939 on a choppy five-day voyage, arriving at Singapore on August 8th. Others embarked on the SS Karagola, which departed Calcutta on September 15th, reaching Singapore on September 28th.[5] The battalion was initially accommodated with the Loyals in Alexandra Barracks on a low hillside overlooking Keppel Harbour.[6]

Ian Stewart arrived in Malaya from India on August 25th 1939 as 2 i/c 2nd Argyll and Sutherland Highlanders with clear ideas about mobility that derived from his experiences in the First World War, together with some experimental ideas about jungle tactics. The battalion's commanding officer was the dashing Lt Colonel Hector Greenfield who returned to the UK on February 20th 1940 to take command of 15th Brigade. Stewart was appointed battalion commander in his place.

The officers of the battalion came mainly from south of Scotland's Highland faultline, some even from south of the border. David Boyle, who later commanded D Company, was the son of an Air Commodore from Guildford though his uncle was the Earl of Glasgow. Sandhurst-trained, 'the Big Boyle' rose very fast in the Argylls and had the reputation for a sharp mind. He arrived in a 1940 draft and Stewart was clearly impressed by him for in April 1941 Boyle was promoted straight from 2nd Lieutenant to Captain and Company Commander.

Several officers were university graduates or had interrupted university studies to join up with the approach of war: Adjutant Angus MacDonald educated at Winchester and Magdalen College, Oxford; subsequent Adjutant Ranuld Beckett, educated at Glenalmond and Oxford University; Mike Bardwell of Stowe and Jesus College, Cambridge; Bill McLean and Ernest Gordon were St Andrews undergraduates.[7]

The other ranks, known as the Jocks, were mainly recruited from the industrial belt between the Forth and the Clyde: from Falkirk, Stirling, Edinburgh and Port Glasgow.[8] These were areas haunted by poverty and many were from broken or deprived homes. As many as 40% were orphans or were not in touch with their real parents. Others came from more rural areas further north – from attractive lochside towns like Dunoon, Lochgilphead and Sandbank as well as outlying Argyllshire farming communities. Originally, from the 1790s until 1883, the battalion had recruited almost entirely from Gaelic speaking Highlanders and commands had to be given in the Gaelic tongue.

Many who joined the Argylls were escaping the abject poverty of the industrial cities. Jockie Bell explains, "A lot of lads were joining the Highland Light Infantry just to get a square meal but I'd been making my own way since I was sixteen, so I was managing. I was maybe a bit lightweight but not stupid. The Army paid me so little that when my wife had our son, and she wasn't very well with him, she ended up having to leave the bairn for her mother to look after, and she went to work alongside her father in the shipyards. I never wanted to be a soldier but I tried to make the best of it."[9]

John 'Nick' Carter originally joined the Durham Light Infantry in 1934 along with his brother to escape poverty and "to get a pair of boots." These were the years of the Depression when dole money was 7 shillings and 6 pence. John's nickname derived from Nick Carter the famous detective but initially he was called 'Bobbajee.' He won an award as the smartest recruit but in the same year he transferred to the Argylls because he wanted to be in a Scottish regiment like his father who had served with the Seaforth Highlanders in World War 1. Nick served and was wounded in India. As his mother had taught him to cook he became a battalion cook and was sent for training at the Army School of Cookery in Poona. "In the Cookhouse I looked after the boy soldiers – well they were boys and boys are always hungry."

Nick arrived in Singapore as a Lance Corporal in A Company before voluntarily relinquishing his stripe following ragging from a Platoon Sergeant who was in the habit of teasing Sassenachs. "I never liked to be an NCO and I didn't want it any more so I dropped it. Joe Lonsdale picked up the stripe."[10]

To many of the Jocks this was the family regiment: for example, there were the three McDougall brothers, Alex, Hughie and Tommy; the three McPhee brothers from Campbeltown, Alex or Sandy, Duncan and Malkie; and many pairs of brothers within the battalion including the Dohertys, the Gibsons, the McDougalls (Jim and Billie) and the McVeys. Billy Doherty was in fact the twenty-year-old half-brother of Jimmy, the battalion Quartermaster, who was more than twice his age. This family link also applied to some officers: 2nd Lt Sandy Stewart had two brothers serving in other Argyll battalions, one was a POW in Germany and the other with the Highland Division in Egypt. Many officers like Captain David Wilson and Lt Derrick Montgomery-Campbell were also the sons and grandsons of former Argylls.

Sgt Alex McDougall of B Company, born at Fort George and brought up by his grandmother in Clydebank, was the son and grandson of Argylls. Alex said: "I made the mistake of joining the Kosbies (King's Own Scottish Borderers) and when I told my father I'd joined up he said 'Which did you do?' When I said, he went doon right away frae his work and got me oot of the Kosbies and intae the Argyll and Sutherland Highlanders – that was 1933, and I didn't go to the Castle – the Depot, until 7th January 1934. That's where I did all my training. We left there and went to Edinburgh and from Edinburgh to Tidworth, and went abroad then when the old King died in 1936."[11]

Jimmy McLean, then a 2nd Lieutenant, comments on the Jocks, "They were very hard men but they had a wonderful reputation amongst most other people during the Campaign, and we did a lot more fighting than many of the troops who were there. I had a Cpl (Alex) McDougall in my platoon who was an absolutely first class fellow from Clydeside. My home is in Greenock so I knew the types and had a quick rapport with them although it could have been difficult for officers coming from places elsewhere. But Greenock was Clydeside and I knew these people – I knew them as workers in the shipyards and I knew their fathers, and I knew how tough they were. Captain Lapsley from the Bearsden area for instance would have come across this type too. Most of my communication with them was in jungle training – and then in action they were absolutely first class. You could rely on them absolutely, and if you had a chap like McDougall in your platoon, no-one stepped out of line. He made sure things happened and people did what they were told so there was no difficulty."

Jimmy McLean also observed a sense of propriety and a certain dignity about the sort of men who joined the Argylls: "The type of chaps they were and the social groups they came from I knew quite well. They worked at the shipyards and came home at 5.30 p.m. to the tenement buildings. They'd have high tea, and then get dressed up – everything highly polished, spick and span, shining shoes, and then they'd go out and meet five or six others and stand at the same spot the whole evening, just talking. And then go home without having gone anywhere else! Occasionally, they would go to a pub, perhaps on a Saturday night or to a football match on a Saturday afternoon. Otherwise regularly during the week there was this routine of dressing up and meeting, chatting, then going home. I saw it during my growing up days, the chaps standing on the corner, and they'd greet me – it always struck me as odd, all my life, the dressing up. The Argyll Jocks belonged to this social group of people."[12]

What makes a good battalion? The 2nd Argylls were like a close-knit family with its internal squabbles and disharmonies yet totally bonded by shared experience. Eric Moss compares life in the battalion to life in his home village of Glencoe. Highland soldiers sometimes refer to "the family of the Regiment." There was tolerance and unity, a sense of community and communal lifestyle; considerable toughness and the ability to transform into an effective fighting machine. Angus Rose saw the Argylls' Esprit de Corps as the voluntary submission of the individual to the requirements of his unit or the battalion, with the voluntary state only achieved by forceful methods in the initial stages. This spirit was achieved through personal example, by tradition, by public opinion and honour. It entailed total selflessness but really became exhilarating and reaped rewards when it came to wartime action.[13]

Most old Argylls would agree that three factors contributed to the strength of the battalion: tradition, good discipline and good senior NCOs. The Old 93rd were well known for their good discipline, which in the battalion's early history was considered due to recruitment parish by parish. Each parish was expected to produce so many men and any man guilty of ill discipline would have his name posted in the parish kirk in his home glen. The original 93rd Sutherland Highlanders were raised as a Regiment of Foot in 1799 in Sutherland on the authorisation of King George III. Major-General William Wemyss, the nephew of the last Earl of Sutherland, recruited the regiment by calling meetings in every parish at which all available men would be lined up. The General, carrying a silver snuff mull, incidentally lost during the Malayan Campaign of 1941–2, went along the ranks offering snuff, 'the King's Bounty Money' and a dram of whisky to every man who signed on.

In his 1949 regimental history Lt Colonel G.I. Malcolm of Poltalloch writes: "All who saw them were struck by one thing especially – the complete absence of crime among the men... they were first classified by parishes with the conviction thereafter that anyone behaving ill would not only be in personal disgrace but would bring dishonour upon the parish."[14] In 1881 the 93rd were united with the 91st Highlanders who had been raised by Duncan Campbell of Lochnell in both Argyll and larger Lowland communities. It was embodied at Stirling Castle five years before the 93rd – in 1794 – and then referred to as 'the Argyle Regiment'.

The backbone of any good battalion is its senior NCOs and in this respect the 2nd Argylls were well served. Battalion RSM Alexander 'Sandy' Munnoch came from Bannockburn Village near Stirling; a village not lacking in historical significance, for it was here in 1314 that Robert the Bruce thrashed the English army. Munnoch was a '21 year' regular soldier who had been RSM at Stirling Castle for three years before joining the battalion in India. Sandy Munnoch was a tough man, unpopular with some, but one who took a deep interest in the welfare of individual soldiers and was good at handling difficult young men of whom the Argylls had its fair share. He would take the latest arrivals on route marches to acclimatise them. He refused to allow them to drink from their water bottles while they were out marching and would check every water bottle at the end of a march. "Take your bloody hands off those waterbottles!" he'd growl.[15] Alex McDougall says of him, "He wouldn't tell you to do things he couldn't do himself."

Sandy Munnoch was well known for his lively sense of humour. Nicknamed 'the Bull' he became somewhat perturbed when Walt Disney studios brought out a popular cartoon called Ferdinand the Bull. "I've been known as the Bull all my days, and I'm effed if I'm going to listen to anyone call me Ferdinand!"

CSM Alexander 'Sandy' McTavish of HQ Company came from Edinburgh and was a strong determined personality, later to distinguish himself in captivity. He had joined the Argylls in 1924 as a drummer and was to retain the nickname 'Drummie'. He was also a keen footballer. After serving with the 2nd Battalion in the West Indies, he had a long period of service with the 1st Battalion, the 91st, and spent several years at Stirling Castle, drilling the Jocks along the Castle esplanade. A photo of the time shows young Sgt McTavish on parade being inspected by an elderly King George V.

Sandy McTavish rejoined the 93rd in India and became CSM D Company. David Boyle wrote of him: "He had the perfect combination of strict discipline, tact and complete understanding of other people's problems; he was a devoted family man and when off duty asked for nothing more than good company, a pipe and a pint."[16]

In Sgt Percy Evans, an Englishman, the Argylls enjoyed a cheerful, gifted and much talked about rations sergeant and entrepreneur. Indeed, Percy Evans was something of a legend. "A great character. The best type of QM Sergeant who would conjure up stores and supplies out of a hat, and no questions asked. He was full of fun and quite tireless," comments David Wilson. Others thought him mean and arrogant. There were strong doubts as to whether all his activities were above board. "A rogue!" said another old Argyll. Here are some comments made by various Argylls fifty-six years later:

"He had an Indian work gang, some Hindus and some Muslims, who apparently were a great help to Percy Evans in his headquarters."

"He was a bigshot in the 2nd Argylls and he looked after the stores sent to the various cook houses."

"He must have finished up a millionaire!"

"Percy Evans was a fat little chap. His shorts came to under his knees. He kept himself to himself. He could buy the battalion out of his own bank account. He used to come down to the ration hut and he would take food out then take it back. I caught him at it. I didn't report him but I watched him. If he'd come in front of me and it was in action, I'd have shot him!"

"Do you remember the wee vans that used to come in and out, the contractors Wah Hin and Company? That's Percy Evans! They were wholesale provision merchants and the regulars used to say 'That's Percy Evans' firm.' He was a bandit! He was that! We drivers did a week at the time bringing in rations. You had to be up at Percy's ration stores dead on six o'clock a.m. And when you got there he would say to you: 'Do you want gunfire or the bottle?' This was a wee half of whisky. Gunfire was a mug of tea. Most of the time I had the gunfire, but this morning I said I'd have the bottle. But you want to see the amount of meat that we collected from the RASC and handed in to Cold Storage to keep – the perishable foods. But when we went back at night, we got out a couple of trays of mince. I said to Percy 'Where's the rest of it?' 'Nothing to dae wi' you' he says.

"But we were taking note of everything. We put butter into the Cold Storage, and we got margarine out, and different things like this. But this time I says to him 'Percy, that's not right! We handed butter in here!' He says 'You shut up – you're drunk!'." Vast quantities of butter delivered to Cold Storage had miraculously turned into margarine when the drivers returned to collect it. Once Percy Evans lost

$500 in one of the trucks, a small fortune to the Argyll drivers, and didn't even bat an eyelid when the money wasn't found. Percy Evans had a stock of little wristwatches with a red 12 on them that he handed out to favoured Argylls at a discount price but nobody was quite sure where they came from.

Some Argylls were sent to Percy Evans for a 'gumsy diet' after having teeth removed. Jockie Bell was one of them. "I said to him 'I've had my teeth out and I'm waiting on dentures.' I was waiting on dentures when the war broke out and I was waiting on them when it ended, but you can eat rice with nae teeth and you never got much roast beef from the Japs! Anyway, he says 'Just a minute. Here!' and he handed me a couple of packets of Jacobs cracker biscuits and a packet of Oxo cubes! I felt just about an inch tall, and he'd a great big store of tucker, you know!"[17]

Ernest Gordon remembers Hogmanay 1941 when Percy Evans was outmanoevered by a cunning Jock: "The tactics of attacking on the rear and flanks was learned well by the Jocks. That was evident at New Year when Pte Thompson siphoned off 80 gallons of Mr Evans' McEwans beer from the barrels in the NAAFI!"[18]

If Ian Stewart knew of Percy Evans' activities, and it seems likely he did, no action was taken for Percy was good at his job and always delivered what was required. Both in the Malayan Campaign and the Captivity he was to show no lack of courage.

Other outstanding senior NCOs included CSM Alexander 'Sandy' Biggarstaff of B Company and RQMS J. Fleming who worked closely with Percy Evans and the battalion Quartermaster 'Doc' Doherty.

There was less social distinction in the Highlands and West Coast of Scotland than in other areas of Scotland and the United Kingdom, but military requirements necessitated probably no more social interaction and fraternisation between officers and men in the Argylls than in other regiments, but there was a strong mutual respect which did not exist in many other battalions. Retired Lt Kenneth McLeod comments: "I would say the relationship between officers and men was first class." Former Pte Duncan Ferguson agrees. McLeod explains one point of contact: "You could be on the sports field playing with the men, but you wouldn't call them by their first names. You had to be careful. You couldn't be too familiar because you had to give orders and had to get obedience. You never asked the men to do something you were not prepared to do yourself – and you should always be prepared to do it." A newcomer to the Argylls was serving as Orderly Officer and made a disparaging remark about the Jocks. He was punched on the nose and floored by a fellow officer.

Bridging the gap between officers and NCOs were two commissioned officers who had been sergeant-majors in India. It was no easy task for a former NCO to settle in as an officer in the Argylls. One officer says: "It wasn't common in pre-war days for officers to come through from the ranks. He had to be a gentleman and be able to enter into any type of society and be accepted by all and sundry."

Battalion Quartermaster James 'Jimmy' Syme Doherty MBE from Edinburgh had enlisted in the Argylls in February 1917 as a fifteen-year old boy soldier and was a Sergeant by the age of 22. He had served in Ireland, Jamaica, China – as Battalion Provost Sergeant in Shanghai, Hong Kong, then India. By 1934 he was QM Sergeant, 2nd Argylls and in 1935 was appointed Battalion RSM. Doherty was a stalwart of the Regimental Kirk. He had not wanted to become an officer but was commissioned and in December 1941 promoted Captain following the award of an MBE.

Eric Moss describes Doherty as "a smart soldier, not very tall, slightly built, straight backed and alert with eyes that never missed a trick." In Ian Stewart's words, Doherty was "a persuasive obtainer of necessary supplies." The Argylls in Malaya were never to be short of ammunition, or, as Ian Stewart insisted for his battalion, "Something hot every four hours."

Doherty was often called upon, even after his commission, to sort out particularly difficult soldiers. One day he called in a troublesome 'hard case' in A Company, told him that he was getting into bad company and that he would beat him up himself if the young man did not sort himself out. There was no further trouble from this individual.

Doherty was well known for going round the dining hall and asking the men at the end of the tables if there were any complaints about the food. The expected answer was 'No,' but one day a man complained. "Well, it's the bully beef." "Bully beef?" retorted Doherty, Bully beef is good for you! We fought the last war on bully beef." He was always keen to remind younger Argylls that he, like the Colonel, had served in the Great War.

"Aye," replied the young Jock, "but it was fresh then!" This is an RSM tale familiar to most regiments, but indicative of the affection felt in the battalion and in later years in Stirling town for 'Old Doc'. Doherty was a keen tennis player and both a ballroom and a Highland dancer. He took a keen interest in battalion boxing, tug o' war and football.[19]

Captain Tam Slessor, the Battalion Transport Officer, a great footballer and battalion centre-half, had a reputation throughout his long career as a morale builder. Enlisting as a private soldier in 1932 he served in India as a PSM and was commissioned in December 1940, moving straight to the rank of Captain. He was known as 'Tam Crickey Jings' on account of the fact he never swore; he'd always say 'Crickey Jings' or 'Good Gordon Highlanders' but after a few drinks some said that he could turn the air blue. Civvy Cameron, one of the battalion football team and also All India Hockey player, thought him "a terrific bloke – he would help people out. He wasn't aloof and he could deal with both sides, both the military and the discipline and the off-duty side."[20]

Another former NCO was Gaelic-speaking Captain Eric 'No Socks' Moss from Glencoe, the former Battalion Pipe Major. His nickname derived from the fact that since the 1930s, indeed to this very day, he wore no socks except on social occasions. The son of an Argyll killed at Passchaendale in the First World War with an unknown grave, he attended St. John's Episcopal School at Ballachulish then joined the Argylls in 1925 at the Isle of Wight as a fourteen-year-old boy soldier. He served around the world with the 2nd Battalion including in the West Indies, China and India. He did very well in musketry and small arms courses and served as Pipe Major 1937–8. As an accomplished piper he composed two marches for the Argylls: 'The 93rd March to Peshawar' and 'The Shaktu Valley March.'

Moss was then a CSM before his initiative and experience led to a commission as a full lieutenant. In September 1940 he was promoted captain. He briefly commanded A Company before being sent to Movement Control. Devoted to the battalion, there is no doubt that this last move saddened and frustrated him.[21]

Ian Stewart wasted no time in taking the battalion up-country into mainland Malaya for intensive training, leading his men through jungle and rubber tree plantations, across rivers and leech-infested swamps. A photo of the time shows Stewart with RSM Sandy Munnoch and then Adjutant Captain Angus MacDonald, later the Brigade Major, leading the battalion through the mud of Kranji Creek on Singapore's north-west shore – an Argyll training ground and the very point where the Japanese landed and infiltrated months later.

Sgt Alex McDougall of B Company remembers how the news of the outbreak of war with Germany arrived during Church Parade: "I had a broken leg from playing hockey. The battalion was in church and I was in my hospital blues, and we were shouting out as they marched past 'We're at war wi' Germany!' But they wouldna' believe it – 'Don't tell us a lot o' daft things!' They went away roond tae get dismissed. I was sitting in the Corporals' mess when they came in. I just turned on the news bulletin and it told them. They said 'You were right enough!' That was 3rd September."[22]

When Captain, later Major, Angus Rose and the then commanding officer Lt Colonel Greenfield returned in October 1939 on the SS *Duchess of Bedford* to rejoin the battalion after a long home leave, Ian Stewart already had the battalion in the jungle up-country, much to the disapproval of Malaya Command where Stewart was regarded by many senior officers as little more than a crank.[23] Other battalions in Singapore including the 2nd Gordon Highlanders (Lt Colonel W.J. Graham, then Lt Colonel John Stitt MC) and the 1st Manchesters (Lt Colonel E.B. Holmes MC) packed up work at mid-day. While they slept and rested the Argylls were out training "in the mid-day sun" developing their tactics, efficiency and aggressiveness.

Some Argyll officers felt that he was remorselessly overdoing it and was totally obsessed, even mad with tactics. Eric Moss, then a Captain in the battalion, says: "We were worked really hard at jungle warfare. I think it is fair to say it was sometimes night and day. I remember one of our senior Majors saying to the CO: 'Oh, for Christ's sake, Ian, give us a rest!' but on we went. We never really got much rest, but we were ready for them."

Younger officers resented their weekends being spent in training when they wanted to pursue other interests such as the Flying Club and yachting. One young officer, later a big admirer of Stewart, thought about quitting the battalion and told the CO, "I really don't want to go but what I do want is to get away from you!"

Eric Moss felt that right from the beginning the Argylls were tougher and more prepared than the other battalions in Malaya: "We'd come from India. Although we had respect for the sun, we never gave way to it. It was common in India for chaps in some regiments not to do any work after 8.00 a.m. because it was too hot. So from 8.00 in the morning they were confined to their barrack rooms, and this wasn't a good thing. I know of one regiment in the same garrison as we were, who paid too much attention to the sun and were confined to barracks all day. Now that regiment was full of suicides and homosexuality just because they'd nothing to do all day.

"We would go out and march at 8.00 in the morning, get back at 3.00 in the afternoon, through the heat of the day, 128°F in the shade, that sort of thing. When we got to Singapore the Gordons naturally tried to tell us all about it – they'd been in Singapore, they knew Singapore, you don't work after 10.00 in the morning, it was too hot. This is what they were telling us. Of course, we didn't do that. We got straight out into the jungle and trained. And time and time again Stewart would arrange an exercise, along with the CO of the Gordons. It would be cancelled at the last minute. We never went out with the Gordons yet. But we did with the Loyals

– the Loyals were quite keen, they weren't a bad regiment at all. Most of the exercises we did it was the Loyals who were the enemy. But there was none of them trained like we did. We used to get fed up day after day doing the same damned thing, but it did train us."[24]

Topees, the tropical pith sun-helmets of the British Empire, were not the Wolseley helmets worn when they first went to India and which were still worn by the Royal Marines. The pith helmet did not contain cork and was much cheaper to produce. The Argyll topees carried a diamond shaped flash in green and yellow, the battalion colours. Officers' topees had a flamboyant white hackle made of feathers, which was tucked in behind the flash (see the group photo of Argyll officers). Duncan Ferguson explains Argyll tropical headgear: "We wore our sun topees on all the jungle marches. In action we wore 'tin topees' (literally topees reinforced with tin). When we were driving we wore the Glengarries. The Tam-o'shanters, TOS we called them, were worn for going out – dresswear, or the Glengarries. We kept them in our kitbags. Stewart wore his Glengarry all the time and he was told off often enough by his batman! Stewart was the one standing up while he was telling others to take shelter!"

'Bonnets TOS' are the large, round khaki berets with the 'tourie' or bobble, on top: the Tam-o'shanter, in a coarse material. Officer versions for Sergeants upwards are in finer material and are called 'Balmorals'. The troops referred to both as Balmorals. The Glengarry is the fore-and-aft cap with a chequered, or diced band around it, with ribbons. Here too the subtle difference of rank. The officers' Glengarries had ribbons with nicked ends at the back, whereas the troops' ribbons were cut straight. In the 2nd battalion the Glengarry was worn at a slight angle, whereas 1st battalion wore it straight. Colonel Stewart, and later Lt Col 'Gertie' McKellar, wore theirs throughout, distinctively emphasising pride in the battalion, knowing it would be remarked.

The A&SH silver cap badge was equally remarkable, being the largest in the British Army. The design carries the Boar's Head with the motto *Ne Obliviscaris* meaning "Do not forget", and a Wildcat with the motto *Sans Peur* meaning "Without Fear". The Boar's Head was the badge of the Duke of Argyll's family who raised the 91st Highlanders and the Wildcat the badge of the Sutherland family who raised the 93rd. Recruits in Scotland, unlike those in England, were immediately badged to their Regiment the moment they went for training. "You got your Balmoral the day you joined up – regulation issue Balmoral and cap badge", Jockie Bell said. This system was considered to produce a better Esprit de Corps.

Jockie remembered his topee being stolen from his cabin on the ship. "We'd been told how to sponge them lightly with just a little water along the puggaree, to keep them clean. If you put on too much water the cork showed through and they turned brown. Someone stole mine; sometimes they claimed they'd blown overboard. Anyway, I was to go ashore in Singapore wearing my Balmoral – the old soldiers laughed at me. They were telling me that in that terrible heat I'd get sunstroke and everything else that was going, and I was getting worried – here, what was I in for now! But there was a band to welcome us – and what were they wearing but Balmorals and KD shirts and shorts and drab hose."

Before departure from Scotland, Jockie had been issued with KD (Khaki drill) tropical gear – shorts, long sleeved shirt and 'dingy' hose. On the voyage they changed into the tropical shirts at Bombay. In Singapore he acquired a pair of tartan trews, which were worn with a blue patrol jacket. At a time of shortages it was very much a case of beg, borrow or steal. "Some of the fellows would take a pair of trews to the Indian tailors," Jockie said, "and get a piece inserted on the inside leg which gave them a bit of flare, but that wasn't regulation issue so you couldn't wear these on parade or you'd be hauled up if the Sergeant felt like it. You needed slacks at night to keep the 'mozzies' off, and some got white suits made. I couldn't afford any of that. We had our greatcoats with us, hanging by our beds at Tyersall until they took them away. I just had one pair of boots issued. Most had two pairs, and I was accused by the QM of having sold a pair along the road, which I hadn't."[25]

The Argyll shorts included the type that could be unbuttoned at the leg and unfolded to make trousers, giving more protection against mosquitoes at night. These were more practical than the Gordons' smart cotton drill trousers. Khaki hose, the 'dingy' hose, were worn over socks and had elastic garters carrying two red flashes with nicked ends. Pipers wore diced hose.

The Argylls' dark green and blue kilts with badger-head sporrans for Officers and Sergeants were handed in by the Jocks in December 1939 and dispatched back to the UK. They had ceased to be battledress issue for Highland Regiments. The 'Battledress only' order was ignored by one battalion, the 1st Queen's Own Cameron Highlanders who were still wearing them at Dunkirk in May 1940, but the Argylls sadly obeyed orders.

The Pipe Band, the heart of any Highland Regiment, of course continued to wear the kilt as did officers for walking out in Singapore or on special occasions such as Governor's receptions on the immaculate lawn of Government House (today the Istana, official residence of the President of Singapore, on Orchard Road). The tartan of officers' and sergeants' kilts was of a finer quality and finish than that of the Jocks.

The kilt is made from six to eight yards of cloth with the pleats cut out at the top so that it is shaped to the waist. The Argyll tartan was No. 2 Government Tartan, (now 1A). It was slightly different from the Black Watch (43rd Regiment of Foot) No. 1 Government Tartan, first issued in 1739 when the Independent Companies raised in Scotland in 1725 for policing duties, became the first kilted regiment. The original kilts worn were of the belted plaid type, a more engulfing garment than the modern kilt. Except for its texture the tartan has changed little since the 18th century. A firm in Bannockburn, Messrs. William Wilson and Sons, Tartan Manufacturers, were contracted by the Army in the 1770s to produce Highland cloth, and did so for the 93rd. Originally the tartan was coarse in texture with the wool combed and the threads hard twisted. In 1872 Queen Victoria ordered the introduction for other ranks of a softer tartan made with carded wool with the threads loosely twisted. Officers and Sergeants had already been wearing this tartan since the 1830s. The kilts were originally made of only three yards of tartan with broad pleats. It was not unusual for men to add an extra yard at their own expense. The Regimental officer's kilt has a special green silken panel sewn onto it. The panel is about five inches wide and stretches two-thirds of the way down from the waist where the opening of the kilt falls on the right hand side. Sewn onto this panel with green silk threads are 'Princess Louise's Favours', tailed rosettes made of fine green tape – originally bestowed by Princess Louise, Colonel in Chief of the Regiment. These originally kept the kilt apron closed. There was a thistle also on it now an "8" in memory of the 8th battalion,

Officers, like other colonial gentlemen in Malaya, were expected to leave their visiting cards at Government House and with other senior officers. They could then expect invitations to balls, tea parties and other social events where they would hopefully meet eligible young ladies.

Officers had to purchase their own uniforms and the battalion had its own tailor, Noor Mohammed, the Regimental Dhurzi, and his half-dozen or so assistants who went wherever the battalion went. "They made the tunics, jackets, trews, and the white sharkskin jackets with the gold epaulettes worn on Mess night," said Kenneth McLeod.

Noor Mohammed was a Punjabi, originally employed by the battalion in India. He came with them to Singapore. "He was employed to work for the Regiment, probably for Wazir Ali, one of the biggest contractors," Eric Moss said. "The NAAFI didn't operate in India, so various worthy Indians came to seek a contract with the Regiment which would then employ them to look after the Regiment – not only to supply the canteens but if they got the chance they supplied barber shop and tailor shop as well. One of the biggest was Wazir Ali who had the contract for the Highland Regiments. He didn't run the barber's shop but had tailors. I don't know what happened to Noor Mohammed."

Equipment – pouches, belts, gasmasks and capes – were basically World War I vintage and weaponry was outdated and in short supply. "Do you know, before the Jap war started, we'd nothing like a 2 inch mortar and do you know that the Pioneers had to make 2 inch mortars out of wood painted grey, just to carry around for training, just a kid-on."

Throughout 1940 and 1941 parties of replacements were making the long journey from Stirling Castle to Singapore. In November 1939, Pte Duncan Ferguson was in a party of twenty-eight men under a wealthy nineteen-year-old 2nd Lieutenant. They were despatched from Stirling Castle, which was still the Regimental HQ of the Argyll and Sutherland Highlanders when war broke out in Europe.

The Castle rang to the clattering boots, shouts, bugles and bagpipes in its draughty corners of history, exposed to the wind up on the rock above Stirling town. The ramparts face north to the Highlands, to Ben Lomond in the northwest and to Ben Ledi and Ben Vorlich in a crest of mountains the Scots call 'hills.' Below is the River Forth winding beside the Wallace Monument, built to commemorate one of the old heroes of Scotland. The Forth curves through the flat farmlands below the Ochils to become the Firth of Forth as it approaches Edinburgh City on its south shore. It is crossed by the fine old Forth Railway Bridge, as famous as San Francisco's Golden Gate, and wearing the same red paint.

As a working castle, soldiers were drilled out on the esplanade in front of the great gates. CSM Sandy McTavish, drilling the Jocks there in the 1930s, bawling at them in a very correct manner, was often barracked by the ladies of the Top o' the Town: "Leave them soldiers alone – you great bullying b....... !"[26]

The ladies were equally fierce down in the Raploch, the cluster of council houses that sits below the Castle, smoke curling from the lums (chimneys) each winter morning. The Raploch folk had a reputation for being "nae blate in coming forward" (not slow in speaking their mind) as Duncan Ferguson who had joined the Argylls on the outbreak of war and did his training in the Raploch, recalled. "It was dead winter 1939, reckoned to be one of the worst winters in years, and we were taken out for PT in singlets and shorts, along the road and down in front of the council houses in the Raploch – this woman, what a mouthful she gave Sergeant Gunn, the training sergeant, and Corporal Morgan: 'Get out, you dirty basket! Get these laddies away and let them get their claes oan! They're bloody frozen there – their wee tossles'll be broken off!' Around the field there we went: 'On Guard! High Port!' And there was wee Pate. He was to come on the same draft as me, but when we got our embarkation leave, he never came back. I always used to get at the back of him – and see! – when he was marching, his two arms were up at the same time. The Sarn't used always to get onto me! 'Keep in step, Ferguson!' I'd say 'Pate! For Chrissake – ONE of your arms at the time!'."

Duncan recalls a bizarre start to a bizarre journey as they marched out from the Castle gates, over the garden moat, across the esplanade and down the snow-dressed cobbles leading down the steep hill from the Castle to the railway station. The ground was covered in a foot of snow yet much to their indignation, instead of wearing their practical Balmorals, the marching soldiers were wearing tropical topees on which the snow flakes gently settled. The band was playing as they marched, passing the Castle Inn, the Jocks' pub; and the Golden Lion, the officers' pub, down to the railway station. They were in the khaki battledress that had replaced the kilt as a fighting garb.

"The snow was up right over the top of our boots, marching down with our sun topees on. It must have been our young Lieutenant's idea. Instead of strapping them on our backs we were wearing them! We got to Stirling station, we were all there waiting for the train – and his mother comes, and she gave every man, twenty eight of us, a big bar of chocolate and a 20 packet of cigarettes each! Every man! Then we got to Edinburgh, and he took us to that big hotel at Waverley Station and we got a meal and he paid for it."

Duncan's party first sailed to Cherbourg then on by train to Marseilles. "We were going to get the train that night," Duncan says, "going across France to Marseilles to get the boat, and our rich Lieutenant says to the Sergeant, 'You can take them out and show them around the town – but keep them together. Don't let them stray!' So the Sergeant is marching us through the town, he was going to take us all about, and gradually two's away and two's away, and when he got back to the station the Lieutenant says 'Where's the Draft?' Well they came drifting in – and you want to have seen some of the things they had! There was yin o' them had a grandfather clock on his shoulder! Others had big trays o' cakes, and things like that! They'd been in the shops, and the Lieutenant says 'Right! Get a meal. I'll see you later about this!' So we'd to walk along and get our tea." They never did get their tea. Someone spread a rumour as to the Frenchified contents of the stew and the brave lads all walked out.

In the South of France they embarked on a twenty-one day voyage on the *SS Andes* with the rich young man, now well under the thumb of the Jocks, continuing to hand out their beer money: "He gave it to us every three days, and he never marked a ha'penny in our paybooks! Not a ha'penny."[27]

A year later, in October 1940, four officers and about two hundred men were despatched from Stirling Castle as further reinforcements. The four officers in this party, all subalterns, were thirty-one year old Bal Hendry, a powerfully built Watsonian who had played rugby for Edinburgh and was a Scotland rugby reserve; Gordon Schiach from Dunoon, soon to be Battalion Intelligence Officer; Kenneth I. McLeod and Sandy Stewart. They departed from Liverpool on a Polish ship, the *SS Batory,* joining a huge convoy to Cape Town. One problem on the ten week voyage to Singapore was keeping the men occupied: PT and running round the boat deck, lectures and a route march in Cape Town all helped.

Also on board but not yet knowing he was going to the Argylls was twenty-eight year old Padre Robert Hartley Beattie, the son and grandson of Presbyterian ministers from County Donegal in Ireland. He recalled the same excitement of experiencing a new world that he had felt when the *Batory* had stopped at Capetown: "Nothing like this had ever been seen before and the eye overflowed the brain in the attempt to comprehend. There was an anti-climax when we streamed down the gangway into dirty, noisy sheds. These were the same in any language. There were boxes, shouting men, spilled flour and tarry rope.

"As we rode in the taxi along the waterfront and past the airport, I wondered what the next three years would be like. The old sweats had told me on the boat that Singapore was a three-year station and that after the first year one got used to it. I found the heat all it was cracked up to be. It was simply unbearable at the beginning. I was always looking for a spot either to lie or to sit. Standing was a fatigue in the smallest doses.

"This was indeed a city of contrasts. Large American limousines flowed up and down the main streets, invariably Malay drivers at the wheel – Syces they were called. Riding comfortably in the back were Chinese and European men, well dressed and cool. On the other hand Chinese coolies, barefooted and perspiring, sweated between the shafts of rickshaws, no better than beasts of burden. One noticed Chinese women too. They were the builders' helpers, carrying bricks and mortar up ladders. Indian Tamils, bent double, pulled great two-wheeled carts and chanted and grunted as they strained.

"All of Singapore was new and exciting. It was the perfect antidote to belt-tightening and blackouts. How pleasant it was to drive through the lighted streets and to feel free of all the other Blighty restrictions."[28]

Kenneth McLeod, arriving with Beattie on the *Batory*, had joined up in 1938: "A government notice came out that those of us of a certain age group had to do six months training, and then I had to sign on again and that was me in for the duration." After officer training at Bulford, McLeod had written to Major-General Gervais Thorpe, Colonel of the Argylls, asking for a posting to the Regiment. "I got orders to go up to the Castle from Alva and get kitted out, revolver and compass and so forth, then go down to Auchengait camp. I went there with Bal Hendry, Gordon Schiach and Sandy Stewart. I was still the senior 2nd Lieutenant. I called a parade for kit inspection and told the Sergeant Major in the camp that they must all be properly kitted out, especially with tropical gear. I held this inspection and the fellows had nothing at all, so I asked the Sergeant Major what was in the Quartermaster's stores but they hadn't got the necessary kit. So we trucked these men along to the Royal Scottish Fusiliers barracks and asked for the CO but he was not there and I got the Quartermaster and told him I needed to obtain tropical gear. There was a bit of an argument with the Fusiliers who weren't going to comply without this and that forms and permissions, so I said to Bal Hendry we would just go over and play a round of golf and then come back, which we did, and that got sorted out. Within a few days we were away."[29]

On arrival in Singapore, McLeod, trained in the use of the new 3-inch mortar, was put in charge of the Mortar Platoon with PSM Hugh Sloan. Having played golf and curling for Scotland and being an accomplished hockey and badminton player, McLeod also became battalion Sports Officer. In Singapore, he also discovered he was a good runner; he trained on the running track at Raffles College ground as anchorman in the mile relay.

Many of these new arrivals with the battalion were Geordies from England who had trained for eight weeks at a Highland Light Infantry camp at Auchengait near Troon. They had Highland Light Infantry numbers and were taken by the Argylls to make up the numbers. In all some 20% of the 2nd Argylls were Geordies. They are distinguishable on the regimental roll by the numbers commencing 332. Regular and Scottish Argylls had the numbers 298 and 297. Derrick Montgomery-Campbell explains the strange logic behind the policy of putting English soldiers into Scottish regiments: "After Dunkirk the Durham Light Infantry lost a lot of men there, and I remember I was elected to take a draft of Argylls down to Durham. I remember those lads practically had tears in their eyes... The idea was a lot of Scots used to go absent without leave because they came from around Edinburgh and Glasgow way, just too handy. So the British government decided to take a lot of English recruits into Scottish regiments and vice-versa."[30]

Joe Lonsdale from County Durham was one of the 'Geordie' Argylls. It was no great shock for him to be in a Highland regiment as his grandparents came from Edinburgh. He learnt to shoot in the Church Lad's Brigade and early in 1940 found himself in A Company's 9 Platoon under the care of C.Sgt Bing.[31] Jimmy McLean comments on these Geordies: "They were very fine soldiers and they had quite a rapport with our Jocks, from their lives as civilians. There still is a connection between the Newcastle people and the Scots in civilian life, and that would be found in the Army."[32]

Pte Jockie Bell was in a party including 2nd Lt David Boyle and Lt Montgomery-Campbell that arrived on the SS *Orion* via Capetown in September 1940. Recently married but barely shaving, Jockie hadn't expected to be sent abroad, having only been graded B3 'for light duties'. However he thought he was on a cushy billet going to Singapore. Having arrived by train from Stirling, the party embarked on the troopship at Liverpool and was somewhat surprised to find themselves the next morning at Greenock on the Clyde. Most of the Argylls were single men, so Jockie Bell was often ribbed about being married. A few months after arriving in Singapore he received a telegram from his wife to say that he had a baby son – a boy who was already five years old before Jockie first saw him.[33]

Following the end of the Phoney War in Europe, the lull between Hitler's invasion of Poland in September 1939 and his attack in the West in April/May 1940, came the first Japanese invasion scare. The first task of 12th Indian Brigade was to resist any Japanese landings on the beaches at Mersing on the east coast of Johore. The landings never happened and the area around Mersing and Endau became one of the Argylls' main training areas as well as a delightful spot for evening sea bathing.

Former Argylls are unanimous in their opinion of Ian Stewart who was regarded as never asking anything of his men that he would not do himself. "I am very proud to have served with him," comments former Lt Montgomery-Campbell. "The men would follow him to hell and back," says Duncan Ferguson.

The Argylls were fiercely loyal but they didn't fight for their CO or for King and Country; they fought for the Regiment, just as their Highland ancestors at Culloden had fought not for Bonnie Prince Charlie but for the Clans. Regimental spirit was everything.

All officers arriving with the battalion were expected to do three weeks training with the Jocks. Any officer not coming up to expectations or suffering major health problems in the tropics was quietly sent back to Singapore and found a staff post.[34]

Certainly, with a steady flow of keen young officers arriving from the UK, Ian Stewart took the opportunity to remove some of the older officers to other Singapore postings. This didn't always make him popular. In fact, he quickly replaced all four Company commanders, including Cunningham of A Company and the able 'Scruff' Elliot of B Company, with younger men. The new generation of company commanders was coming in – young Territorials like Mike Bardwell, David Boyle, Ernest Gordon and Robert Kennard. "They had to be given their chance" as Eric Moss observed.

Ernest Gordon, a sailing enthusiast from Dunoon, had joined the RAF in 1937 but had fractured his skull and spine in a flying accident. On his recovery he went to St Andrews University to study History and Philosophy.[35] In the summer of 1939 he joined one of the Argyll Territorial battalions and quickly got a posting to join the 2nd Argylls in Singapore, arriving in January 1940.

Kennard, the Marlborough educated son of a Royal Navy Captain from Linlithgow, fair-haired and of medium height, was a quiet, shy man who gave the appearance of being rather sleepy, but was athletic and intelligent enough. Unlike Boyle or Gordon he was thought to have little charisma or fun about him, but got on well with Ian Stewart. Perhaps their similar English public school backgrounds contributed to this.

Kennard had served with the 7th Territorial Battalion since 1930. In 1939 the 7th Battalion split in two; the east half containing Kennard and the Falkirk Company became the 10th Battalion and did not go to France with the Highland Division in 1940. Instead Kennard found himself on a reinforcement draft bound for Malaya, arriving a few months after Gordon. There is some confusion as to Kennard's rank while in Malaya – it seems that he was in fact a pre-war Major in the Territorial battalion but this rank was non-substantive so he was ranked as a Captain with the regular 2nd Argylls. Following the Malayan Campaign he was promoted Major.[36]

Many Argylls suffered severe bouts of malaria. Lt Kenneth McLeod, an outstanding golfer and all-round sportsman who arrived with the battalion in 1940, went into hospital with malaria and turned on the ceiling fan. He awoke with facial paralysis on the side of his face nearest the pillow; his speech was affected and from then on he did only light duties in HQ Company, but did later fight with the battalion.

In June 1941 the Argylls headed for the agreeable little coastal town of Mersing on the southeast coast of Malaya. Here and at nearby Endau they trained, built beach defences and in the evenings relaxed. Padre Beattie remembers that one evening a Malay officer Mohamed Bin Amin took some of the officers to a Malay soirée then the next day for tiffin at the Corporals' Mess of the Malay Regiment.

After two months at Mersing the Argylls, accompanied by two officers of the Johore Military Force and led by two pipers and a drummer, made an eight-day 116-mile trek from Mersing to Singapore. Officers marched with their men. Ian Stewart offered fifty dollars to the best marching platoon with the best bivouacs at the end of each day's march. The prize went to 13 platoon of C Company. Any drivers spared the march in order to keep the battalion supplied had later to march the same distance of 110 miles around Singapore Island. Stewart's 2nd Argylls were nothing if not 'fighting fit' and supremely efficient.

Duncan Ferguson remembers that Ian Stewart was in front of the battalion all the way from Mersing: I bet he did more than twice that journey because he went back and forward to see his men were alright."

Ferguson also recalls a little dog that marched ahead of the Argylls all the way to

Singapore. Actually, according to the Straits Times there were three little dogs accompanying the Mersing march: Jock, Jill and Sheila, and A Company's dog was photographed at the head of the march. One Argyll brought back in his ammunition pouch a baby turtle as a pet. Lt Montgomery-Campbell was near the front of the march, acting as a guide to the marching units: "I had four men with me and we went on two or three miles on compass marches, finding out what beaches to direct the marchers to. The rations came into the beaches by boat. I had to go ahead, plan exactly what beach it was, and put stakes in to give guidance through the jungle sections."

Sgt Alex McDougall recalls the Mersing march as an arduous experience: "You had to walk through jungle with a platoon in front cutting their way through with machetes and they had to be relieved every hour."

The Mersing march was reported in the Straits Times of July 24th 1941 under the headline 'Highland Regiment's Great March: Mersing to Singapore in 8 Days'.

Again Stewart saw the importance of large mugs of hot sweet tea five times a day to combat the enervating climate. The men were not allowed to drink from their waterbottles while route marching. The waterbottles were filled with treated water from small tanker lorries driven by Argyll drivers Tommy McVey, Fred Murray and Geordie Gilfillan. Fred Murray was also Ian Stewart's driver. Some surviving Jocks today remain sceptical that they ever received their full ration of hot tea.

Interviewed by a Straits Times reporter as the Argylls marched back to Tyersall Park Camp, Stewart, "a man whom the correspondents loved to interview,"[37] and certainly a man who didn't shun publicity for his battalion, described the march as "nothing heroic but just part of the training scheme which has put my men among the fittest fighters in this part of the world."

The Mersing march had another significance which seems to have passed unnoticed by the readers of the Straits Times and most at HQ Malaya Command: it proved to those like Stewart who doubted Singapore's impregnability just how vulnerable the island was to a rapid infantry advance from the north. There was no impenetrable jungle barrier protecting the northern approaches to Singapore. If the Argylls could make such a march then so could the Japanese and that very month the Japanese had completed their occupation of French Indo-China, a move which brought them so much closer to the east coast of Malaya and Thailand.

The march clearly showed what a fit, jungle-trained battalion could achieve. As the Argylls' experience of the jungle developed, the jungle and its wildlife ceased to be a terror and became a friend, or that was the theory. In the jungle there were delightful creatures like the Mouse Deer but also more feared animals. Alex McDougall remembers close encounters with jungle wildlife: "I was sitting in a motor car by the side of the road out on patrol near Mersing when a tiger leapt right over the top of our car – talk about fright! We met snakes on patrol; I'd just gone past, turned back and suddenly saw it just about to strike – it was hanging from a tree, the tail down, and of mammoth size – if it got anyone round the neck it would have strangled them. The last man shot it."

Nick Carter remembers the monkeys. "In jungle training we were trained to take every opportunity to nod off as you didn't know when you'd sleep again, and then to tap the next person on the shoulder when you were moving off. We were told to watch what monkeys eat – what they eat you can eat! A school of monkeys in the early morning is an education to watch. They sit in a circle with one in the middle in charge. You can see him pick out one and punish him – he must have given the wrong answer. If you make a noise they vanish. But I've watched them."

The Argylls spoke of 'average,' 'close' and 'open' jungle, never impenetrable jungle. They quickly discovered that the jungle grew thickest at the road's edge and gave the false impression of being impenetrable while in reality the primary jungle a few yards back from the road was by no means impassable. The Argylls developed techniques of moving through jungle in single file, the front man cutting the way with his parang, the second widening the path, the third checking the route with his liquid compass. In Malaya's dense primary jungle there was 30–40 yards visibility and few landmarks to navigate from except for the rivers and roads.

Ian Stewart recognised that movement in the jungle and rubber plantations would have to be by compass. Untrained men would quickly become exhausted in the enervating, hot, humid climate; soon they would be lost and mentally depressed. Stewart could train his Argylls to progress through such jungle at a thousand yards an hour.

The arrival of Lt General Percival in Malaya in May 1941 saw to an extent a shift in policy towards the Japanese threat with the Governor, Sir Shenton Thomas, no longer having the dominant say. Eric Moss explains: "Shenton Thomas' policy was to keep things as normal as possible. When Bond left and Percival came in, there was a shake-up in Malaya. We had to make Malaya realise there was a war on. Shenton Thomas' policy was to keep things as normal as possible, don't alarm the natives, don't do anything to reduce the war effort, keep producing rubber and tin as fast as we can, but Percival came in and said 'No, you can't keep this up. We're at war and the Japs are likely to be coming in at any time,' so he shook things up… and they conscripted civilians, increased the Volunteers right round. Very soon all the weekend was given up for exercises for the Volunteers and we went out umpiring these."[38]

Tyersall Park Camp, the 2nd Argylls' home since December 1939, lay south of Bukit Timah Road and north of Tanglin barracks. On the west side of the beautiful Botanical Gardens, the site reverted to jungle after the war. The land is still the property of the Sultan of Johore but remains overgrown, undeveloped and inaccessible. 200 yards from Napier Road is the rusted remains of Argyll Gate and further on another side entrance. On the hillside to the south of the camp area are some fine houses including the French Embassy. In those days it was a hastily constructed hutted camp erected on land belonging to the Sultan of Johore accomodating two battalions, the other being 9/14th Hyderabads, a Brigade HQ and the Indian Military Hospital.

The attap roofed bamboo huts were of reasonable quality but made pretty crude comparison with the more permanent Tanglin barracks. The huts were built on piers to keep out snakes and wildlife and were about forty yards long with a verandah running the full length. Each contained 30 beds, 15 down each side, allocated according to rank.

Junior officers lived in similar huts but with cubicled sleeping accommodation. There was a small cold water cubicle at the end of the hut for ablutions. They usually employed on a sharing basis Chinese 'Boys' to look after their uniforms and generally tidy up.

The Jocks had to keep their quarters and uniform immaculate without anyone to tidy up after them, the blankets absolutely squared, the kilt on its proper peg, the topee and flashes placed just perfectly. Duncan Ferguson, then a driver, remembers with a strong sense of injustice the consequences of having a split boot. It had split at the back, a common occurrence with heavy driving, and he had gone to the stores for a replacement pair.

There were no boots of his size so he was given a chit to get a replacement pair as soon as they came in. However, come the next inspection the split boots were spotted and he was told to report to his Company Commander, Kennard, who was in no mood to listen to explanations. Duncan received seven days CB and was marched straight out. At night he was "on jankers" – called out for inspection at the double; once inspected he was given the next order, "Highland Dress!" At the double back to quarters to change and return for inspection, which was followed by the order "Full Marching Kit!"

One problem with the huts at Tyersall was that they were mostly built on soft, uneven ground so the wooden poles supporting them, which were supposed to be two feet off the ground, could be four feet high on one side and less than a foot on the other. This sinking tendency was especially evident at the bar end of the Wet Canteen!

Perceptions of Tyersall Camp differed. To many Jocks it was "a pigsty of a place" – an unwelcome return to the deprivation they had joined up to escape. To some officers living there it was a Boys' Own adventure and was no more grim than public school accommodation, but another describes Tyersall as "an absolute dump" with poor toilet and washroom facilities. There were dry toilets with wood and corrugated tin surround. The cold water showers had no roof but were surrounded by an attap screen. There was a separate shower for men suffering from foot rot.

However, they were able to create a reasonably comfortable if flimsy Officers' Mess on Tyersall Mound, overlooking the camp, and a homely Sergeants' Mess. There were two canteens: the dry canteen where Jocks could get tea and a 'wad', and the wet canteen, which sold beer. Eventually, a camp cinema opened. During the rainy season of November to February, when the breezy monsoon known as the Sumatras hits Singapore, the camp often became very muddy.

Captain Kenneth McLeod remembers: "We entertained the Naval Base, *HMS Glasgow* when they were in, and we entertained the Gordons. Yes, the regimental silver would be out for that. We were always outside with the Officers' Mess. We had the band playing at one end of the 'lawn' as it were, with the fairy lights all around the palm trees, and we'd all be out there, drinking and talking and the band playing. A very pleasant evening."

"We had beautiful silver," comments Major Moss. "It was in both the Officers' and the Sergeants' Messes. In our amalgamation of the 91st Argyllshire Highlanders and the 93rd Sutherland Highlanders it was the 93rd that had the name, and the charisma, and most of the silver. We didn't inherit much from the 91st. The 91st weren't kilted and the 93rd were; the 91st for a long time had no Scottish identity except for a thistle on their badge. Their depot was in Pembroke in Wales. The Highland Regiments, consequent of the Clearances and so forth, had changed a lot since they were formed, and in 1883 the 93rd was the most Highland of all the Highland Regiments – almost entirely Highlanders and Gaelic speaking. But after 1883 they were recruited in Clydebank and Port Glasgow. They were a good regiment just the same."

On Mess Guest Nights, the Pipe Major would write out a Pipe Programme which would be put on the dining table. A typical programme would be a Slow March,

Strathspey and Reel, concluding with the 2nd Battalion's regimental march 'Hielan' Laddie.' Eric Moss explains: "The Pipe Banners which are carried by the Pipers have on the obverse side the Arms of the particular owner, usually a company commander, like the Stewarts who had the unicorn with the motto 'Wither Way' written in the old Scots. On the reverse side were the regimental tartan and the regimental coat-of-arms. To expose the reverse side, the Pipers went out in reverse order – in other words the Pipers came in led by the Pipe Major, and walked round the table showing the obverse side of the banner. They stopped here, played the Strathspey and Reel, and then to show the reverse side of the banner they went out back the way they'd come, led by the Pipe Corporal, and they played Hielan' Laddie."

Kenneth McLeod describes the relationship between officers in the Mess: "We were all very pally. Various officers arrived out at different times and Ian Stewart would see them and pick the men he wanted in the battalion. The only time we would really meet was at meals – you came into your own Mess with your own batman serving as waiter, and you sat anywhere, not always next to the same person – but even then it would not necessarily be meals at the same times. Otherwise we met in the evenings or at sports. We all harmonised but during the day you hardly saw one another."[39]

The evenings saw a good deal of drinking and ragging in the Mess. A popular activity was diving headfirst through flimsy wall partitions. As Mess President it was frequently Angus Rose's job to call in the Pioneers to remove and replace the damaged partitions, then explain away the missing walls to Ian Stewart as alteration work. Stewart thought it odd that nothing ever seemed to be different.[40]

The Jocks at Tyersall were allowed to keep pets. CSM Archie McDine was very attached to his canary. Duncan Ferguson recalls other pets: "One of the boys had a duck he called Donald and it waddled after him everywhere. Another had a monkey, and when he went out it was kept on a chain by his bed, and the lads would give it saucers of beer until it was drunk. Davy Heeps from Lauriston, a hard man, had a dog. It was the most obedient I ever came across. When Davy went out the boys would tease it so sometimes Davy's things were in a right mess. He'd come back and tell it 'You're on a charge! Three days CB!' There was a box there, so the dog would jump into it and stay there."

Security at Tyersall was not particularly tight. Passwords were issued but not taken too seriously. Padre Beattie remembers: "Sometimes when some of us were returning to Tyersall of an evening, the sentry, always a Hyderabad soldier, would challenge us and Bal Hendry would reply 'Swiss Navy' and the sentry would allow us in."[41]

Nick Carter recalls how meals were cooked at Tyersall: "It was done in a cement-floored block about the size of two rooms, with open sides and an attap roof with stoves all around it – but no ovens. If I was on duty they got meat pie. I mixed the dough and then opened tins of McConnechie stew, and stirred it round in a bath with a paddle and put some thickening in. You made your pastry in a bath and rolled it out, put your containers upside down on it and cut out the lids. You got your Army frying pan, which could fry 100 eggs at a time – and then you put the pastry in there. You'd give the heat a quick bump up with the petrol gun and bake it – the petrol gun was like a Bunsen burner, but using paraffin you could pump it up to get a high heat. Then you'd put your hot stew on a platter, and put the lid on top. It's mind over matter you know – I've seen many a kettle of strong tea put up as gravy, with gravy salt and thickening – and they've enjoyed it!"[42]

Fresh meat was a rarity for the other ranks; it was a tin of McConnechie between two men. Duncan Ferguson says, "We used to go to the Gordons for a good feed. They got steak and eggs and chips! We didn't – we got bully beef, hash and McConnechies. Percy Evans had a whole hut piled up with stores – a hut the size of our sleeping quarters!"[43]

In the Married Quarters were the wives and families of married officers, the RSM, all but one of the CSMs and other NCOs. Any soldier over the age of 26 and any officer over the age of 30 could be considered for having his family with him. Eric Moss recalls: "There was always a quota and usually a waiting list. It didn't mean because you were 26 you automatically got quarters. You automatically got marriage allowance right enough, but you had to wait for quarters to become available. And if you could find private quarters you got an allowance to help with that but you never heard of soldiers in private accommodation. Officers you got marrying 'under strength' for instance, when they didn't get any marriage allowance, they paid for a private house out of their own pocket. Under strength means – well, an officer wasn't given official sanction to marry unless he was 30. In my Regiment an officer was presented with a silver statuette of an officer in full dress uniform, but if he was under 30 he didn't get that statuette, he was given something else like a silver salver – a regimental thing. He had to conform to Army rules before he got the statuette. Sometimes, if the Colonel thought that the marriage was not suitable he would try to stop it, write to the parents or something like that."[44]

One of the Jocks, Pte William McDougall of the Motor Transport section, married his sweetheart Elsie, the daughter of a wealthy Eurasian Singapore planter. William's brother Jim, who had transferred from the 1st Argylls to be with and look after his younger brother, was best man at the wedding. In the months that followed a limousine would drive to Tyersall Camp to deliver lunchtime sandwiches for William.[45]

CSM McTavish's daughter, Rose, remembers her childhood in Singapore as a very happy experience. She attended the Army School at Alexandra Barracks and the family was first quartered at Changi and Selarang and finally a terraced house near the Botanic Gardens, very close to Tyersall Camp. They had a very pretty young Chinese amah that the visiting young soldiers would chase in fun. Rose remembers how the young men and her father's friends, like PSM Hoostie McNaught, would come round with a piper and give them a party or take them for a picnic at one of the east coast beaches.[46]

Today only the names of Tyersall Avenue and Tyersall Road remind us of the site that was once a barracks. Few Singaporeans today are aware that there was a large Army camp there.

In October 1941, the battalion was photographed carrying out Anti-Fifth Column exercises on Singapore Island. It was fun as the men dressed in assorted mufti; some wore sarongs. A photo of the group of 'Fifth Columnists' includes the very tall figure of D Company's Lt Ian Primrose from Campbeltown, Argyll. He came from a well-known London-based stockbroker family. Sgt Major Hoostie McNaught, Sgt Jimmy Love and the adjutant Captain Ranuld Beckett were also there. Few of them realised what a serious problem Fifth Columnists would be in the campaign that was soon to follow. In November there were further exercises with the battalion's armoured vehicles, which were also photographed by a visiting Army photographer.

The Armoured Car Platoon formed No.4 platoon, HQ Company. It was to provide the vital mobility upon which Stewart's tactics depended. The platoon consisted of five, later four, old and temperamental Lanchester armoured cars, acquired by the battalion in 1940 as training vehicles, and three South African Marmon-Harringtons. There was also a Carrier Platoon with fourteen bren gun carriers. These carried the bren, a .303 Vickers machine gun and a .45 Thompson machine gun.

The armoured car situation compared favourably with the two Indian battalions in the Brigade who had only three armoured cars and eight carriers each with no armoured car platoon as such. The Lanchesters were among twenty-two delivered to Malaya before the war. The Marmons, of which some 175 were delivered to Malaya, were brought down from Kuala Lumpur by Lt Montgomery-Campbell and four drivers early in 1941. Each Lanchester had a crew of four men: commander, gunner, hull gunner and driver. The hull gunner should also have acted as wireless operator but there was no wireless, not that wirelesses were of much use in jungle conditions. Signalling was done with flags. Montgomery-Campbell remembers: "Wireless sets were absolutely useless – they hardly ever worked. They were ineffective in the wet weather. We had trouble with the valves and the range was limited to half a mile or so."

Wireless and telephone communication was to prove a serious problem in Malaya. Royal Signals units sent to the north of Malaya soon discovered the difficulty of making reliable wireless links and found they had to bring up cable trucks working under terrible weather conditions. Trying to erect telephone posts in monsoon conditions or climbing trees covered in red ants to make fixings for cables was irksome, painful work. In the end, many cables were laid down the sides of roads and only further south were they able to link to public telephone lines.

To deal with breakdowns and recovery the Argylls' Armoured Car Platoon had a Light Aid Detachment or LAD consisting of a 3-ton vehicle and a motorcycle. Recovery included the finding and recovery of armoured cars abandoned and left derelict by other units. There were also three 3-ton support vehicles carrying ammunition and rations.

The Lanchesters, built by the Lanchester Motor Company of Coventry in the period 1927–31, were armed with twin Vickers machine-guns and a .5 anti-tank machine gun. Each Argyll Marmon was armed with a single Vickers machine-gun and a Boys .55 anti-tank rifle – a heavy long barrelled rifle with a five-round top-mounted magazine and fierce recoil. Invented by a Captain Boys in the 1930s, this weapon was already obsolete though not to prove entirely useless. Both Lanchesters and Marmons also carried a .45 Thompson machine-gun.

The armoured cars had four purposes in combat: aggressive patrolling of rubber estate roads; close support to the rifle companies; spraying the rubber estate trees to clear enemy snipers lurking in the branches; and forming a firm base from which to fight.[47]

Captain Timothy Turner, the thirty year old Armoured Car Platoon Commander, had previously gained experience training the Armoured Car Squadron of the SSVF (Straits Settlement Volunteer Force) nicknamed "the Saturday night soldiers," an unfair description as their training commitment went well beyond weekends and was combined with full time work. The son of an Army colonel in the Cameronians, Turner had participated in the 1938 Empire Games in Sydney as Stroke in the winning English rowing Eight. After serving with the Bengal Lancers, he returned to civilian life in Malaya, arriving in Singapore in his magnificent Lancers uniform complete with turban. He worked for Wearne Motors as manager of their used cars department in Singapore until volunteering for the Argylls mid-1941, shortly after their arrival in Singapore. His expertise with temperamental vehicles and Lt Montgomery-Campbell's knowledge of machine-guns led to their appointments in the armoured car platoon. Turner was considered the man most likely to be on the receiving end of a Japanese bomb on account of his habit of directing the armoured cars at night while dressed in a white evening suit.[48]

The Marmons were not as useful and well armoured as the Lanchesters and the carriers could frankly be described as deathtraps – very vulnerable to a tossed grenade or sniper up a tree. Armour-piercing bullets could also penetrate their flimsy sides.[49] Ironically, this was commented on to the Argyll officers by a well-known Japanese photographer who came to photograph Singapore-based battalions and who everyone thought was Chinese. It was later discovered that he was a retired Japanese colonel and spy!

The Lanchesters were commanded by Sgts Albert 'Dunky' Darroch and Harry Nuttall, Cpl Robert King and Lt Montgomery-Campbell. The three NCOs had served with the Transport Platoon in India. Cpl Andrew Wilson later commanded one of the vehicles. Each armoured car was named after a castle of Scotland. Cpl King and his crew, including Ptes J. Harcourt and D. Porter, were photographed in front of their Lanchester *Dumbarton Castle* on the Tengah Road. Another good photo shows Sgt Darroch and his crew enjoying a refreshing coconut drink in a Malay village. The armoured car crews were issued with two pairs of dungarees worn over their normal khaki shorts. It was highly uncomfortable in the armoured cars in the hot, humid weather. With no air-conditioning, the men sweated profusely in the confined space.

Other Lanchesters were named after Stirling, Glamis, Inverness and Blair Castles. Montgomery-Campbell commanded *Glamis Castle*. It is something of a mystery as to what happened to the Lanchester *Blair Castle* as it did not serve with the battalion in the Malayan Campaign. The Marmons were not allotted names but were referred to by the last of their registration numbers e.g. Car 24 or Car 68.

Some Argylls loved the tropics and the excitement of Singapore. Others, like Pte Jockie Bell who arrived in September 1940, hated the humid heat and the smells of 1940s Singapore, which was not the clean, hygienic place we know today. It was said that Singapore had twelve different smells, few of them pleasant. Captain Eric Moss found the climate harder to cope with than the dry heat of India and also missed India's vast open spaces. Many suffered from prickly heat, which was treated with calamine lotion and recommended sea bathing.

In Singapore many colonials viewed the Argylls, like most soldiers, with distrust. The Jocks had a reputation for brawling. Pte Duncan Ferguson of C Company remembers with some pleasure the punch-ups with members of English regiments such as the Loyals and the Royal Artillery and Royal Signals around the Union Jack Club. Norman Catto, a sergeant in the Gordon Highlanders, comments on the Argylls: "They were a wild crowd at times, but they were mostly town people, whereas the Gordons were mostly country folk – we got along not bad, but you know they were paid on Wednesday to keep them out of Singapore on Friday nights."[50]

In Singapore, the Union Jack Club, more recently the Omar Kayam Rest Home, was located behind the Palladium Cinema, adjacent to St Andrew's Cathedral. It was staffed by Chinese barmen and a Royal Navy bouncer known as 'Big Kelly'. Food and drink were cheaper here and they needed to be for Army pay was meagre. A married private in the Argylls earned only five Straits Settlement dollars a week. At the time there were approximately eight Straits dollars to the pound. Jockie Bell said, "Peanuts we were paid! I was a married man with a wife and one child and I got S$5, and even an officer standing there watching me go up and salute said 'Can you not give Pte Bell another couple of dollars, Quartermaster?' 'No, no! That's all he's allowed.'... The money we got was a scandal – the British Army was the worst paid, or nearly worst, perhaps the French or maybe the Chinese were worse!"

Duncan Ferguson, then a single man, describes his weekly pay: "My wages were S$3 a week – 7 shillings – and I had to leave half of my pay to my mother, and off of that S$3 I had to get Brasso, Blanco, boot polish, laundry, toothpaste, and the highlight of my week for a long, long while was payday. At the finish of payday I had eleven cents left, and I used to get a bottle of orange pop and one banana. The bottle of pop was 10 cents and the banana 1 cent. How did I manage? Well you adjusted."

It was by "mucking in" that an Argyll managed. Every Argyll had a 'Mucker'. Duncan Ferguson explains: "I passed my driving test and was put to the MT (Motor Transport Section), and there was a chap, Willie Eckford – also from Falkirk – who came along and said: 'Are you going out, Fergie? Come on, come with us' – him and 'Big Ben' (Cpl Aubrey Bentley, an Englishman; like Willie Eckford he would later die in captivity). And I said, 'Going where? Where can I go with eleven cents?' He said, 'Come on, muck in with us,' so they took me and we'd muck in together and you'd get maybe S$20, S$25 from Ben, and S$10 or S$15 from Eckie and I'd look at my eleven cents and they'd say: 'Are we going out tonight then mucker?' And I'd say 'Ye-es! We're going out tonight!' And that's when I started getting out into Singapore with Cpl Bentley."

Often Argylls did not know men in other Companies or even platoons. They stuck with their own particular group of friends. This was also to apply in subsequent actions, escapes and captivity. Some post-war Argyll friends never met each other in the years 1941–1945.

In the words of a private in the RASC: "The Argylls ruled the Union Jack Club." Once, while up-country in Selangor, some Argylls descended on the Red Shield Club in Kuala Lumpur. While their officers were dined at the Selangor Club, quite a battle commenced at the Red Shield with men and furniture thrown out of windows and into the river. Rivalry was particularly strong with the Australians when they ventured from their own Anzac Club. There was the famous Battle of the Union Jack Club and an Australian soldier was killed in a similar fight in what became known as the Battle of Lavender Street in Singapore.[51] Alex McDougall believes he was responsible for starting the Battle of the Union Jack Club: "I was the one that caused it – I got the jail, I didn't half. It was something that was said – it was an Australian guy; I poured beer over his head... And we had another riot; a wee pub place and dance hall down Lavender Street where all the troops used to go. It was full of Australians. They said something. Before you could say 'Jack Robinson' a riot started there an' all."

"That was our day out, a Wednesday. What a battle! We were in the Union Jack Club and there were a lot of Aussies in," recalls Duncan Ferguson, "and John McFadyen started it off there. An Aussie came in and said something to him, and Alex Carruthers was there and Big Ben, and of course Alex put one on him. And

John just sat in this chair. 'Pass them over here,' he said. And he had his steel topee on, and he just hit them with that – Bang! And out the window! And Big Ben's tunic was covered in blood. Davy Smith, the Phantom Bugler, was outside, sat on the top of a taxi and blowing the Argyll Call on his bugle, and in they came. And you heard the whistles going for the Redcaps and they were coming in at the front but Big Ben had gone out the window, then came in again – how they didn't notice his tunic was covered in blood! 'What, has there been trouble in here?'"

As for the Lavender Street Battle, Paul Gibbs Pancheri, a civilian and SSVF Volunteer, remembers observing its aftermath: "Returning at about 11.00 p.m. I went to turn off Kallang Road into Lavender Street to go up Balestier Road and into Norfolk Road where I lived. The entrance to Lavender Street was closed off by a number of Military Police vehicles, so I got out of the car to have a look. There were a number of very belligerent Jocks being rounded up by the Military Police and herded into the trucks, whilst numbers of Australians were being loaded into ambulances. What had happened was that on payday the Jocks had gone to visit their usual haunts only to find the Diggers in full occupation. It appears that a fierce contest took place, the much smaller Jocks, being in better condition, had 'put it across' the newcomers in a big way."[52]

Jimmy McLean's view is that in their time off the Argylls behaved no worse than other battalions: "When they were loose and drinking they could get a bit wild. They had a reputation for that and I think it was probably quite true... They knew how to look after themselves and they came into the Army pretty streetwise. The two regular Argyll battalions would have different types to the territorial battalions and they were a different type altogether from the more rural recruits of the Gordon Highlanders."

To minimise trouble the Argylls were paid on Wednesdays and other regiments on Thursdays. One Argyll died of alcohol poisoning after a heavy Hogmanay drinking bout. He was one of six of the battalion to die prior to hostilities. These men lie today in Kranji War Cemetery alongside those who died in the campaign.

One dollar could buy a whisky and a small bottle of beer. A rickshaw ride back to Tyersall barracks from town was 25 cents and 50 cents would purchase ten dances with pretty Chinese girls at one of Singapore's three Entertainment Worlds: New World, Happy World and Great World. Two dollars guaranteed a good time in the supposedly off-limits red light districts in Bencoolen or Lavender Street. Some Argylls took up running after Sunday's Church parade and, clutching their two dollars, headed across town to these areas. However, there was often a heavier price to pay from VD, though the Argylls were up-country training so much, that this kept them out of these establishments more than the garrison troops who suffered much higher rates of VD. The Argylls reckoned that another Scottish battalion that came to Malaya from Shanghai and were then fairly quickly moved to India in 1940, had 75% VD cases!

It wasn't just the Jocks who were considered socially unacceptable by many colonials. At the exclusive Tanglin Club, officers could pay a greatly reduced entry fee, but some junior officers like Bal Hendry felt cold-shouldered.[53] In fact, the civilian members had seen their club virtually taken over by senior Army officers who seemed to see it as their preserve. When civilian members joined the Volunteers many did not hold officer rank. They found themselves barred from entering their own club in uniform!

Many junior Argyll officers found more agreeable occupations in swimming and yachting. Others including Padre Beattie were in the battalion Rugby team – one of the best in Singapore. Some, like Captains Ernest Gordon and Mike Blackwood, were already experienced yachtsmen from their schooldays and joined Singapore Yacht Club. Others joined the Flying Club or frequented the nearby Garrison Golf Club or the Royal Singapore Golf Club on Sime Road.[54]

Captain Eric Moss observed the reaction of civilians to the Argylls and compared it with his previous postings. He found the civilians in Hong Kong "absolutely dreadful" to the troops and those in Peking not much better. Those in Shanghai and Tiensing had been very welcoming. The Singapore civilians were not considered welcoming. The planters in Malaya were much more so, though there were always exceptions: when the Argylls were at Mersing one particular English planter became a thorn in their side. He objected if they played football on a Sunday. "He objected to this, that and the next thing. He was a bloody pest!"

Battalion boxing matches were popular and prize money encouraged contestants. The team organised by Lt Bell and trained by CSM Archie McDine, travelled about giving exhibition fights. The battalion champion was L.Cpl Patrick 'Sophie' Stewart. Other fine fighters included the team trainer PSM Hoostie McNaught, C.Sgt James Wailes, Cpl Alex McDougall, Pte A. 'Lanny' Ross, little Pte Tom 'Skin' McGregor, Pte 'Naught Naught' Anderson from Falkirk (so called because of his number 298000), Pte Jim McCuaig and Lt Ian Primrose. Primrose, a very tall, athletic man from Campbeltown, knocked out the Manchesters' heavyweight champion in the first round of an exhibition fight. Alec Carruthers, whose rank swung wildly between Sergeant and Corporal, had been boxing trainer until returned to the UK with those who were overdue leave from India.

Alex McDougall, who once knocked out Hoostie McNaught, describes how an army boxing team provided funds to charity and how, years before, he had become a boxer: "Before the Japanese came into the war, we organised a boxing team of all the different regiments in Singapore. I was the Corporal in charge and Lt Bell was the officer in charge and we went all over Malaya giving exhibitions of boxing – to the Malay Regiment, the Police and so on – collecting money for the Red Cross. We raised quite a few thousand dollars.

"I learned to box at a Catholic Boys' and Girls' School – and I'm a Protestant. I went to a Protestant school, but it was these two boys that were in the Argylls along with me, George Murphy and Jake Farlow – I used to run about with them when I was 15. I went to Dundee the first time and fought in the Caird Hall when I was 15 for the Maryhill Boys' Parochial Hall. The RCs had all the equipment, and George Cranston, Murphy and Jake Farlow told the priest, Father Murphy, I was not a bad scrapper – I was always scrapping at school. So they got me up to St Mary's Boys Guild and this Father Murphy says 'Put the gloves on, McDougall and I'll have a wee spar with you.' I was sparring, just the way you would when you were fighting with the boys at school, and I let one go – and he had a white surplice on, and he had a fountain pen in it – and that's the first time I was ever K.O.'d – really K.O.'d – he let one go and he belted me!"[55]

Lanny Ross had a dark secret that Pte Duncan Ferguson discovered when he drove Lanny to the General Hospital following a bout with Hoostie McNaught; a bout won by Lanny with a knockout. Ferguson overheard the nurse ask Lanny his first name and to hoots of laughter from Ferguson he replied "Blackadder". The curtain opened and the fierce Lanny glared at Ferguson: "See if you tell anyone that,

I'll knock your block off!" However Lanny Ross was a good man to have beside you on the streets of Singapore. Duncan Ferguson remembers: "Lanny Ross says 'Come on, Fergie, we're going out.' So we were going up the road to the Union Jack Club, and there are two big Aussies coming towards us you see. And they say 'Off the f... pavement and let us pass!' Lannie says: 'You get off the pavement and let us pass.' And they say 'Come on sonny, on you go.' Bloody sonny! Just two wallops, and the two of them were out cold."[56]

Boy soldiers Civvy Cameron and Alfred Booth were members of the Highland Dancing display team that gave performances not only in Malaya but also in Java and Sumatra. The battalion 2 i/c Major K.D. 'Mali' Gairdner was also a fine dancer. Battalion Sports Day was an opportunity for Highland dancing. Eric Moss explains: "We used to aim every Sports Day to have the four Sixteensome reels, one reel for each Company, and in the middle a Thirty-twosome for HQ! You have more people dancing in the larger reels, so it takes the same amount of time, but you needed a lot of practice for a Sixteensome. I taught a Sixty-foursome to some of the 2nd Battalion. But there was little time for this in Singapore. Stewart was trying to turn every Lance Corporal into a Divisional Commander! He went to Woolworth's and bought up every penny compass they could provide so that the chaps could navigate."[57]

The battalion football team was one of the very best. The team was a finalist in the Rovers Cup, Bombay in 1938 and the same year won the Secunderabad Area Cup and travelled afar to win the Honolulu Cup. PSM, later CSM, Hoostie McNaught was an outstanding goalkeeper. Pte William 'Hooky' Walker was so nicknamed because of his prowess on the football field – he played right or left forward and took the penalty kicks, never missing in three years. Walker, whose father had been in the Black Watch, had joined the Argylls as a seventeen-year-old in India in 1935. There was also a battalion Hockey team and both officers and Jocks had access to Tanglin Swimming Club as well as Garrison pools. Nick Carter enjoyed water polo, cross country running and hockey.

Besides the sportsmen, there were others who kept up the morale of the battalion often at their own expense. One such was Colonel's Bugler, Davy 'Smudger' Smith from Bridge of Allan near Stirling. Duncan Ferguson recalls him as the Phantom Bugler: "A fire call would go out at 3.00 a.m. in Camp, and he would have us all running about with fire buckets of water and sand, and it was him sitting up in a tree! Just amusing himself! He was always in detention. When we were having that scrap at the Union Jack Club, it was him sitting on top of a taxi playing the chant from the Argylls that was calling the rest of us down there! And when he was on Fort Canning Guard there came one day a Foreign Legion General inspecting them. Some of the fellows were thinking they recognised the face! It was him inspecting the Guard. He did detention for that."[58]

Although streetwise, twenty-four year old Jockie Bell, was not one for the action of either Lavender Street or the Union Jack Club. He had only started shaving the year before while training at Stirling Castle. At first he didn't smoke, he drank lemonade then later graduated to shandy. The camp canteen didn't sell spirits but there were barrels of Younger's beer. Here Jockie 'Ting-a-ling' Bell became one of the Canteen Singers and was rewarded with lemonade. More genteel entertainment was provided by Mrs Gibson, an Australian lady of Scottish descent, who lived in a fine residence on Cluny Hill at the back of the camp. Jockie was not averse to tea with Mrs Gibson. "Every now and again you were invited over and there was always maybe a couple of Navy, a couple of Manchesters and a couple of Argylls. CSM McTavish came to me because at first I was of quite a good character – I didnae drink – so he sent me to the bunfights, free tickets, and I used to go there, and she gave you a couple of bottles of McEwan's Blue Label, and you got your tea, and I would start on the pineapple juice and the cakes. She had a tennis court and you could have a good laugh. And I used to go around taking the fags, filled my pockets, a few here, a half dozen there, from those round tin containers with smokes. There was a full size snooker table in the house. It was beautiful, Mrs Gibson's party. I wonder if those two got back to Aussie? They always invited folk up, had friends there and you met them all – they were la-di-dahs, we were just the common type. Maybe she just liked to do you a good turn."

Jockie was also entertained at the Presbyterian Church Lecture Hall on Orchard Road. The Presbyterian Church had been approached by Padre Beattie of the Argylls and asked to form a club to meet the needs of the soldiers. The Argylls were predominantly Presbyterian and the battalion was unique in having its own Kirk, recognised by the General Assembly of the Church of Scotland and the Royal Army Chaplains Department.

Two ladies at Singapore's Presbyterian Church, Mrs Cassells and Mrs McLare, were particularly active in welcoming the Argylls and arranging games, concerts, dances and even organ recitals. Sgt Ross formed a harmonica band. Jockie remembers visiting the Hall: "I was sent with another chap called Jeremiah McGuiness from Springburn, big Gerry, big gawky sod, and away we goes to the party and go in and this lady says 'Just come away through here boys,' and they had us doing fatigues in the back, helping, giving us an apron! It was bacon, eggs and beans, nae drink, a wee club for the soldiers with soft drinks. Another time we were invited to go to this Scotch Club at the Caledonia (in Seremban) when we'd finished our chores. The chap who invited us said 'Well, you've got your collar and tie but you're not dressed to get in, but I'll get you in round the back', and you had to climb in through the toilet window and from the toilet into the bar. I'm standing at the bar and he bought us a 50 drum of cigarettes. The band was playing and you could see people dancing – who comes in but Big Boyle (Captain David Boyle commander of D Company). He says 'What the hell are you doing here?' The bloke we're with says 'It's my fault. I'm a member and I've brought them in as my guests.' 'Well, as long as you don't start singing like you do in the canteen!' Boyle says. 'The CO's in there!'."[59]

Sometimes the reaction of the civilian population could be surprising. On Christmas Eve 1940 Alex McDougall attended a Midnight Mass in Singapore with his Catholic friend George Murphy: "I was copying what he was doing – blessing himself, bending the knee – and a bottle of whisky fell out of my pocket, right on the floor and went splat, and the old Catholic priest was looking down. Well, after he'd got done, he said 'Would the two soldiers stay behind please.' So we stayed and he came up – and he replaced the bottle of whisky for me – the heid man of the Church. I'll never forget that."[60]

The popular song known to all the troops in late 1941 and forming the title of this book was 'Moon over Malaya.' The song was sometimes called 'Terang Bulan' as the idea for it, but not the tune, came from a popular, romantic Malay song of that name which had for many years been the Perak state anthem and was much later, in 1963, chosen by Tunku Abdul Rahman as the national anthem of Malaysia. The Argyll song went thus:

'Palm trees are swaying in the moonlight
Casting their shadows o'er the sea
What then will greet us in the morning
Just stay a while and listen here to me.

For a moon is shining on Malaya
Stars twinkle down from up above
Girls in their sarongs and kabayas
In their kampongs they sing their songs of love.

You can hear Terang Bulan and old Sarino
Songs their mothers sang in days gone by
From Penang to Ipoh and Malacca
You can hear those enchanted lullabys.

For the guitars they are strumming in the moonlight
And the echo of those kronchongs never die
There's a moon shining brightly on Malaya
And to think someday we're going to say... Goodbye!'

Later, in the prison camps they would add the words: "And thank Christ we're going to leave it by and by!" An Argyll, Cpl James Greig, possibly assisted by Bandsman Reg Taylor, created this song. They never said 'Goodbye' to the Far East for they both died in captivity, Greig in Thailand and Taylor in Singapore.

Officers enjoyed a hectic weekend social life when in Singapore. Saturday night was the only night that the city's nightlife went on till well after midnight. Dressed for dinner, many officers headed for Raffles Hotel then after more than a few drinks on to the Tanglin Club. On Sunday morning they played golf or went sailing, and there followed perhaps three hours of drinking followed by fierce curry tiffin. After that all but the strongest characters headed to their bedrooms for an afternoon siesta, which was referred to as 'lying-off.' Angus Rose always tried to play a round of golf after his curry tiffin but found it a very painful experience.[61]

One young officer who arrived with the battalion early in 1940 had too much money to spend. Eric Moss remembered him. "He was an utter little rascal and he was always in trouble, and always wrangling himself out of it. I had a lot of trouble with him as I was senior subaltern at the time. He got into trouble with his brother officers. It was learned that he had taken a girl out and kept her out till 1.00 a.m. – and that was very bad form. It was bad behaviour especially when she was so young. It brought the officers into bad repute in the eyes of her parents, although he did marry her in due course. He had access to too much money. We were in KL when he bought himself a big Chevrolet estate car, and he pranged it. He couldn't wait for it to be repaired, and went out and bought himself a brand new one. He came down to my room and asked me to come and have a look – a light blue Chrysler Royal, brand new. I said 'But you haven't got white wall tyres on it!' Oh, I don't think that's necessary,' he said. But half an hour later there was the car with white wall tyres. I said 'No radio?' 'Och, I don't think we need a radio,' he said, but damn me, he called me out again, and here he had a radio. I said 'What – you haven't got a shaver? That would save you time shaving in the car in the evenings when you're going to meet your girlfriend.' Then there was a shaver. He asked the CO's permission to marry and the father told the CO to stop the wedding at all costs, but he couldn't. He was sent a 21st birthday present by his mother that he didn't like, so he went to a jeweller in Raffles Square and bought an expensive birthday present for himself."[62]

Sgt Alex McDougall formed a friendship with an officer, Captain Ian Lapsley. McDougall was sent to meet Lapsley off his ship from the UK. Lapsley in civilian life was a journalist with 'The Scotsman' newspaper. At New Year 1941, after a wee dram, they got into big trouble together: "I was reduced to the ranks and then I was reinstated. I was a Corporal at the time... I was busted twice. That Captain Lapsley, he wasn't busted. It was New Year's time. He was very friendly – it was him that got me my promotion to Sergeant and him that got me my promotion to full Corporal. I was a Lance Corporal when I went down and met him at the Docks and brought his gear up. He was promoted to full Lieutenant and right up to be a Captain in nae time. Well, we broke through all the Officers sleeping quarters, raked through all their kit and threw it all over the place. And we were caught. He was put under house arrest, I was put in the Guard Room. I got sentenced to a court-martial. I got the court-martial on a Tuesday. I was promulgated on a Wednesday – reduced to the ranks. But I was reinstated Saturday. And to Corporal on the Friday. Lapsley went up and told them that it was him that was to blame for everything."[63]

In Malaya there were some 18,000 Europeans, half of them women and children. Many of these colonials were of Scottish descent. Some of their families had been in Malaya since the 19th Century but most had arrived to make a new life for themselves in the 1920s and 30s. There were distinct differences in social lifestyle between the more relaxed, more racially integrated British Malayans and the more formal British Singaporeans. Singapore was the headquarters of the major trading and estate managing companies and it had a more formal, sophisticated lifestyle than the more rurally isolated Europeans on the mainland. Almost all the Europeans spoke a local language, usually Malay. Some three hundred members of the MCS (Malayan Civil Service) and about two hundred white police officers administered the country. They worked hard and at the weekend they played hard. Social life often revolved around the Club but the Europeans were not alone in having their clubs – the Chinese businessmen had the richest clubs, the Indians had their clubs too and the Eurasians more clubs that anyone else.

Malaya in 1941 was 70% jungle or, as we say today, dense tropical rainforest, much of it mountainous and considered impenetrable. The country produced a third of the world's tin and half the world's rubber. Both industries had suffered greatly in the Depression years of the 1930s when supply far outstripped demand.

Even Singapore Island was then largely covered in rubber trees. Malaya's population was about five and a half million: Malays, Chinese, Indians, Eurasians and Europeans – each community with its distinct characteristics, religious practices and customs. The gentle, calm and colourful Malays were thought of by the Europeans as rather lazy but capable enough administrators, and the Chinese as rather loud, but industrious, natural businessmen.

The ports of Singapore, Penang and Malacca had since the 1820s formed the Straits Settlements, a Crown Colony since 1867. The central Malay states of Perak, Selangor, Negri-Sembilan and Pahang had since 1896 formed the Federated Malay States; each had its own Malay Sultan but with power very much in the hands of a

British Resident presiding over a British administration system. The four northern Malay states, until 1909 vassal states of Siam, and the state of Johore in the south, formed the Unfederated Malay States each ruled by a Sultan with a British Advisor who, unlike the Residents, had strictly limited power.

Up-country the Argylls met and socialised with Scottish rubber planters and tin miners, many of whom later served in the FMSVF (Federated Malay States Volunteer Force) and other volunteer units such as the Johore Volunteer Engineers which were mobilised a week before the Japanese invasion. Some FMSVF officers had formerly served with the Argylls: Brigadier Robert 'Bobby' Moir DSO MC i/c FMSVF units; Lt.Colonel James 'Gertie' MacKellar MC, CO 4th (Pahang) Battalion FMSVF, and RSMs T.B.M. Dinnie, formerly of 1st Argylls, and T. Ingles, who had served with the 93rd in India.

Brigadier Moir, who took his dog everywhere with him, always wore his Argyll Glengarry, disdaining a tin hat. MacKellar, the son of a clergyman, was educated at George Watson's, Edinburgh, where he excelled as a footballer. He joined the Argylls in 1914 and twice earned the Military Cross in the First World War. After the war he served in Ireland but left the Army in 1922. He went bush-whacking in Australia then tea planting in Ceylon. In 1940 he volunteered to serve with the Argylls in Malaya and arrived in Singapore complete with his First World War officer's sword. He served in the Argylls with the rank of Captain. Shortly afterwards, his services were requested by Brigadier Moir and the FMSVF and he found himself with the rank of Lieutenant Colonel. The nickname 'Gertie' was on account of his fair complexion, blue eyes and rosy cheeks.

The Argylls, together with 4/19th Hyderabad Regiment (Lt Colonel E.L Wilson-Haffenden) and 5/2nd Punjab Regiment (Lt Colonel Cecil Deakin), also of 12th Indian Infantry Brigade, formed the mobile HQ Command Malaya Reserve. The two Indian battalions were among the best in India but had suffered from the loss of many experienced officers and NCOs to newly formed battalions when the Indian Army was expanded following the outbreak of war. Replacement officers were often inexperienced and some did not speak the native tongue of their battalion; new conscripts were very young and inadequately trained. The Hyderabads, being a regiment under the jurisdiction of the Maharajah of Hyderabad, reputedly one of the richest men in the World, were not strictly Indian Army but State Infantry.

If the Japanese invaded the job of 12th Indian Brigade would be to relieve the exhausted frontline troops. For three infantry battalions to fulfil this role was something of a tall order since any Japanese landing was likely to be at least in divisional strength. The Brigade Commander was the popular Brigadier Archie Paris MC, an athletic, realistic, shrewd, plain-speaking officer who was to show remarkable coolness and courage under fire and communicated well with the Jocks. Ian Stewart considered him a wise and sympathetic leader with an exceptional understanding of military morale; a commander who only demanded from his troops the absolute minimum necessary to achieve an objective and who gave great moral support to his subordinates.[64]

Ian Stewart aimed at developing amongst all Argylls aggressiveness, moral resourcefulness and speed. Every man had to be competent in different roles, from driving an armoured car to handling an anti-tank rifle. To ensure this was so, Stewart changed their jobs around every three months.

Ingenious solutions were found to technical problems. For instance, the problem of using a bren gun in a rubber estate where grass and undergrowth obscured a clear line of sight. To overcome this a motor cycle chain was attached to the bren gun so that it could be tied to a tree, thus supporting it above the undergrowth and giving a clear line of sight for the bren gunner sheltering behind the tree.

Montgomery-Campbell explains the nature of jungle fighting: "In the jungle it is the quality of the man far more than the quality or quantity of weapons that counts; his psychological, physical and tactical training; his morale, his toughness, his discipline. When the man becomes the deciding factor it is the infantry that decides the battle. The jungle is certainly impassable for non jungle-trained troops. It offers a universal covered approach. It enormously increases difficulties of control at all levels, for it prevents visual means of communication and visual connection with the enemy beyond the rifle section."[65]

To Ian Stewart the crucial factor in Malaya would be control of the road 'in depth', i.e. domination over a fairly long distance of road. If the Japanese attacked Malaya they would advance down the roads and only resort to the jungle to outflank the British defenders. The jungle prevented visual control; and wirelesses corroded in the damp and were useless in mountainous jungle. Maps and compasses were also scarce. So control depended on keeping open the road, and battle was therefore always for that purpose.

Stewart realised that static defence was useless in such conditions. The enemy could walk round entrenched positions, could encircle and come out behind you on the road. Flanks were not secure and an enemy could not be forced into a frontal attack. This forced the defender into either attacking or delaying the enemy through gradual withdrawal. The narrow frontage of the road did give the defender a greater concentration of artillery and machine-gun fire, which would have the effect of scattering the enemy into the jungle on either side of the road, so losing them all means of control.[66]

Derrick Montgomery-Campbell, who was 2 i/c of the Armoured Car Section, had joined the battalion in September 1940. The son of an RAMC officer from Argyllshire, his father often abroad, he had been educated as a boarder at Dollar Academy and in 1938 was studying engineering at Edinburgh University. A member of the University Regiment, which became part of the Militia during the September 1938 Sudetenland crisis, he went on to attend the short course at Sandhurst after which he was commissioned into the Argylls. He says: "The straight main roads were vital ground and each little bridge was vital to us. Also to have the heaviest fire down the road so that you dispersed the enemy to the side of the road. Once you had done that he was cut off from his supplies. We were also fighting him the way he was fighting us. We did the same movements, getting in at the back of him and shooting up his supplies."[67]

Every Argyll learnt to operate in three to five man Tiger Patrols, a concept first devised during training at Mersing. The purpose of Tiger patrols was to harass the enemy's communications up to twenty miles behind their lines with the basic tactic of "fix frontally then encircle" – the tactic also used at platoon, company and battalion strength. Tiger patrols were not intended for reconnaissance; they were there to find the enemy, break his morale and destroy him. These patrols could lie low in the jungle for days and strike when the opportunity arose. They existed mostly on very basic rations of biscuits and bully beef. The biscuits were extremely hard "teeth-breakers" that only became digestible when soaked in water. A tin of bully beef was shared between two.

Tiger patrols wore long trousers, sleeved shirts, gym shoes and bush hats. One man usually carried a tommy gun, the others rifles. Some Argylls had doubts about the value of Tiger Patrols. Kenneth McLeod explains: "The terrain was against Tiger Patrols. You had to carry a parang and if you are going to have to force your way through the jungle you are not going to go very far or fast. You can go through rubber but to get in behind enemy lines you had to get into the jungle; you had to be very very careful because you could get lost, with the tin playing havoc with your compass. Bal Hendry with three or four Argylls was lost for a day and a half on one of these exercises and we had search parties out looking for him – and he had a compass. Credit to him that he did manage to get out on his own after a while. But you certainly also had to know where your own men were." (see Ch.2 for a Tiger Patrol that nearly ended in disaster).[68]

Before departure on jungle training expeditions Argylls received their emergency rations: "You got your biscuit and dry tea, and sugar in a wee bag,"Jockie said, "and then you got your 'Take a Chocolate,' and you were told 'You're not going to take your chocolate until the officer gives three blasts on his whistle – that's an emergency ration!' So the old soldiers were saying, 'Ach, eat it up!' And we were rookies, we were all abroad, up the jungle, and saying, 'Chocolate? What's the game?' So we ate it, and then the scheme was cancelled... and we had to hand it all back again when we got back to barracks, but there was none left!"

Ian Stewart developed a method of attack called 'filleting' – cutting off the enemy's control of his battle by an encircling attack on the road or by swift, aggressive frontal attack straight down the road which would split his forces. These tactics were very similar to those developed by the Japanese in French Indo-China as they prepared to invade Malaya. Stewart's thinking about the jungle was also similar to that of Freddie Spencer Chapman who arrived in Malaya at that time as senior instructor at 101 Special Training School (Lt Colonel JML Gavin RE), Singapore, and employed several Argylls as instructors. After the war Spencer Chapman wrote his famous book 'The Jungle is Neutral'. At HQ Malaya Command, Stewart continued to be widely regarded in the words of one Brigadier as a "crank". Some referred to him as "Mad Stewart." Undeterred he continued to prepare his battalion to function for long periods in the jungle away from the normal supply lines and free from the fear of prolonged isolation and jungle wildlife.

The Argylls made considerable efforts to improve the military maps of Malaya which were based on civilian maps and quite inadequate for their purposes. Great work was done by Lt Pat Noone of the FMSVF, an anthropologist and expert on Malaya's aboriginal people, who knew the jungle well. He had a Cambridge 1st in anthropology and worked for Taiping Museum. Noone was then attached to Brigade HQ and was later to serve alongside the Argylls of C Company. His brother Richard was an intelligence officer attached to 3/16th Punjabs. Both were with the Volunteer Border Patrol.

Montgomery-Campbell was appointed Battalion Intelligence officer shortly after his arrival in Malaya in 1940. He found himself for months on end up-country away from the bright lights of Singapore, mapping jungle paths with the aid of forestry maps, and marker patrolling – placing identification marks along jungle routes. This work brought him into contact with Pat Noone. Monty says, "My reports had to go into Brigade HQ and he used to vet these. All we had were maps of the forests, just giving where the different woods were, of teak and so forth. They had the two main roads that came down from east and west and that was it. Where my area was,

Mersing and Endau, we had to fill in all the little bits and pieces for the Brigade, so we had all this area to map again. I used to take my little Zeiss camera and take photographs of the tracks and smaller roads and put in a report. This was where Pat Noone had a look at it, and he got maps in from the Punjab Regiment and the Hyderabads and the Argylls. And he had to vet these to make a bigger map."[69]

The 2nd Argylls earned the nickname 'the Jungle Beasts.' Stewart was loved and feared by his men. A strict disciplinarian with piercing blue eyes, he was also a man who possessed immense charm. Young officers were filled with trepidation at a summons to see their Colonel. They secretly called him 'Busty' on account of his amazingly thin chest and skinny body, but marvelled at his incredible fitness and the fact that he never seemed to sweat however great the heat or exertion. The nickname 'Busty' appears to have been given him by the wartime troops, not the old regulars. Everyone in the Argylls had a nickname.

The battalion was involved in the belated construction of land defences known as the Kota-Tinggi Line in southern Johore. Their labours were constantly observed and photographed by numerous Japanese 'tourists.' Angus Rose, then commanding D Company, wrote: "These Nips would follow along behind us taking all the measurements and carefully writing them down in their notebooks, so, in order to give the little men more homework, we used to stick in extra pegs."[70]

Captain C.E Collinge, commanding the SSVF armoured car unit in mid-1941, had an even more bizarre experience while training near Mersing. He saw a Japanese Colonel in full dress uniform emerge from a car, make his way to a riverside jetty and onto a launch driven by a Malay. The boat headed for the sea and, presumed Collinge, a waiting Japanese submarine. Collinge quickly reported the incident to Malaya Command and received a visit from the GSO 2 (Intelligence). He was told that Malaya Command was aware of the presence of Japanese officers in Malaya but the instruction was "do nothing to create an incident."[71]

Intent upon constructing a machine-gun post with a clear line of fire, Angus Rose came into conflict with the local colonials when he attempted to cut down a few banana palms obstructing the view.

Despite Lt General Percival's 'shake up' there was still military complacency among some of his subordinates, despite clear evidence of Japanese intelligence gathering, and the evidence from the Argyll jungle bashing that the jungle and mangrove swamps were not the impenetrable barriers some liked to assume: a comfortable theory which promoted Fortress Singapore as a secure and safe haven in the public image, and allowed the Colonial Office orders for increased tin and rubber production to proceed up to the end.

The big guns at Fort Connaught, Fort Serapong and Fort Siloso on Blakang Mati island, and at Berhala Point Battery and at Changi and Labrador Park, would take care of any Japanese attack from the sea on Keppel Harbour or Singapore. The RAF and the Royal Navy would deal with any attempted landings on the east coast of Malaya. Lt General Arthur Percival, the new GOC Malaya Command, seemed to hold the view that defences to the north of Singapore island were bad for morale and would cause alarm to the civilian population. He had a military justification for not defending Singapore's northern coastline in that the natural defences for the Naval Base lay in Johore and if the Japanese took Johore Bahru they could take the Naval Base.

There is no doubt that everyone, including Ian Stewart, underestimated the military capability of the Japanese. Air Chief Marshal Sir Robert Brooke-Popham, the C. in C. Far East, in a letter to Major-General Ismay wrote: "I was amused by one battalion commander who while we were standing together looking at his men, said, 'Don't you think they are worthy of some better enemy than the Japanese?' I also got a similar remark from the Colonel of the Argyll and Sutherland Highlanders yesterday; he has trained his battalion to a very high pitch for attacking in the type of countryside one gets near the coast, and said to me, 'I do hope, sir, you are not getting too strong in Malaya, because if so the Japanese may never attempt a landing'."[72]

The Argylls needed bringing up to wartime fighting strength. Experienced soldiers were regularly being redeployed from the battalion to other units including the Military Police and others were being sent home, their time with the battalion having expired. In all 116 Argylls served with other units in Malaya. In April 1941 twenty-four Argylls were taken away to help form the 1st Independent Infantry Company that later fought with distinction alongside the Argylls in the north of Malaya. The selection of these Argylls was a matter of some controversy for Stewart received a severe written reprimand from Brigadier Paris for choosing, perhaps understandably, to get rid of some difficult Jocks. An officer who saw the reprimand letter comments: "They were tough blokes, usually the people who get into trouble fighting and so on, but they were unreliable, had no loyalty." In this redeployment the Argylls' football team lost its talented but troublesome goalkeeper, Pte Dan Quinn, who had replaced Hoostie McNaught who was busy training the battalion boxing team.

One officer and twenty men, including Cpl Sammy Moffatt from Paisley, were, for their sins, taken to serve with the Military and Field Security Police. PSM Maurice Edmonson was commissioned into the East Surreys and was later killed in the Singapore fighting. Four men joined Spencer Chapman's staff as instructors at 101 Special Training School (for SOE operatives), while a section of Argylls including Cpl J. McDonald were sent to Johore Bahru to secure the Sultan of Johore's splendid palace against Fifth Column attack.

Lt Ian Stonor, who had been with the battalion in India, was appointed ADC to Lt General Percival and saw little of the battalion in Malaya. One day he invited Eric Moss to dine with him and Percival at Malaya Command. Percival was a physically unimpressive man who spoke quietly and listened carefully. He had a reputation of kindness and consideration both to junior officers and the troops. He was also dismayed at the lack of progress made in defending Malaya since his previous tour of duty as Chief of Staff in 1936 and spoke of them as wasted years. Moss says: "I met Ian Stonor in Singapore one evening and he asked me along for dinner. I said I was a bit diffident about it. 'Oh, come along,' he said, 'there's only the General and myself in tonight.' So I went along. It was blackout time, so it was dim inside. It was a fairly long table and Ian Stonor and I sat at one end and a few chairs further up was the General, sitting alone having his meal. Tall lean chap, no chin, buck teeth, he looked a rabbit, but he wasn't. Anyway, Ian Stonor and I were chatting away at one end of the table, Percival sitting paying no attention, but I happened to mention the disgrace it was that civilians weren't being protected – there were no aircraft and so forth, and Percival said, 'You're quite right. It is a disgrace'."

Looking back, Moss comments on Percival: "My own personal view of the man, and I got to know him fairly well, is that he was an able and a nice man. Through reading since the war, I realise what a task he had."[73] George Patterson, who was to succeed Stonor as ADC, shared this view and admired Percival without reservation.

Shortly before the Japanese invasion of Malaya, Ian Stonor found himself acting as 'officer's friend' to Captain Loveday at an interesting court-martial. Eric Moss explains: "There was a chap in the Royal Engineers responsible for accepting the tenders from the various Chinese, and it was noticed by the other wives that his wife was beginning to be expensively dressed and wearing jewelry, and this got round. This chap was tried by court-martial on 27 counts involving thousands of Singapore dollars. Time and again in the evidence for the prosecution it would come up that there'd be a meeting between this chap and the Chinese contractor, and his wife was always present, and she took the money and put it in her handbag. It ended up he was found guilty on all charges and he was cashiered, deprived of his rank and committed to five years hard labour, and he was in Changi jail when the war ended, but his wife escaped and got home and still had all this money."

All these men – experienced India veterans like Ian Stonor now being lost to the Argylls – needed replacing. Major Lindsay Robertson, the able, plain-speaking 2 i/c of the 93rd had come with them from India but was returned to the UK in mid-1941. He managed to get himself quickly back to Singapore when he was appointed ADC to Mr Duff Cooper, Chancellor of the Duchy of Lancaster and after the Japanese invasion, self-styled chairman of the Far East War Council. Duff Cooper arrived in Singapore on September 9th 1941 and departed on January 3rd 1942.

Other Argyll officers including Captains David Wilson and Michael Blackwood, both colonels' sons who had joined the battalion in India, were sent to the OCTU (Officer Cadet Training Unit) as instructors in Jungle Warfare. Lt Bill Bruce was sent to Sarawak to advise the White Rajah and joined the Sarawak Rangers. Lts Hugh Munro and Stuart Law, with Captain Moss, were on Movement Control duties but were to see a great deal of the battalion in the forthcoming campaign. Major Angus Rose was appointed as a GSO 2 (Training) at Malaya Command.

Replacements in the form of sixty-two men and five officers arrived barely fit after a long voyage and with no jungle training as late as December 1st 1941. They were formed into a Draft Company under CSM Alexander 'Sonny' Porter and other experienced NCOs like Sgt David Alston and Cpl 'Hoot' Gibson. They were kept well away from the action until reasonably acclimatised and trained, on December 20th.

In late November 1941, the Argylls prepared to move to Port Dickson for intensive training. A popular location on the west coast, just north of Malacca, Port Dickson provided a yacht club, golf club and long sandy beaches. Among the Argylls Port Dickson was known as "the holiday camp." It compared very favourably with a so-called rest-camp at Endau that Duncan Ferguson visited. "It was supposed to be a rest-camp. You lay on three boards in your tents to keep you off the ground – and here was this big snake curled up underneath my three! Gawd's sake! Just where we had our tents there was a wee kampong house, and you should have seen the size of the python they had in this cage! It could have swallowed us, nae bother. I said to the Malay – made him understand – I hope that's bloody safe! Then tied up just about ten yards from our tent they had a big iguana. If you went near it could have whipped your leg off with it's tail! A rest camp? You'd tae sleep like this – with one eye open!"[74]

Jockie Bell describes an earlier trip to Port Dickson: "I was asked by the Sergeant Major if I wanted to go to Port Dickson holiday camp. 'Oh, d'you get tea and buns and a' that, and cakes?' 'Oh, aye!' So I says, 'Right, I'll go,' and he says 'Put all your gear in store and take your rifle wi' you and away to Port Dickson.' And I'm up there and it comes payday. It's all English officers up there with the wee funny hats and striped troosers, you know, and he hands out 10 bucks. I signs. Thank you! The next week, 10 bucks, that's OK. The camp was great; nae fatigues, nothing, and you could gae oot in wee boats. Big McCutcheon wis there and he used tae gae oot fishing in the sampan and there was a roller skating place, and boys to do all the chores, and help yourself to the lime juice, ice cool, and the tucker was quite good."[75]

One night Jockie went with some Argylls, English boys and a Gordon Highlander to see the lights of Kuala Lumpur: "We finished up in a big cabaret, the Great Eastern, and we met these civvies, so they got their photos taken with the Glengarries on. We missed the bus to take us back, so we found an empty bus at KL station to have a kip there, but the police came along and got the MPs. They told us to get the train up to Seremban and get a lift in a truck. There were Aussies at Seremban and they said '—— off out of here! Are you deserters?' And we said: 'No, we're Argylls from Port Dickson.' So they let us jump in the back of the ration truck. When we got back to our own camp in Singapore we were up in front of Big Boyle (Captain David Boyle OC of D Company) and the officer said, 'You were missing for 48 hours and you didn't clock out at the Guardroom.' We didn't know we had to, so we were absent without leave. So Boyle asked me to explain, and then he asked what the holiday camp was like and did we enjoy ourselves? 'Well, as a matter of fact, sir, I did.' 'Well, dammit,' said Big Boyle, 'did you not go there to enjoy yourself? Case dismissed!'."

There were no more fun and games in that last week of peace, first at Seremban then at Port Dickson. It was a period of intense training. The Argylls were training on firing ranges in Malacca when, on Saturday November 29th, they were put on 'Second degree of readiness.' This was not for the first time, but this time the feeling was that this was the real thing. In the words of Angus Rose, "The Jocks were in very high spirits and spoiling for a fight."[76] Tom Wardrope reflected "We wanted to get up and at 'em. We were young and full of fire. We thought the Japs would be a pushover."[77]

1. Obituary notices in the British national press (the Times, Daily Telegraph and Guardian); Burkes Peerage; Argylls magazine "The Thin Red Line" (TRL) 1987. Japanese incident in Shanghai and family/Clan details from Major Eric Moss, Maurice Edwards, David Wilson and Henry Steuart Fothringham OBE 1997
2. Rena McRobbie 1997
3. Tom Wardrope: Sayonara Mine Enemy
4. Civvy Cameron
5. QMS Aitken's Record Book at Stirling Castle. (Aitken)
6. Rose
7/8. Ernest Gordon: Miracle on the River Kwai (Gordon).
9. Jockie Bell 1997
10. John Carter interview 1998
11. Alex McDougall interview 1997
12. Jimmy McLean interview 1997
13. Rose
14. G.I Malcolm's History.
15. Obituary notice TRL and Duncan Ferguson interview.
16. Obituary notice TRL and letter from/interview with RSM Mctavish's daughter
17. Jockie Bell
18. Wilson and Gordon letters and numerous Argyll recollections
19. Stewart/Alex Bean/Doherty/Ferguson/Moss
20. Slessor information from Obituary TRL 1996 and Civvy Cameron. Eric Moss information from Audrey McCormick interviews
21. Moss 1997
22. Alex McDougall interviews
23. Rose/Ivan Simpson
24. Moss
25. Bell
26. Mrs. Rose Denny 1997
27. Duncan Ferguson
28. Hartley Beattie 1998
29. Kenneth McLeod
30. Montgomery-Campbell
31. Joe Lonsdale
32. Jimmy McLean
33. Jockie Bell
34. Bal Hendry
35. Gordon
36. Kennard obituary in TRL and Moss/Wilson recollections 1998.
37. "The Straits Times" July 24th 1941 and comment on Stewart by Ian Morrison in "Malayan Interlude" 1942. Recollections of Montgomery-Campbell, Alex, Duncan Ferguson and Hartley Beattie 1997–8
38. Moss
39. Information on Tyersall from all Argyll and Royal Marine interviews
40. Rose
41. Beattie letters 1998
42. John Carter 1998
43. Duncan Ferguson 1997
44. Moss
45. See photo of the wedding. Jim McDougall was later killed-in-action (see Roll of Honour).
46. Rose Denny interview 1997
47. Wilson article on the Lanchesters in TRL. Montgomery-Campbell conversation on the armoured cars 9.97
48. Information on Turner from Chye Kooi Loong, Major Montgomery-Campbell and Audrey McCormick
49. Wardrope and Rose
50. Norman Catto to Audrey McCormick1997
51. Information on the Union Jack Club from various Argylls and Arthur Lane
52. Pancheri: Volunteer
53. Bal Hendry
54. Rose
55. Alex McDougall
56. Duncan Ferguson
57. Moss
58. Duncan Ferguson
59. Jockie Bell
60. Alex McDougall
61. Rose
62. Moss
63. Alex McDougall
64. Stewart
65. Montgomery-Campbell
66. Stewart
67. Montgomery-Campbell 1997
68. Kenneth McLeod 1997
69. Montgomery-Campbell conversations 1997–8
70. Rose
71. Collinge letter to Hugh Bryson 11.2.67 British Association of Malaya papers. (University Library, Cambridge/ NA Singapore)
72. Ismay memoirs
73. Moss
74. Ferguson
75. Jockie Bell 7.97
76. Rose
77. Wardrope: Sayonara Mine Enemy

COMMAND STRUCTURE

2ND ARGYLL AND SUTHERLAND HIGHLANDERS
December 8th 1941

Commanding Officer	Lt Colonel Ian Mac A. Stewart OBE MC
2 i/c and OC HQ Company	Major K.D. 'Mali' Gairdner
Adjutant	Captain Ranald Beckett
Orderly Room Sergeant	QMS George Aitken
	Sgt David Adamson
Quartermaster	Captain James Doherty MBE
RQMS	RQMS J. Fleming
Rations Sergeant	Sgt Percy Evans
RSM	RSM Sandy Munnoch
Transport Officer	Captain Tam Slessor
Mortar Platoon Commander	PSM Hugh Sloan
Armoured Car/Carrier Platoon Commander	Captain Timothy Turner
2 i/c	Lt Derrick Montgomery-Campbell
Signals Officer	Lt Richard Webber
Pioneer Platoon Commander	PSM F. Colvin
CSM HQ Company	CSM Alexander McTavish
CQMS	CQMS D. Walker
OC A Company	Captain Ernest Gordon
CSM	CSM Arthur Bing
CQMS	CQMS A. Baird
OC B Company	Captain Michael Bardwell
CSM	CSM Alexander Biggarstaff
CQMS	CQMS James Johnstone
OC C Company	Captain Robert Kennard
CSM	CSM Archibald McDine
CQMS	CQMS James Ditcham
OC D Company	Captain David Boyle
CSM	CSM Hoostie McNaught
CQMS	CQMS Ronald Steele

LANCHESTER ARMOURED CAR

TECHNICAL DATA

VARIANT:	Mark I Mark IA	Mark II Mark IIA
Weight:	7.4 tons	7.05 tons (Mark II) 6.95 tons (Mark IIA)
Crew:	4	4
Length:	5.99m/19' 8"	6.10m/20' 0"
Width:	2.11m/6' 11"	2.02m/6' 7 1/2"
Height:	2.77m/9' 1"	2.82m/9' 3"
Track:	1.57m/5' 1 3/4"	1.57m/5' 1 3/4"
Wheelbase:	3.73m/12' 3"	3.68m/12' 1"
Armor:	9mm	9mm
Armament:	One 12.7mm/.5-in Vickers MG One/Two 7.7mm/.303 Vickers MG	

Ammunition:	500 rounds, .5-in S.A.A. 4000 rounds, .303 S.A.A. (Mk I/Mk II) 3000 rounds, .303 S.A.A. (Mk IA/Mk IIA)
Engine:	Lanchester 40 HP Six-cylinder, gasoline 6.180 liter 90 BHP @ 2,200 rpm Water-cooled
Fuel capacity:	100 liters
Range:	320 km (road)
Maximum speed:	72 kmph/45 mph
Turning circle:	8.08m/53'

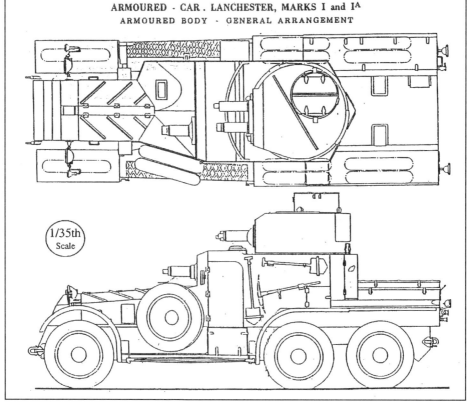

ARMOURED - CAR . LANCHESTER, MARKS I and IA
ARMOURED BODY - GENERAL ARRANGEMENT

1/35th Scale

Miles 10 5 0 10 20 30 40 50 Miles

M A L A Y A

Main Jap thrusts shown thus
Location dates are those of 2nd. A. & S. H.

10th DEC.

S I A M

Jitra

Alor
Star

8th. DEC.

10th. DEC.

Kota Bharu

Gurun

Sungei Patani

14/15 DEC.
Baling

Kroh

Kuala
Krai

Merbau Pulas

15/16 DEC.
Kupang

MUDA R.

Titi Karangan
17 DEC.

Kuala
Trengganu

Grik

PENANG

17/18 DEC.

Terap

19 DEC.
Sumpitan
20 DEC.
Len Gong
Kota Tampah
21 DEC.
22 DEC.

CHENDEROH
LAKE

Taiping

Kuala

Salak. N.
23 DEC.

Kangsar
18 DEC.

Chemor
24/27 DEC.

Ipoh
17/18 DEC.

Goeping

Antoun Bridge

26/29 DEC.
Dipang

Kampar

1st. JAN.

Telok
Anson

Bidor
30/31 DEC.

1/3 JAN.

Trolak
4/7 JAN.

Slim

Jerantut
11/12 DEC.

Kuantan

ABOUT 1st. JAN.

Tanjong
Malim

Rasa
8 JAN.

Kuala
Lumpur

10/12 JAN.
Setul
MANTIN
PASS

26th. JAN.

Seremban

Gemas

Endau

Port Dickson
8/9 DEC.

13 JAN.

Mersing

Labis

Malacca

Muar

Kluang

19th. JAN.

8th FEB.

Johore
Bahru

13
JAN

1/15
FEB.

SINGAPORE

CHAPTER TWO

THE BATTLES IN THE NORTH: DECEMBER 1941

"Cuimhnich gaisge agies treuntas ar sinnsear"
(Remember the Valour and Brave Deeds of our Forefathers)

ON DECEMBER 8TH 1941 the Japanese 25th Army under the command of Lt General Tomoyuki Yamashita invaded Malaya and southern Thailand. Units of Lt General Takuro Matsui's 5th Infantry Division, transported from Hainan island in Southern China, landed at Patani and Singora, today Songkla. Opposition was limited to some local Army and Police units and three brave Thai pilots whose obsolete aircraft were quickly shot down by Japanese fighter planes.

The Thai Prime Minister, and in effect military dictator, Pibul Songgram, had made a secret deal with the Japanese, believing that they would win the coming conflict and that an alliance with Japan was the best opportunity for him to preserve Thailand's independence. A strong nationalist, he also regarded this as his best opportunity to win back the Northern Malay States of Kedah, Kelantan, Trengganu and Perlis granted to Britain by the 1909 Bangkok Treaty, as well as territory lost to the French in Laos and Cambodia. Pibul knew that the Thai armed forces were no match for the Japanese and resistance would bring the same cruelties upon the Thai people as these same Japanese divisions had inflicted on China's population. Although outwardly he appeared pro-British, he deliberately ignored an appeal by Britain's wartime Prime Minister Winston Churchill for him to resist the Japanese and absented himself from the meeting of the Thai Cabinet on December 7th 1941 so that no instructions were issued to the Thai Armed Forces.

On December 6th, four days after mobilisation, Lt General Arthur Percival MC DSO, General Officer Commanding Malaya, was warned of the approach of Japanese ships heading in the direction of Thailand's Kra Isthmus. Percival can hardly have been surprised at the direction the Japanese invasion fleet was taking. Some four years before, as GSO1 HQ Malaya, he had written a report that predicted Japanese landings at Patani, Singora and Kota Bahru.[1] Percival issued 'Action Alert'.

The Argylls were ordered north from Port Dickson, where they left their heavy baggage, then travelled light by train north-eastward to the little town of Jerantut in the Central Highlands of Pahang in anticipation of Japanese landings at Kuantan on the east coast. As their train drew into the little station at Jerantut an aircraft was spotted in the distance. The train was hastily evacuated and bren gunners assumed an anti-aircraft position. The plane that flew over them at low level turned out to be an old Tiger Moth of the Singapore Flying Club. It seemed to say everything about British airpower in Malaya.

A reconnaissance mission including armoured cars was sent eastwards, a distance of a hundred miles to Kuantan, where the beaches were defended by 2/18th Royal Garhwal Rifles, but there were no Japanese there. Whether or not Japanese patrols did attempt to land at Kuantan is uncertain. The basis of the rumour of a major Japanese landing, which also led to the approach and subsequent loss of HMS *Prince of Wales* and HMS *Repulse,* may have been a herd of cows straying onto a minefield.

Lt Montgomery-Campbell was on the mission to Kuantan and believes he had a Fifth Column experience on the evening of December 10th, the day the Prince of Wales and the Repulse were sunk by the Japanese off Kuantan. This incident has never been explained satisfactorily: "There was an incident at Kuantan where we motored overnight and took up positions there. From what I saw there were no particular landings there at that time, but there was a civilian car which came up to the road block I was at. I asked this naval officer for his identification, and got talking to him. He was in white uniform with a naval hat on. So he then said to me – and I had Corporal MacDonald with me, a tall chap – 'I have some very important information to give headquarters,' so I asked him where he had to go and he said Kuala Lumpur. So I repeated that I wanted some identification from him. He said, 'Look here, I'm not prepared to give any identification,' and he produces this .303 revolver at me. I was getting ready to go for my .45 when MacDonald straight away put the tommy gun at his head. I sent this man to HQ and I don't know what happened to him after that, but you had to be very careful indeed. From what I gathered afterwards, it appeared he was in charge of a lighthouse down there and was giving a Morse code signal to Japanese ships."[2]

The Argylls then continued northward by train and lorry to the mining town and Army base of Ipoh in Perak State. They arrived here in a very tired condition after their vigorous period of training followed by long journeys, on the late afternoon of December 13th. That evening they received a very fine bacon and egg meal, for Captain Eric Moss (now of Movement Control) had mobilised the local wives led by a police officer's wife, a Mrs. Marriott, to cater for them. Moss's responsibilities included managing the movement of troops through Ipoh railway station and seeing that units moving up to the frontline did not run into the enemy lines.

The following afternoon the 5/2nd Punjab Regiment arrived at Ipoh. For the time being the Hyderabads, the third 12th Brigade battalion, remained in Kelantan State on the east coast of Malaya in an attempt to block the Japanese advance southwards from Kota Bharu.

Ian Stewart had a number of concerns at this time: thirty very experienced Argylls had been lost to the battalion just before leaving Singapore, demanded by Command HQ (located at Sime Road and later at Fort Canning Hill's 'Battlebox'). These jungle-trained India veterans were to serve as orderlies for the first four weeks of the Malayan Campaign. Even worse, the four Lanchester armoured cars, upon which Stewart's 'battle for the road' tactics depended, had been taken away from the Argylls on their arrival at Port Dickson.[3] There was also some confusion as to exactly what the role of the Argylls was to be, shock troops or rearguard? One officer said: "Initially we were supposed to be shock troops – if there was a breakthrough we were supposed to hold the line for our troops to re-form behind us and then we were to withdraw, but that policy couldn't materialise fully. We weren't really the Mobile Reserve intended at all."

As the Argylls were no longer being called the Mobile Reserve it was decided by the 'powers that be' that they no longer required their armoured cars. These were handed over to the 3rd Indian Cavalry Regiment who had recently arrived from India minus armoured cars, which were scheduled to arrive later.[4] The 3rd Indian Cavalry were, on paper, the divisional reconnaissance regiment, but amounted to squadrons of dismounted men, many of them poorly trained recruits. Fortunately for the Argylls, the Lanchesters proved too temperamental for their new owners to handle, refused to work for them and were, with the exception of the armoured car *Blair Castle*, quickly returned before the Argylls saw action.

Stewart was summoned to 3rd Indian Corps HQ at Kuala Lumpur to receive his orders for the battalion. The picture he found at Corps HQ was depressing: there was the British failure (due to a lack of political nerve) to implement Operation Matador, a plan to occupy south-east Thailand before the Japanese landed;[5] there were the successful Japanese landings at Kota Bahru on the north-east coast of Malaya; the 11th Indian Division under Lt General David Murray Lyon MC DSO (formerly of the 4th Gurkhas) was defeated at Jitra and Asun on December 11th /12th and was about to be defeated at Gurun thirty miles further south. The great warships HMS *Prince of Wales* and HMS *Repulse* were sunk off Kuantan; two highly experienced Japanese divisions, the 5th and 18th, were advancing into Malaya from Thailand, while a third Japanese division, the inexperienced but tenacious Imperial Guards, were moving southwards from Bangkok, and Japanese mastery of the air was already total, with the northern airfields already in Japanese hands.

Only the one-armed Corps commander, Lt General Sir Lewis Heath who had soundly defeated the Italians at Keren in Eritrea, gave any impression of calmness, control and stability, but he already looked exhausted.[6] Although an able commander, 'Piggy' Heath did not get on with Percival. Eric Moss explains: "He was senior to Percival and was jealous of him. You'd expect someone of that rank to conquer that sort of thing but he didn't, he wasn't big enough. Heath wrote a book in which he doesn't leave Percival with a name. Percival wrote a book, and when he did mention Heath he does so nicely, and he doesn't pass any criticism. Heath was capable, there is no doubt about it, but he shouldn't have been jealous and so obstructionist and personally disloyal to Percival."

A disagreement had already developed between Heath and Percival. Heath wanted to quickly pull his Corps back across the Perak River, delaying the Japanese through demolitions. Percival insisted on a continued defence of the Muda River further north. The position of 11th Division on the west coast road was not only threatened by the Japanese advance to the north but also to the east, along the road from Patani in south-east Thailand to the border town of Kroh. While 11th Division was tied up at Gurun, 12th Brigade's task was to defend the Kroh and Grik Roads and protect 3rd Corps lines of communications, which centred on the town of Kuala Kangsar.

From Ipoh on February 14th the Argylls were hurried north west into remote, mountainous and jungle-covered countryside. The battalion's instructions were to take up defensive positions in support of KROHCOL – a battalion-strength British thrust across the Thai border by Lt Colonel Henry Moorhead's 3/16th Punjab Regiment, which was intended to occupy 'the Ledge' (a piece of high ground some 35-40 miles into Thailand from which they could deny the Japanese access to Malaya). However, the Japanese had moved too fast and successfully occupied the high ground. KROHCOL also met strong resistance twenty miles north of Betong from the Thai border police and some Thai convicts released and given Japanese rifles. When three Japanese battalions and tanks joined the fray, the fate of Moorhead's force was sealed despite some brave resistance. They retreated, hotly pursued along the mountain pass at Kroh by the Japanese Ando Detachment (Colonel Tadao Ando's three infantry battalions of the 42nd Infantry Regiment supported by two artillery companies and a tank company) that was soon to be met by C Company of the Argylls.

These Japanese battalions after landing at Songkla smashed their way across the Thai border into Malaya. It was the view of Angus Rose that Moorhead's unit and other Indian Army battalions suffered from the Indian Army peacetime Northwest Frontier attitude – that avoiding casualties was the prime consideration. Casualties were bad for morale, got into the newspapers and led to questions being asked in Westminster. (But this was an over-simplification, certainly.)

From behind enemy lines Freddie Spencer Chapman observed the purposeful Japanese advance in the north of Malaya: "The majority were on bicycles in parties of forty or fifty, riding three or four abreast and talking and laughing just as if they were going to a football match. Indeed some of them were actually wearing football jerseys. They seemed to have no standard uniform or equipment, and were travelling as light as they possibly could. Some wore green, others grey, khaki, or even dirty white. The majority had trousers hanging loose or enclosed in high boots or puttees. Some had tight breeches, and others shorts and rubber boots or gym shoes. Their hats showed the greatest variety: a few tin hats, topees of all shapes; wide-brimmed planters hats or ordinary felt hats; high peaked jockey hats; little caps with eye shades or even a piece of cloth tied round the head and hanging down behind."[7]

They helped themselves to bicycles or had them supplied by Malaya's Japanese bike repairers who also supplied them with maps of carefully reconnoitered routes. On they rode. When the tyres wore out they rode on the metal rims, the noise sounded like approaching tanks to an increasingly bewildered and alarmed enemy.

An American intelligence report dispatched from Singapore on December 28th 1941 described the Japanese tactics: "The Japs show great physical endurance and ability to cross difficult terrain including streams, swamps and jungle. In encounter, leading elements immediately fan out right and left to locate flanks, and attack simultaneously with the main body when it comes up. Their attitude is consistently aggressive and they infiltrate rapidly round any resistance met. In moving through jungle they are guided along paths by Japanese civilians formerly resident in Malaya. A company column is usually preceded by an advanced patrol split up into groups of one or two men with tommy guns, who allow any British counterattack to pass through them and then open fire on them from the rear... they show great stamina and move through undergrowth, climbing trees to avoid or ambush hostile patrols, and may lie hidden in bush or paddie for hours waiting for a chance to advance or join up."[8]

At Jitra, the British and Indian defenders fought from a conventional line of trenches which was heavily flooded with rainwater. Communication between units was poor and soon broken. The Jitra forces fought hard but the Japanese simply outflanked, then destroyed, pockets of resistance.

On General Heath's orders on December 14th, the main body of the Argylls left Ipoh by train and bus and took up positions to defend the road westwards near Baling. These were A, B and D Companies. The Argyll C Company under the quiet Territorial, Captain Robert 'Bobby' Kennard, augmented by a section of ten men from D Company, was sent north to Grik to obstruct and delay a Japanese advance along a small road which ran south from Kroh to Grik and onwards through Kuala Kangsar. When at noon on December 13th General Heath gave Colonel Moorhead's KROHCOL force permission to withdraw from the Thai border west towards pre-prepared positions at Baling, this left open the entry to the road south. It was the local Chief of Police at Kuala Kangsar, C.W.D. 'Bill' Hall, who alerted the Army to the urgent need to 'plug the gap' along this road.

The result was that on the 13th, while waiting for Argyll C Company, someone crazily ordered sixty lightly armed police constables from Ipoh with six of their officers, (one in tie, jacket and long trousers) to head north and hold Grik "at all costs". Harvey Ryves, the police officer responsible for the Grik area, intercepted their buses half way along the road between Grik and Lenggong. He telephoned Bill

Hall to say he thought the position of the police party sent to Grik was useless as they were neither trained nor equipped to take on a highly professional Japanese Army. Fortunately for them, the police contingent was withdrawn to Sumpitan the next day without having met any Japanese. Here they joined the Hyderabads, though PC 1051 Hashin agreed to return with the Argylls as Malay interpreter. Captain Kennard also collected a local tin mine manager, a Mr. Coffey, who knew the border paths and roads very well and spoke Malay.

The Japanese were still expected to pursue Colonel Moorhead's Punjabis along the main road west. However Brigadier Paris now withdrew the Punjabis to the Baling area, some nine miles west of Kroh, withdrawing through the Argylls. There was no pursuit. The Argylls remained there until the 16th, disturbed only by a Japanese patrol at Kupang, on the night of the 15th, while to the north and west of them, one disaster followed another. The Argylls orders were to delay the enemy 'subject to not being committed', a military euphemism for not allowing themselves to be encircled and become involved in a costly engagement.

It was on the 15th that the invaluable Captain Douglas Broadhurst, the Baling police chief, joined the main body of the Argylls there. Broadhurst, thirty years old, had been in Malaya since 1929. He spoke Chinese dialects, Cantonese and Malay and obviously was familiar with the locality. He offered his services without seeking permission from his superior. He had also given his revolver to a local planter he felt needed it more than he did. With him were two local rubber planters, Bob Symes and George Taylor, both Malay speakers and very robust individuals. Broadhurst explains: "The civil government in Kedah collapsed very quickly and no police job was left for me to do there. So I went with Symes and Taylor to Baling and offered our services to Colonel Stewart. He readily accepted because, as far as I know, none of the three regiments in the Brigade, that is the Argylls, the 5/2nd Punjab Regiment and the 4/19th Hyderabad Regiment, had anybody in them who could speak Chinese or Malay or any well-used local language."9

At this time, Pte Jockie Bell was 'CO's Escort'. Armed with a tommy gun, he and his companion rode in the back of a Ford V8 Estate Car. One of their jobs was to organise billets for the Argylls coming north. "We met civvies up there and they said 'Oh, Hello, how are you doing?' And all that. And I said 'Well, you'd better take a wee bit of cover because that's Two Stroke Charlie coming ower' – this was that wee Jap plane that used to come round regularly, and they said 'Oh, the RAF will sort that. ' When you were bursting the doors open in these bungalows, Indians were coming over, you know, the collar and tie ones, saying 'Mr. Thing will be very angry. This is irresponsible.' 'Tell him we're taking over!' And when we went into those houses as billets, they were immaculate; the mozzie nets were up on the beds, big wardrobes full of sheets and white suits, shotguns and fishing rods, even motorbikes and cars lying at the back door."

Meanwhile, the disastrous events on the Kroh to Grik Road had been seen by Richard Noone, one of the Frontier Patrol personnel in the area, whose brother Pat was assisting the Argylls while he, Richard, was helping Colonel Moorhead's 16th Punjabs. Richard Noone was sent out of the Baling area with a patrol to reconnoitre the road to Grik, "to see if it was being used by the Japs". He took the patrol by jungle paths to above Klian Intan, a kampong (Malayan village) between Kroh and Grik. There they saw "the Japs streaming south in cars and trucks," with nobody to stop them but the Argylls at Grik. It seems likely that this was early on the 16th.

By the evening of the 16th at Baling, all had changed. After a withdrawal "to conform to other battalions" the main body of the Argylls found themselves on the evening of December 16th at the little kampong of Titi Karangan. This was the same day that the nearby island 'fortress' of Penang, Britain's oldest possession in Malaya, was abandoned after several devastating air-raids on the capital Georgetown, the European population being evacuated, and eight northern aerodromes including Butterworth supposedly demolished, though the Japanese were quickly to make good use of them and the bombs and other ammunition left in the hasty retreat south.

TITI KARANGAN

Titi Karangan lies on the Karangan river thirty miles east of Penang Island. It is on the site of a small road bridge over the river. The road runs westward from the border town of Kroh then southwards to Taiping. The Karangan River is a tributary of the great Muda River which is spanned by the Pekaka bridge some six miles north of Titi Karangan. The Pekaka Bridge was held by 5/2nd Punjab Regiment whose commanding officer had orders to hold it against the approaching Japanese until early on the morning of December 17th.

The countryside around Titi Karangan is hilly with rubber trees spaced evenly on the sloping hillsides and patches of thick jungle that the Argylls would call 'average' jungle with a visibility of thirty or forty yards. The road to Titi Karangan was extremely quiet except for demolition squads of the Indian Sappers and Miners setting explosive charges in culverts and on bridges.

The Argylls prepared to meet the advancing battalions of the Japanese 5th Division. They got into position in torrential rain on the pitch-black night of December 16th. The river was overflowing its banks. December sees particularly heavy rains in this area with frequent flooding. Sleep was impossible that night. Ponchos and overhanging trees gave little protection from the downpour. The men were soaked, tired and in little mood for a battle as they were breakfasted in the early hours with the statutory hot sweet tea. Ian Stewart was to ensure that his Argylls were always breakfasted before dawn in anticipation of a battle.

Ernest Gordon remembers the arrival of an impudent Argyll Don-R despatch rider who strode into A Company HQ and loudly asked "Where's Gyppo?" (Gordon's nickname with the Jocks, though apparently derived from "Hippo" on account of his size and being slow on his feet). Gordon overheard the Don-R and emerged from his concealed position to challenge the bold Jock's insubordination: "What did you call me?" The Don-R was not the least bit ruffled: "You should hear what the others call you!"

The Japanese attack was preceded by rumour though the rumour was not too exaggerated. Ian Stewart recollected: "Just before dawn an excited message came to say that the Japs had driven through to our right, and that a vital bridge had been prematurely blown up and a few more cheery things like that. They were exaggerated as these rumours always are when things are going badly, but they weren't exaggerated very much."

Stewart set up his advanced HQ amongst the rubber trees on the east side of the river with a good view of the road to Merbau Pulus, the likely route of the Japanese attack. With Stewart were RSM Sandy Munnoch; Stewart's batman/bugler Drummer Albert Hardie; his runner Pte Rocky Wanless; Pipe-Major John McCalman; and battalion adjutant Captain Beckett.[10] Two rifle companies, A and B Companies, were also deployed on the east side of the Karangan river with D

Company under Captain David Boyle on the west side of the flooded river. D Company was to see no action that day. The Argyll mortars and machine guns were well camouflaged but there was no artillery support and no radio contact. By dawn the whole area was set up as an ambush designed to meet and damage the initial Japanese thrust down the road and the predictable Japanese outflanking movement.

Two armoured cars supported A Company which was astride the road to meet the Japanese advance head-on and "frontally fix" them. The road came through a narrow jungle covered valley some fifty yards wide. B Company on the flank, some 700 yards east of A Company and 200 yards further forward, was hidden in the rubber. They would deal with the encircling attack, then counter-attack. The patrolling armoured cars linked the different companies and were prepared to cover any withdrawal. The Transport Section was four miles down the road with the 2i/c Major K.D. 'Mali' Gairdner. The fighting companies would reach there at the double on foot.

The disadvantage to the Argylls was that they were on a very wide front of some four miles, about three times more than was considered normal or safe for a battalion.

At 10.00 a.m. the battle commenced when the Japanese advance party, dressed in an assortment of native attire including sarongs, straw hats and T-shirts, began to emerge from the jungle close to the road. An ambush was attempted by tired and somewhat confused Argylls with a lot of shouting and nerves on both sides. Unsure if it was the Japanese or local rubber tappers, the Argylls hesitated. The Japanese advance party fired first but with no accuracy, then pulled back rapidly to deploy through the jungle in an outflanking movement. One Argyll managed to shoot himself in the foot, some thought deliberately. Sgt Alex McDougall remembers: "I was standing up shouting 'Look at those... !' You couldn't see the Japs because they were in behind the hedges. Colonel Stewart was shouting to me 'Get down you bloody fool, you!' I was shouting at the Japanese for the boys to get onto them with the machine guns!"

It was then that the Japanese got into trouble. At the same time as pushing with their first battalion down the road and into the devastating fire of A Company, the second Japanese battalion attempted an outflanking movement, turning off the road onto a rubber-covered hillside of the Karangan Estate. Here some two hundred Japanese fell straight into B Company's trap and found themselves caught at the very close range of seventy-five yards by the machine guns, tommy guns, rapid rifle fire and mortars of the Argylls. Alex McDougall recalls: "Then the force of the bullets was blowing them up – knocking them up high from behind the hedges they were hiding behind! They were being flung up and down!"

The surviving Japanese were in confusion and bunched under the heavy attack. Scores fell, including a European in a peaked cap who appeared to be giving them directions. This man took cover behind a tree, but was shot through the tree by an Argyll using a Boys anti-tank rifle. According to the journalist Ian Morrison, the Argyll was in civilian life a professional golfer.[11] The European's identity was never established but he was one of three such Europeans killed and four such encountered by the Argylls in similar circumstances. Indian soldiers reported similar cases. One theory is that these Europeans were German members of the French Foreign Legion's 5th Regiment from French Indo-China, recently occupied by the Japanese. Given the choice of going into prison camps with the French or fighting

49

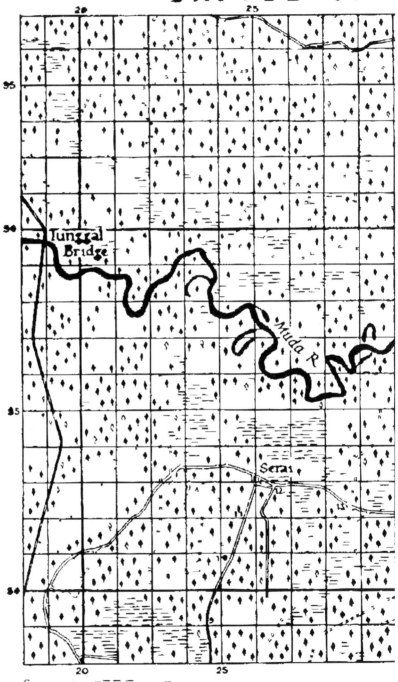

Swamp
Rubber
Jungle

Scale

Furls ┆ ┆ ┆ ┆ ┆ _____ 2 _____ 3 Miles

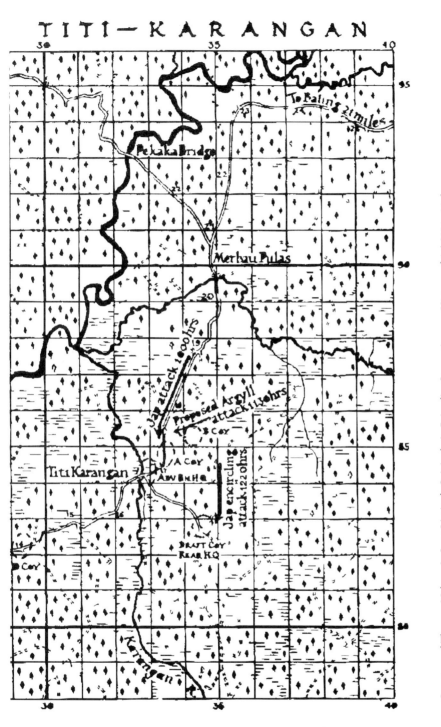

TITI-KARANGAN

Dispositions are the final ones as at 0800 hrs

for Germany's ally Japan, they threw in their lot with the Japanese.

Who shot the German at Titi Karangan? There were a number of fine golfers among the officers of the 2nd Argylls, in particular Kenny McLeod and Eric Moss, but neither was at Titi Karangan.[12] It is known that Cpl King in his Lanchester shot a Fifth Columnist with his machine gun (see on) at about this time, but he was with C Company on the Grik Road. Certainly the anti-tank rifles were issued to the armoured car section. The mystery remains.

The Japanese hurriedly regrouped and continued their attack. At 10.45 a.m. Captain Ernest 'Tiny' Gordon was wounded in the right arm while commanding A Company. Because his flank was open he thought he should check to see what was happening; "I was wounded by an LMG from a section of Nips. I thought it could be the vanguard of the encircling movement."[13]

Ian Stewart moved his Battalion HQ forward to A Company's position on the road in order to direct the battle. The Argylls 2-inch mortars were knocked out by very accurate Japanese 4-inch long-range mortar fire. Twenty-six year old Sgt Victor Hookey of A Company, twice wounded and very angry, was last seen advancing alone against the enemy with fixed bayonet.[14] Joe Lonsdale, a Lance Corporal in A Company, comments on Hookey: "He was a very nice fellow from Greenock, very smart. He was getting fed up, we all were, with withdrawal, forever on the move, and I think it was getting to him."

Other Titi Karangan casualties included Pte Robert Currie who was never seen again, and L.Cpl W. Gray who was among the wounded. Captain Bal Hendry, like Gordon a Territorial, a big formidable man and keen rugby player, was sent forward to take command of A Company. Hendry had just returned from a visit to Divisional Headquarters thirty miles down the road. Here he had been shocked to find a cocktail party in full flow. The gathered staff officers reacted with some dismay when Hendry suggested they arrange a meal for his tired and hungry driver, but in the end they did.[15]

Stewart now had to do some quick thinking. He later confided to a friend who had served with the battalion in India that the real pressure and stress on him throughout the campaign was constantly having to anticipate the next move of the Japanese in fast flowing battles. Where and when would the next outflanking movement fall? In spite of their heavy casualties, the Japanese were keeping up the pressure and a wider outflanking move could be expected to develop very soon. To avoid encirclement, it was time for the Argylls to put in motion a pre-planned aggressive attack. Such an attack, with the Argylls leaving their well-prepared positions and engaging in close hand-to-hand fighting, would inevitably result in heavy casualties to A and B Companies.

A curious conversation took place between Stewart, wearing his distinctive Glengarry – he was always reluctant to wear a tin hat in battle in spite of constant requests from his subordinates – and Pipe-Major John McCalman, as to the appropriate tune for the pipers to accompany the advance. Stewart explains: "We discussed first 'The Highland Laddie' or 'The Blue Bonnets' and I'm afraid I suggested 'The Highway',[16] which happens to be the march of my own clan." Stewart had chosen *Gabaidh Sinn a Rathad mhor* that translates as 'We'll take and keep the Highway'. Drummer Hardie, Stewart's loyal batman, was ordered to blow the Regimental Call followed by the Advance.

"The Signal," Stewart explains, "was to attack and to attack with all we'd got –

and that was precious little. He sounded the regimental call, and like a good bugler always does, he was wetting his lips, to get a good blow for the Advance when a dispatch rider came dashing up the road. I stopped the bugler just in time – just as he was beginning to play – while I had a look at the message."[17] The dispatch rider from Brigadier Paris' HQ came up the road with a written message for Stewart: *"You may withdraw at your discretion."* It was 11.30 a.m. A relieved Stewart hastily ordered Drummer Hardie to blow 'Stand Fast'. "It had been a matter of seconds," wrote Stewart, who put into action a quick withdrawal.

B Company pulled back first. Small groups of men, encouraged by Stewart and RSM Sandy Munnoch, moved swiftly through the rubber and along the road. These men were fit from up to two years of jungle training and they moved at speed. As the wounded Tiny Gordon, a very big man, was assisted back Stewart approached him. According to some accounts Gordon, far from receiving any congratulations for A Company's efforts, was fiercely and very publicly reprimanded for allowing himself to be wounded so early in the battle. A year of jungle training wasted! Ernest Gordon has no recollection whatever of this being Ian Stewart's reaction: "I never received a scolding from Ian Stewart. He expressed his sympathy for my wound."[18] The wounded, including Gordon and L.Cpl Gray, began the long journey back to Singapore.

Captain Mike Bardwell's A Company withdrew at 11.45 covered by a Lanchester armoured car near Titi Karangan. No sooner had they cleared the village than a section of fifteen Japanese followed in hot pursuit, attempting to rush the last of the Argylls. The Japanese failed to see the well-concealed Lanchester, which was camouflaged with freshly cut branches. Camouflage netting was rarely used as it impeded movement and restricted the use of weapons. The Lanchester swung forward and opened fire with its twin Vickers and mowed down the Japanese. Not one escaped. The firepower of these Lanchesters against an enemy as yet unsupported by tanks was devastating.

As the Lanchesters withdrew down the road, they came into contact with the wider Japanese encirclement on the hillsides above the road – again Japanese dressed in an assortment of native dress. The Lanchester machine gunners sprayed the hillside keeping the Japanese heads down. Back along the road, the transport was waiting to take the very tired but excited and well-satisfied Argylls ten miles to the rear for a well-earned rest. They cleared the area without further difficulty.

The Battle of Titi Karangan lasted barely two hours. The Argylls manned the road to the north with A and B Company and inflicted great damage on the advancing Japanese, estimated to be at least six times their own number. D Company was defending the road into Titi Karangan from the southwest, whilst C Company, as already mentioned, was in action on the Grik Road away to the north. According to Stewart's estimate at least two hundred Japanese lay dead or dying along the road and across the rubber covered hillside. Ernest Gordon's estimate was higher. It is still his view that between 200 and 400 Japanese were killed by A Company's bren gun fire. The Argylls had suffered eleven casualties: two missing presumed killed and nine wounded.

The Japanese tactic was now clear: frontal fixing; local encirclement to a depth of a thousand yards, followed by a wide, deep encirclement of up to four miles, all at incredible speed. The Japanese soldier travelled light and was lightly armed with useful close quarter weapons like the tommy gun. The Argylls, with their combination of mobility and aggression, had dealt the first blow to the myth of

Japanese invincibility. They had discovered that the Japanese soldier stuck rigidly to plan and if they were rattled the rot set in. A fierce, noisy bayonet charge would often unnerve the Japanese soldier.

Following this battle Ian Stewart ordered "Kid gloves off" in dealing with the problem of Japanese wearing native dress. Anyone was shot who came on the Argyll lines in native dress. "We knew the locals would get away into the jungle and not be in front of our lines," explains one Argyll, but this may have been wishful thinking as the Japanese frequently used local people either as cover or as porters.

There is a story that during this fight the Argylls had worn felt bush hats similar to those worn by the Australians and the Loyals. When Ian Stewart heard that the Australians, who were still in Johore, were getting the credit in the newspapers for holding the line he was infuriated and exclaimed, "It was the bloody Argylls! Get your Glengarries on!" The felt bush hats were thrown away and the Glengarries were put on. However this appears to be the stuff of legend. Lt Montgomery-Campbell was at Titi Karangan and maintains that the Argylls wore their Balmoral bonnets except for Ian Stewart in his Glengarry. Steel helmets were later issued but rarely worn. Nevertheless, a few officers including Ian Primrose and 'Mali' Gairdner did wear bush hats for better protection against the sun – perhaps this is how the story arose.

In the fortnight that followed Titi Karangan, the Argylls were to repeat their success in six major engagements and numerous smaller skirmishes with the advancing Japanese along the 150 miles of the Grik Road. Each time they inflicted on a numerically superior enemy casualties far exceeding their own. At Sumpitan, Lenggong, Kota Tampan, Chemor, Gopeng-Dipang and Telok Anson they continued the crucial 'battle for the road' and bought precious time for the retreating 3rd Indian Corps. Not once during these battles did the Argylls see a single Allied aircraft. The Japanese domination of the air was total and the Argylls were under regular air-attack during their determined rearguard 'delaying action'. It should also be realised that in these battles in Malaya, the Argylls and other battalions such as the Leicesters, each numbering under eight hundred men, took on Japanese regimental groups numbering close to six thousand men.

GRIK

While A and B Companies had fought their successful actions with minimal casualties at Titi Karangan, Captain Bobby Kennard's C Company, sometimes referred to as the Irish Company on account of its preponderance of Irish names, were not so fortunate. When sixty-two of them were sent on December 14th to defend the Grik area to the south of Kroh they found themselves not only the first Company of the battalion to see action but also taking on three advancing battalions of the Japanese 42nd Infantry Regiment.

The Japanese aim was to seize Perak's royal capital, the small town of Kuala Kangsar on the Perak River. Here they would control the vital road junction with the main north-south trunk road, thus severing supply lines to British forces in the northwest of Malaya and trapping these units.

The area around Grik and Kroh in Upper Perak was very remote hill country where tigers still roamed in the jungle and roads gave way to jungle tracks. Grik itself is some one thousand feet above sea level. 13 platoon plus the Section from D Company were under the recently arrived 2nd Lt John MacInnes of Iona who had hastily rejoined the battalion after a bout of illness. They were immediately sent by

Captain Kennard to patrol the road between Kroh and the Thai border to look for Japanese infiltrators, while C Company HQ was set up in Kroh, some twenty to thirty miles north of Grik. Sgt Albert Skinner was in command of D Company Section. Also in the area was PSM Jimmy Love with a Tiger Patrol from A Company.

Duncan Ferguson was driving the 15 cwt. Ford V8 supply truck for this platoon, bringing up food and ammunition for the forward unit. The track from Kroh to the border was very poorly maintained. To get the truck over the plank bridges, which had only a couple of inches to spare, required the help of an escort. The 'road' was only a winding track, badly maintained by the Perak Government.[19] Sonny Barron, an FMSVF officer who knew it well, confirms this. He was 2 i/c of the FMSVF Special Platoon, an independent jungle unit made up of two Europeans and two sections of Malays. He said the track was only a road trace and very overgrown. He and his Malay guerilla troops found it easier to go by the jungle.

At one stage, towards evening on that first night of the 14th, Duncan's truck became stuck in a ditch. Unable to extricate it, he and his companion cat-napped there, exhausted and fearing the Japanese would arrive. They were found by the men of 13 Platoon who lifted the vehicle from the ditch. They told Duncan that they had been over the Thai border and had seen Japanese troops massing in great numbers. "And that was the last time we saw any of those poor fellows," comments Duncan.[20]

John MacInnes' platoon was particularly successful that night, December 14th-15th, ambushing Japanese patrols, probably accounting for sixty or seventy of the enemy. But they were lost when the Japanese rapidly advanced in strength.

The next day, December 15th, Duncan, following his night on the road, was sitting outside the Company HQ in a Malay kampong house near Kroh. He was hungry and tired and was just starting on a piece of bread and some bully beef when he was called to take the truck back up the road. His reluctant response was interrupted when an exhausted runner came in with the news of 13 Platoon's disaster. "The Lance Corporal came running down and he came in to Captain Kennard and told him that the men had been cut off," Duncan said. "Kennard said this was more than an infiltration of Japanese and the Lance Corporal told him 'Oh! They're coming in strength! There are mobs of Japanese.' Kennard asked him if he was returning to the unit and he replied that there was no use in going back up there. They were finished. Captain Kennard said, 'Right! Out! Back!'."

Duncan was perturbed that Kennard was so agitated and shouting rather than giving quiet commands as expected of Argyll officers. "There definitely was a panic reaction by Kennard. 'We've got to get out of here. Come on!' He said something about 'getting back to the Echelon,' but there was no Echelon to get back to. 'Get the men in the truck and get back to the next Echelon' is what he told me. But there was a plane above us at the time, machine-gunning everywhere like a mobile bren gun. Men were diving into the jungle for cover. We took shelter behind the trees and the men were saying to me 'You stay put! Don't get in that truck!' They looked as though they would shoot me if I did."[21]

The Japanese plane was still beating up the area with its machine-gun when Duncan was ordered to take the truck and the men south. But Kennard himself remained behind a tree. Duncan said "After you, Sir!" But Kennard did not step out of cover and lead the way with his staff car and driver. "When the plane went away he asked if there was anyone else who could drive a truck and, when one fellow said he could, Kennard ordered him to take mine. I said, 'Sorry Sir, you can't do that! I signed for that truck and that's my truck!' The other driver said to me 'What can I do? He ordered me to take it.' So I said 'Well take it – and I'll report the two of you when I get back'."

Duncan joined the others in the truck but they didn't get far: "We hardly went a couple of yards, actually about fifty yards, when it went right over into a monsoon ditch. All the men piled out and headed down the road, each man for himself, and left me with the driver. The driver said to me 'What are we going to do?' I said 'You don't know what to do to put a truck out of action?' So I took the carburettor out and threw it into the jungle and then stood back a bit, put two or three rounds into the petrol tank and up it went. It was like a Laurel and Hardy film – the road was very twisty and we were running and we got so far when Ping! Ping! Ping! It was Jap snipers. I was getting round the corners pretty fast. Then there was this extraordinary moment – I came across this Argyll cook, sitting on a low wall at a bridge, tucking into bully beef with an open crate of bully beef beside him. He suggested I stop and have some. 'Those are Japs coming down the road behind me!' I told him. Then somewhere, some way on, I got hold of an old Chinese lorry, with high wooden sides on it for carrying rice sacks. I cannot remember how or where. It was a wreck, but I used it for carrying the boys. I had to have someone with me all the time to get it started – I had to have a man heaving away on the starting handle, and keeping the radiator topped up with water."

The Argylls were now drawn together into a fighting retreat. Down the road between Kroh and Grik they started operating a system of running ambushes. Duncan remembers the Sergeant picking out the best places: a steep precipice on one side, a steep hill rising on the other and the road twisting around sharp corners. This made it difficult for the Japanese to surround them. There were 35 men. The ambushes were seven men to each position down the road, about a hundred yards apart, each unit in action for a ten minute period, then collected by Duncan and taken to the end of the next ambush unit, where Duncan stopped. Duncan waited there to withdraw the front seven again in his "bloody old Chinese lorry", with its constant demand for water, while the men from the lorry ran on to the end of the ambush units and took up a position for their next turn.

As soon as the first seven contacted the enemy and started blasting away, Duncan had a man heaving on the starting handle to get the old truck going. This leapfrog system, seven, seven, seven seemed never-ending. "It went on, it seems, for a long, long time, maybe a day and a night," Duncan said. Exhaustion began to tell: "The Corporal asked me 'Fergie, will you keep your eyes open for us? I'll let the men get a wee kip' (sleep). I was bleary eyed and falling asleep. Then the Japanese were onto us again. I says to my assistant 'Get out! Get on that handle!' He says 'The Japs is no' coming!' I says 'Get oot there and dae as I say!'."

The person responsible for organising this invaluable delaying tactic was most likely the CSM, that experienced India hand, Archie McDine. Kennard was not present and left with his driver separately, ahead of the truck. The police at Lenggong, near Grik, got a message from Kennard on the 15th that contact had been made with the enemy and the fighting was hard, and at 6.00 p.m. that night the District Officer ordered the evacuation of the police establishment of 120. (The next morning was when Richard Noone saw the Japanese traffic on the Kroh Road.)

In the old Chinese lorry Duncan brought out 35 men, all alive, almost all that remained of the C Company expedition. A detachment of the 1st (Perak) FMSVF who had been occupied in defence of the northern airfields, were in Grik when Kennard first passed through. This was the first relieving force C Company met as they now returned to Grik. The Volunteers began firing as this odd vehicle appeared but their FMSVF officer was out on the road. He climbed on the running board, shouting to them to hold their fire. The Argylls stopped at a bridge by a road junction, utterly exhausted, as the first regulars arrived, with an Argyll Lanchester armoured car under Cpl Bertie King, and a 3 inch mortar. With them were Indian troops. Duncan was sitting by the bridge when the Lanchester came up, and in the conning tower was a well-known figure – Fergie's mucker, Cpl Aubrey Bentley.

The return to the battalion was highly emotional to these men who had stared death in the face. "I'm not ashamed to say that I was greetin' (crying) when I saw our armoured car, and the Hyderabads, the Independent Company, the Punjabis coming up... I was greetin' and I wasn't alone," Duncan said. "We were all the same. That bit of road from Kroh to Grik, where we were swopping round, I was completely knackered, and afterwards I was sitting against this wee bridge when all of a sudden I heard 'Hello, Mucker! How're you doing?' I looked up at the armoured car and there was Big Ben, my mucker, up in the turret. And when my mucker Ben says 'Hello Mucker' the tears were rolling down. He calls out 'Here ye are, Mucker' and throws me half a bottle of whisky. But from that day to this I never saw Ben again. A great big bloke he was too. A great bloke altogether."

And what of the lost 13 Platoon? The men were forced into the jungle. They were assisted by the FMSVF Frontier Force officer, Lt Pat Noone, a well-known anthropologist who lived among the Temiar – aboriginals who inhabited the Highlands of Northern and Central Malaya. Noone was one of five European officers of this Force, set up in January 1941 to patrol the border with Thailand and to spy on Japanese activity there. He operated in mountainous jungle that he knew well, having spent three years mapping out the area with the assistance of the FMS Survey Department. He used elephants for transporting baggage and supplies. Now he was accompanied by his cook boy Puteh Bin Awang, two Dyak trackers, and the thirty aborigines and their families, whom he was returning to their homelands after their assistance with the Patrol. A few days earlier a wireless message to his advance base at Tapong on the Upper Perak River, had summoned him to join the Argylls at Grik. First however, he was directed to go up to Kroh to join MacInnes' platoon. He was either with them when the Japanese overwhelmed them or encountered them later in the jungle.

Lt Pat Noone and the remainder of 13 Platoon however, were only starting to come down from the border fracas onto the road from Kroh to Grik. They were actually behind the main force of the Japanese. They had a firefight at Kampong Kerunei, a small village about six miles south of Kroh. The Japanese were driven off but two Argylls were wounded. It is known that about 24 men had been collected by Pat Noone and were coming south with him. By the time they got to Grik it was entirely deserted and down by the river a Chinese shopkeeper told them everyone had gone. At this point the party divided. One group went with Noone and the aboriginals he was collecting. They were going to move east then south in a large loop, then head south down the mountain ranges in the direction of the Cameron Highlands.

The other group chose to head down river in the hope of reconnecting with the frontline troops more quickly. Most of the men in this group were almost certainly drowned trying to raft down the fast flowing Perak River in an old ferryboat. It is known that many Argylls, especially more recent arrivals in Malaya, could not swim. The possibility of even a strong swimmer surviving a capsize or break-up in the fast waters of the Perak River was remote. [22]

The group of four who remained with Pat Noone, Sgt Andrew 'Matte' Connelly, and Ptes George Bolt, William Richardson and Edward Westhead, were led through the jungle near Jalong in the mountains east of Kuala Kangsar. One of them dropped his rifle in the Piah River, little more than a stream, but it delayed their trek for two hours until the rifle was recovered. There was no question of an Argyll leaving his rifle behind.

When they arrived near Sungei Siput, the cook boy, Puteh Bin Awang, was sent into the town to telephone for a vehicle to pick them up. They were shocked to learn from him that the Japanese were there before them. By this time they were all exhausted and their boots were worn through. The Argylls were ill. They spent Christmas in the Tanjong Rambutan area then continued their journey.

At this time Noone's party was joined by another Volunteer Frontier Force officer, Lt H.C. Dolman, a forester in civilian life, who had brought two East Surreys out of the Baling area. Sgt Andrew Connelly, the fittest of the Argylls, wanted to press on to the Cameron Highlands with their two Dyak trackers, but he didn't get beyond a nearby Christian mission house and later gave himself up to the Japanese. Ptes Richardson and Westhead died from malaria. Noone and the surviving Argyll Pte Bolt and the Temiar set out again but Bolt fell behind. Noone pressed ahead leaving Bolt with one of his trusted guides, a man called Uda, to move at his own pace. Some hours later Uda reported to Noone that Pte Bolt had collapsed and died going up a steep slope. It is somewhat ominous that he had been left behind with a tribesman who in November 1943 was to murder Pat Noone.

PSM Jimmy Love and Sgt Albert Skinner, A and D Companies respectively, also cut off in the area north of Kroh, managed to get away. The two Argyll sergeants met up with a sergeant from the Leicesters; they went native, dressing unconvincingly as somewhat heavily bearded Malays – more like two dreadful looking ruffians – with Love in patent leather dancing shoes. They daringly made their way undetected through the garrison town of Taiping, already occupied by the Japanese, and rejoined the battalion three weeks later some one hundred miles further south after encountering Major Angus Rose who was conducting Special Operations on the west coast of Malaya. Rose wrote, "The next thing I knew was that a heavily bearded Malay had slapped me on the back exclaiming at the same time, 'Oh,Christ! Fancy meeting you here, Mr. Rose.' For a moment I failed to recognise the identity of PSM Love of my own regiment behind his natural disguise. Then turning to a red-bearded Malay I extended a hand with the traditional observation of "Dr Livingstone, I presume.' 'Aye,' added Love, 'and Mr. Rose was ma' platoon commander when we was in Edinbrae'."[23]

Lt John MacInnes was captured and died at Taiping jail on February 19th 1942. Whether he was wounded or in the jungle for a period of time is not known. Four of his men also died of appalling neglect in Taiping jail as did Fergie's mucker, Cpl Bentley, captured some days later. Pte Hugh Benny got as far as Ipoh but died in the jungle.

From Grik the retreat of C Company survivors and their relieving units continued, hotly pursued by the Japanese on their bicycles. Sonny Barron of the FMSVF explains how the Japanese forces came in strength at such speed down the road trace from the Thai border. Their trucks had winches mounted on them that enabled them to lift logs to improve the bridges. Barron recalls these Japanese trucks which he later observed more closely on the Death Railway: "They were 2 and 3 ton, short and long wheelbased chassis, cab vehicles, fitted with drop-sided flat top bodies with optional canvas topped canopies. The winches were fitted on a reinforced platform immediately in front of the radiator and just above the front bumper bar. These were driven by a gearbox power-take-off unit. The vehicles were very similar to the Marmon-Harrington trucks used by the American and Allied forces in World War 2 and probably based on copies of them. However the 2 ton version of the Jap trucks were unique in that they had two extra axles fitted with rail wheels, mounted betwixt and between the conventional front and rear axles that were fitted with tyred road wheels. These extra axles could be raised or lowered by hydraulic power and operated independently of the road wheeled axles, thus making it possible for them to be used on either road or railway. In the latter instance as a light motorised personnel carrier. I personally only saw them operate in this manner at Ban Pong railway junction although other POWs claimed to have seen them being used by Jap railway engineers on the Wampo section of the Siam-Burma Railway."

The road south of Grik was of better quality. It headed southwest almost parallel to the Perak River. Fergie, still in his old lorry, managed to come out as the tail to Cpl Bertie King's Lanchester, which should have been behind them covering their retreat. Duncan, looking from his driving seat at Bertie in his Lanchester turret, pulled faces at the cheerful Corporal: "Bertie – oh, he was a nice chap. Came from Clydebank… awfy canny – sort of Christian bloke you'd never think he'd become a soldier… I was making faces at him as we went along in the Chinese lorry. And then I saw the turret of his Lanchester swinging round and the machine gun coming down and it looked as if it was pointing direct between my eyes! I says: 'Christ, Bertie, I'm only kidding!' And I was crouching down, huddled up, when I heard the machine gun going and saw the flames coming out. When it stops I get up. 'I'm only kidding, Bert!' I'm yelling, and he's pointing to behind me. When I looked back, he'd cut seven Japs in two, coming down on their bikes. He was quick. That was Bertie, he was great."

Derrick Montgomery-Campbell in the Lanchester *Glamis Castle* witnessed some more sharp-shooting by Bertie King's machine gun that day: "I was in the second armoured car. First was Cpl Bertie King. We had to move forward and Bertie King, knowing the area, went ahead. It was he who fired at this German using a machine gun, not an anti-tank gun. How did I know he was a German? I suppose I didn't, but he was a person in white and he was on a verandah, signalling with his arms towards the Japanese. Bertie King shot him from the car. That was the very first time we came across a white officer on the other side of the fence, so to speak."[24]

Duncan's Chinese lorry was now finally packing up and refusing to restart. He was left behind and later a truck arrived to give him a tow. This was driven by Pte R.Wood, who was attached to the Field Security Police, and was better known as 'Neep-heid,' meaning Turniphead. So Duncan said to him: "Now listen, Neep-heid, I've no bloody brakes. There's no water in the radiator because it's bust. So take it easy! Go slow!' So he gets in that truck, and he's whooping down the road and I'd no brakes. Finally he stops dead. And I went right into him. I said 'What did you do that for? I told you I'd no brakes!' He said 'There's an aircraft.' I said 'Where?' and I look. He points 'There!' And it was at least 30,000 feet up in the air! 'Did you stop for that? That's got nothing to do wi' us! That's going away to bomb somewhere, you nanny-goat, you!'."

They then had an altercation with a sergeant trying to set up a roadblock: "This Sergeant comes down and tells us 'Get that truck shifted down the road! We're making a road block.' I told him it'd not move. 'Get that truck moved out of here,' he says, 'I'm telling you!' 'How can I move it when it'll no move?' And he says – this is a Sergeant – he shouts to someone and he tells him 'If they don't move that truck- shoot 'em!' That's true! Shoot me! The truck cannae move and it's not my fault!"

They abandoned the Chinese lorry and then got a scolding from Captain Quartermaster Doherty for leaving it behind full of land mines and gun cotton: "Well Doc, he blamed me for everything from Dunkirk right on! And I'm standing there thinking 'How do I deserve this?' and he goes on and on! Then he gets a couple of fellows and says 'Now you two men – go with him! Get all that stuff off our truck.' I ask Doc if he's coming with us: 'Sir, that sergeant will still be there.' 'Get going,' he says. So we go back and tell them 'Our Captain Quartermaster sent me up – you'd better not give us any more threats or he'll be up here to bother you!' We get it all into this other truck and get it back to the echelon, and when we get it there it was getting dark – we left the old thing behind and shouted 'Sarn't you can bloody use that now!' When we got back the boys were sitting round with a fire and they had a dixie of tea – so I asked 'Where's Neep-heid? Any of you ken where he is?' I was in that mood I'd have bloody shot him ...with all this hassle with Old Doc blaming me for Dunkirk on, ranting and raving at me... and I wasn't even near Dunkirk!"

Duncan was in an evil temper and continued to look for Neep-heid but never did find the man. He was also perturbed to see other troops later lighting fires to cook by – a clear invitation to the Japanese. But Fergie obtained another lorry with the assistance of Captain Tam Slessor "who never swore when he was sober – 'Good Gordon Highlanders! Starch my shirt buttons!' This was the sort of thing he used to say."

C Company with 50% casualties was only able to rejoin the battalion after Titi Karangan. They regrouped south of Sumpitan. Major Fearon with the Independent Company sent to relieve C Company, commented that they were "absolutely exhausted, sleeping on their feet." C Company was pulled back to rest at Lenggong. Their experience was a sobering lesson to the Argylls on the swiftness of the Japanese advance but their achievement had been great. The Japanese had been stopped from fighting their way west into south Kedah and Province Wellesley to cut off the retreat of 11th Division. Not one of the 35 Argylls who fought the long delaying action received any recognition for their valour. Ian Stewart wrote a few months later: "For four days this Company, with the gallant assistance of some Volunteers, delayed the advance of at least three enemy battalions until the remainder of our Regiment was moved to that particular front to back them up. They did their job and did it very well."[25]

In 1943, while a prisoner in Thailand, a Japanese officer who had fought on the Kroh to Grik Road approached Duncan. "How many men?" he asked. Fergie scratched on the ground with a stick the number '35'. The Japanese officer added two zeroes to the 35. Fergie was persistent and scratched them out. There had only been 35 Argylls delaying the Japanese along the road from Kroh to Grik, he insisted. His persistence cost him a bashing from an insulted and disbelieving Japanese.[26]

On December 19th the battalion was given its next task: to deny the town of Kuala Kangsar for three or four days to the Japanese approaching down the Grik Road, until 11th Indian Division completed its withdrawal southwards. Kuala Kangsar on the Perak River is an ancient Malay royal town and home of the Sultan of Perak. Most importantly, from a military point of view, it was the site of the crucial road junction with the main north-south road. If the Japanese were quick enough in taking the junction, much of 11th Indian Division would be trapped in northwest Malaya.

SUMPITAN

The Argylls, supported by the Malayan Independent Company, drove thirty miles from Kuala Kangsar up the mountain road to Lenggong village, arriving there at 8.30 a.m. on December 19th. Four miles further up the road was the village of Sumpitan and approaching it in strength were the Japanese. Stewart decided to attack up the road rather than wait for the Japanese to arrive at Lenggong. He ordered the as yet unblooded D Company to lead the advance. They were supported by A and B Companies. The tired and depleted C Company and inexperienced Draft Company were kept out of the action. Ian Stewart called for maximum aggressiveness with immediate action on contact with the Japanese. Morale was high as the Argylls embussed again and, led by a Lanchester armoured car, the advance began towards mid-day.

Two platoons of the Independent Company had arrived in Sumpitan ahead of the Argylls at 10.30 a.m. and had not anticipated that the Japanese advance unit had already infiltrated the village. As they left their vehicles in the centre of the village, the Independent Company was ambushed and suffered some twenty casualties. They responded with a bayonet charge, shouting their Pathan and Sikh war cries as they drove the Japanese across the stream that ran through the village.[27] Several Japanese were shot trying to retrieve equipment dropped in their flight. The Japanese responded with their mortars. 2 platoon, the Pathans, ran out of ammunition, and the situation was looking critical when the Argylls D Company under "the Big Boyle" (Captain David Boyle) smashed into the village taking a large number of Japanese completely by surprise. Again, the Lanchester's twin Vickers machine-guns gave devastating fire. It was now the turn of the Japanese to take heavy casualties.

While D Company mopped up the Japanese in the village of Sumpitan the two supporting Argyll companies, B Company forward, formed defensive circles or 'Porcupines' down the road back to Lenggong. A flexible defence in depth was created, each company a self-contained unit ready to fight for possession of the road. Tiger patrols were put out to find the enemy and the patrolling armoured cars linked the different units. More Japanese launched an assault north of Sumpitan and began attacking D Company down the road into the village. The Japanese infantry were supported by the usual accurate mortar fire.

At 2.30 p.m. Stewart called in a short supportive but fairly ineffective Howitzer and mortar barrage. The Artillery support was provided by 22 and 15 Field Companies (Majors Clegg and Muir) attached to 12th Indian Brigade. At 3.00 p.m. elements of D Company attacked up the road with their armoured car, hoping to drive the numerically superior Japanese back. Under pressure, the Japanese were confused, disorganised and failed to exploit the situation. Bunching in and around trees they took thirty to forty casualties. The Argylls advance continued successfully for a quarter of a mile until a tree felled on the narrow road by the gunfire stopped the advancing armoured car.

The main purpose of the attack, to disorganise the Japanese and to delay their advance, had been achieved. The fighting went on until early evening when the Argylls avoided encirclement and successfully withdrew to Lenggong. They had lost three men and the Independent Company one officer wounded and twenty other-rank casualties, mainly killed. An Argyll serving with the Independent Company in the early weeks of the Malayan Campaign was Pte Civvy Cameron who recalls: "We spent quite a lot of time in the jungle searching for these blighters – the Japs. Whenever we took up a position you had to machine-gun the trees around it automatically, because their snipers used to sit up in the trees. We killed quite a few of them this way. I remember an occasion when we were at the side of the road. An officer told me to hold my fire until he gave me the word. And the Jap patrol was coming nearer and nearer, and I was still never firing my bren gun. We had Gurkhas there, and there was a Jap officer just coming towards me, and the next moment he was advancing with his head off! The Gurkhas with their khukris – absolutely no mucking about!" [28]

Duncan Ferguson shared Civvy's admiration for the Gurkhas describing them as "great little chaps" who rejected any weapon except the khukri. The Gurkhas hated the bren gun carriers and seemed in the habit of cheerfully ditching them at every opportunity. They weren't particularly fond of rifles either. It wasn't unusual for them to go into attack wielding khukris and leaving their rifles on the ground behind them.

The Argylls at Sumpitan had been forced to abandon an armoured car hit by a mortar bomb. One of the carriers became bogged down in a ditch. Prompt action by Sgt Malcolm McPhee and his crew in another carrier led to the recovery of the first and its guns and the rescue of the crew. Under heavy fire, McPhee dismounted, attached a chain and towed it away. He was later awarded the Military Medal.[29] Japanese casualties in the village ambush and the road attack were around one hundred. The Argylls withdrew from Sumpitan under cover of darkness without any follow-up from the mauled enemy.

LENGGONG AND KOTA TAMPAN

On the morning of December 20th, the day after the successful action at Sumpitan, the Argylls were instructed to keep Kuala Kangsar open for three more days. Three strong Japanese battalions were advancing down the road from Sumpitan and approaching Lenggong. Captain Bal Hendry's A Company, confident after their action at Titi Karangan, was instructed to ambush and delay the advancing Japanese. The Independent Company was again in support.

At dawn on December 20th the first successful ambush was made. A patrol of twelve Japanese fell to the bren guns of A Company which then withdrew, probably too soon to fully exploit the situation. Encirclement was always the 'fear factor' that could lead to hasty withdrawals. At 8.30 a.m. Captain Bardwell's B Company came under pressure. There was some light Japanese shelling and an armoured car was hit. While the Argylls were engaging a Japanese battalion frontally on the road another battalion was encircling at great depth. In the late afternoon reports from local Chinese farmers indicated that the Japanese were heading in strength down the wide, fast and muddy Perak River in all available river craft, including boats they had manhandled from the east coast, and on foot along the river bank towards the settlement of Kota Tampan. There they hoped to cut off the Argylls by setting up a road block to their rear. Successful negotiation of the river would also enable them to by-pass Kuala Kangsar.

"Hardly a very pleasant position," wrote Stewart. "In our battalion we'd been brought up on two watchwords: aggressiveness and speed, to an extent that sometimes got a laugh from other people but anyhow on this occasion it saved us."

Police officer Douglas Broadhurst takes up the story: "I think it was at Kota Tampan that a Chinese walked into Battalion HQ – I was still then with the Argylls – and told us that the Japanese were making for the Causeway between milestones 55 and 56. If the Japanese took this Causeway, the troops north of it and all the transport and equipment would have been cut off and very likely would have been wiped out. But fortunately, the information came in soon enough for Colonel Stewart to send reinforcements to the Causeway and repel the Japanese attack."

There is a story among the Argylls that the source of information of the forthcoming Japanese attack was in fact Pte Davy Heeps who was in a party of Argylls already captured by the Japanese: "Davy was taken prisoner up-country and they were made to carry the wheels of the big guns, and Davy was tied to a wheel at night. Well, he got away one night and crossed the river to warn the battalion of the Japanese plan. So as not to endanger his fellow prisoners or give the game away, he swam back and went under the wheel again. The Japs went down in sampans but the battalion was waiting and blootered them."[30]

Stewart sent a despatch rider four miles south to alert Major Gairdner at Rear Battalion HQ. He then sent back two armoured cars and the carriers to attack the Japanese. The despatch rider arrived first at 4.00 p.m. Gairdner sent Intelligence officer Gordon Schiach to muster Kennard's C Company, some fifty men, and the Draft Company, some sixty men, to defend the Causeway – a narrow strip of road which crosses the west bank of the Perak River a mile north of Kota Tampan and nearly five miles behind the Argylls forward positions. Schiach hitched a lift in Padre Beattie's Riley car.

Today, Kota Tampan is a peaceful riverside town famous for its stone-age caves, but there was little peaceful about it on December 20th 1941. At 4.55 p.m. Sgt Willie Hamilton's bren-gun carriers moved onto rough and swampy ground and met the Japanese on a track half-a-mile from the river. Pte Tom Wardrope received a serious head wound when his carrier was ambushed.[31] Captain Kennard had left C Company in the care of Lt J.H. Smith and gone ahead in his car to assess the situation and make contact with a platoon of Punjabs who were holding a position on the river bank. Realising that he was cut off from his company by the Japanese advance he abandoned his car and took to the jungle only to be shot in the right thigh by a Japanese sniper.

Kennard then found himself caught in crossfire and for some hours he hid under large lotus leaves cut with his parang. From his hiding place he heard Japanese voices on one side and Scots voices on the other then Japanese machine guns and the reply of the bren guns. Lt Smith had brought up the Company. He heard the Japanese clapping their hands and shouting 'Punjabi, Punjabi!' The trick seemed to work for the Argylls held their fire and were compelled to withdraw when Japanese reinforcements from the river came in on their northern flank. The Japanese could be heard collecting their wounded.

Under cover of darkness Kennard staggered on but each time he put his weight on his right leg his knee bent and he fell over. Unable to reach the road he lay down in the long grass and slept till morning. He met some frightened Tamils who showed him where two small canoe-like sampans were hidden among the reeds. He managed to capsize the first of these and waded back to the riverbank. It was here he encountered a party of eleven Argylls who had been cut off in the fighting the previous evening. They included Lt Robert Orr with compass, map and revolver; Cpl T. Collins, L.Cpls Patrick Stewart and McEwan, a bren gunner who had enjoyed considerable success in the previous day's battle.

The Perak River is broad and fast flowing. Two of the men from the Draft Company could not swim. An attempt to launch the second sampan ended in disaster and the party proceeded on foot, soon finding another larger sampan that was successfully launched. They returned to British lines two days later after boating down the Perak River. One problem they encountered was the new phenomenon of hostile Malays. The rural Malays in the past had always been friendly and smiling. Further downstream they reached Lake Chenderoh, a vast artificial lake created by the damming of the Perak River. Here was the Perak Hydro Electric generating station. Their sampan was fired on from a jungle hillside by Indian machine gunners from 5/2nd Punjabs. Eventually they were found by Cpl Bertie King, patrolling between the river and the road in his Lanchester armoured car. (For about thirteen miles the road borders the western side of the lake.)[32]

Kennard was returned to Johore then Singapore in a crowded hospital train with the dying 2nd Lt Kenneth MacLean. Also among the wounded was L.Cpl Joe Lonsdale, wounded in the leg while giving covering fire to men pulling back into a rubber plantation. He spent two weeks in a Johore Bahru field hospital before rejoining the battalion with other 'walking wounded.' Further down the line, Angus Rose, still on Special Operations with the Australians, encountered this train: "As I was very anxious to obtain news of my regiment, I went over to the platform and enquired from an orderly in the rear coach if there were any Argylls on board. 'Argylls,' said the orderly. 'Yes, sir; we're stuffed full of Argylls.'... I walked up the whole length of the train. Apart from Argylls, of whom there were a large number on board, there were also a good many Indian troops. The atmosphere was like a Turkish bath and the poor nursing sisters looked as if they were at the end of their tether. I met Bobby Kennard lying up in the front coach and clad in a Lance Corporal's shirt. Bobby had a bullet wound in the thigh, but seemed cheerful enough and had had a miraculous escape. There was another Argyll called MacLean, lying below Bobby. He was badly wounded and, although smilingly cheerful, looked terribly weak and frail."[33]

To go back to the main action in the rubber near Kota Tampan, fierce fighting ensued between the Japanese and C/Draft Companies. The Draft Company performed magnificently in this, their first action. Japanese casualties were heavy, some shot out of trees in which they had taken up sniping positions. Tree spraying with brens was often productive to the Argylls. Pte Stan Roberts says, "They came round the back of you and they were up in the trees but they weren't good shots, their rifles weren't great."

Again the Japanese could be heard shouting "Punjabi, Punjabi!" This was an oft-repeated confusion tactic to flush out the Argylls but proved less than convincing. Again a European, presumably a German, was shot while advancing with the Japanese.

At 5.15 p.m. the Argylls at Lenggong began withdrawing to Kota Tampan with A and B Companies covered by D Company who were ready to ambush the pursuing Japanese. The anticipated pursuit was immediate and was dealt with by the ambush parties. Lt Ian Primrose's D Company platoon made a successful night ambush on Japanese trying to cross the now demolished Causeway, killing fifteen of them. Again the Argylls had successfully denied the road south to the Japanese without allowing themselves to be encircled and destroyed. Argyll casualties that day were three officers and fifty men, mainly wounded.[34] The Japanese casualties were around 350.

The Argyll officer casualties, in addition to the wounded and at that stage missing Captain Kennard, were Lt Robert Orr from Dumbarton, missing and wounded, and the recently arrived 2nd Lt Richard Armstrong reported missing presumed killed. His empty car was found at the roadside. Armstrong was twenty-one years old and the Oxford-educated son of an Army colonel. A Malayan Civil Service cadet in Perak since January 1941, he had briefly served with the Hampshire Regiment. He volunteered to serve with the Argylls when the Japanese invaded Malaya. Armstrong was one of forty MCS members to die in the War. Their names are inscribed on a plaque in Singapore's St Andrew's Cathedral. NCO casualties that day included the powerfully built, pugnacious former PE and boxing instructor CSM Archie 'Dinah' McDine of C Company, who was killed by mortar fire and had been the likely leader and organiser of that delaying action at Kroh.

The following morning the Japanese Ando Regiment made another assault on Kota Tampan, rafting down the river, but was met with artillery and machine-gun fire. At 8.00 a.m. a Japanese company supported by close range artillery attacked the Argylls left flank which consisted of A and D Companies. The attack was repelled. Argyll casualties were seventeen men including Lt Bell of A Company who was wounded in the right arm, and Sgt J. Haggart of D Company. Among the dead was Alex McDougall's brother, Tommy: "I wasn't with him when he was killed, but this boy Skin McGregor came down. He says 'Your younger brother's had it, Alex.' Duncan McPhee from Campbeltown says 'Come on, I'll run you back up the road now.' The Japs had withdrawn after the battle. We went up there and I got my younger brother. He was lying at the side of the road. What happened was he got hit directly with a shell – and you know how they wear these pouches of ammunition – well all the ammunition went off and killed nearly all the men in his section. And he was – oh! He was blown to smithereens – but his watch was still going, and it was the watch he was presented with for swimming. And the Japanese stole that off me an' all. Well there were eight blokes all lying there, so we buried them in wee shallow graves there – me and Sandy (L.Sgt Alan) McPhee and his brother who was in charge of the Motor Transport Section, and Wee Skin McGregor of D Company. The local people marked them off and I believe there is a statue of remembrance there."[35]

The Argylls' instructions that morning were to deny Kuala Kangsar to the Japanese for two more days. At 1.00 p.m. they were permitted to withdraw from Kota Tampan, passing through the positions of 5/2nd Punjabs, but Ian Stewart delayed the withdrawal to attempt one more crack at the Japanese. Sure enough, at 2.30 p.m. the Japanese attacked Advance Battalion HQ/C Company's positions and were effectively dealt with. At 6.30 p.m. a Japanese section was wiped out by the bren guns of PSM Colvin and Drummers McShane and Blythe. Under cover of darkness the Argylls withdrew six miles down the road.

The Argylls were now very tired but so were the Japanese who failed to follow up the Argyll withdrawal with their usual alacrity. Argyll losses that day were two officers and twenty other ranks. They included the highly regarded CSM Alexander Biggarstaff of B Company killed in action. Japanese losses were at least two hundred. The exhausted battalions of the Ando Regiment, depleted by its bruising engagements with the Argylls, were pulled out of the battle for northern Malaya by Lt General Yamashita who had ordered units of Lt General Nishimura's Imperial Guards Division south from Thailand to replace them.

Exhaustion was starting to tell on some Argylls. Jockie Bell remembers the case of Bobby M. "We had Japs around us at this time, and we were going through the rubber estates, and Big Boyle said to us 'Right boys, you'll need to jog-trot through all this.' He'd got information from a couple of coolies that the Japs were all around, so we were all jog-trotting through the rubber estates hell for leather. We'd got a 15 cwt truck coming through with the wounded on it, and Boyle looks, and here's Bobby lying in the back of it, and Boyle called him all the names. 'Get out you!' He got his big .45 out and said 'I'll blow your head off right now!' Bobby said 'I've got a bit of shell shock... malaria, Sir.' 'You march with the boys!' Boyle tells him, 'You march with the boys!'."[36]

December 23rd was a day of general and confused withdrawal. Japanese reconnaissance planes flew ridiculously low as if to show their contempt for possible attack. They were followed by low-level air attacks and a further artillery attack on the Argylls' transport near Salak on the Perak River, which caused twenty-five casualties including Rations Sgt Percy Evans and L.Cpl Michael Friel who lost a leg. Four Argylls and two mess boys were killed. Pte Stan Roberts remembers: "We didn't see any of our planes. Theirs flew in at 300 feet high, you could see the pilots."

Bandsman Robert Taylor distinguished himself that day and was later awarded the Military Medal. The citation read: "His great devotion to duty during bombing and machine-gun attacks was an example to all. At the height of activity he was exposed to great danger in carrying casualties to the ambulances."[37]

Duncan Ferguson remembers two "sweeper" boys who accompanied the battalion: "We had two boys who were sweepers to the battalion, just clearing up. A young Chinese boy and a Malay. The Malay boy introduced me to his sister, Mona – oh, she was lovely. Well these two young laddies were with me, and they were only boys of about 15 or 16. What were they doing here, I asked them. They wanted to be with us. I told them to keep an eye open, I wanted a sleep, I was bleary-eyed. I lay down and they watched over while I had a sleep. Well, they woke me up and they had a meal made. Oh, a lovely meal that. Rice and things. When I went back to the echelon I told the lads they'd better go back. If any of the officers saw them they'd be very angry – go back because it's dangerous! I saw them once again... I was carrying ammunition in my truck and across the road were big caves that you could go down into – no, not the Batu Caves. You went up to the Batu Caves; you went down into these. There were some soldiers down there sleeping, but I was on the other side of the road, and I said to the two boys I was going to the back of the truck to have a sleep. It wasn't long before someone was shaking me. 'Hey! Mucker! There's artillery shells blasting us!' 'Where?' 'Listen!' I could hear the bang. I said 'That's our 25 pounders firing!' They said 'No, that's the shells landing!' An argument started, but then they listened again. You could hear the noise of firing then whoosh! Three of them landed and one right across the road. The ground shook and there was a fearsome explosion – it went down among the caves and some Argylls were killed. The two sweeper boys were crying and one Argyll was shell shocked."

Sometime later Duncan organised a lift south for the two sweeper boys. He didn't see them again in the Campaign but they were to meet again on the Death Railway.

One day Duncan was coming from a day's work on the railway when he passed a group of Asians heading up the railway as forced labour – and the two boys were among them. His heart sank when he saw them, because "they were great wee lads". He gave them all the money he had on him which happened to be $5, as he was in funds at the time. But he never saw the boys again.[38]

Japanese mortar fire could be both accurate and lethal. Padre Beattie recalled an incident at this time where one of the Companies and Rear Headquarters were occupying a broken down sawmill. He had just left the mill when a Japanese mortar shell fell clean through the roof causing seventeen casualties, most of them seriously wounded.

Pte Nick Carter recalls how he was wounded: "It was by a hand grenade thrown from a plane, which got me with splinters and shrapnel down one side, and then he hit me with a bullet in the thigh. I was rescued by Hugh Irvine and ex-Boy Hyslop who carried me off the field. I'd been cut off at Grik with the cookhouse – sometimes the cookhouse was in front of the frontline and sometimes it was behind it! You couldn't always keep up! But I got myself out and joined the battalion again. Then when I was wounded I was in and out of hospitals down Malaya to Singapore and was posted as 'Missing believed killed.' My mother and I were close and she just didn't believe it. When the war ended some friends saw me in a Pathé newsreel on a Cambodian airfield, and she said 'I told you so!'."

The battalion arrived at Chemor, seven miles north of Ipoh, on the evening of the 23rd. On December 24th Major-General David Murray-Lyon was relieved of his command of 11th Indian Division. He was a brave, competent officer in a hopeless situation; certainly a scapegoat for the defeats in the north of Malaya. On Murray-Lyon's departure, Brigadier Archie Paris took the divisional command and Ian Stewart assumed command of 12th Indian Brigade with the temporary rank of Brigadier. Major Gairdner took temporary command of the Argylls, a great challenge after the thankless role of 2 i/c, which in battle left the holder at rear battalion HQ with the medics and transport, ready to move up the line if the commanding officer became a casualty.

Many Argylls viewed Ian Stewart's departure gloomily: "Stewart should have stayed in charge of us, instead of that he was made Brigadier and in charge of three battalions – that was a cockup as far as I'm concerned. He couldnae be with his ain boys."

Christmas Day 1941 did not pass without extra rations and whisky courtesy of Sgt Percy Evans. Douglas Broadhurst says, "The retreat continued southwards following the main road with actions at Siput and near Chemor. And I think it was on Christmas Day that I went into Ipoh in army transport and found the place seemingly deserted and a large department store, like Robinson's, selling groceries and drinks like that which appeared to have been bashed about a bit. We loaded our truck with goodies such as bottles of whisky and other things to take back to the battalion."[39]

Quartermaster Captain James 'Doc' Doherty and his team were able to replenish supplies from Army and NAAFI stores abandoned in the hasty retreat from Ipoh. The trucks, however, were under constant threat of Japanese air attack. Duncan Ferguson remembers: "We always had a boy watching for the aircraft, and he had to shout 'Aircraft!' and we'd pull off the track. There was once when we'd pulled up and there were two or three of the transport pulled in. My mucker Eckford was with us. He pulled in to the side and we went in behind trees, and I heard 'Get away and get a tree o' yer ain!' Saying to this laddie Trainer. I says 'Let the laddie alone! Shouting at him like that!' 'Are you wanting him? Go over there beside Fergie – go away with Fergie!' Well, I don't know how this boy did it; we were at the back of this big tree and when the plane came down, dive-bombing, he was right underneath me. I was perched on top of him! When the planes went away I went down to get my truck, but it was a wreck, just a skeleton."[40]

Jockie Bell takes up the story of his namesake, also of D Company: "He wore glasses and was an awfy decent kind of bloke, but he'd always wanted to be a driver, and he took three different driving courses in the Argylls and he failed in two. Whether he passed the third I don't know, but when we were in Ipoh, it was at night, and we were loading magazines from the bren guns, opening up boxes and someone came round in the dark shouting 'Any drivers here?' So someone said to me 'There's your chance. You took a course.' But I said 'I want to stay with the boys.' It's funny. You get a feeling you want to be with the boys so I wouldn't go and volunteer. But John Bell went. He always wanted to be a driver and yet in the end it was his death."

"I'd been getting a lift from him down the road, and looking out for him for aircraft. His truck radiator was steaming. It was a big civvie truck he was driving, with landmines and gun cotton, but he always stopped and he had a bottle for filling the radiator with water from the ditch, and his specs were always steaming up. But you know how you got caught up in the traffic jams, and there were these other trucks coming down the road so I jumped onto one of them instead. And, poor soul, it was just after that we came across him. He was lying half way up an embankment, as if he'd been trying to climb up it. He was black, absolutely black." [41]

CHEMOR

Chemor, fourteen miles south of Kuala Kangsar, lies in a tin mining and rubber plantation area. The main northern military base of Ipoh was being hastily evacuated. The Argylls passing through the town at night could see the big oil tanks of the Standard Oil Company burning fiercely. Ipoh eventually fell to the Japanese on December 26th. Again, just as at Kuala Kangsar, the Argylls were called to act as rearguard north of Ipoh. They now faced the inexperienced but tenacious, numerically superior and fresh Japanese Imperial Guards Division. A Japanese officer described the soldiers of this division thus: "Their morale was very high and they were well-motivated, though their training was inadequate and their constitution not the best."

There was a night of skirmishing in which Argylls returned from Tiger patrols with trophies including a Japanese sword and machine-gun. However some Tiger patrols nearly ended in disaster. Alex McDougall nearly got killed on one. They were out on a long distance patrol for some days. But a day later Alex's brother, a Corporal in D Company, also set out on patrol. "We were coming back in," explains Alex, "when we heard a shuffle going on in front of us and I shout 'Halt! Who goes there?' The word I got back was 'The Campbells is coming!' But the password when I went out was 'the 93rd,' so two different passwords. So all my men are putting shots up their barrels when a voice comes out 'Is that you, Sanny?' Meaning Alex – they called me Sanny. It was my brother. The two of us were within seconds of shooting each other. I read the riot act when I got back into camp. He'd come out a day later than me on a different patrol and a different Company and they'd changed the password and none of us knew."[42]

The next morning at Chemor an opportunity presented itself for an Argyll counter-attack supported by 4/19th Hyderabads with artillery support from the 25 pounders of 137th Field Regiment RA. The terrain, with some high limestone cliffs overlooking the road, was eminently suitable for tempting the Japanese forward then ambushing and filleting them.[43] The plan, however, got into trouble early when the Imperial Guards advanced further and sooner than anticipated. The Argylls' chance of attacking up the road was lost and they saw little fighting. A Japanese encircling movement was however dealt with by the 4/19th Hyderabads.

Ian Stewart had the highest regard for the Hyderabads. After the war he was to reprimand Angus Rose following the publication of Rose's book 'Who Dies Fighting' which contained criticisms of this "very gallant regiment." Rose was told that he should apologise.

GOPENG – DIPANG

The Argylls' next major action and most bruising one to date was on December 28th-29th between the once prosperous tin town of Gopeng and the kampong of Dipang (Kuala Dipang), five miles north of the Chinese town of Kampar. The Argylls' task was to guard the northern approaches to Kampar and delay the Japanese in time for the British Battalion (an amalgamation of the Leicesters and East Surreys), Gurkhas and FMSVF units to prepare an effective defence of Kampar.[44]

12th Indian Brigade was defending the road in front of Dipang to a depth of five miles, 4/19th Hyderabads forming a frontline then withdrawing through the Argylls' positions before nightfall. The plan was to draw the Japanese into the little town of Gopeng then set the guns of 137th Field Regiment RA onto them. Again, however, the Japanese moved quickly and were onto the Hyderabads as they withdrew. By 2.00 p.m. the Argylls defending the railway line southwest of Dipang were engaged.

It was on that day that Bal Hendry, commanding A Company, led his well-known assault on the railway station at Kota Bahru village (not the place of the same name on the north east coast where the Japanese landed on December 8th). Hendry, together with his batman, Pte James 'Big Jimmy' Anderson from the East end of Glasgow, and the tough, fearless but mild-mannered CSM Arthur Bing were visiting A Company's forward positions, delivering food by armoured car to a section of seven men watching the railway line seven miles to the west of the battalion.

Sure enough, they observed a party of fifteen forward-patrolling Japanese, led by a Malay guide, come up the railway track and enter the little railway station. Hendry decided to make a surprise attack with maximum Argyll aggressiveness. While the armoured car and section of seven men fixed the Japanese frontally, Hendry and his two companions approached the railway station from the right flank. They ran into two Japanese and shot them. They then went back and successfully approached from the left flank.

The Japanese were taken completely by surprise as the three Argylls stormed the railway station. CSM Bing emptied his tommy gun magazine into five of them in the waiting room then used the tommy gun as a club on the sixth man. Bing burned his hands on the hot barrel in the process. Pte Anderson shot or bayoneted those who tried to escape while Hendry shot two Japanese in the ticket office then bashed two more insensible with his steel helmet. Not one of them escaped.[45]

With a company of Japanese coming down the railway line with machine gun and mortar support, it was time for a hasty departure. One shaken Japanese soldier was brought back as a prisoner for interrogation at Brigade HQ. He received rough handling from an Argyll who had just heard that his brother had been killed in action.

Pte Stan Roberts comments on the ability and ingenuity of the Japanese to move swiftly down the railway lines: "I saw them coming down the railway in trucks, with the tyres off, and they had tanks with wheels on the sides, so they could come down on the rails."

At nightfall on December 28th most of the Hyderabads were able to disengage and withdraw behind the Argylls. One Hyderabad Company was still in front. The Japanese follow-up ran into an Argyll ambush at 25 yards, again using an armoured car with its devastating firepower. The Japanese had artillery and air support with intense low level bombing. It was the constant attacks from the air that undermined the morale and rattled the Indian troops, trained for a very different type of warfare. Jimmy McLean remembers these attacks: "These Jap fighter bombers were coming over at Dipang with no opposition, and they were bombing from treetop height. There was absolutely no answer to it – nothing the fighting men could do. We couldn't get our heads up."

December 29th began quietly enough but it was to be a difficult and stressful day for the Argylls; the day when exhausted men came up against Japanese tanks. That morning the Times journalist Ian Morrison visited Battalion Headquarters, which was in an impressive colonial house near the main road – perhaps not the wisest choice for Battalion HQ as it was an obvious target. In fact one Indian Army battalion commander made a point of never locating his HQ in comfortable European houses and was consequently never attacked.

Morrison spoke with CSM Bing about the previous day's assault on the railway station. While he was there two Argylls brought in an elderly Chinese man for questioning by the Intelligence officer. They had found beside his house banana leaves laid on the ground in the shape of a large arrow pointing straight at battalion headquarters. The man's story did not add up and according to Morrison he was taken out and shot.[46]

In fact, two suspected Fifth Columnists were shot. The job was given to Cpl Alex McDougall whose brother had been killed at Kota Tampan: "The Adjutant came out and said 'I want you to take these prisoners out and do what you want with them,' so I took them out. I don't know whether you know what banana leaves are – they're like big arrows. Well, they'd taken banana leaves off the trees and were showing the Japs where we were billeted and the Japs could see them from the air and that's how the Japanese bombers came in. Charlie Brandon got killed. I took the prisoners out and I'd no intention of shooting to kill them at the time. I let them go. The Sergeant says to me 'It's up to you. Do what you want with them.' Maybe he thought I was going to get a little recompense after losing my brother. We were in a big plantation – that's where this bombing raid was. Yes, I shot them in the end. There were two of them. I fired two shots over their heads and let them go. Then I don't know what came over me. They fell down in the big high grass. When they came back up I just took a bead on them and bumped the two of them."[47]

Such incidents were frequent and had been common in the fighting in Kedah, an Unfederated State where there were more hostile Malay attitudes to British rule. Lt Colonel Moorhead of 3/16th Punjabis ordered a man shot who, waving a white topee, appeared to be directing Japanese dive bombers and when arrested and searched was found to be carrying in his pockets long strips of white cloth of a kind used for ground markings. Another was shot for sniping at a despatch rider. Curiously, a high proportion of these Fifth Columnists were Malay teachers.

At 1.00 p.m. the Argylls withdrew through the Hyderabads. At 2.30 p.m. they were again the forward battalion as the Hyderabads withdrew across the Dipang River. During the early afternoon, in response to intelligence reports of Japanese tanks in the vicinity, two small 2 pounder anti-tank guns from 15th Anti-Tank Battery, the first such guns the Argylls had seen in the campaign, appeared in support of the Argylls.

At 3.00 p.m. the Japanese attacked. They were easily held until eight tanks and motorised infantry, all guns blazing, came rapidly down the road in an attempt to fillet the Argylls. The Japanese tanks carried 5 machine guns, a 2 pounder cannon and sometimes mortars. Faced with an enormous firepower, including alarming 8 inch explosive bullets, B and D Companies scattered off the road in some confusion and panic. Alex McDougall remembers: "I was hiding behind a tree. Quite thick trees these rubber trees. A shell from a tank split the tree further up. If it had hit the tree a bit lower, I wouldn't have been here today. It just split the tree like that. That was the first time the tanks hit us."

The two anti-tank guns proved useless. The Lanchesters were pepper-potted by Japanese armour piercing bullets. Sgt Albert Darroch was mortally wounded in his Lanchester while taking on the tanks. He refused to leave the already wrecked vehicle and was later awarded a posthumous Distinguished Conduct Medal. The citation read: "He displayed such skill and courage in the handling of his armoured car that the company was able to break off the engagement without casualties. Later he kept his car under heavy enemy fire for ten minutes in an attempt to clear the road."[48]

Darroch's driver, Pte Archibald Hoggan was awarded the Military Medal for coolness under fire. During the action he was able to reverse the wrecked armoured car although Darroch was leaning heavily on him. He cursed Darroch and pushed him away, unaware that Darroch was mortally wounded until he saw an eye lying on the floor of the vehicle.

Sgt Willie MacDonald, a big shy soft-spoken man and "a real Highland gentleman"[49] was a leading member of the Argyll Kirk. He was severely wounded in the neck when his carrier was attacked. Sgt Malcolm McPhee, also of the carrier platoon, was awarded the Military Medal when he stopped his carrier under fire to shield another carrier that had become bogged down in the mud, so allowing the other crew to be rescued.[50]

Jockie Bell witnessed the fate of one armoured vehicle: "There was an air raid and we were taking shelter in a rubber estate, and one of these armoured cars came running in there beside us. The next thing is someone says to me 'You want to go and have a look at that?' John Todd was a runner, and they had push-bikes, so he dumped the push-bike and got a lift in one of these buggies. A Jap tank came up the back of this wee buggy thing, and they fired a missile, and it went through and flew around inside and you could see where it had smashed the wireless, with holes inside the buggy as if it had been drilled with a drilling machine. It was a shame – he gets a lift down the road and gets killed for it."[51]

The Battalion Intelligence Officer, Lt Gordon Schiach was wounded in the backside by a mortar fragment but decided to take himself to get medical attention and deliver maps to Battalion HQ on the way. Driving down the road he ran into a Japanese tank and was machine-gunned. In spite of terrible abdominal injuries he arrived with his wrecked car and maps at Battalion HQ. Padre Beattie says, "I was standing in the ditch at the side of the road. I heard a loud clanking noise and looked up the road to see an old Austin 10 come zigzagging towards me. I recognised it as the one Gordon had picked up and was using in his capacity as Intelligence Officer. The tyres were smashed, the glass was smashed and the roof was hanging on precariously. As he slowly passed I shouted to him. He turned a very white face and attempted a smile. I saw that he was hit so I ran after him. He slowed down to a halt and when I got to him he said in a low controlled voice, 'Hartley, old chap, I'm hit. Will you help me out?'"

"I lifted him out of his car and laid him on the side of the road. He had a nasty cut on his head and a large gaping wound at the top of one of his buttocks." Schiach died a month later in Singapore's Alexandra Hospital. His maps never did get to the CO An over-zealous Padre Beattie decided to destroy them with the car to prevent the Japanese getting them. His efforts to torch the car nearly resulted in him burning himself.[52]

The Argyll Reserve under the cool, smiling Major Gairdner, supported by 5/2nd Punjabs, came to the rescue of B and D Companies, but not before the leading Japanese tank had fired on Brigade HQ killing Argyll Sgt Ronald Baxter. The tank was then knocked out by one of the 2 pounders. RSM Sandy Munnoch and HQ staff made a fighting retreat down the road.

It was during this savage battle that Hokkien Chinese volunteer ambulanceman and stretcher-bearer Pte Ban Tsan Chuan, affectionately known to the Argylls as Joe, calmly collected the Argyll and other wounded from the battlefield and took them to safety. He was later awarded the Military Medal. Padre Beattie recalled the popular ambulanceman: "He was an extremely pleasant man of about twenty years or so, well-spoken, well-educated and good-looking. His father, he told me, was a warlord. Joe was driving an old Morris 12 behind me. We had decided to make the journey together for our mutual protection. This Morris had been picked up at the Telok Anson waterworks by one of the young officers. Joe was taking the vehicle for a coat of camouflage paint.

"As we sped down the road I thought we'd seen the last of the Jap plane. Soon, however, I heard Joe's horn hooting feverishly. Joe came to stop behind me, jumped out of his car and ran to tell me his news. He was greatly excited and managed to convey to me in several languages that a Jap plane was following and trying to attack us. We had been on a very bending road and travelled as fast as we dared, knowing that the plane would have trouble hitting a car moving round left and right hand corners. It did not take long for the lesson to sink in. The occupants of both cars were out of them and running like stags into the rubber trees alongside the road. We lay flat on our faces for half an hour until the atmosphere became quiet and then Joe and I resumed our journey."

After the war, Ban Tsan Chuan wrote in a letter a little of his story: "When war broke out I was sent up to Ipoh, then to Grik and was attached to the Argylls. I was the only Chinese attached, and in the capacity of an ambulance driver I was interpreter in addition to driving. It was rearguard action all the time and I had a very tough time, with the others. It was a useless fight simply because there was no air support, and it was a terrible crime to have sent men to their doom. Tiger patrols were sent out on reconnaissance, but very few returned alive.

"My ambulance was machine-gunned and bombed and even six bombs could not find their mark. I barely escaped with my life. Because of my unfailing and unceasing work at the wheel of my ambulance through fire, shell and bombs, I was, I'm most glad to say, mentioned in Dispatches. Brigadier Stewart shook hands with me and said 'At this rate you will soon get the DCM.' Imagine how proud I felt and how happy I was." [53]

Eventually the Japanese were halted at Dipang. The Argylls withdrew over the Kampar River bridge at 6.15 p.m. and the iron bridge was blown at the fourth attempt, destroying the two central spans. Some of B and D Companies had still not returned after being scattered off the road. Bal Hendry gathered up these men, about 120 of them, and led them in the growing darkness to the river, which was wide and fast flowing, much more fearsome than the rivers they'd practised crossing only weeks before.

On the south side of the Kampar River those who had crossed by the bridge prepared to help non-swimmers over the river. It looked like a hopeless attempt to swim to the far bank and secure the rope to help others across, but Hendry, attached to a long rope, bravely plunged in. To great amusement, Hendry emerged mid-stream standing somewhat dazed waist deep in four feet of water. There was no difficulty wading across. [54]

Argyll casualties in the Gopeng-Dipang battle were three officers killed or mortally wounded (Gordon Schiach, twenty-three year old Lt Alex 'Sandy' Stewart from Ardpatrick, and 2nd Lt Kenneth MacLean) and sixty other ranks killed, wounded and missing. Lt Rab Mundy was reported missing, last seen being machine-gunned by a Japanese tank but he took to the jungle and reappeared at Bidor two days later none the worse for his experience.

Jimmy McLean was also wounded. He remembers: "I was cut off at Dipang beside the Kampar River. I was a B Company platoon commander under Mike Bardwell. The Japs broke through B Company front with tanks. I had gone forward to help Sandy Stewart who was with the forward platoon and got wounded by rifle fire from one of the tanks, which broke right through the middle of our lines. They were shooting to right and left. Sandy was ahead, near the right side of the road and I was to the left. I heard him call out and went forward under cover, but the Japs passed his position and where I was, and there was nothing to be done. Those of us there when he was killed were caught up, unable to withdraw except to get into the jungle. I found the Japs had got round behind me and I couldn't go back. Their infantry fanned out from their trucks and were right across the road and I was behind their lines. I was on the edge of the jungle under cover, and made my way to the river. I hid amongst them. I could hear them moving about before I got into the river and swam across. It wasn't very wide but was in flood. Then I swam down it. I picked up a Corporal who was wounded and tried to take him back with me. We got so far and then he made a burst of it by himself – he was in a bit of a daze, in shock, and he wouldn't stay with me. He was hit just shortly after he left, a chap from Newcastle. I found out afterwards he managed to get to the Casualty Clearing Station but he died just after he got there. Just as I came out of the river and was heading for my own side, I got shot too. They must have heard me, as there was a burst of firing. I was hit down my right arm and side but not my legs so I was able to carry on. There were some troops on the rocks. I saw somebody near the middle of a metal bridge preparing to blow it, a sapper, and I called up to him. [55]

"I was taken back to the Casualty Station which I think was the one beside Kampar. The battle there hadn't started so it must have been about the 29th of December. I recall very clearly the MO, Dr Alfie Roy MBE RAMC, took me in and put me on this operating table and said there was a compound fracture and two bits of my right arm were sticking out. I remember saying to him couldn't he just stuff them in and put a bandage round it, and he laughed. The Japs were bombing the place, and he had several people helping him when suddenly there was this air raid and everybody else cleared off, except me on this table, and Dr Roy. I looked round – I hadn't had the anaesthetic yet – and said 'Where's everybody gone?' He said they were just a little frightened. He didn't turn a hair – he was a very fine chap! I wrote afterwards to Sandy Stewart's parents who lived near Tarbert in Argyllshire, to tell them I had seen Sandy killed, but there was nothing could be done about it."

The Argyll dead recovered from the battlefield, including Lt Stewart and Sgts Baxter and Darroch, were buried in the College grounds in the town of Tanjong-Malim, fifty miles north of Kuala Lumpur, and after the war were reinterred at the beautiful Taiping War Cemetery.[56]

The battalion was bussed back 25 miles to Bidor for what was expected to be three good days of much needed rest but only amounted to two days and a Hogmanay dinner including whisky and tinned Australian ham. Captains Doherty and Slessor (i/c Transport) saw the Jocks were never short. Four lorry loads of good food had been recovered from abandoned stores and NAAFIs, champagne and chocolate included. Padre Beattie remembers that Hogmanay at Bidor: "The group of which I was one was billeted in one of the rooms of a nice new school building obviously for the use of Chinese children. We all sat round the walls of the classrooms and feasted on the ham and pickles. We told stories and sang songs. RSM Munnoch got his hands somehow or other on the instruments of the school band. Trumpets, cornets and the like were blown. The highlight of the evening however was when Munnoch sitting cross-legged on the floor with a drum between his knees, gave his impression of an Egyptian soloist rendering his repertoire. It was well into the night when we stretched out on the floor."

Clearly some good drinking went on for one officer refers to "getting the battalion sober and moving off again."

TELOK ANSON / BIDOR

Telok Anson, today called Telok Intan, is the chief town of Lower Perak. It is a market town and tin port located on the wide Perak River some twelve miles before it reaches the Indian Ocean. The Argylls fought here on January 2nd, 1942.

15th and 28th Brigades were holding a strong position at Kampar, defended by units including the Gurkhas and the British Battalion, survivors of the Leicesters and East Surreys who had been badly mauled in the north of Malaya. The British Battalion was commanded by Lt Colonel Charles Esmond Morrison DSO MC, CO of 1st Leicesters and formerly military adviser to the Sultan of Johore. 12th Indian Brigade was in reserve. The task of the Argylls was to prepare positions at Bidor for the Kampar defenders to retreat through and to keep an eye out for coastal outflanking attacks in the Telok Anson area, fifteen miles to the west of the Argylls' main positions up the Perak River. FMSVF Armoured cars patrolled the Kinta river area.

In the early hours of January 2nd, while the Battle of Kampar raged, the Japanese did infiltrate into Telok Anson in strength, more likely down river as at Kota

Tampan than by sea. They massacred a number of the local population, some of whom fled into the jungle and mangrove. The Japs were then intercepted and shot up by the Independent Company, led by Major 'Shep' Fearon of 5/14th Punjabs, and supported by two Argyll armoured cars. At first the Independent Company withdrew from the town but then returned with the armoured cars and caught the Japanese reforming in the main street of the town. The Japanese took heavy punishment from the armoured cars' Vickers machine guns before forcing a withdrawal.

At daylight on January 2nd the Japanese engaged Bal Hendry's A Company south-east of Telok Anson, making the usual outflanking movements. At 8.15 a.m. Hendry's company began to slowly withdraw, demolishing as they went. An Argyll armoured car assisted the Independent Company to extricate itself.

That afternoon the Argylls came under Japanese air-attack. The fighter-bombers strafed with their machine-guns. Hendry was badly wounded in the head and shoulder.[57] Captain Ian Lapsley took over command of the Company. An armoured car was destroyed and several vehicles set on fire and wrecked. Major Gairdner, the acting CO, took control. He withdrew A Company through D Company three miles down the road. The Japanese follow-up was caught by the Argyll machine-guns, 137th Field Regiment's guns and 5/2nd Punjabs fighting patrols. As darkness fell, D Company withdrew one mile to hold an already blown bridge. A Japanese night attack was held.

The next morning the Japanese avoided close contact and concentrated on wider encirclement. The guns of 137th Field Regiment again gave them heavy casualties in the open tin-mining country. The Argylls, sometimes under heavy bombing, spent the day leap-frogging back before the advancing Japanese.

That night 11th Indian Division withdrew, perhaps prematurely, from Kampar. For two days the battle had raged with much hand-to-hand fighting in the trenches, bunkers and foxholes of Green Ridge just north of Kampar with the Japanese Kawamura Brigade (Major-General Saburo Kawamura's 9th Infantry Brigade, 5th Division which came from Hiroshima) suffering hundreds of casualties and close to retreating.[58] The British Battalion (formed of East Surreys and Leicesters) particularly distinguished itself and even today two streets in Kampar are named after two of their officers. The Argylls covered the defenders' retreat until 11.00 p.m. when all were clear of Kampar and heading for Slim River.

12th Indian Brigade, including the Argylls, was moved under cover of darkness twenty miles back to Trolak on the Slim River. They were exhausted but with only twenty casualties could feel well pleased. Douglas Broadhurst remembers: "We continued southwards to Kuala Dipang where there was another short action, then through Tapah and Trolak. Trolak seemed to be what might become a fairly stable position. The fore battalion was the 4/19th Hyderabads. Behind them the 5/2 Punjabs, and behind them the Argyll and Sutherland Highlanders. We had already received information from a Tamil that the Japanese had tanks coming up to attack us. So we were not unaware of what was going to happen. Defensive positions were set up."[59]

It should be mentioned that during these battles in northern Malaya the Argylls received praiseworthy logistical support from the only Australian unit deployed north of Johore. This was the 93rd MT Company of Lt Colonel Chris Black's 2/3rd Motor Transport Battalion whose mature soldiers were popular with the Argylls. The '93rd' was a curious coincidence. Duncan Ferguson pays them this tribute: "They took chances those boys. They came right the way up and grabbed us when we should maybe have been miles further down the road, but they came up for us." Eric Moss remembers: "They were mostly elderly men, elderly by our standards. I remember one chap there, Tony. I said 'You're an old Etonian, Tony?' 'Thatsrigh!' 'You don't speak like it, Tony!' 'Well, you soon forget that back home'."[60]

In March 1942, Ian Stewart scripted a radio broadcast made in Bombay. In this he made clear that Transport did not mean that the Argylls had an easy time: "Withdrawals were often by motorised transport. It sounds grand to say that you have been using Motorised Transport but it usually meant six hours in the dark or more to do twenty miles, for the traffic congestion on the roads at night was simply dreadful. You were dumped off in some village, which you had never seen before, to grope your way round and find somewhere to lie down and sleep till dawn. At dawn you had to get up and get things extended out before the Jap bombers arrived."[61]

1. See Clifford Kinvig's biography of Percival "Scapegoat" and Ong Chit Chung: Matador
2. Montgomery-Campbell interview 6.97
3. Stewart
4. Montgomery-Campbell
5. Stewart. See Ong Chit Chung's "Matador" for an in-depth study of Operation Matador.
6. Ian Morrison: Malayan Postscript 1942
7. Spencer Chapman: The Jungle is Neutral
8. US Military Observer, Singapore Report no.141. 28.12.41 (PRO WO170/19)
9. Broadhurst interview (Singapore National Archives Oral History Unit). The planter Symes was Bill Symes, manager Pataling Rubber Estates, Kuala Katil Estate, Kedah. (Chye Kooi Loong letter 8.97) Taylor was Kedah planter George Taylor who was a Captain in the Volunteers. (Beattie memoirs)
10. Most details of the battle from Stewart and Rose's accounts
11. See Ian Morrison: Malayan Postscript and Peter Elphick: Singapore: the Pregnable Fortress. According to PRO CO980/217 Cpl Archie Hoggan MM (Darroch's gunner) shot the German and brought out the body on his Lanchester.
12. Montgomery-Campbell
13. Gordon letter 4.98.
14. Stewart
15. Hendry
16/17. Stewart
18. David Wilson heard this well-known story. Gordon letter 4.98 says otherwise.
19. Ferguson/Sonny Barron. The state of the road is also confirmed by Alex Mackenzie, a civilian expert working for Malaya Command and blowing bridges in the area with the assistance of a small number of local Volunteers and labour. Diary of Kuala Kangsar police officer Harvey Ryves also consulted in this section (Imperial War Museum)
20/21. Ferguson interviews 6.97, 1.98 and 10.98
22. Chye Kooi Loong: Jungle Journey; Denis Holman: Noone of the Ulu and Richard Noone: Rape of the Dream People
23. Rose
24. Montgomery-Campbell
25. Stewart
26. Ferguson 1997
27. War Diary of the Independent Company
28. Civvy Cameron interview 1.98
29. The Straits Times 31.1.42
30. Broadhurst interview (Singapore National Archives). Davy Heeps story from Duncan Ferguson 1.99
31. Wardrope: Sayonara Mine Enemy
32. Kennard's account published in Stewart's history
33. Rose
34. Stewart
35. Alex McDougall interview 12.97
36. Jockie Bell 10.97
37. Straits Times 31.1.42
38. Duncan Ferguson 11.97, Hartley Beattie 2.98 and Nick Carter 1.98 on Japanese air attacks
39. Broadhurst interview. (Singapore National Archives)
40. Duncan Ferguson 1997
41. Jockie Bell 1997
42. Alex McDougall 12.97
43. Stewart
44. Chye Kooi Loong has written a detailed history of the British Battalion/Battle for Kampar
45. Stewart/TRL obituary to Bal Hendry/ Jockie Bell
46. Ian Morrison
47. Alex McDougall interview 11.97
48. Straits Times 31.1.42
49. Wardrope
50. Straits Times 31.1.42
51. Jockie Bell
52. Wounding and death of Gordon Schiach from Stewart, Gordon, Moss and Beattie
53. Ban Tsan Chuan letter to Rev. G.B. Thompson 1946
54. Stewart
55. Jimmy McLean interview 11.97
56. George Aitken's Record Book/ Commonwealth War Graves Register
57. Stewart/Hendry obituaries in TRL
58. See Chye Kooi Loong's excellent History of the British Battalion
59. Broadhurst interview (Singapore National Archives)
60. Views on Australian 93rd MT Company from Stewart, Ferguson and Moss
61. Stewart broadcast script

Sergeants and Warrant Officers of the 93rd Highlanders (2nd Argylls) at Secunderabad, India, January 1939. Only 17 of these came to Malaya, 5 as officers. They include Sgt F. Colvin (top left); 4th row: Sgt John McCalman (4th from left), Sgt Bill Bruce (4th from right), Sgt D.Walker (3rd from right), Sgt James Ditcham (5th from left), Sgt George Aitken (centre); Sgt Alexander Biggarstaff (3rd from right). 2nd row: Sgt J. Fleming (3rd from left) Sgt J. Smith (2nd from right); Pipe Major Eric Moss (right), Seated: CSM Sandy Munnoch (2nd from left), RSM James Doherty (6th from left), Lt Colonel Greenfield (centre), CSM Joseph Allen (4th from right). (Courtesy of A&SH Museum, Stirling Castle)

Junior NCOs of the 93rd Highlanders (2nd Argylls) at Secunderabad, India, January 1939. Albert Darroch is alone on the back row left. Hoot Gibson is the moustached figure 4th row, 2nd from right. **Ian Stewart** is front row centre wearing a topee. To his right is David Wilson. Sgts include 5th and 6th from the right Biggarstaff and McTavish.

(Courtesy of A&SH Museum, Stirling Castle)

Officers of the 93rd Highlanders (2nd Argylls) at Secunderabad, India, January 1939. Only half of these officers came to Malaya. They include: back row: Ian Stonor (left), Mike Blackwood (3rd from left), David Wilson (4th from left), Peter Farquhar (5th from left). Middle row: Jack Hyslop, (4th from left), Angus MacDonald (centre), Angus Rose (3rd from right). Seated: Lindsay Robertson (2nd from left) **Ian Stewart** (4th from left); Hector Greenfield (centre), then CO.
(Courtesy of A&SH Museum, Stirling Castle)

Argyll Pipes and Drums in Secunderabad. Eric Moss (front left) is Pipe Major. Busty Simpson (centre) is Drum Major.
(Courtesy of A&SH Museum, Stirling Castle)

Singapore 1941: Ernest Gordon (left) with Lt Colonel Selby of 2/9th Gurkhas and SSVF officers.

CSM Sandy McTavish in younger days An inspection by an elderly King George V. The King is escorted by the then Colonel 'Babe' McMillan.
(Courtesy of Mrs Rose Denny)

The Argyll football team in India. Back row: Hooky Walker (left), Hoostie McNaught (centre). 2nd row: 'Doc' Doherty (right). Front row: Lt Colonel Greenfield (3rd from left) Tam Slessor (centre) and Alec Carruthers (right). The latter, also a keen boxer, left Malaya before the Japanese invasion but was a POW in Europe, twice escaping. (Courtesy of Hooky Walker)

Lts Montgomery-Campbell (back left) and Schiach (back right) with men of 11 Platoon, A Company. They include on the back row L.Cpl Tony Hodgson, (2nd left) Ptes A. Fergus (4th left), J. 'Rocky' Wanless (4th right) and H. Grainger (3rd right) (Courtesy of Montgomery Campbell)

93rd Motor Transport Platoon 1938 India included many who featured in Malaya. Back row: Pte (later Cpl MM) John Jennings (left); Pte (later Sgt) Harry Nuttall (4th from left); Pte (later Sgt MM) Malcolm McPhee (6th from right). Middle row (standing): Pte (later Cpl) James Flynn (2nd from left). Front row seated: Lt (later Major) Angus Rose (6th from left); Lt Colonel Greenfield (centre); 2nd Lt (later Captain) David Wilson (5th from right). Seated on the ground: Pte (later Cpl DCM) R. King (left); Pte (later Sgt DCM) Darroch (right). (Courtesy of A&SH Museum, Stirling Castle)

River Crossing. Cpl. Aubrey Bentley (Bareheaded) assists men to cross.
(Courtesy of Imperial War Museum)

At Tyersall Camp: Kenneth McLeod (left);
Bal Hendry (right)
(Courtesy of K. Mcleod)

Duncan Ferguson 1941

On the *SS Batory:* Back row Lts Kenneth McCleod (2nd Left), Gordon Schiach (right) Bal Hendry (seated extreme right) (Courtesy of K. Mcleod)

The wedding of Pte William McDougall in Singapore 1941. His brother, James, is on the left. (Courtesy of family)

Jockie Bell 1941

MOON OVER MALAYA

An Argyll, Cpl James Greig, possibly assisted by Bandsman Reg Taylor, created this song. They never said 'Goodbye' to the Far East for they both died in captivity, Greig in Thailand and Taylor in Singapore.

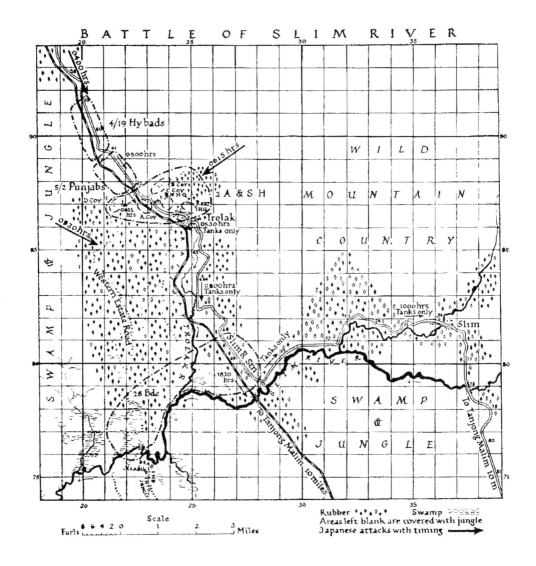

BATTLE OF SLIM RIVER

0400 hrs

4/19 Hybads

0500hrs

0615 hrs

W I L D

5/2 Punjabs
D.COY
0615 hrs A.COY
0930hrs

B COY
BN.HQ
Rear
HQ
2 A & S H

Trolak
0530 hrs
Tanks only

M O U N T A I N

C O U N T R Y

0800hrs
Tanks only

1000 hrs
Tanks only

Slim

Slim R Stn
Tanks only

Western Estate Road

TROLAK R

RIVER

1830
hrs

28 Bde

S W A M P

SWAMP

To Tanjong Malim 10 miles

&

J U N G L E

To Tanjong Malim 10 m

J U N G L E

Scale

Furls 8 6 4 2 0   1   2   3 Miles

Rubber ••••• Swamp ------
Areas left blank are covered with jungle
Japanese attacks with timing ➔

CHAPTER THREE

SLIM RIVER JANUARY 7TH 1942

THE SLIM RIVER FLOWS ALONG THE BORDER between the former Federated Malay States of Perak and Selangor. The river is some thirty miles north of the Federal capital of Kuala Lumpur and about the same distance from Ipoh. The area is hilly with rubber plantations and jungle.

As early as December 22nd 1941, the Chief Engineer Malaya Command, Brigadier Ivan Simson, recognised Slim River as a good position for anti-tank defence but at that time there were no troops in the area, so little follow-up was made to Simson's observations. The area was in fact a poor defensive position compared with that abandoned at Kampar.[1]

On December 31st Ian Stewart, as commanding officer 12th Indian Brigade, was visited by Generals Percival and Heath. All agreed that their aim must be to stop the Japanese over-running the central Malayan airstrips at Kuala Lumpur and Port Swettenham before Allied reinforcements – the British 18th Division – arrived at Singapore in mid-January.

Brigadier Paris, now commanding 11th Indian Division, set up his Divisional HQ at Tanjong Malim, some ten miles south of Slim River. He had two brigades to hold the Slim River position: the 28th under the popular Brigadier W.R. Selby, and the exhausted 12th Brigade, which included the Argylls, under acting Brigadier Ian Stewart. The two brigades moved into position at dawn on January 4th.

12th Indian Brigade was situated in the plantations forward of the river and north of the village of Trolak on the obvious route for a Japanese advance. 28th Brigade was defending the Slim River railway station, north of the Slim River and one and a half miles south of Trolak village. The British intention was to hold these partially prepared positions for three days until the night of January 7th/8th. The weakness of 12th Indian Brigade's positions was clearly the lack of any anti-tank defences north of Trolak. There was also nowhere on the newly constructed road to create demolitions.[2]

At Trolak, three miles north of Slim River, the main west coast road and railway are only a few hundred yards apart. They run parallel until reaching the river, which is crossed by the railway, whereas the road turns five miles to the east before it crosses the river. Trolak village consisted of a single long street at the end of which was a narrow bridge with a narrow stream, the Trolak river, flowing at right angles to the street, winding south to join the Slim River. Just before the bridge and parallel to the river a track ran off to the left down to a rubber factory and Tamil coolie lines about a mile away. B Company, whose task was to defend the Trolak road bridge, were billeted in the huts deserted by the Tamils. The men rested, washed their clothes, chatted and swam. Bully stew and hot tea arrived three times a day.

By this time the Argylls, who had borne the brunt of the fighting in the north, had suffered about 25% casualties – some 250 men including 13 officers – without receiving replacements. The battalion had far fewer malaria casualties than other units, but the four rifle companies were down to sixty men.[3]

Lt Montgomery-Campbell was ordered to take six drivers and collect armoured cars from the Ordnance Depot at Kuala Lumpur. "We arrived just after breakfast after a very slow night journey. I paraded myself to the officer in charge of the armoured fighting vehicles (AFVs). I remember I saluted this major, introduced myself, told him my unit, and requested six armoured cars. To my horror he gave me an awful dressing down for not shaving and being scruffy looking, whilst he was in a beautifully laundered uniform. Sarcastically I replied 'You do know there's a war on?' 'Yes! I bloody well know that!' There was silence. 'Now what do you want?' 'Six AFVs,' was my reply. 'Where's your written authority?' I told him what my orders were. His reply was 'Sorry!' I stormed out and went to the Brigadier. I got the six AFVs, of which three were dispatched back to the battalion, whereas the other three had to be serviced. Padre Beattie, who'd been visiting Divisional HQ, got a lift back with me."

On the evening of January 5th the Japanese pushed down the railway line from Bidor, pressing the rear-guard of 4/19th Hyderabads, but were dealt with by the Indian troops in a very effective dawn ambush. That night Montgomery-Campbell and Padre Beattie, returning from Kuala Lumpur, arrived at Trolak. In the darkness they nearly drove straight through Trolak and into the frontline.

January 6th was a quiet day with the Argylls in reserve. However a local Tamil told Stewart that he had seen a hundred Japanese tanks on the road north of 12th Indian Brigade's positions. Even allowing for exaggeration this was an alarming development. Stewart decided to withdraw his forward battalion, 4/19th Hyderabads, at first light – a delay that was to prove fatal. He ordered his reserve battalion 5/14th Punjabs up the road to Trolak and alerted the Argylls who were blocking the road north of the village.

The Argylls were now commanded by the energetic, jungle-trained Lt Colonel Lindsay 'Robbie' Robertson, known to the Jocks as 'Uncle'. A former 2 i/c of the battalion, he had reluctantly been Mr Duff Cooper's ADC during the minister's visit to Singapore.

At 2.00 a.m. on January 6th nearly a hundred Argyll replacements arrived. They were a mixture of veterans, some wounded early in the campaign, and green replacements. Thirty of these men were not new conscripts but the experienced men taken from the battalion for staff duties at the start of the campaign.[4] They returned in good spirits with Captain D. Drummond Hay, Lt Kenneth McLeod and PSM Jimmy Love, rested after his jungle adventures.

Dug in defending the railway line to the west of the road was Napier's A Company. D Company was in the rubber west of the railway line, C Company on the rubber estate road east of the main road, and B Company defending the Trolak road bridge. The roadblock was defended by the Argyll armoured cars under the command of Captain Timothy Turner.

It was a dark, rainy night. Douglas Broadhurst remembers supplies of food coming up, including very hot, sweet tea. After what he described as "the best drink I ever had in my life, I think; very reviving," he lay down on the road for a good night's sleep.[5] Ian Stewart ordered 4/19th Hyderabads to withdraw from their frontline positions at first light.

Suddenly, at 3.30 a.m., three hours before first light, a company of twenty Japanese 16 ton medium tanks, supported by mobile infantry from the 42nd Regiment, began racing down the road in the darkness. Japanese war cries could be heard. The tanks ploughed through the startled Hyderabads, then at 4.30 a.m. they hit Lt Colonel Cecil Deakin's 5/2nd Punjabs. After an hour's fighting, with two Japanese tanks knocked out, the Punjabs folded and abandoned positions that Ian Stewart perhaps unfairly felt were strong enough to hold. The tanks successfully used loop roads to outflank the defenders.[6] These loop roads were in fact part of the old winding road. A new straighter road had recently been built by the PWD (Public Works Department). The loop roads, already obscured by lalang grass and encroaching jungle, featured on the excellent Japanese maps (their agents had reconnoitred the area prior to the invasion) but no one had bothered to put them on the British maps.

The Argylls at Trolak, preparing for an early breakfast, received little warning. Padre Beattie says, "Soon we saw Indian troops streaming down the road and turning down the side road towards us. Ken McLeod went out to try and stem the rush. Turbaned soldiers ducked around him and under his arms and he stood there like a traffic officer to whom no one pays any attention. In the midst of this mad, confused stampede, trucks carrying our breakfast arrived. They had come up from the cookers at B echelon, some ten miles behind. There is no doubt that breakfast would have been bully and tea but none of the men could collect a morsel because of the intensity of the attack."

Telephone lines had been cut since 5.00 a.m. At 6.30 a.m. four Japanese Type 95 light tanks, cannons blazing and machine-guns firing tracer into the early morning darkness, arrived at the Argylls' Trolak positions, sweeping aside the first roadblocks. By 7.00 a.m. it was daylight and they were in Trolak village heading for the river bridge. Again the Japanese attack was supported by accurate mortar fire as they engaged the Argylls in a fierce running battle.

It was an incredibly noisy battle – roaring of tank engines, war cries, exploding mines, intense gunfire. The sky was alive with tracer and flaming Molotov cocktails as the desperate Argylls took on the tanks. L.Cpl Douglas Brodie rushed up to Major Gairdner and asked for a grenade. With two grenades he headed for the ditch to take on a Japanese tank. Until Slim River, the Japanese tanks had played only a secondary role.

Montgomery-Campbell says, "The attack came out of the blue. The Japs brought their tanks down at dawn. They too appreciated that control of the road was vital. The Jap tanks got hold of the small bridges and by so doing they cut off our main supplies. So far as the main bridge went, that was blown up with the withdrawal. I was well forward with the armoured cars – we got hit by tank ammo which, being shells, was more lethal."

Douglas Broadhurst, like so many others, was literally cast off the road and into the jungle by the rapid Japanese advance. The crews of the only three British anti-tank guns in the forward positions fled leaving their two pounders, captured the year before from the Italians in East Africa, to the advancing Japanese. The surprise was total and left many Argylls ill-prepared for a battle. Pte Stan Roberts of HQ Company was asleep in a rubber estate hut, up a side road: "The Japs came in early and we didn't expect them – that's why a lot of us had nae boots on, just bare feet. I was in a group with Captain Lapsley and CSM McTavish. Others got drowned in Slim River. We didn't go that way; we made for the jungle."

Duncan Ferguson was sitting beside his truck on a bridge to the rear of Trolak. Next to him sat a Gurkha. There were six trucks in all. Fergie's truck contained mortars and landmines belonging to HQ Company. Piper Charles Stuart, known as 'Wee Charlie' or 'Boy' Stuart, as he had joined the battalion in India as a boy soldier, was nearby. They saw the Hyderabads come streaming through, followed by the Punjabs. They were not unduly alarmed about this until Argylls started coming through in some confusion.

Suddenly, the Gurkha raised his rifle and shot a Japanese sniper out of a tree. "I said 'Cheerio, Johnnie!' and was going to go on when a wee lieutenant – I don't know what regiment he was from but he wasn't our lot – he said, 'Take this anti-tank rifle and go up to that hut there and take up a position, the tanks are coming round the corner.' 'Well,' I said, 'If you're wanting that pea-shooter for anti-tanks, you go up there and take up a position for I'm nae bloody gaeing to do it!' It was like using a pea shooter against an elephant."[7]

Later Fergie observed men crossing the Slim River under the railway bridge that was later successfully blown. Japanese tanks were already targeting the bridge itself. The river was flowing fast and many men were probably drowned. "It was pandemonium," he said. Men from C and D Company were among those crossing the river. Montgomery-Campbell remembers: "You had to wade across, catch a hold of one girder and pull yourself along to another. When the bridge was blown, with most of the transport on the wrong side, we were cut off. The tanks created havoc." He did not recollect the river being so fast flowing as to create major problems crossing it.[8]

"I think it was Lt Primrose who was there helping to pull us across," says Jockie Bell. "He got wounded through the pocket with a penknife. Yes, I think a number must have got drowned there."[9] Padre Beattie, a strong swimmer, found a good crossing place. He began shouting "This way, Argylls" and vigorously blowing a whistle. He grabbed a revolver and began firing in the air. Argylls began to appear and Beattie demonstrated that it was possible to wade across safely with the water only at waist level. They met CSM McTavish on the other side and Beattie waded across again and found six or seven more men. Major Gairdner and the planter George Taylor were also across the river safely.

Sgt Alex McDougall of B Company, a strong swimmer, was there too. "The river was in spate. They blew the railway bridge and we were on the other side, cut off; we were trying to get out, so what we organised was the strong swimmers were got across first. The Japanese started to fire on us as we were trying to cross, and we were standing on the banking and the river was going by but the whole of the embankment below us was all cut away. Then this bloke jumped in. He had a rope on him to swim to the other side. The current swept him right in below the bank and he never came up – never saw him again; he got drowned. The rope just came up without him... There was a young lieutenant who cut down big bamboo poles, and he strapped them across two big men who were tied together; they swung round with them so they could swing round from one bank to the other, and the ones who couldn't swim held on." Was this Primrose? "Oh, Ian Primrose – NOW you're talking about a man! It was Primrose who organised this thingummy. Well, we got them all across. Smith says 'I think that's all, Sgt McDougall.' I shouts 'Is there anyone left ower there?' Well, Boy Thomson was over there. So I says 'Hang on a minute!' Smith says 'Leave him there! We've nae time – the Japanese'll be in!' 'Don't you f... talk about leaving a boy ahint – I'll blow your f... head off!' That's the way I said it. Anyway, the two blokes went back in the river with the bamboo poles and we got him over. Ian Primrose organised it – he was a wonderful officer and a wonderful fellow. Him and I got blind drunk in London, at the Union Jack Club. By Christ, did we go to town."[10]

Primrose was a popular and very highly rated officer. Padre Beattie wrote: "He was reckoned to be one of the toughest officers in the battalion, and I think he was. I don't think he knew fear. Even his best friend could not have called him a smart officer. Each time I saw him his 'digger' or Australian Army hat was a different shape and his socks were as erratic as his hat. Wherever he went he carried a bren gun instead of the usual service revolver. His men regarded him with feelings of awe, hero-worship and comradeship. He shocked many of them by calling them by their nicknames."

Back at Trolak, when another Argyll armoured car was knocked out Cpl Robert King engaged the enemy and covered the rescue of the crew. King's own Lanchester was soon knocked out with one of his crew killed, and King found himself running for his life through the jungle. For an earlier action Robert King was later awarded the Distinguished Conduct Medal.

Pte Tom McGregor remembered the horror of watching the destruction of the armoured cars at Trolak as they took on the Japanese tanks.[11] The situation was hopeless and he too joined the exodus from the carnage. Everyone was heading for the Slim River Bridge. Pte Finlay McLachlan found having to leave wounded and exhausted comrades particularly harrowing.[12] Many surviving Argylls describe 'the Slim' as more a massacre than a battle and are still haunted by the horror of that early morning, and the desperate retreat that followed it.

For two hours, in savage fighting, they held the Trolak road bridge. Sgt Robert Parry was among those killed. The demolition charges on the bridge failed to explode and no sappers could be found to demolish the bridge. Under heavy fire, Captain Timothy Turner pushed one of the two knocked-out armoured cars onto the Trolak Bridge, but the bridge fell to the Japanese intact.

Lt Richard Webber, the Battalion Signals Officer and a former commander of the ill-fated 13th platoon, had been sent to Rear HQ the night before with Captain Tam Slessor so that they could get a good night's sleep. Returning to Battalion HQ on motorbikes and well forward of the Argyll transport early on the morning of the 7th, they ran into the Japanese tanks coming down the road.

Since the Gopeng-Dipang action Tam Slessor had been acting Intelligence Officer, replacing the mortally wounded Gordon Schiach. Tam jumped off his motorbike and straight into a ditch. One tank, its commander obviously spotting the bike's wheels still turning, approached and fired into the ditch. A bullet creased Tam's upper lip, but when the tank drew off he was able to make his escape.[13]

"We cut across country on a side road to D Company," explains Richard. "Tam was ordered back to Brigade HQ with whom I had got in touch through an old telephone cable, still fortunately connected, and got out. I was told to stay with D Company and we didn't get out, after a very confused battle with the Japs who had got behind us."[14]

Pte James McKnight, a dispatch driver, had a similar experience to Tam Slessor though in the end it proved fatal. Jockie Bell witnessed the incident: "He was going up the road when the Jap tanks were coming down the road. He'd been coming up to take the dispatches and would not have known... We counted thirteen tanks and the Japs sitting on the top as if they were going away on their holidays and they were shooting and blasting. In between these tanks were maybe two dozen Japs with fixed bayonets. This fellow McKnight was going up, and an officer's sword came out and slashed him across the back; he carried on on his bike and must have collapsed up the road and crawled into a bush, because he got picked up by remnants – our boys that were scattered all about the area."[15]

Civvy Cameron had been on ack-ack patrol along the road with his bren gun, looking at the sky and keeping a look out for the Japanese. When the Japanese attack started he joined up with CSM McTavish and worked his way back to the cover of the jungle but had a very close shave when a tank machine gun shot off the sole of his boot. Unlike McTavish he made it back to British lines.

Jockie Bell and Tom MacDonald, of 17 and 18 Platoon respectively, had earlier that morning driven a truck carrying Quartermaster Supplies and ammunition to feed breakfast to Captain David Boyle's D Company. They found the company resting on a laterite side road in a rubber plantation north of Trolak. They were there when the Japanese attack down the main road to Trolak began. By 6.15 a.m. D Company was cut off from the main action at Slim River and were engaged with the enemy. Bell and MacDonald abandoned the truck, expecting to return to it. They took a rifle and bandolier each: "We took cover at the side of the main road and saw a tank come down the side road we'd been on. We took refuge behind a bungalow near the village and saw the natives looting. We watched the Japs go by. They had natives carrying bren guns for them. If they'd had dogs with them that would have been us had it."[16]

On the railway line, Lt Donald Napier's A Company successfully ambushed the Japanese as they advanced openly and confidently down the line. The Japanese casualties were such that they made no further attacks down the line and Napier's Company held their position until the afternoon before making an orderly withdrawal down the line towards Kampong Slim. Napier later told how he met three fully armed men in civilian dress on the railway line. They had called to him, attempted a conversation, then gone on their way. Thinking about it later he was convinced they were Japanese Fifth Columnists.[17]

Kenneth McLeod tells his story: "I was in Rear HQ that morning up in Slim. It was in a schoolhouse. I hadn't joined my mortar platoon, having been in Singapore both for hospital treatment and then told to round up the rest of the Argylls who were scattered around Singapore with other units, on guard duty etc around the island, so I brought this group back to Slim with Drummond Hay's new men – a couple of hundred all told. I didn't know half the men who were in my party – different companies of Argylls, B and C chaps.

"We'd been told that tanks were coming through. I found myself out in the road and met a truck coming down belonging to an anti-tank unit, towing an anti-tank gun behind it – I am told I was waving my arms like a dervish. I got him to stop and told him I wanted him to get into action around the corner as a tank was approaching. I heard his engine revving up and continuing to rev up, and he disappeared without stopping! There was a story I heard later in Changi that someone was getting an award for having got his gun back entire to Singapore. I wondered if it was him… I had been on my way to check up on the Companies who were on the left of the road, to join them and help out as required, and I came on a platoon – there was a hedge across a football field, and I was walking along through the penalty box area when I heard this sound – and a tank appeared behind the goal posts! I took off like a hare without a round being fired. Padre Beattie in fact reported me missing. One of the men was killed beside me and I took off his dog tags, and then lost them and I don't know who he was."[18]

Jockie Bell and Tom MacDonald got caught up in the general retreat south. They were tramping down the road. "If you heard transport coming you jumped into the bush at the side of the road and it was Indians driving but Japs were in beside them with Japs on the lorries because they'd commandeered the transport so you had to watch out."[19] Later they crossed Slim River with others of D Company.

In the Trolak area more Japanese tanks arrived at 9.00 a.m. and the remaining Argyll armoured cars and carriers were destroyed. The surviving Argylls retreated towards Kampong Slim as the Japanese swept on to the Slim River road bridge, ploughing through the reserve battalion ordered up by Brigadier Stewart, 5/14th Punjabs (Lt Colonel Cyril Stokes). The Punjabs, totally unaware of the rapid Japanese advance, were marching up the road in close order, and the two lead companies were totally annihilated. Lt Colonel Stokes later died of his wounds.

The Japanese tanks then caught 2/1st Gurkhas marching up the road. Many of the Gurkhas who survived the massacre on the road were drowned trying to cross the fast-flowing Slim River. Two batteries of Lt Colonel George Holme's 137th Field Regiment RA were also destroyed, and Holme killed. The Japanese tanks crossed the Slim River road bridge after a fierce exchange of fire with an anti-aircraft unit.

South of the river it was the turn of Lt Colonel Alan Murdoch's 155th Field Regiment RA, formerly the Lanarkshire Yeomanry. Murdoch was also killed as he rode forward on a motorbike. The Japanese tanks advanced a further two miles before being stopped at point blank range by a surviving 4.5 Howitzer of C Battery 155th Field Regiment using its last four rounds of ammunition. The gun crew were all killed except for the commanding officer, Captain Gordon Brown MC, who was severely wounded, and a mortally wounded Sergeant who came down the road, had a conversation with the Argyll Quartermaster 'Doc' Doherty and died shortly afterwards. By this time, however, quite apart from the human cost, sixteen 25 pounder and 7.2 pounder artillery pieces had been lost.

Jockie Bell in all this was "crouching as wee as possible, trying to squeeze all of myself under my tin hat, when this officer comes up and says 'Here you are' and hands me these two wee bottles – Molotov cocktails. He says, 'Just rub the match down there, and go down the hill and throw it at the tanks and my men will be waiting!' There were guys with airforce blue shirts, whoever they were, and they were firing bren guns from the shoulder, leaning against the trees. If the Japs had come up behind us, walking, they would have nailed us, but anyway, they didn't. And the Goorkies, their bloody sergeant was talking to them in their ain language and is telling them to spread out and they each get their ain tree. They were all young fellows who'd never been in action and he was punching them and everything – they talk about the brave Gurkhas and all they can do with their big knives is take the top off their boiled eggs. The Molotov cocktails were filled with inflammable oil, and down their sides was what looked like lollipop sticks. You took a matchbox, rubbed it on the side of these and up it went – we never got practice with these things in the battalion... Anyway, this chap says 'I'll just go and get a box of matches.' Well, that was me away and all, shifted my legs. I don't know who he was. An Indian Army officer? Hadn't any uniforms, just rag-tags."[20]

Sgt Harry Nuttall's Lanchester armoured car, supporting D Company, knocked out one leading Japanese tank with three shots from his Boys anti-tank rifle. D Company was joined by the surviving 4/19th Hyderabads battalion headquarters under acting commanding officer Major Alan Davidson-Brown. They blew a small road bridge north of Trolak, delaying the advance of further Japanese tanks till 9.30 a.m. Soon, however, this group was surrounded as they attempted a cross-country withdrawal. Heavy fighting followed with the Japanese coming at them from all sides.

The resourceful, tough extrovert Territorial Lt Ian Primrose, at 6ft 3 inches "a very big, brave man" who had got so many men across the river, volunteered to go forward and check if Japanese or British troops lay ahead of them. He would fire two shots to warn of Japanese. Primrose soon found himself surrounded by

Japanese seeking his surrender. Realising that he must warn his comrades, he fired two shots with his tommy gun into the Japanese officer's stomach. Seconds later the angry Japanese soldiers beat him senseless and tied him to a tree.

In the fighting that followed, Major Davidson-Brown of the Hyderabads and a number of Argylls were killed. Sgt Harry Nuttall escaped down the road in his armoured car, smashing through a Japanese roadblock. He later had to destroy the vehicle when cut off by Japanese tanks but he and his crew returned safely on foot to British lines.

Captain David Boyle, with a Lt Montgomery-Campbell, Lt Richard Webber, a twice-wounded Lt J.G. "Nipper" Smith (who was a former CSM in the battalion) carried by two men, and some of D Company's NCOs including PSM Hoostie McNaught and Cpl Robertson, made their getaway.

The Japanese bayoneted or shot those Argyll and Hyderabad wounded who were unable to walk. Some of these men may not even have been wounded but "playing dead", as they had heard the Japanese took no prisoners. The shocked survivors, including a battered but surprisingly alive Ian Primrose, after digging graves for the dead, were marched northwards to Taiping.

Primrose was made to carry the dying Japanese officer he had shot. He soon became aware that the man had died but wasn't in any hurry to tell the Japanese for fear of retribution. At one stage these D Company survivors were lined up to be shot between the goal posts of a local football pitch. A machine-gun was trained on them. A wry comment from a Jock about never having been asked to play in goal before seems to have broken the tension and the executions were forgotten.[21] Could this remark have been made by Pte Hooky Walker of D Company, an India veteran and keen footballer?

Primrose was not the only Argyll carrying a badly wounded Japanese officer. Pte 'Big Will' Shanks from Falkirk also performed this service and was rewarded with a packet of cigarettes when the officer came to. Will Shanks later died in captivity at Labuan Island, off the coast of northwest Borneo.

The taking of prisoners by the Japanese was a random affair. They recognised that captured officers were a valuable source of information but often small parties of other ranks would not be given quarter. Jockie Bell recalls Roger Hamilton who survived such an incident: "Him and a lad called Coulter were in the jungle and had begged for food at a Malay place. They were given some but the Japs were called to pick up the two of them. They shot Coulter through the back of the head, then they shot Hamilton. But he woke up in a pool of blood. The Chinese picked him up, although he was given up to the Japanese later – they had to or they might all have been killed themselves. Anyway he had a crease around the back of his head. He must have turned his head as he heard Coulter shot, and the Jap officer shot him and didn't check that he was dead. He became an active Christian, and was a male orderly at Ballochmyle Hospital and is still living."[22]

Jockie Bell and Tom MacDonald soon found themselves forced off the road, and trying to follow the electric pylons that ran south through rentices in the jungle. They met up with a Captain Gifford MacDonald of the Kedah Volunteers. He was an Australian rubber planter. "He was travelling fast for short times, then resting, then travelling again. He was a big, swarthy chap. A very fit man. He told us he was travelling light and quick. He carried a rolled up bundle in which he had his gun. His plan was to get to the coast and get a boat – promise them a lot of money when they got to Australia, he said, and those who didn't agree, kill them and throw them over the side. No nonsense. Unluckily for us, with so many people working their way through the rubber, we ended up in a column about 150 strong, taking it in turns for different groups to go first. The morning it was the Indians turn to go first, the Japs opened up on us from some rubber estate housing and we were split up again, so our dreams of getting to Australia in a boat went."[23]

Captain Gifford MacDonald of the Kedah Volunteers was later captured by the Japanese and interned in Pudu jail, Kuala Lumpur. He took part in a daring escape but was recaptured and executed along with seven others.

When it was the Indians' turn to lead and they were fired on by the Japanese, Jockie recognised the familiar sound of bren guns, different from the sharp crack of Japanese machine guns. The Argylls scattered for cover. Jockie recognised Hooky Walker from the tattoos on his arm and pushed the cursing Walker into a thicket. The Japanese passed by, coolies carrying their bren guns. When night fell Jockie heard someone whistling the regimental call "Tippy, Tippy 93rd." He returned the call. Montgomery-Campbell and Richard Webber responded and they found themselves with Captain Boyle's group who were covered in leeches and were busy burning them off. Montgomery-Campbell was in great pain, his feet lacerated, something sharp having pierced his boot. They tried to light a fire but the tinder was hopelessly wet.[24]

In the Slim River disaster thirty Japanese tanks followed by motorised infantry had advanced nine miles, 'filleting' the defenders. They were eventually brought to a halt at 9.30 a.m. by close quarter artillery fire from 155th Field Regiment as described, but not before 12th Indian Brigade had been annihilated and 28th Brigade had been severely mauled, losing the entire 2/1st Gurkhas and much of its artillery. Only 14 officers and 409 men of 12th Brigade escaped the Japanese and returned to British lines. Some 800 were killed, 1200 captured and 2000 were missing – still on the run through the jungle to be captured days, weeks and months later. This was clearly the most devastating disaster of the mainland campaign and the one that lost central Malaya to the Japanese.

Acting Brigadiers Ian Stewart and W.R. Selby, formerly CO 2/9th Gurkhas, held a perimeter around Kampong Slim until nightfall, collecting stragglers. All transport north of the river had been destroyed and the survivors fell back to Tanjong Malim. Fewer than 100 of the 576 Argylls at Slim River were among them: four officers and ninety other ranks, mainly from Lt Donald Napier's A Company and the Transport Section.

At 8.00 p.m. on January 11th 1942 the Japanese entered Kuala Lumpur; central Malaya was lost.

PURSUIT

Lt Colonel Lindsay Robertson of the Argylls was missing, together with his HQ staff. Cpl Gibson last saw Robertson looking as calm as ever, sitting on his shooting stick in the middle of a stream while Signals Sergeant Johnston tried to shelter him from the rain by holding a tin helmet over his head. With an exhausted Captain Beckett, he scrutinised his maps and spoke of heading for Tanjong Malim. Pte 'Big Jim' McCutcheon, Robertson's runner, was also there. Expressing a determination never to be captured, Robertson led a dozen starving and fever-ridden men, mostly Argylls, through the jungle on a mammoth 200-mile trek south. In the area of the Batu Caves the party split up. Robertson's batman, Pte John Bennett, never saw the Colonel's group again. They got as far as Labis where all six, including Captain

Beckett and Pipe-Major John McCalman, were killed in a Japanese ambush the day after Singapore fell.

Angus Rose said, "Robbie had very definite ideas on the subject of surrender and it was his personal code that no soldier must ever lay down his arms, however desperate the circumstances."[25]

Captain Ian Lapsley, sometimes called John Lapsley, OC B Company at Slim River, led an escape column of some three hundred Slim River survivors whom he had ordered into the jungle as the situation at Trolak became hopeless. The column included the remnants of B and C Companies. The Argyll officers included Captain Tim Turner, Captain Drummond Hay (who had been shot in the knee as he went forward to view the battle), Lt Kenneth McLeod and young 2nd Lt John Colliston. Cpl Walter 'Hoot' Gibson was also there. According to the regimental roll and fellow Argylls, Gibson was very definitely a Corporal at this time though in his subsequent two books he claimed to be a Sergeant (see Chapter 6). There were also many wounded including Pte James McKnight, with a sword wound in the back, and Pte Stewart, shot through both wrists. Also in the group was Captain Douglas Broadhurst who had been with 5/2nd Punjabs when the Japanese struck at Slim River. Broadhurst explains: "I, like many others, was cast into the jungle beside the road, and became part of the disintegration that followed that defeat. Having been in what now could be considered occupied territory alters one's outlook on affairs, and one had to consider what next to do. The sensible thing seemed to be to go south as fast as possible, avoiding the Japanese, and come up to rejoin our own forces. At that time, of course, I didn't know that the Japanese had broken through the Argylls and were rampaging on at a fairly high speed. I was at first with one Punjabi soldier until we came upon a few more, and they seemed a bit bewildered to know what to do. And, of course, I can't speak Punjabi or Urdu so there was not much of an understanding between us… So the days wore on. At one time I bumped into some Sikhs who very kindly gave me a chapati. And while I slept on the ground, one of them laid his gas cape over me to keep me warm because one can get quite cold in Malaya at night-time.

"While with the Sikhs I was awakened in the morning by someone standing up and putting his hands up in token of surrender, pointing to some figures in the distance to say 'Oh, Japanese, Japanese!' But on closer examination I noticed that they were British soldiers, two of them. I thought it'd be much better to be with British soldiers than with Sikhs, with whom I really couldn't converse. So I joined these two British soldiers from the Argylls – one was named Johnson – and we went marching south. I don't know if you can call it marching, but it's walking and going south anyway. In time we caught up with larger groups, and at one time we caught up with a company of Argylls commanded by Captain Lapsley."[26]

As they moved south through the jungle, desperately hoping to rejoin their battalion, the men became more tired and hungry. The wounded Captain Drummond Hay was among the first to drop out and another soldier stayed with him. None of the thirty Argyll veterans Drummond Hay had brought up from Singapore two days earlier were to escape from this disaster.

Drummond Hay, in the words of one Jock "the greatest wee man in the world", had served many years with the Argylls. He was not an experienced jungle fighter; he was in charge of the Officers' Mess at Tyersall and was nicknamed 'Pudley' Hay, partly a derivative from the Hindustani word 'Pagal' meaning mad, and his being in charge of alcoholic consumption in the Mess. Needless to say, he had quite a reputation as a boozer, but also a reputation of generosity to the Jocks. In earlier days with the 1st Battalion he had helped organise raffles for the Jocks with good second hand automobiles as prizes.

Padre Beattie and the Medical Officer Eric Bartlett ran through rubber estates from tree to tree until they reached the edge of the jungle. Hiding here they contemplated their next move. Beattie wrote: "I did know that the road, the railway and the river all ran approximately south and all three intersected, in a manner of speaking, at Tanjong Malim, some twenty six miles to the south. We therefore had to get to the west side of the road and, keeping to the jungle, follow a parallel course... We set off again following an elephant track."

At one stage they had a close encounter with four Japanese tanks moving along the road, and on a rubber estate they were fired on by inaccurate sniper fire. From a distance they observed the flash of light from the explosion as a 4.5 Howitzer shell knocked out a Japanese tank and put a stop to the Japanese Slim River advance. As time went on they were joined by some twenty-five Argylls and then ran into Cpl Wilson's armoured car. Eventually they reached Brigade HQ, which had pulled back to a rubber estate in the Kampong Slim area. Here Ian Stewart, Angus MacDonald and Lt Ian Gordon, an Argyll on the Brigade staff, were waiting. Later Lt Donald Napier came in with a dozen of his men. Ian Stewart was unperturbed by Japanese machine gun fire raking the area. He dismissed it with his usual sangfroid: "Pay no attention to these people. They are firing any old where."[27]

Pte Stan Roberts from Falkirk was in HQ Company. He found himself in Lapsley's party. "There were about ten of us. The Chinese were feeding us at times. We were trying to make for the sea or Singapore, but it was a waste of time, the jungle was dense, with a lot of leeches, and we ended up starving and got lost. There was dysentery and malaria and some lost their heads (went mad) and we buried a number of men – two were Argylls."[28]

Kenneth McLeod tells of his experiences: "I was possibly the luckiest fellow in the battalion. We were blazing a trail after Slim, marking the trees, trying to get back to Singapore and we were on the left-hand side of the road. I was in this small party which had split off from the larger bodies and we were keeping the road as a parallel because we didn't have a compass, and in any event the tin mines in the area played havoc with compass readings, so partly we were going by sound – got a bit thrown by thunder because we thought it was the frontline we were approaching. We got near to the Batu Caves where there were Hyderabads and Punjabi troops, making a noise several hundred yards behind us. So I said we would nip over here and keep very, very quiet. We went down the hill there, and here these fellows went past us, and then we heard machine gun fire and they had walked into an ambush. I was the only officer there at that particular time but when we got to Titi (not to be confused with Titi Karangan) I made up with others. That's where Lapsley died."[29]

Montgomery-Campbell had started off with Captain David Boyle's D Company stragglers, about forty men. At one stage they encountered Lt Colonel Robertson and Captain Beckett's group. They ran into a Japanese bicycle patrol led by a German who called out "English. Lay down your arms". Monty explains: "We didn't fire on them as it might have attracted the attention of Japs who were in the village not far away. We withdrew hurriedly into the jungle. I had something wrong with my foot, stood on a nail or something and it was septic. I had to take my boots off, and a couple of lads, Thompson and Kirk, helped me."[30]

Boyle's group encountered Douglas Broadhurst and other Volunteers; "We got to a small coastal town called Sungei Buloh, south of Seremban," says Monty. "There was David Boyle, CSMs McNaught and McTavish and 'Wee Smithie' (2nd Lt John Smith, who had two bullet wounds in his arm and had to be carried). We decided to break up into smaller parties and I had six of them with me, including Kirk, Cpl Robertson, Thompson and Morton, them being in HQ Company. During our journey south, in the hope of making for Port Dickson with the view of getting a boat and sailing for Sumatra, we came across a Spencer Chapman SOE guerilla party of Volunteers, Lts Graham, Van Rennan and Hembry, and a few gunners of 137 Field Regiment. We exchanged information and it was decided to return to Sungei Buloh. Undoubtably, David Boyle and his party must have been taken prisoner the day before our arrival. After a few days we managed to be taken off by a Chinese fellow in a sampan and we sailed for Sumatra. We had a blanket over us, and we had two pots of rice and four coconuts."

Captain Mike Bardwell, with the calm, cheerful Pioneer PSM Colvin and a few others, also managed to pay their way, buying a junk at Jeram and crossing to Sumatra.

When Jockie Bell and Tom MacDonald first joined the Argyll group in the jungle they felt the remainder of the party had little time for them. "Everyone was going off in their own clique," Jockie says, "so MacDonald and I got flung aside. We had nothing... yet we were Argylls!" They also, however, had Argyll persistence. They continued along with Captain Boyle's party, and duly reached Sungei Buloh, walking down the main street where Japanese flags already flew. Local people brought out food for them: eggs, bananas, rice and even cigars.

Near the town they found a small temple surrounded by hundreds of tall sunflowers, on the edge of a mangrove swamp near Sungei Buloh. They sheltered there for one or two nights, accompanied by large crabs that emerged at dusk and the usual thousands of hungry mosquitoes.

Boyle had a valuable wristwatch with which to barter, and possibly by this means he arranged the hire of a boat and a Chinese boatman. Boyle thought for a while, then warned Bell and MacDonald that there were some twenty men and there would not be room for everyone in the boat, but once he and the others reached safety in Sumatra they would persuade the Dutch authorities to send a boat back for the rest. This promise failed to impress either Jockie or Tam. Jockie was wildly indignant that an Argyll officer would consider 'abandoning' two of his men and select only the 'high rankers' to escape. Jockie would make his feelings abundantly clear.

In due course a sampan, rather like a large rowing boat, appeared, its boatman paddling quietly up the estuary and through the mangrove shallows towards them. Boyle's party, including Lts Smith and Webber, CSM Hoostie McNaught, Sgt Acting QM Rab McKirdy, and D Company runner Hooky Walker, moved out to meet him, sinking up to their knees in the stinking mud. And then all hell broke loose. Bell, MacDonald and, according to Jockie, some others who were clearly going to be left behind, were expressing their anger. The startled boatman looked round. He saw the group of men wading out towards him. He saw on the bank, two soldiers leaping up and down, shouting and yelling, waving their arms in rage. One glance was enough. He turned his boat round and rapidly paddled away, oblivious to the further shouts from the men left anchored in the mud.

Boyle was furious, but not beyond words. Jockie was also a little awed at the insults he had just been hurling "at an Argyll officer". But Jockie believed thereafter, quite unforgivingly, that he and MacDonald were being deserted by their officer. Boyle, of course, is not here to answer for himself but a number of his fellow officers would have difficulty with Jockie's interpretation of Boyle's action. Montgomery-Campbell insists that Boyle would have had a good reason for his actions, whether understood by others or not.

David Boyle now squelched back to the two men. "And did he let us have it!" Jockie recalled. But 'Ting-a-Ling' also recalled with considerable satisfaction, "That boatman pissed off with the boat anyway – and Davy Boyle never got it yet!"[31]

Boyle recovered his composure and said that they would have to split into little parties. Cpl Robertson approached Jockie and Tam to ask them if they had any money: "I told him we'd had no pay while we were fighting, so we'd no money and that was when he said we couldn't go with them. Yet we were supposed to be a family regiment, and we'd taken our turn at carrying the big drum that was used for cooking! But we were abandoned."

Boyle's party was later captured while sitting in a Malay village, following the ambush and killing of Lt Colonel Robertson's escape party. Richard Webber, who left with another party, was also captured. Jockie and Tam however now met up with an Indian Army officer who had stood for some time watching the scene. He was wearing a tin hat and carrying a haversack. He introduced himself as Major Baker of the Bengal Sappers and Miners. This unit was in fact officered by Royal Engineers.

Jockie Bell continues: "He said 'Well, boys, it looks as if you'll have to throw your lot in with me, but I can speak the language'. So we mooched about getting food, begging it from the Tamils – they had little themselves but they helped, and we were coming across abandoned villages and living off coconuts and bananas and sometimes a chicken. There were goats running about but we didn't know what to do with killing them, butchering them and getting them stewed up. We hadn't a map and didn't know where we were. We found we had gone round in a circle, finding our own footprints by a stream we had crossed earlier – oh, really that disheartened you.

"So we holed up in a rubber estate, and this Indian man went to get us a map from the schoolhouse. We were sheltering in the house and the Major went to have a bath. This man warned us to get into the woods to hide, and he would bring us food in the evening where we were hiding in this thicket. So we stayed in the woods and he came with a pot of boiled eggs and chicken legs and a map his brother had made up for us because the maps in the schoolhouse had been ripped off the walls. The next day we marched all day, except for a short noon rest. Through the night we saw Jap encampments, where they had fires going, and we were sneaking around them through the rubber."[32]

Ambulance driver Ban Tsan Chuan, who had so distinguished himself at Gopeng-Dipeng as well as acting as a Chinese interpreter, was one of the main Argyll group: "I was eventually left behind because I had a cut on my foot which became septic and I could not walk. Some Chinese people picked me up and cured me. I tried to continue but was unable to since I heard that the Japs were well beyond Johore. At length I borrowed a bicycle and cycled twelve miles to KL to find that Johore Bahru had fallen... I was reported missing in the Malayan Lists of Honour at Singapore. They were quite right in putting it so."[33]

The main Argyll party arrived at Tanjong Malim to find the Japanese already there. Cpl Hoot Gibson was close to dropping out with malaria. Ian Lapsley, ex-cricket captain of Hillhead High School, Glasgow, persuaded him to keep going.

Gibson described Lapsley as "a handsome, quick thinking, popular young officer" who intended returning to Singapore to marry his girlfriend.[34]

On January 14th the party arrived at Kuala Kubu and it was here that they lost Lapsley who had gone forward to recce. Lapsley duly met up with McLeod and others and MPAJA Chinese guerrillas at Titi where Ian initiated guerilla training. But he died of typhoid after drinking from a stream south of Seremban. The group decided to move on in three seperate parties, one was led by Lt Kenny McLeod, another by the 19-year-old Lt John Colliston. Colliston went ahead. He disappeared. He died in the jungle near Titi, as did other Argylls.

Kenneth McLeod found the bites on his body going gangrenous: "I had two lumps like eggs in my groin. I came to this particular kampong and this old Chinese lady boiled water and put some leaves into it and when it was boiling she spat it onto the ulcers. In my wanderings I got some caustic soda and decided to try that, it burnt them off and I was hoping it would dry off the pus. But finally I got some maggots and put them on, wrapping some bits of cloth over them. They became quite tickly, probably as they were eating the pus around the edges, but the ulcers cleared up splendidly after that!"

Eventually, the Japanese captured McLeod and his party. "I was captured after I'd escaped from an ambush. I was still extremely fit and jumped a stream from a standing start. My revolver, shirt etc were hanging over a bush and I had no time to pick up anything. I got to this hill and went to ground in a drainage type of pit and crouched in there and put foliage over me. Then I heard this shouting from the men. 'We've been taken prisoner. Come back or we're going to be disposed of!' I thought 'if I go back we might have a chance', so I came down and waded across this stream and then was grabbed hold of and interrogated afterwards for ages. I surrendered at the very last minute because of the other chaps, but I am afraid that none of them survived the war. I went first into a civil jail in Titi, then to Pudu and into 'the hospital'." He was suffering from ptomaine poisoning, from tinned food he'd eaten that had previously been opened by the Japanese. The 'hospital' was the jail's old cookhouse. "It was full so I was put in the corridor which was open, and I just lay on the tiles without a shirt. Then I shared a cell with an Indian officer."[35]

Stan Roberts tells of his capture at Titi some time after the Fall of Singapore: "We ended up being captured by Malays, and the Japs came up. They were carrying heads in bags and they were saying 'That's your pals' – you couldn't see who they were, they were covered in blood, but they were different regiments and Chinese. One bag had six heads in it. Our hands and necks were tied with wire and we were beaten up. They were cruel folk, them. They were tying men to trees and using them for bayonet practice. You couldn't do nothing about it. They had the heads on poles in Kuala Lumpur too."[36]

Jockie Bell and Tom McGregor spent fourteen days in the jungle before being given away to the Japanese by Malay villagers. Many Malays felt little loyalty to the British and a combination of intimidation, rewards and propaganda usually delivered fugitives to the Japanese. Prisoners caught in such circumstances faced prolonged and brutal Kempetei interrogation, and few survived. Jockie, fifty-six years later, still suffers from recurring malaria that can be brought on by hot summer weather – the legacy of his jungle experience. He takes up the story of their capture: "We were in a bad way with lacerated legs, lumps in the groin and limping badly. We felt very fatigued so we lay down on the grass and fell asleep. We awoke to Japanese bayonets pushed in our faces, and Major Baker shouting, 'It's all finished!' He'd got up, met some natives who told him to wait outside and they would get him some food cooked, then they had fetched the Japs.

"They came up in two private cars, one was a Morris, with two Indian civilians driving them. They took us down through the rubber estate to the cars and took us to Klang to a shop house where they kept us. A great big woman came out with a Jap officer, and what a peacock he was with cavalry boots and all that. The Jap talked to the woman in Malay, and she spoke to us in English. She was a big stout woman and she was hitting Major Baker and all he was giving was his name and number. She asked me how many Japanese I had killed, and I said I hadn't killed any, I was a truck driver. But there was a young Indian boy sweeping the floor, and he came nearer and nearer us and managed to tell us we would be taken to Kuala Lumpur and there were a lot of our comrades there, so this was encouragement.

"This woman gave us a big plate of corned mutton and rice and cigarettes. Then we were taken to Kuala Lumpur and there the Japs gave us bread and a big tin of jam and a pile of sugar and tea to drink. To my way of thinking these were administrative troops who came along behind, mopping up and collecting all the supplies. They put us in a British Army truck and took us to Pudu jail, and there were two Argylls lying wounded in the truck. One had a lot of tattoos on him and that was John Crone from the Regimental Police, and I recognised the other as a chap who'd come out with me, Private 'Dinky' Day, the old soldier who'd served his time in India. A smart Jap officer spoke perfect English and he was speaking to us, so Day said 'Don't tell him anything.' All the Japs wanted to know was where we'd been and who'd fed us, so they could catch anyone who'd been helping us... and where was Colonel Stewart. So that's how we got to Pudu, and I was only there a couple of days before I collapsed."

Capt Tim Turner had taken over the leadership of the third party from Tiri, which contained Douglas Broadhurst. Two thirds had dropped out through fever, starvation and exhaustion. Their group arrived at the Batu Caves in a party of twelve men. Here they encountered the Japanese and scattered, running for their lives. Six of the fugitives escaped. Three more Argylls joined them: L.Cpls Jock Gray, Hugh Falls and Pte Johnston. The group continued to Benut on the west coast of Johore, where they were supplied with food, quinine, a shotgun and ammunition by a forty-two year old Chinese Port Dickson police clerk, Siow Ah Kiew, who along with other police staff at Port Dickson had been paid off by the local police chief J.B Masefield, a nephew of John Masefield, the Poet Laureate, and advised to head south.

Siow Ah Kiew fed the Argylls and tried to get them a boat. He was betrayed to the Japanese by an informer and beheaded along with twenty other Chinese in the area. Still, his wife and daughter Angela assisted the Argylls: "I will never forget my 15th birthday" said Angela, "for that was the day on which the Japanese killed my dear father and my weeping mother took me aside and said 'Angela, you must go into the jungle. We can't abandon those poor British soldiers'."

Mrs Siow scribbled a note, tucked it in the hem of Angela's skirt and told her to deliver it to Captain Turner. Heading for the rendezvous where her father had previously met Turner, she found the Argylls very tired but in excellent spirits. They firmly believed that the war against Japan would be won and their predicament was only a setback. Captain Turner and his men took every precaution for Angela's safety, escorting her into the jungle and out to the jungle's edge. Benut was under dawn to dusk curfew and the Japanese were everywhere, rounding up and killing

Chinese. Angela carried food to the Argylls in small baskets.

The valiant efforts of the Siow family were not forgotten by the Argylls. In September 1946 Brigadier Stewart wrote to Mrs Siow to thank the family and recognise Ah Kiew's sacrifice. He enclosed an Argylls' cap badge and later sent an engraved silver plate. Subsequently the British High Commissioner presented Mrs Siow with a letter of appreciation from Lord Mountbatten. When the Argyll & Sutherland Highlanders returned to Singapore in February 1964 for the first time since 1942, they again made contact with the Siow family.[38]

Eventually, Captain Turner and five other Argylls were surrounded in a hut and captured by the Japanese. Racked with malaria, they were later brought to Changi POW camp, Singapore. Turner never really recovered his strength and died of cholera in Thailand. Another Argyll officer who had been in the jungle, 2nd Lt R.B. Marriott, was court martialled by the Japanese, no one was sure why, and taken away to Singapore's notorious Outram Road prison where he endured torture and starvation before being returned to Changi in a very bad state. Thirty-six other Argylls remained at liberty in the jungle as late as July 1942, but only two were to escape captivity or death.

One of the last to be captured was Alex McDougall: "I was in the jungle when the whole of Malaya had collapsed. Sgt Robert Kerr and I started off with 27 men, after Slim, but we finished up with 18 of us left. We were living in a place outside of a leprosy colony by the Batu Caves – and there was a doctor from Dundee (Authors: most likely Doctor Gordon Ryrie, Superintendent of Sungei Buloh Leprosorium who stayed behind following the evacuation) – he was giving us a wee bit of sugar, things like that. We heard at the start that the Japs weren't taking prisoners, they were just shooting them out of hand. Rab Kerr was senior to me and said 'we can't take all these men and give ourselves up'. I said 'Rab, we can't last any longer'. My other younger brother Hughie, who died later on, he and another guy started fighting and were trying to drown one another in the river. They were doowhacky, that's all. You get jealous and selfish, and there were fights among the men – someone's got something more and they want it. You don't know how human beings... they come to such a low pitch they don't know what they're doing. So we gave ourselves up. Yes, we had all our arms with us in the jungle after Slim. That's why the Japanese belted me and knocked out my front teeth... they brought out about two battalions to take us in."[39] They were taken first to Taiping jail, then on to Pudu jail, Kuala Lumpur.

Cpl Gibson's group received help from local Chinese, particularly Dr Koo of Ulu Lungut . They also met the young son of a Dr Osman, a Malay evacuated from Sungei Patani, who recognised Broadhurst. From his family they acquired a useful AA map of Malaya. In early February Pte Johnston died. Gibson, Gray and Broadhurst continued their journey with a young Chinese guide, Lim Siong.

Gibson, formerly a piper and boy soldier, had served seventeen years with the Argylls in both China and India. A short, pipe-smoking man with a big moustache, he had an air of calmness and energy about him. Twenty-two year old John 'Jock' Gray from East Lothian also had a reputation for calmness but was a quieter, less abrasive character than Gibson. Broadhurst says: "Gibson was a fiery character who was all go, go, go all the time. His greatest words were 'push on, push on,' when other people gave up the struggle."

This determination did not always make him popular with fellow Argylls. One recollects an occasion, probably at Lenggong, when Gibson had urged a bayonet charge through the jungle at the Japanese. "Remember your forefathers!" he exclaimed. His companions greeted the suggestion with derision.

On February 4th they were at Kachau, on the 10th at Betang Benar and on the 13th they arrived on the coast at Chuah, six miles north of Port Dickson, from where the Argylls had set out a month earlier to do battle. Here they obtained a boat and sailed the 150 miles to Sumatra where they found Lt Montgomery-Campbell, Sgt Colvin, Cpl Robertson and other successful escapers. The resourceful Colvin had served seventeen years with the Norfolks before joining the Argylls in India.

Lt Colonel Robertson's youthful batman, Pte John Bennett from Glasgow, "a big, quiet chap", originally a driving instructor in the MT section, found himself with Pte Douglas Stewart of the Argylls, two gunners and two sergeants. They joined the guerrillas in the Batu Caves area. Only Bennett and Stewart survived the 300-mile trek south and the years of disease and danger, moving from camp to camp, frequently ambushed by the Japanese. Bennett became extremely ill and in June 1945 Stewart went down with dysentery to add to the effects of malaria and beriberi. However they both survived to emerge from the jungle near Segamat in September 1945.

In January 1946 Bennett featured in an article in the 'People's Journal' under the heading: "Snake soup, monkey stew and elephant steaks – these were the foods that kept me alive in the Malayan jungle". An emaciated Bennett had been smuggled out of a Muar hospital by members of Force 136 and handed over to an RAF Regiment unit. Evidently the MPAJA guerrillas were contemplating shooting him because he knew too much about them.[40]

In April 1942, Bennett's party met Freddie Spencer Chapman who in 'The Jungle is Neutral' mentions an Argyll sergeant 'Andy' Young – in fact, L.Sgt James Young of 15 Platoon. After Slim River Young had escaped to the Gemas area and joined the guerrillas near Titi in Negri-Sembilan State. The Argyll sergeant had taught the MPAJA guerrillas bayonet practice and become quite a legend after killing a senior Japanese officer in an ambush. The guerrillas in their singsongs enjoyed his fine tenor voice. Young was well known in the Argylls for his guitar playing. Racked with beriberi, malaria and tick typhus, he died in the jungle in early 1944.[41]

In all, some 40 Argylls are listed as 'died in the jungle' following the Slim River disaster; many of them were buried at Titi after they had met up with Chinese guerrillas. Other Slim River casualties are listed as 'missing' and 'killed in action' 7.1.42 or 13.1.42. Exact figures are hard to establish. Of 576 Argylls some 75 were killed in the immediate battle; 40 died in the breakout; about 30 got to Sumatra; nearly 300 were captured, mostly 'on the run', and 94 returned to British lines.

The Slim River disaster would have been the end of the story for any other battalion, but this was not to be the end of the Argylls and their rear-guard role in the battles in Malaya.

NOTES

1. Brigadier Ivan Simpson: Singapore: Too Little, Too Late
2. See S.W. Kirby's official history
3. Argyll casualties by 6.1.42 estimated from George Aitken's Record Book / Casualty figures given by Stewart and Commonwealth War Graves registers
4. The identity of the 30 Argylls brought up to the battalion on the eve of the Slim River battle draws different opinions from historians. According to Stewart they were experienced veterans. Others refer to them as raw recruits, a version that is supported by some surviving Argylls. Jockie Bell met two young Argylls in Pudu who didn't even know which company they were in. They told him that they had just arrived on the train from Singapore.
5. Broadhurst interview (Singapore National Archives)
6. Kirby
7. Ferguson interview
8. Montgomery-Campbell interview
9. Jockie Bell interview
10. Alex McDougall interview 11.97
11. Tom McGregor interview
12. Finlay McLachlan interview
13. Jockie Bell
14. Webber letter 1.98
15/16. Jockie Bell
17. Stewart/Beattie
18. K. McLeod interview 1997
19/20. Jockie Bell
21. Stewart
22/24. Jockie Bell
25. Rose
26. Broadhurst interview (Singapore National Archives)
27. Beattie
28. Stan Roberts
29. Kenneth McLeod
30. Montgomery-Campbell
31/2. Jockie Bell
33. Ban Tsan Chuan letter to Rev G.B. Thompson 1946
34. Gibson
35. McLeod
36. Stan Roberts
37. Jockie Bell
38. Gibson/Chye Kooi Loong/ Audrey McCormick
39. Alex McDougall interview 11.97
40. Article on John Bennett in 'The People's Journal' and letter to Argylls Regimental HQ from RAF Regiment
41. Spencer Chapman

CHAPTER FOUR

RETREAT, REORGANISATION AND ESCAPE

ON JANUARY 8TH 1942 the surviving Argylls who had returned to British lines gathered at Rasa, south of the bomb-damaged town of Tanjong Malim. They numbered four officers (Captain Tam Slessor of the Transport Section; Lt Donald Napier of A Company; Lt Arthur Wilkie of the Signals Section and CQM James Doherty) and ninety other ranks, mainly the men from A Company who had shot up the Japanese along the railway line and avoided encirclement.

Padre Beattie writes: "When we arrived at Tanjong Malim we found that some of the Argylls had been ahead of us. These men were lying like corpses on the verge of the roadway. In fact bodies were everywhere, every man out of the world. At this point motor trucks began to arrive from the south. These were driven by Australian soldiers and belonged to their transport corps. They had been ordered to pick up those of us who had made our way to Tanjong Malim. The tall Australian drivers stood by their vehicles or talked in little groups. They were quiet but efficient. Soon the Aussies called the sleeping to take their places in the trucks. The back door of each vehicle was lowered and men were half lifted and half pushed in by strong Australian hands. When a fat man came along facetious remarks would be passed and unprintable epithets would be heard in the darkness.

"As each truck was filled the driver would take his place and without shouting or ado the truck would slip off down the road. Before each got going however the driver would come aboard carrying a mug in one hand and a bucket full of water in the other. Whether you were officer or man a mug was pushed at you and a nasal voice would say, 'Here mate, drink her up, you may not get another.' These Australian drivers seemed to be men over forty and were ideal motor transport personnel. I do not think I ever saw a crashed Australian vehicle as the result of poor handling."

General Wavell had arrived in Singapore by Catalina flying boat on the morning of the Slim River disaster. He flew to Kuala Lumpur then drove to the Batu Caves where he spoke about the disaster with Brigadier Paris and a shocked Ian Stewart, exhausted to the point of incoherence. He then visited the Slim River survivors at Rasa where they had spent the night in deserted Chinese shops.[1] It was here that CQMS Baird discovered for the first time that he'd actually been wounded the day before at Slim River – a severe flesh wound in his buttock.

Two Argyll armoured cars, both badly shot-up Marmons, and half the transport had survived the battle. These vehicles transported the remaining Argylls south to Kuala Lumpur early on January 11th.

Two Argyll officers who had served with the battalion before the Japanese invasion arrived to join what was left of the battalion. Twenty-five year old Captain David Wilson was formerly the Battalion Transport officer and very much a son of the Regiment for his father Lt Colonel Robin Wilson DSO had commanded the 1st Argylls and his grandfather General Sir Alexander Wilson KCB had been Colonel of the Regiment from 1920 till his death in 1938. In 1938 Wilson had trained at the Tank School in India and Ian Stewart at first put him in charge of the Argyll armoured cars. He was a humourous and energetic officer whose nickname 'Chuckles' gives some indication of his cheerful nature. A man of many talents: he could play the bagpipes, drive a railway engine and at Tyersall had operated the cinema projector.

With Wilson was a fellow Captain and Colonel's son, who had also served with the Argylls in India, the brave, sensitive 23-year-old Michael Blackwood. In Singapore during the early weeks of the Malayan Campaign they had served as jungle warfare instructors at the OCTU (Officer Cadet Training Unit), teaching such skills as camouflaging, constructing kapok bridges and assembling and using collapsible boats. They then managed to get themselves posted a little nearer the action, Wilson employed by 3rd Indian Corps as a sort of liaison officer to select good rearguard positions and arranging Rear Area HQ accomodation, and Blackwood as 12th Brigade's staff captain. Wilson was to be commanding officer of what was now scarcely a weak company and Blackwood to command the armoured car/ carrier platoon.[2]

The Japanese were now advancing simultaneously down the main road and along the west coast. The west coast was defended by units of the FMSVF under the command of Argyll Brigadier Robert Moir. General Wavell ordered Lt General Heath to plan a 150 mile withdrawal to Johore and plans were made for a final mainland battle on the so-called Mersing-Muar Line, bringing in the unblooded AIF 8th Division (Major-General Henry Gordon Bennett) and fresh British troops from the Singapore garrison – Gordons and Loyals.

The remnants of 12th Indian Brigade were to hold the Mantin Pass, four miles north of Seremban, covering the retreat of 9th/11th Indian Divisions then acting as rear-guard as far as Gemas. At Mantin Pass the Argylls prepared an ambush. David Wilson explains: "We were disposed in a good ambush position at the head of the Pass, on a steep and twisting metalled road. If the Japanese had blundered upon it in haste, they might have received a nasty shock, but if they had come up round our left flank the position was not so good for defence. But that approach would have been up very steep hillsides with thickish jungle and undergrowth and they would have had to waste time, perhaps a full day or so to use it, and this would have delayed them, which was the whole object of the exercise.

"There was a battery of 25 pounders in support and they had ranged on the road in front of us and could have been of great help if need be. We spent a bit of time digging ourselves in and camouflaging the positions. No movement was allowed in daylight; all our feeding was done at night. During the day the odd Japanese recce plane came over and we crouched down under cover hoping we were not spotted, and oddly enough I don't think we were, for although they would circle round suspiciously, they never came for a really close look and we were never attacked."

Unfortunately, the order for withdrawal came before the Argyll ambush could be sprung. At one stage during the withdrawal the Argylls were trapped for two hours by a prematurely blown bridge. Later Captain David Wilson and Sgt Harry Nuttall demolished an important railway bridge at Seremban without assistance from the sappers. David Wilson says: "Sometime on the afternoon of the 12th, I was sent for from my lair by Ian Stewart, still in command of what was left of 12th Brigade, and was told that we were to withdraw that night all the way to Gemas, about 50 miles further south, and I and the two armoured cars with a platoon of Argylls was to act as rearguard for the first ten miles blowing three bridges en route. A flimsy bit of handwritten paper was the authority which I would hand to the engineer officer in charge of each demolition. It was quite a responsibility to be the last of an Army!"

The Argylls withdrawal was timed for 8.00 p.m. but a tropical storm and lightning strike had struck a demolition further down the road. There was a delay till 10.00 p.m. The Argylls left their positions and marched very quietly down the far side of the pass, embussing into their 15 cwt and 30 cwt trucks. Ian Stewart wished Wilson good luck and departed leaving the young captain with two armoured cars and two trucks to carry his platoon. They drove slowly south through Seremban.

"It was all a bit spooky," recalls David Wilson, "not a soul to be seen anywhere, not a light; debris caused by bombing all over the roads, telegraph poles askew and fallen down and lines threatening to wind themselves around truck wheels, and yet somehow you felt unseen eyes watching you through the windows and half-destroyed houses, but there was no opposition."

The Argylls rearguard approached the first bridge, a large steel girder bridge carrying the railway over the main road, on the southern outskirts of Seremban. Wilson ordered most of the party to proceed to the second bridge four miles on while he remained with Sgt Harry Nuttall and the armoured car.

"The explosive charges were all in position, linked by cordtex and junction boxes and all ready to blow, but no one to blow the bridge. The engineers were nowhere to be seen. But what about us? Surely, we could do something? After all, Harry and I had both been on a short mine and explosives course run in Tyersall Park by our Madras Field Company of Indian Engineers, not all that long ago, and so we worked out a plan. We found a large 'junction box' packed with squares of gun cotton from which a large number of cordtex leads ran to the main charges, lashed to one of the main girders which faced south down the main road. With a length of electric cable we lashed a 36 grenade securely to the girder and the junction box, and I got a bit of string and tied the grenade lever-down. Holding our breath we pulled out the safety pin, and tip-toed off the bridge."

Wilson and Nuttall backed the armoured car 150 yards down the road, stopped and fired a long burst of the Vickers machine-gun at the bridge girder. The vibration broke the string holding the grenade. The grenade exploded setting off the charge in the junction box. The whole bridge went up in a terrific explosion showering the armoured car in debris.

Two very happy Argylls quickly surveyed their handywork then drove on to the next bridge where Ian Stewart was waiting for them. "We felt very pleased with ourselves. We thought Ian Stewart would be pleased with our work. Not so! He was almost incandescent with rage!" David Wilson explains Stewart's anger: "In those days we had no communications at all and he was quite in the dark with what we had been up to, so when he had heard the machine-gun fire and the explosion of the bridge, he naturally assumed we had run into trouble, and had possibly been wiped out, and when he heard us coming down the road with no lights on towards him, he thought we might well have been the advancing Japanese! So I was practically roasted alive by him!"[3]

During the last stage of the withdrawal south the Argylls' job was to ruthlessly push on the exhausted 11th Indian Division – roughly waking sleeping drivers and keeping the traffic moving. Fine work was also to be done by the Movement Control Officers including Eric Moss who got two divisions through Segamat in one night and dispersed them into new positions by daylight. On January 13th the Argylls took the train south from Gemas to Singapore where on arrival they received a great reception from waiting friends. That evening they were back at Tyersall Park Camp ready for refitting.

The Padre, Captain Hartley Beattie who reportedly swore like a trooper, was described by one Argyll as "just one of the boys."[4] When the Argylls had arrived in Singapore they had no padre of their own as padres in India did not move around with the battalions. At first they shared a padre with the Gordons. Beattie had served with the battalion since November 1940 and was known to participate in Tiger patrols during training. Returning to British lines after Slim River, he returned to Singapore in his newly acquired Morris Oxford, giving a lift to Captain Doherty. At Doherty's house his wife was waiting with bacon and eggs for the two of them.

On the first Sunday after the return to Tyersall about a hundred people, mostly returning Argylls, assembled in the camp gymnasium. Families of some of those who had not returned were also there. A service was held. Lt Donald Napier played a voluntary on the piano. Ian Stewart read from St. Paul and they sang the Old Hundredth and the 40th Psalm.

Padre Beattie's frequent companion at the Regimental Aid Post, the Battalion Medical Officer, Captain Eric Bartlett RAMC also escaped at Slim River. Bartlett was a medical graduate of Aberdeen University and the son of an Episcopalean clergyman from Aberdeen. During their time in India and Malaya the Argylls had a succession of Medical Officers, unlike Bartlett mostly Irishmen from the Indian Army Medical Service who hadn't wanted to join the English RAMC.

Lt Robert Mundie also rejoined the battalion from the staff of 12th Indian Brigade. Earlier in the campaign he had been missing in the jungle for many days but had got back to the battalion.

Following the retreat into Johore the 9th and 11th Indian Divisions were amalgamated under the command of Major-General A.E. 'Bill' Barstow. When Barstow was killed in action, Brigadier Berthold 'Billy' Key, an Indian Army officer, took the divisional command in preference to British Army Brigadier Paris. Paris, who in Stewart's view had done a brilliant job in the divisional command, returned to the command of 12th Indian Brigade. Paris had recognised the futility of defending bridges across the Perak River and had pulled his division back into tin mining country with clear fields of fire for the machine guns and artillery. It was in artillery that the British had their superiority to the Japanese.

Ian Stewart came back to the Argylls with Major Angus Rose as 2 i/c and David Wilson as adjutant. Argyll sick and wounded returned to the battalion from Singapore hospitals as did those on staff appointments until the battalion numbered 250 men: two rifle companies and a small HQ Company with armoured cars, carriers and mortars. Sixteen young, enthusiastic Chinese volunteers acted as stretcher bearers, freeing Argylls for the rifle companies.

On January 21st thirteen temporary commissions were given to FMS and Straits Settlements Police officers, members of the Malayan Civil Service (MCS) and FMSVF (Federated Malay States Volunteer Force) officers. From the police: 2nd Lts John Leahy, Douglas Weir, Hubert Strathairn, Neil Stewart, Robin Calderwood and Lt Bill McLean.[5] From the MCS: Lt John Love, 2nd Lts Stewart Angus, Walter Cole and Patrick (or Philip) Wickens. The Argylls gave Cole the Malay honorary title 'Dato'.

From the Volunteers of the FMSVF: Lt Albert Gispert, a chartered accountant from Kuala Lumpur, and 2nd Lts CR McArthur of the Straits Trading Company and CSN of the Perak Battalion, and Noel du Boulay, a copra planter from Torkington Estate, Selangor, who was irreverently called 'du Boulay Beef' by some Argylls. From the Kedah Volunteer Force, Irish rubber planter 2nd Lt John O' Callaghan, a man "proud to wear the Argyll trews," and a fourteenth officer was to be Lt WGA Morrisson from the AOER (Army Officer Emergency Reserve).

Douglas Weir and his friend Hubert 'Strath' Strathairn from Crieff joined the Argylls in late January, shortly before the evacuation of the mainland. Weir had already encountered the Argylls during their visit to Kuala Lumpur in 1940 and later in December 1941 while Weir was working with Dalco, an intelligence group under Colonel John Dalley, consisting of men with a knowledge of Malaya and its languages. Dalco officers participated in special reconnaissance patrols and formed guerrilla stay-behind parties. As the son of a Scot, Weir was brought up on tales of the Argylls; the battalion was the natural choice to join for the final battle, and he requested release from Dalco for that purpose.[6]

Of the two other 'Argyll police officers' Neil Stewart was a Police Cadet officer based at Ipoh and Robin Calderwood was an Assistant Superintendent in the Detective Branch, Kuala Lumpur. Here Calderwood had raised a Police Mobile Column of over three hundred men who went on anti-looting patrols. Another civilian who joined the Argylls on the mainland following the fall of Kuala Lumpur was Albert Gispert, a Londoner of Spanish origin. He worked for the accountancy firm of Evatt and Co, first in Singapore then Malacca and Kuala Lumpur. He commanded a machine-gun company in the 2nd Battalion (Selangor) FMSVF in which he held the rank of captain. A popular, athletic man, he founded the Hash House Harriers, a cross-country club still going strong in Singapore today, though sadly today's members know little of their founder. The club was originally based at the Selangor Club, known as the Spotted Dog, in Kuala Lumpur. Holidaying in Australia when the Japanese invasion of Malaya began, Gispert hurried back to Singapore for early January.[7] As a Lieutenant in the Argylls he commanded the Mortar Platoon.

Stewart Angus of the MCS, an Oxford graduate, had arrived in Malaya in 1935 and was Assistant District Officer in Ipoh, Perak. W.D. (Bill) McLean worked for Harper Gilfillan Ltd, Kuala Lumpur. C.R. McArthur was the Seremban manager for the Straits Trading Company Ltd and John O'Callaghan was the Assistant manager of the Harvard Rubber Estate in Bedong, Kedah.

The arrival of these officers gave the battalion a very top-heavy total of 23 officers. Ian Stewart formed some of the new arrivals into a Tiger patrol platoon supported by battle-experienced Argylls. Douglas Weir's patrol consisted of Cpl J. Jennings MM, Ptes A Fowler and Henderson. Jennings had won his Military Medal in the north of Malaya. Together with Sgt Thomas Purves (later died of wounds) "under heavy machine-gun and mortar fire... covered the withdrawal of their section, inflicting heavy casualties and finally forcing the enemy to withdraw." The new officers offered the added dimension of good local knowledge and linguistic skills. Douglas Weir spoke Malay.

Captain Doherty, the Battalion Quartermaster, QMS Fleming and Sgt Harry Nuttall were busy salvaging armoured cars left derelict by other units. An over-enthusiastic Harry Nuttall actually pirated a Lanchester belonging to another unit, locking up the crew in their guardroom "for not using it properly." Nuttall, the son of a circus family and a Barnardos (orphanage) Boy, had joined the Argylls in 1935 as a piper. He went out to India with Lt Colonel Hector Greenfield and became a driver in the transport section, graduating to Lanchesters in 1940.[8]

Captain Eric Moss was busy collecting ammunition. He describes a visit to the Alexandra Munitions Depot, which even at this critical time was operating a five day week. "I was given the job of taking a convoy, mostly Australian drivers, up to this depot to load up with field artillery ammunition. While we were there, there was a raid, and the Australians jumped off their trucks into a ditch at the side of the road. We eventually got going again, and the ground was littered with debris, including a lot of detonators. The Australians wouldn't take their trucks in there. So I think it was our own chaps who drove the trucks through, took a chance. We got to the doors and they were locked. I remember myself and a young sergeant from the Ordinance Corps, blowing the locks off to get in. We loaded the ammunition but we had no help whatever from the Australians. It was the old funk bit."[9]

Moss was to make a sadder visit to the Alexandra area to visit the dying Lt Gordon Schiach who had been terribly wounded at Gopeng-Dipang. Ernest Gordon in his book describes visiting Schiach and gave him a book of Scotland's prose and poetry. Schiach picked out 'the Canadian Boat Song'. Eric said "I went to visit him in Alexandra Hospital just before he died. I met the nurse in the passage and she said he was very, very ill. I knew what that meant. She let me see him and Gordon was lying back on his pillows. I remember his hands were down each side of him, lying on the covers, and they were very, very white, all the flesh had disappeared. 'Hello, Eric,' he said. He was too weak to raise his hand. 'Got a mortar bomb up my jaxie and bullets across the guts but I'm doing all right.' But he died that night."[10] At Gordon Schiach's funeral at Singapore's Bididari Cemetery, Piper Stuart played 'Flowers of the Forest'. After the war his remains were interred at Kranji War Cemetery.

By the time the Japanese invaded Singapore the Argylls had two 3 inch mortars with 700 rounds; 4 carriers; 6 armoured cars and numerous machine-guns and tommy guns. Like the Japanese they found the tommy gun particularly useful for close-quarter fighting in jungle and plantations.

The period January 15th–25th was one of intense training and saw the arrival at Tyersall towards the end of the month of some 200 Royal Marine survivors from the Prince of Wales and Repulse. A Scottish Singapore SSVF MG company moved into Tyersall Camp on January 19th together with the MG platoons of 2nd (Selangor) FMSVF and trained with the Argylls at this time. The plan was evidently to amalgamate them and the bren carrier platoon of the Gordons into a force of 'Storm Troopers' to make hit and run forays against the Japanese, but the amalgamation never took place. The FMSVF platoons were sent to relieve the Manchesters, at the beach defences on Blakang Mati Island.

Other new arrivals, the Royal Norfolks from the British 18th Division were also billeted at Tyersall. Duncan Ferguson remembers a group of new arrivals looking at an Argyll armoured car, Harry Nuttall's *Stirling Castle* parked near the main gate. "'What's all these marks on it? Is that camouflage?' 'That's bloody bullet holes on it.' They said 'Machine guns?' I said 'Aye – we've lost all the rest of our carriers and armoured cars. It's the only one that made it!'."[11] Padre Beattie also remembers these men: "They had just arrived in the country and they were sent off almost immediately up country to fight the Japanese. They certainly did look straight from home with their ill-fitting tropical kit and their over-sized topees. Strangers to the tropical climate and the jungle conditions, their experiences were anything but happy."

Paul Gibbs Pancheri, one of the SSVF volunteers calling in at Tyersall writes: "Conditions at Tyersall were dreary. Everything was wet and muddy and the Norfolks and Cambridgeshires dispirited. The Jocks tried to cheer up the new arrivals in their own fashion, and when one newly arrived warrior gloomily remarked 'I think it'll be another Dunkirk' the reply came pat from the Argyll, 'Dinna kid yourself laddie, there's nae place to go frae here'."[12]

Most of these new arrivals were ill-prepared for fighting the Japanese and too late anyway. The 5th Beds and Herts (Lt Colonel D. Rhys-Thomas OBE MC) did not arrive at Keppel Harbour until January 29th and were hurriedly billeted in Birdwood

Camp. One of their officers wrote: "Our thoughts turned to jungle. No one aboard had ever seen jungle; no one had the least idea what a Japanese soldier looked like, nor were there any books or pamphlets which might enlighten us. Thus our imaginary schemes and lectures had to be based largely on guesswork, and they were not very good guesses either."

On January 26th Ian Stewart received orders from Malaya Command to use his Argylls to hold the Singapore Causeway while all British, Indian and Australian forces in Johore were evacuated.

ESCAPE ACROSS THE CAUSEWAY

On January 27th 1942, the day 22nd Indian Brigade was lost north of Layang-Layang, twenty-eight year old Naval Lt John 'Joc' Hayes, formerly Assistant Navigator and Signal Officer on HMS *Repulse,* was sent for by Rear-Admiral 'Jackie' Spooner, the senior naval officer in Singapore and formerly a popular Captain of HMS *Repulse.*[13]

Spooner told Hayes that he was needed as a naval liaison officer on Lt Colonel Stewart's staff; that he was to gather "anything that floated" ready for the evacuation of Johore. These craft would be needed if the Japanese bombed the Causeway before or during the intended evacuation.

The following morning as Rear-Admiral Spooner ordered the demolition of Singapore's Naval Base with its vast oil-storage tanks, Hayes found himself at Ian Stewart's Johore bungalow headquarters. "Such as remained of the 93rd (2nd Argylls), which was two weak companies and our beloved armoured cars, was to be put into Johore itself, to stop behind and fight it out, so that the Causeway could at any rate be blown up successfully," says David Wilson. "It was going to be a real 'Death or Glory' party and our hearts sank lower as the full horrors of the scheme became apparent. I know mine was being squashed under the soles of my boots every time I took a step on the way up."

Stewart explained his evacuation plan to Hayes. There was to be a timed withdrawal of all British, Australian and Indian troops on the mainland with an outer perimeter of four miles held by the Australian 22nd Brigade (Brigadier HB Taylor) and the Gordon Highlanders (Lt Colonel John Stitt MC). The inner perimeter of less than one mile in depth was to be held by the 250 Argylls, temporarily commanded by Major Angus Rose while Stewart took overall charge of the operation. 3rd Indian Corps, resisting the Japanese on the west coast of Johore, would withdraw in three columns along three main roads into Johore Bahru, passing through the outer and inner bridgeheads. The operation had to be completed in one night, Saturday January 31st, if the Japanese pressure could be contained, and on Thursday January 29th if things went badly. Stewart knew that it would be impossible to complete the evacuation within the hours of darkness so there was every possibility of the inner perimeter Argylls being lost if the Japanese attacked and it became a race for the boats.

Later in 1942 Hayes described the days before the evacuation in a BBC radio broadcast: "They were beautiful, those last days in January; brilliant and cloudless; and at night the moon was waxing to full. The cavalcade across the Causeway and into the island had already begun, an unending train of private cars, big cars, little cars, black cars, tawny cars, all piled high with the pathetic personal trappings of refugees. The stream, moreover, was not helped by the demolition squads, already preparing to cut our line of retreat as soon as we had finally crossed. Pneumatic drills clattered continually. Cylinders of concrete littered the side of the Causeway. And below the waterline, the Navy was laying its depth-charges. At the northern end of the Causeway was a lock with inner and outer gates. Since the Navy was most anxious to use either side of this lock as boat points, it wanted at least one pair of gates left intact until the last moment."[14]

On January 28th the Argylls got into position. David Wilson takes up the story: "Immediately after we arrived a large party of Jap planes appeared and deluged us with a good deal in the way of large bombs. We picked up one fragment with 'GR VI' on it which we sent to the RAF HQ with our compliments, as it was obviously one that the Japs had picked up off one of our own airfields up north."

While touring the area with Angus Rose, Wilson drove over a suspicious looking hump in the middle of the road: "As we went over it Angus said 'Do you know, I think that must have been an unexploded bomb. It looks just like the pictures one sees in books about them' but we thought no more about it. Later on in the afternoon we came back in an armoured car. I was sitting on the turret with Michael Blackwood, and we happened to be looking the other way at the time. We stopped to get a wheel disentangled from some telephone wires that had come down as a result of the bombing, when I looked round and saw the same bomb, with a large notice up, 'DANGER.' So we piled into the armoured car, and told the driver to drive very carefully and slowly forward, and when we had got fifty yards, we told him to go like hell. I was told later that the bomb went up about two hours after that."[15]

On the morning of January 29th a further air raid came on the Argylls positions. Predictably, the raids always came at 11.00 a.m. with twenty-seven aircraft each carrying eight to ten bombs. Trenches were well prepared for these "Diarrhoea" attacks.

Scottish rubber planter Douglas Telfer, who worked for Dunlops, was serving as a Don-R with the FMSVF Armoured Car Regiment at this time. He recollects the first time he saw Ian Stewart: "I can remember the infantry were up on the hill slope up to the right of us. It was a mixed bag, but there was one character in his kilt and his tammy, strolling up and down with his shooting stick. I was speaking to my officer, Jack Tovey: 'Who's that goddammed idiot up there?' He says 'That's Stewart of the Argylls.' I've never seen as brave a man in all my life. The bullets were flying everywhere. The troops were there and I remember him shouting to this machine-gunner: 'Murdoch, I say! Murdoch!' 'Yes, Sah!' 'I think if you can come out here with your gun you'll get a better view and you'll get a chance to close these Japs down. You'll get a better view here!' Murdoch, a big, tall lad, came right out into the open and got down into position. 'That's right, Murdoch, you'll be able to close them down there.' Colonel Stewart strolled down the line. I never saw anything like it. That was the Argylls. That was 'Busty' Stewart – that's what they called him."[16]

A particularly dangerous occupation was being a battalion runner – an easy target for sniping and there was always the danger of running straight into an enemy patrol. Early in the campaign an Argyll runner, a Corporal, shot himself in the foot to get his ticket back to Singapore. Duncan Ferguson encountered another looking for a way out: "We were doing the rearguard over in Johore, and the officer came to me and says 'Take Boy Stuart back to Tyersall. He's to get a motorbike.' Well, this runner came to me and said 'Fergie, are you going back to Singapore?' 'Aye' 'Well see when you're going,' – it was to be dark at night – 'slow down going down the brae and I'll get on there.' I says 'What do you mean? Deserting?' He says 'I'm getting out of this. I've had enough of this.' 'Och, a great battalion runner,' I said,

'I'll dae it – I'll slow down, but you're the battalion runner – you can pass me!'."

Another FMSVF man there was Sgt Cecil Lee, from the FMSVF Armoured Car Regiment. He wrote: "The evacuation of the mainland was planned for the morning of the January 31st 1942, and our section of four cars was informed that as we were lame ducks and expendable, we would be attached to the famous Argylls for the rear-guard at Johore Bahru, whence we now moved – to a hill and bungalow overlooking the Straits of Johore where the HQ of the Argylls was established. Here on January 30th, whilst wandering out of curiosity in Argyll lines, I saw for the last time my old friend 'G' Gispert, who fresh from leave in Australia had joined the Argylls as a platoon officer – his usual cheerful and delightful self.

"Here with the Argylls we came into direct contact with the real army. Though much reduced after their disasterous experience at Slim, where they had lost two-thirds of their number, they were, under their now famous Colonel Stewart, still an effective fighting force.

"That day the Japanese came over and dropped their bombs on us. There was a move to the slit trenches and I heard one Jock calling to his pal, 'Dinna run, dinna run.' Their colonel had enjoined that there was to be no scramble to slit trenches, but a solemn drill movement in normal time. Panic is so infectious that it is easy to see the wisdom of this and I noted it."[17]

Meantime, Hayes gathered his boats: two large pleasure steamers, sampans and ferries. Some he placed to the west of the Causeway, close to the Sultan's magnificent palace, with three good embarkation points. Some boats he placed to the east of the Causeway. Four naval beach parties were on both the Johore and Singapore shores. An MTB stood by to assist the escape of the Johore parties.

The Causeway in 1941–2 (today much widened) was a very solid concrete structure carrying both a road and a railway line running along the side of it. The Causeway was some 1100 yards long and 40 yards wide. Also running down the side of it was (and is) the vital pipeline supplying Singapore's reservoirs with its water. Still today, Singapore depends on this pipeline for most of its water.

The engineers were completing the laying of explosives under the arches of the Causeway's northern drawbridge lock gates and, assisted by the Navy, laying depth-charges and gelignite beneath the central area of the Causeway. Final plans for the Evacuation were made in a beautiful bungalow on Straits View Hill east of Johore town and overlooking the Causeway. As Ian Stewart gave out final instructions the Argylls dug slit-trenches across the immaculate lawn. Stewart and Hayes drove down to the Causeway. Every Argyll was issued with a smoke generator to cover their escape if the Japanese attacked.

Hayes found the atmosphere in Johore unsettling. "Apart from artillery fire, which one's imagination insisted was getting closer, there wasn't a sound in the town of Johore Bahru. For three days now it had been empty, the shops in many cases left open. Early in the night I went round to visit the beach parties, riding pillion behind a motorcycle despatch rider. The noise of a motorcycle in that empty, silent town was shattering. It was a long night for us all. We could not believe that the Japanese did not understand exactly what we were doing, the night was brilliant enough; and in that case why didn't they knock hell out of us? They would, of course, in the morning. We expected that, but why so quiet now? The stillness was eerie."[18]

As darkness fell the motor-transport began to appear: lorries, ambulances, carriers and motorbikes. Generals Percival, Heath and Gordon-Bennett supposedly made an undignified withdrawal in an ambulance and observed events from the Singapore shore. It was a full-moon night with a clear sky. Some artillery fire could be heard in the distance and searchlights and sporadic anti-aircraft fire from across the Straits in Singapore. During the night a suspected Fifth Columnist was detected, fired on and killed when he ran away from Argyll positions. He was not the first Fifth Columnist suspect shot by the Argylls. Everyone prayed that the Japanese would hold off. Sgt Cecil Lee of the FMSVF continues: "Whilst we waited for what we thought would be a sticky rear-guard, it all turned out very peaceful. Gispert told me with a rueful smile he had got the job of leading the last platoon and had to lay an ambush, but contact with the Japanese was broken, and the Argylls retired without molestation. On the bright morning of January 31st, feeling quite cheerful, we were ordered over the Causeway on to Singapore island, whilst Australian troops, forming part of the bridgehead garrison, marched over, as on peacetime manoeuvres, and the Australian brigadier in charge, Taylor, waved us over."[19]

"It was a moonlight night," says David Wilson,"and headlights were not needed at all. The whole show would have made a sitting target for the Jap airforce, but as usual they failed to take their chance, and it is strange how often they did not do anything at all at night."[20]

The motor transport was followed by the infantry battalions; their feet tramping on the asphalt road. The operation was going quicker than expected. As the sun came up the Australians, then the Gordons, the 92nd Highlanders, marched across. A single Argyll piper piped the Gordons across to 'Blue Bonnets over the Border' and their regimental march 'Cock o' the North'. By 7.00 a.m. over 30,000 men had crossed without loss. Only the 250 Argylls remained.

Angus Rose described the scene and his feelings as daylight came up: "Every bit of movement was covered by fire from some concealed position. Armoured cars glided from one position to another, halted and traversed their turrets. Two flights of Hurricanes tore over our heads. The sight was quite unprecedented. This was a cake walk. All I wanted were the Japs but, alas, no Japs came. It was a disappointing anti-climax, after having keyed ourselves up to concert pitch."[21]

The Argylls had anticipated a four hour hold for stragglers but with the sun up and it getting warm, it was clear that their mission was completed. Joc Hayes describes the final moments: "Then we ourselves went down the bank to the drawbridge. As an air-raid shelter I was allotted a hole filled almost entirely by a gigantic pinion wheel, well surrounded by gelignite charges. One by one the machine-gun posts were called in, and then the anti-tank guns and the armoured cars. Our boat was sent away, and a few minutes later I realised that the front line of the British Army in Malaya consisted of two bren gun posts. The sun was well up now, and the day was warming."

Thus at 7.30 a.m. on Sunday February 1st the Argylls began crossing the Causeway to Singapore to the pipes of Piper Charles 'Boy' Stuart and Piper McLean. They played 'A Hundred Pipers' and the Argyll quick march 'Hielan' Laddie' as the Argylls withdrew in open order. David Wilson remembers: "We then got our orders to withdraw, which we did rather like the last act of the Aldershot Tattoo. I was across about fifth from last, and Ian Stewart actually gave the order for the Causeway to be blown."

Major John Wyett, an Australian 8th Division staff officer, crossing the Causeway from the Singapore end some hours before, had to threaten a sapper sergeant with his pistol to prevent a premature blowing of the Causeway before the Argylls and many other units were across. He reported the incident to Stewart who seemed disinterested: "Good show. Keep me informed, won't you; we're going to be the last across." During the final moments Wyett joined Stewart again on the Johore side and asked him why the pipers were playing. Stewart replied: "You know, Wyett, the trouble with you Australians is that you have no sense of history. When the story of the Argylls is written you will find that they go down in history as the last unit to cross the Causeway and were piped across by their pipers."[22]

As a young subaltern in 1914 Ian Stewart had been the first British soldier of the BEF on French soil; he was determined to be last across the Causeway to Singapore. Heavy machine-guns and anti-tank guns were called in, leaving only two bren guns, one manned by Ptes Finlay McLachlan and Tom McGregor who had also covered the withdrawal through the Mantin Pass. On Stewart's orders the bren-gunners then hastily retired across the Causeway with company commanders Slessor and Gordon. RSM Sandy Munnoch, the pipers and Sgt Harry Nuttall's Lanchester armoured car Stirling Castle driven by Pte Joe Russell, followed.

The scene is excellently portrayed in Peter Archer's painting 'Sans Peur' to be found in the Argyll's Regimental museum at Stirling Castle: the tall, lean figure of Ian Stewart in glengarry, conversing with each man in turn as they filed past in extended order. Each man received a friendly, encouraging word.

Stewart, Hayes and Drummer Albert Hardie remained to scamper across the Causeway before either the Japanese descended or the charges were blown. Stewart, by his own admission, was not one to hang around, but Hardie, all 5 ft 3ins of him, had no fear of the Japanese and showed no inclination to run. "Dinna hurry, man," he chided the Colonel.[23]

No sooner were they across than at 8.15 a.m. the Causeway was blown by Indian Army sappers. Ian Stewart gave the order "Blow!" and what followed he described as "a colossal explosion that chucked rocks about three quarters of a mile." The drawbridge at the Johore end disappeared in a cloud of smoke and seconds later the middle of the Causeway disintegrated, blowing a far from comforting 60 to 70 ft gap and rupturing the Pipeline.

Joc Hayes also describes that moment: "We arrived on Singapore Island at the southern end of the Causeway in time to hear 'Take cover.' We waited. Dead silence. Then the drawbridge disappeared in a cloud of smoke. A few seconds later and the middle of the Causeway disintegrated. The Straits for some distance on either side was a sheet of spray from falling rock. The depth charges had done their work. The smoke of the demolitions died away. The drawbridge, too, had disappeared, and the water flowed through a large gap in the centre of the Causeway."

The Argylls were back at Tyersall for breakfast at 10.00 a.m. If Stewart was surprised at the speed of the withdrawal, more surprised were the Japanese. They had planned an attack on the Causeway from the west coast using the Imperial Guards Division but when their forward troops cautiously moved into Johore Bahru they found it deserted. It seems that they had become increasingly cautious following successful and costly ambushes by the Australians in Johore.

On the morning the Causeway was blown the Singapore newspapers carried the announcements of military awards for the campaign in mainland Malaya. These had been published in the London Gazette a week earlier. Of thirteen awards made, eleven went to the Argylls. Ian Stewart was awarded a Distinguished Service Order (DSO), regarded as a near miss for a Victoria Cross: "By his skilful handling, his battalion was disengaged and brought through the enemy with very few casualties after a very effective delaying action. Later, while still acting as rear guard, he effected a further 24 hour delay which was most valuable in permitting readjustments to be made in the main position. Throughout the operations his leadership and clear-cut decisions have been of outstanding value and his calmness under fire an inspiration to troops under his command."

Other awards to members of the battalion were based on Ian Stewart's recommendation but fell well short of his original list: Distinguished Conduct Medals (DCMs) were awarded to Lanchester commanders, Sgt Albert Darroch and Cpl Bertie King, and Military Medals (MMs) to Sgt Thomas Purves, Sgt Robert Robertson, Sgt Malcolm McPhee, Ptes John Jennings (an India veteran known as 'Big Jennings' on account of his height and famous for having the longest handlebar moustache in the Argylls. Jennings had three times been cut off behind enemy lines and three times returned), Archibald Hogan, John Harkins, Harry Carroll, and Bandsman Robert Taylor, their deeds of valour recorded in short citations.[24] A Military Medal was also awarded to Private Ban Tsan Chuan, attached to the Argylls from the 3rd Malayan Volunteer Field Ambulance Corps. Captain David Boyle was subsequently awarded a Military Cross (MC).

Fifteen Argylls were mentioned in dispatches: three company commanders, Captain Bobby Kennard, Captain Bal Hendry, Captain Tiny Gordon; Captain QM James Doherty; Lt Ian Primrose, RSM Sandy Munnoch, PSM F. Colvin, Sgts Harry Nuttall, R. Donaldson, W. Smith, W. Malcolm; Cpl J. Sloan, L.Cpl T. Barnfather, Ptes B. Drunsfield and A. Bruce.

One might wonder why CSM Archie McDine was missing from the honours list, but he was killed and the story of the Kroh Road went unrecognised. Also, to this day no one quite understands why Bal Hendry, particularly after the action at the railway station near Gopeng Dipang, never received an MC.[25]

Ian Stewart celebrated his DSO with a game of after-lunch golf with Angus Rose. Their play was interrupted but not marred by Japanese shelling.[26]

NOTES

1. Stewart/Wavell letter
2. Wilson/Beattie
3. Wilson
4. Wardrope/Beattie
5. Weir/Stewart
6. Weir/Chye Kooi Loong
7. Audrey McCormick
8. Obituary in 'The Thin Red Line'
9. Moss
10. Accounts of visiting Schiach from Gordon and Moss and funeral from Beattie
11. Ferguson/Beattie.
12. Paul Gibbs Pancheri: Volunteer
13. Hayes memoirs: Face the Music
14. Hayes 1942 broadcast
15. Wilson. See also Rose's account
16. Douglas Telfer
17. Diary of recollections of Cecil H. Lee
18. Hayes 1942 broadcast
19. Lee
20. Wilson
21. Rose: Who Dies Fighting
22. Wyett memoirs: Staff Wallah
23. Stewart and Hayes radio broadcasts
24. Straits Times 1.2.42
25. The opinion of many Argylls interviewed
26. Rose

A group of HMS Prince of Wales Royal Marines with 3 U.S Marines, taken off Newfoundland 1941 at the time of the historic meeting between Churchill and Roosevelt. The photo was taken by Mne Peter Dunstan using the camera of Mne Peers Crompton (2nd row from the front; 3rd from left). Cpl Charles Miller (2nd row from the front; 3rd from right) and Mne Tom Webber (back row right) also appear.

A photo taken aboard HMS Prince of Wales 1941 during a visit by the Princess Royal. Captain Aylwin RM escorts the Princess. Behind him Captain John Leach RN. Sgt Terry Brooks is front right on the Guard of Honour and Mne Tom Webber 3rd from right.

Men of A Company, rest in a rubber plantation. Sgt Albert Skinner, back left, drinks from his mess tin. In front of the tree L.Cpl Budd and Pte Grainger. The L.Cpl in the centre is Tony Hodgson. On the right of the picture is Sgt Bluff Wallace. In the background eating bread is a Pte Smith, and behind him to the left is 'Wee Tomintoul' L.Cpl Tom Jarvie.

Lt Colonel Ian Stewart (front centre) with Captain Angus MacDonald (left) and RSM Munnoch (right) in the mud at Kranji Creek. (Courtesy of Imperial War Museum)

Cpl Bertie King (front left) and his Lanchester crew
Sgt Darroch (left) and his crew rest in a Malay village.
(Both courtesy of Imperial War Museum)

Marine Maurice Edwards 1941

Marine Peter Dunstan 1941

At first this photo was unrecognised by Argyll veterans as being of 2nd Argylls in Malaya. Then faces were recognised and names remembered. Lt Ian Primrose is the very tall figure 6th from the left of the back row. Grouped on the extreme left at the back are Cpl Budd, and with towels round their necks, PSM Jimmy Love and CSM Hoostie McNaught. Seated 2nd row left, identified by his brother, is Cpl Tom McDougall and 4th to 6th from left Captain Beckett, Pte Willie Guthrie and L.Cpl Billy Doherty.

CHAPTER FIVE

THE PLYMOUTH ARGYLLS – SINGAPORE

ON DECEMBER 2ND 1941 the new battleship *Prince of Wales* and the old battlecruiser *Repulse* arrived off Singapore with four escort destroyers but without their 'air cover', the new aircraft carrier *Indomitable,* which had run aground off Kingston Harbour in the West Indies.

The presence of these two great warships boosted the morale of colonists and garrison alike and encouraged the belief in Singapore's invincibility. The Times newspaper boasted of Singapore as 'the island of many warriors'.

Aboard each of the two warships was a detachment of Britain's elite 'Sea Soldiers', the Royal Marines, whose motto is *Per Mare, Per Terram* – By Sea and Land. Most of these Marines had already seen action in the North Atlantic and the Mediterranean Sea, the *Prince of Wales'* Marines having participated in the action against the German battleship *Bismarck*. They had also witnessed the historical meeting of British Prime Minister Winston Churchill and US President Franklin D. Roosevelt off Newfoundland in July 1941.

The Royal Marines traced their history back as far as the year 1664. Throughout the 18th and 19th centuries they were employed aboard Royal Navy ships to repel boarders, as marksmen, and to provide landing parties. In 1704 they seized Gibraltar and held it against the French and Spanish for eight months.

In 1855 the Royal Marines were divided into Royal Marine Artillery and the Royal Marine Light Infantry, but the two were reunited in 1933. Their function by the 1930s was to provide detachments, in peace and war, to man guns on warships and to provide a strike force immediately available for amphibious operations. As their motto implied, every Marine was trained to fight on land and at sea and was able to handle a wide range of armaments including light artillery.

There were three Royal Marine Divisions based at Chatham, Portsmouth and at Plymouth. Like the Argylls, the Marines were tough, well-trained men, proud and loyal to their unit and its traditions. These Marines should not be called Royal Marine Commandos; Commandos were not formed until mid-1942.

On duty at sea in the tropics the Royal Marines wore khaki drill and khaki hat with white top instead of their traditional dark blue uniform and white helmets. On deck they wore khaki shorts and sandals. In action and while working in the gun turrets they wore anti-flash gear and blue denim overalls.

At dusk on December 8th the two great ships and escorting destroyers left Singapore Naval Base in heavy rain and headed northwards into the South China Sea. Their mission: to find and destroy a Japanese troop convoy destined for Singora in southern Thailand, so entirely disrupting the Japanese invasion of the Malayan peninsula. Admiral Sir Tom Phillips KCB on *Prince of Wales* asked for continuous air cover but was told this was not available.

On December 10th at 11.00 a.m. Force Z, as this Royal Naval force was known, was attacked off Kuantan by ten squadrons of Japanese naval aircraft flying from Saigon. The Royal Marine detachments on both warships manned the 14 and 15 inch, 5.25, 4 inch AA, pom-pom and Bofors guns during the attack. A survivor from *Prince of Wales* said of these RN (Royal Navy) and RM guncrews, "I thought they were heroes because they fought non-stop and there were shell cartridges lying all over. They were kicking these over the side into the sea from the smaller AA guns, notably the Oerlikons and the Pom Poms; the shell case which is approximately six inches long, could easily be kicked out of your way. Those shell cases were lying all over and they never stopped firing right to the end."

Repulse avoided nineteen torpedoes but at 12.20 was struck amidships and sank at 12.42 after four more hits. Forty-seven minutes later Prince of Wales went down.[1] Some of the ships' crews were lifted from the deck by escorting destroyers that came alongside; others like Captain Bob Lang RM and Lt Geoffrey Hulton RM were eventually lifted from the water. They were covered in fuel oil.

Sgt Terry Brooks, a turret captain, ordered his guncrew to remove their boots and inflate their rubber lifejackets. He then went down to the magazine to bring out three of his men before they all jumped overboard. Nineteen year old Marine Peter Dunstan, one of Brooks' guncrew, discarded his steel helmet, overalls and boots and leapt over the starboard bow sixty feet into the water. They were picked up by *HMS Express*. Cpl Charles Miller had been showering when the Japanese attack begun and he was called to Action Stations. There was no time to put on his uniform and when the time came to abandon ship he entered the water naked. Eight hundred and forty men including Admiral Sir Tom Phillips perished. Twenty-seven Marines from *Prince of Wales* and forty from *Repulse* were among those who lost their lives.

Survivors were picked up by the three escorting destroyers *Electra*, *Express* and *Vampire*; the fourth destroyer, the old *Tenedos* having been dispatched back to Singapore because of fuel shortage before the Japanese aircraft attacked.

The survivors were quickly returned to Singapore. At the Naval Base a fleet of 140 ambulances waited to take the injured straight to hospital. The uninjured survivors received a tot of rum and a shower and were bedded down on the floor of wooden huts just off the parade ground. Many officers were well looked after aboard *Exeter*. The next morning the survivors were paraded before Vice-Admiral Sir Geoffrey Layton for a poorly received 'pep-talk' interrupted by a Japanese air raid. The talk was not resumed – the Admiral had disappeared. Two hundred and ten fit Royal Marine survivors (6 officers; 204 other-ranks) were re-kitted at the Navy Supply Stores in the Naval Dockyard and other naval establishment and formed into a 'Naval battalion'.[2]

Captain Bob Lang later wrote: "Each NCO and man received a stand of arms although, in many cases, the condition of the rifles left much to be desired. The light armament weapons were somewhat varied and included a few bren guns, some Lewis guns and a Hotchkiss gun, all that were available at the time from RN sources. These deficiencies were later made good from Army sources."

Each man received $20 and officers $100. Twenty four year old Cpl Charles Miller RM came from Southport and had joined the Corps in January 1936, serving early in the war with the New Zealand Navy before joining *Prince of Wales*. He recalls the rekitting at Singapore as somewhat basic: khaki shirt, shorts and webbing with not enough steel helmets, razors or Royal Marine badges to go round. Later, on his return to guard the Naval Base against Tamil looters, he found no looters and precious little left to loot. Exploring the deserted godowns he did find the impressive blue-banded, gold leafed Admiral's crockery, carefully stored away for future use.[3] Royal Marine band survivors were among those evacuated from Singapore on December 19th[4] though two boy buglers, 17 year old Liverpudlian Charlie Gomery of *Repulse* and W.K. James of *Prince of Wales* remained.

The trauma of the loss of the warships followed by the evacuation of many of the survivors drafted back to the UK certainly had its effect on the morale of those left behind in Singapore. Captain Lang later reported: "It may be said that during the action many men went through great physical danger and mental strain with natural reactions to the nervous system. In certain cases this effect remained up to and even after the fall of Singapore, but in the large majority of cases it ceased to be noticeable after a comparatively short period. In quite a number of cases there appeared no adverse effect whatsoever. It was noticeable during the operations that men who stood up well to artillery, mortar and small arms fire frequently showed a tendency to jumpiness during air raids… Large numbers of the ships' companies being drafted home to the UK followed by the inevitable rumours and counter rumours resulted in a tendency to leave the men in an unsettled state of mind with doubts and apprehensions for the future."

The Naval battalion Royal Marines had two basic duties: firstly to form a mobile anti-parachute force for the protection of the Naval Base area northeast of the Causeway that links Singapore to the mainland; secondly to provide guards for the Dockyard and other naval establishments both inside and outside the Naval Base.[5]

At this time there was obvious Fifth Columnist activity in the jungle around the Naval Base. Flares were seen being fired during Japanese air raids. Patrols of Marines, Naval Personnel and Naval Base Police were sent out to find the elusive Fifth Columnists. A mock air raid was even staged to try and catch them. No Fifth Columnists were caught but the Chief of Police commended Sgt Thomas RM for his conduct.

Some seventy-five Royal Marines under 26 year old Captain Claude Aylwin RM, CO of the *Prince of Wales* detachment, and Lt Charles Verdon RM, were sent to the north-west coast of Singapore island to defend the Royal Navy Wireless Transmission station at Kranji on a hill close to the shore where the Japanese were to land a few weeks later. Here they joined a Royal Signals unit and constructed defence posts, dug trenches and erected barbed wire. It was at first an agreeable enough place to stay, with a football pitch, but being only 500 yards from the shore became somewhat dangerous once the Japanese had seized Johore Bahru and British artillery was firing across the Straits with the Japanese responding with small-arms fire.

Fifty Marines under Lt R.J.L. (Jim) Davis of *Repulse* were sent to guard the Royal Navy Armaments Depot while the remaining 75 Marines under Captain Bob Lang RM, CO of the *Repulse* detachment, defended the Naval Base area. Lang, the senior of the two Royal Marine captains, had very narrowly escaped drowning on December 10th after a long, exhausting struggle in the sea, but had soon recovered from his ordeal.[6]

Lang explained the secondary role of his group of Marines: "During night raids by enemy aircraft it was observed that lights and flares were being fired by Fifth Columnists from the rubber plantations and scrubland surrounding the Naval Base area. The Police asked for the assistance of the RMs to subdue this activity. A system of RM patrols with Police representatives was instituted to operate during the hours of darkness. Although no Fifth Columnists were actually caught red handed, their activities declined with marked rapidity and it was clear that this system of patrolling was amply justified."

On December 24th forty Marines were withdrawn from Kranji and after a week's inadequate jungle warfare training were sent up-country under Lt Jim Davis RM in the first week of January 1942. This up-country party was intended to be employed in patrolling rivers and raiding the coast behind the Japanese lines. They were to be part of 'Roseforce' together with the Independent Company, an armoured car squadron from the 3rd Cavalry and various other Indian units and artillery and engineer support. Roseforce was also to act as flank guard and rearguard during 11th Indian Division's retreat to Johore. It was to work closely with Brigadier Moir's Lines of Communication FMS Volunteers.

Angus Rose described the young Davis thus: "He lined up about six foot six inches and had a side-hat some two or three sizes too small, from which emerged a crop of unruly hair. He had the heart of a lion and his shy, uncertain manner disappeared completely when there was any danger in the air. His sense of humour was as constant as his untidiness."[7] Jim Davis recalls: "I didn't understand much that was going on at that time from my lofty position as a junior lieutenant. Angus was a great leader determined to get his DSO at our expense, but I would have followed him anywhere."

The up-country party went by train to Kuala Lumpur then on to Port Swettenham, today Port Klang, where they were met by Angus Rose and Colonel Alan Ferguson Warren DSC RM. Warren had been a GSO1 for the War Office in the Ministry of Information and was sent out to Malaya in May 1941 as Liaison Officer for all Far East Secret Operations. His foresight led to the setting-up of an evacuation escape route across Sumatra.

The speed of the Japanese advance and the Japanese control of the air led to the Roseforce base ship, the coastal steamer Kudat, and their fast Eureka launches being sunk by Japanese aircraft. The men would serve mainly as demolition parties, smashing vital equipment and blowing ammunition dumps, buildings and abandoned ships. On January 4th they were at Jeram; on January 7th in Kuala Lumpur breaking up factory machinery with sledgehammers and burning down smokehouses. They also rescued a number of Army personnel cut off by the rapid Japanese advance.[8]

This party was under regular air attack and took some casualties at Telok Datok on January 10th. These received further injuries when the ambulance returning them to Johore Bahru was involved in an accident. Angus Rose's car was destroyed in one of the air-raids but was replaced by one from an Argyll serving with the Independent Company, which the enterprising Jock didn't particularly need.

At Telok Datok the Marines held an important iron river bridge, covering the Army retreat and civilian evacuation which progressed in three columns towards Segamat. Cpl E.C. Lilley was a particularly steady character as he had been manning the guns on *Repulse*. That afternoon the Marines waited, hoping to attack a Japanese advance reconnaissance unit, but were ordered back before the opportunity arose. They blew further bridges along the road to Malacca, then proceeded to Muar, then Labis.

During the aborted up-country operations Angus Rose was still one of Percival's GSO2s. His original Roseforce had included six naval officers – all survivors from Force Z – and six of the Malayan Volunteers and fifty AIF (Australian Imperial Forces) men led by Lt Ralph Sanderson of 2/19th Battalion. The naval officers were responsible for the sea and river craft used including the base ship *Kudat*.

Roseforce operated in two platoons in the Trong area of Perak. They were armed with a liberal supply of tommy guns but had been disbanded after a partially successful mission at the village of Temerloh, west of the Perak River, in which Rose had ambushed and shot dead a Japanese major-general with a .303 rifle. Rose had found the Australians particularly difficult to work with because of their tendency to 'do their own thing'.[9]

We can only guess at Rose's feelings about the whole Roseforce experience. Here was the epitome of the professional man of action put in charge of assorted units:

difficult Australians then relatively untrained Volunteers, the assorted Independent Company including some tough but difficult Argylls, and Royal Marines hardly prepared for this type of jungle warfare. Added to this there was little moral or logistical support. No one at HQ Malaya Command had any real idea of how best to employ Roseforce behind Japanese lines. Rose's original plan submitted on December 17th to Lt General Percival and Captain Tennant RN, formerly of *Repulse,* had been to land an entire battalion behind Japanese lines, seriously damaging their lines of communication. Two platoons could hardly achieve this. Rose must have felt frustrated and undervalued.

Much to the relief of all concerned, Roseforce was disbanded at midnight on January 12th. The Independent Company headed for Malacca to assist the Acting Resident in the task of evacuating civilians. The up-country Marines returned to Singapore's Naval Base on January 14th 1942. On January 29th the Royal Marines evacuated the Naval Base. Captain Bob Lang later reported the background to this: "Shortly before the evacuation of the Naval Base the Naval Police were disbanded and replaced by RMs. As senior RM officer I took over all keys of the Dockyard and operated directly under the command of Captain Atkinson RN, Captain of the Dockyard, who remained until the end. Before finally evacuating the Base it was our sad duty to destroy all liquor, a duty that was performed without relish. We left the Dockyard on 29th January for Tyersall Camp, taking with us 30,000 rounds of ammunition and an assortment of weapons including the 3.7 Howitzer, which had to be abandoned as it unfortunately fell to pieces. The Naval Base was turned over to representatives of the 9th and 11th Indian Divisions which were taking over that sector for the defence of Singapore Island."

PLYMOUTH ARGYLLS

On February 2nd 1942 the amalgamation of the 210 Marines with the 250 Argylls began. Whose idea this amalgamation was is unclear but some surviving Plymouth Argylls today hold the view that it was at the suggestion of Lt Colonel Alan Warren RM,[10] the man who introduced the tommy gun to Malaya as a useful weapon for jungle fighting and who had been already active in Malaya organising Special Operations and Stay-Behind Parties.

Warren, who had co-ordinated the successful but highly controversial evacuation of European civilians from Penang, was already making plans for a major Singapore evacuation operation and may have seen a role for the Argylls and Marines in this operation. The Royal Marines with their knowledge of boats would have been particularly useful. They may have also been considered as suitable for 'stay behind' parties which were being put into the jungle at this time.

The Plymouth Argylls were not a unique example of collaboration between Argylls and Marines. The composite battalion quickly took the name 'Plymouth Argylls' after the well-known football club, as all the Marines were from the Plymouth depot. Links between the Argylls and Plymouth dated back to the 1880s when the Argylls were stationed in Plymouth and the admiration of a local man for the Argylls' style of football play eventually led in 1903 to the creation of the Plymouth Argyle football club. Then in August 1940 the 8th Argyll Territorial Battalion, the most Highland of the territorial battalions, was posted to 101 Royal Marine Brigade at Plymouth and for the next two years served as part of a Royal Marine Division in North Africa and the Mediterranean. When their CO Lt Colonel George McKellar suggested to the divisional commander, Major-General R. Sturges

RM, that his Argylls should wear kilts for ceremonials, the Royal Marine general very quickly produced 990 sets of kilts and service dress tunics.

Both 12th Indian Brigade commander, Brigadier Archie Paris MC (he was the son of Major-General Sir Archibald Paris KCB of the Royal Marine Artillery who had led the Naval Brigade at Antwerp and the Royal Naval Division at Gallipoli in the First World War) and Ian Stewart quickly earned the respect and confidence of the Marines. Captain Bob Lang RM commented on Stewart: "Never do we ask to be commanded by a finer, more courageous officer."[11] Stewart wrote of the Marines: "It is scarcely necessary to say that they were troops of the very highest quality, and the Argylls are indeed proud that it was to the 93rd (2nd Argylls) that the Marines asked to come."[12]

In training the Marines in his battle tactics Stewart emphasised two points. Firstly, the necessity to spread out with much greater distances between men and sections than was normally the case. This was in order to prevent heavy casualties from air or artillery attack. Dispersal was to be at 10 paces between each man, 150 yards between sections and 30 yards between platoons. Secondly, the cooperation between armoured cars and infantry.

Commenting on the initiative shown by the Marines, Stewart described them as "grand fellows" and is supposed to have said that every one of them should have been an NCO. Stewart made clear from the beginning that neither unit would be subordinate to the other and each would be equal in all respects. Lang wrote: "Lt Colonel Stewart, his officers and men will always be remembered with gratitude by those of us who realised the difficulties that may have arisen."

At Tyersall the five Royal Marine platoons moved into five attap huts, but the officers' quarters were full and Lang and Aylwin found themselves sharing a tent. On the first night at Tyersall Marine Peter Dunstan remembers: "After we were dismissed and got settled in that evening in the NAAFI, there was a right sort out between us and the Argylls. I can't recall who started it but it was a good sort out." Duncan Ferguson also remembers this incident: "That was only once. You never, ever knew who started any argument. If John McFadyen was there that was all it needed! It was just a wee argument, it wisnae a big battle, just in the canteen. It was all over in no time! Aye, somebody just blew apart... a bit of rivalry. It wisnae a pitched battle."[13]

Marine Tom 'Jan' Webber of the *Prince of Wales* detachment found the Argylls very friendly, but conversation between broad Scots and West Country Marines was sometimes difficult. Some Jocks could switch their speech from vernacular to an easier Scots-English; others remained pure 'Glesca'. Marine Maurice 'Bungy' Edwards, also of *Prince of Wales* detachment, comments on the Argylls: "They were obviously shaken by their disaster at Slim River. They had lost some very good men there."[14]

Some sources refer to a football match played at Tyersall Park Camp between the Royal Marines and Argylls – the Marines winning. Some have no recollection of this match, but former Captain David Wilson of the Argylls confirms that it took place on the Tanglin ground, beside St George's Garrison Church, on the opposite side of Napier Rd to Tyersall Park and he was there to see it.[15] Certainly the Argylls had an outstanding football captain and centre half in the person of Captain Tam Slessor, but their excellent goalkeeper Hoostie McNaught was posted missing since Slim River, as was goal scorer Hooky Walker. According to Captain Lang it was an inter-company competition and C Company (Marines) won.

Most Argyll families, including Angus Rose's wife and daughter, had left Singapore in early January. CSM McTavish's daughter Rose remembers: "We had a choice of going to Australia or back home; my mother chose to come home. We were a big family, four girls, and big families went first so we were put on a Dutch ship on January 1st 1942, and had to change ships in South Africa. There were a lot of sailors on board from *Prince of Wales* and *Repulse,* and I remember they were recalled from South Africa and had to go back. We were given money to buy warm clothes there because we didn't have any." As the bombing intensified the last Argyll family, the Johnstones, left Tyersall for Keppel Harbour and the evacuation ship *Empress of Japan.* Passengers were dismayed when they heard the ship's name. She was later renamed *Empress of Scotland,* said to be in honour of the Argylls. As for the Johnstones, Jessie and her children would never see CQMS James Johnstone again.

Walter Green of the RAF was stationed at RAF HQ Sime Road. He describes the intensified bombing sometimes by as many as 130 bombers at the time: "The Japanese came over Singapore almost regularly at 10.00 a.m. and I recall one particular morning we were told that they had dropped their entire load on Tengah airfield and I believe destroyed all the planes we had on the ground. This was the method they invariably employed, the leader of the squadron would signal when over the target and the whole of the bombers would drop their bombs altogether. I know it made one hell of a mess of Tengah!"[16]

Marine Maurice Edwards from Newbury had been Key Board Sentry aboard *Prince of Wales* and at Action Stations during the Japanese attack had been at a position above the magazines supplying the Bofors and Pom Pom guns. Now at Kranji Wireless Station, on the northwest coast of the island, he was also observing the raids: "The main receiving aerial mast had a crow's nest near the top and we Marines kept aircraft watch from that post. We watched Tengah getting a pasting and of course other places. Jap planes came over in groups of twenty-seven but when they had captured the southern airfields of Malaya, often the groups would be increased to fifty-four together with fighter escorts."

Tengah airfield received a further pounding on February 13th, but this time from the British 9.2 inch guns of Fort Connaught on Blakang Mati Island (today Sentosa), firing off the last of their armour piercing ammunition stock. The shells passed over Tyersall Park and were heard clearly enough by Argylls and Marines. Contrary to popular belief, some of the big guns of Singapore were traversed to fire northwards, but unfortunately had the wrong type of ammunition.

The Argylls' regimental funds and the Colours, symbolically containing within its folds the 'Spirit of the Regiment', were dispatched to the UK. The regimental silver, later looted by the Japanese but recovered in September 1945, was stored in sealed boxes and deposited with Messrs William Jacks of Singapore.

'Tiny' Gordon had briefly resumed his command of A Company before the evacuation of Johore but was now ordered to depart Tyersall with thirty men to work on the docks at Keppel where coolie labour was rapidly deserting. Later, a platoon of Marines was put on similar duties at Keppel Harbour.

The Plymouth Argylls consisted of four rifle companies with A and D Companies made up of Argylls commanded respectively by Lt J.H. Smith and Captain Mike Bardwell. Twenty-three year old Mike Bardwell, formerly a tea planter in Assam, was Angus Rose's cousin.[17] On the run after Slim River, he had escaped the 150 miles by sea from Jeram on Malaya's west coast to Sumatra. Once there, he insisted that the Dutch allow him to fly back to Singapore so that he could rejoin his battalion and marry his fiancée Kate Lundon, a New Zealand nurse. She was the daughter of Frank Lundon, the senior partner of Singapore architects Swan and MacLaren and Commodore of the Royal Singapore Flying Club. In fact, it was a Malayan Volunteer Air Force Tiger Moth, not a Dutch aircraft that flew Mike Bardwell from Rengat in Sumatra to Kallang Airport, Singapore.

B and C Companies were Royal Marines commanded respectively by Captains Lang and Aylwin. B Company was predominantly *Repulse* Marines with troop commanders Lts Geoffrey Hulton and Jim Davis. *Prince of Wales* Company troop commanders were Lts G. Sheridan and Charles Verdon.[18] The Sergeant Major was Colour Sergeant J.L. Stokes of *Repulse*.

Back up included a mortar platoon, signals section made up mainly of Marines, six armoured cars and four carriers. Cpls Bailey and Glover commanded the two RM armoured cars *Glamis Castle* and *Dunvegan Castle*. Marine Jack McPherson DSM was detailed to C Company bren gun carriers with Marines O'Shaughnessy, Parkinson and Summer. A former *HMS Hood* Marine, McPherson had won his DSM in the Norwegian Campaign.[19]

The RM Rifle companies had been supplied by the Royal Navy Armaments Depot with .303 rifles, Bruno .300 Light machine guns[20] (a predecessor to the bren with rimless bullets), .303 bren guns, a few American tommy guns and plastic grenades. Tiger patrol units were formed. Marine Peter 'Tiny' Dunstan was selected from the *Prince of Wales* detachment for Tiger patrolling together with Marines Anderson, R.W.C. Brown, E.D. Harry and Westgate.[21]

During the period of intense training with the Argylls Captain Lang was instructed to hand over one officer and fifteen Marines from B Company for other duties: "A few days after joining the Argylls I was sent for by Rear-Admiral E.J. Spooner DSO (then Rear-Admiral Malaya) and told that due to looting taking place in the evacuated Dockyard – believed to have been perpetrated by British and Australian troops – the whole RM unit was to be sent back to the Naval Base for guard duties.

"I pointed out to Admiral Spooner that if this was done it would place Lt Colonel Stewart in a difficult position and completely upset the battalion he had just reorganised. I was anxious also that the troops who had settled down well to their training with the Argylls should not be taken for outside duties. I was of the opinion that it would be a matter of days only before the attack on the Island commenced in which case the Marines would presumably have to be withdrawn from their guard duties to take their positions in the lines of fighting troops. Admiral Spooner finally agreed they would not go back to the Dockyard but insisted that a guard of one officer and fifteen other ranks would be sent there."

INTO BATTLE

On Sunday February 8th at 1.30 p.m. the Japanese preliminary bombardment including 8 inch shells began across the Straits of Johore. This was accompanied by intensified air-raids with as many as 135 aircraft coming over in formation. That evening Stewart gathered his officers. "You had better get what sleep you can now as I think this is the real thing." Angus Rose wrote: "The Colonel looked grave... I know neither of us had confidence in the beach defences." Rose checked his equipment and filled his water bottle before going to bed.[22]

Eight miles north of Tyersall at 10.00 p.m. the Japanese made their assault across the Straits of Johore landing in various areas north-west of the Causeway that had been used by the Argylls in their training exercises only three months before. The first landings were at Lim Chu Kang and Sarimbun on the north-west tip of Singapore island, followed by Kranji. The area was covered in mangrove swamp with thick jungle inland. Lt General Percival is held to have believed that the attack would come in the northeast of the island where he had stationed his fresh British 18th Division troops and where Japanese feints were being made. According to Angus Rose, Ian Stewart also may have held this view and certainly on the weekend before the landing he told his officers to go out and explore the northeast of the island and get to know its roads. Brigadier Paris correctly believed the Japanese would land on the northwest coast.

However, Lt Colonel Ashworth, one of Percival's staff officers whose observations are in the Imperial War Museum, recalls that at a conference of senior officers the GOC did accurately predict the point of attack. General Bennett ignored until too late, General Percival's orders for night patrols to investigate enemy activity heard across the straits opposite the AIF sector.[23]

In any event, the Japanese were faced by tired and demoralised Australians who were greatly weakened by the introduction of large numbers of untrained reinforcements who now experienced a very terrible bombardment. Also present were the exceedingly brave but poorly armed Dalforce Chinese volunteers.[24] The Australian 22nd Brigade's 2/18th and 2/20th battalions,[25] together with the Dalforce Volunteers, defended a front some four and a half miles long. They fought hard and took very heavy casualties but failed to hold the Japanese landings of vastly superior numbers. By 12.05 a.m. on Monday February 9th the Japanese had secured themselves on Singapore's northwestern shore and the defenders were retreating. Demoralised Australian reinforcements sent forward in support disintegrated. The Japanese were soon able to begin the process of floating tanks across the Straits to the Lim Chu Kang beachhead.

At 4.00 a.m. at Tyersall those of the Plymouth Argylls who had managed to sleep through the distant but incessant Japanese bombardment of the northern shore were awoken and put on one hour's notice to move. Officers visited the men to tell them that they were going out to give the Japanese one last shock.[26] There was a delay. "By 6.00 a.m. no message had come through," explains David Wilson, "and after 7.30 we went back to the mess and had some breakfast, or rather a second one, as we had stuffed some down at 4.30 in the morning. At 8.30 a dispatch rider dashed up on his motor-cycle waving a message at me, which we all seized, but it read: 'Your allotment of the grenade range on the following dates has been cancelled' which was a bit of an anticlimax."[27]

At 10.30 a.m. the order to move eventually came through. Lt General Percival ordered 12th Indian Brigade minus 5/2nd Punjabs to move to Keat Hong village, today part of Choa Chu Kang HDB township[28] near Tengah airfield, and, as Command Reserve, reinforce the Bukit Panjang-Keat Hong Road to the right of the Kranji-Jurong Line. This defensive line ran from Kranji in the north of the island to Jurong in the south west. It was intended to deny the Japanese access to Bukit Timah and so protect Singapore City from a Japanese advance from the West.

Outside Tyersall's Argyll Gate a long line of lorries and buses each spaced fifty yards apart and sheltering under the trees at the roadside waited to receive the Plymouth Argylls. Each company had six lorries, one for weapons, ammunition and supplies, and also a recce car. By midday the convoy of vehicles was moving at 20 mph up Bukit Timah Road. Their intended route was northward then turning westward along Choa Chu Kang Road towards the Neck and close to the abandoned and largely destroyed Tengah airfield that had been the first objective of the Japanese. Despite intense Japanese air activity they were not attacked, but sporadic shelling of the road caused some panic among drivers of other units, causing them to break formation and swerve across the road. Marine Maurice Edwards remembers that even the Argyll drivers ordered them to "bail out" when the Japanese aircraft flew overhead.

As the Japanese artillery, known to Argylls as "the long range snipers", intensified their shelling, the Plymouth Argylls debussed at Bukit Panjang village and the advance continued westward on foot, led and encouraged by Ian Stewart and a lone Argyll piper, Piper Charles Stuart. As they advanced through the rubber they could hear and see the burning oil tanks at Kranji. A petrol storage dump was hit some half a mile from the advancing units, causing a great roaring fire and attracting more Japanese artillery fire. The Royal Marine companies were heavily bombed in two high level air attacks and took some casualties in the rubber adjacent to the Choa Chu Kang Road. Sgt Tommy Locklin, commanding 14 Platoon, was wounded in the hand. Six of his men, including Cpls Fluck and Scantlebury, were also wounded. Lt Sheridan, commanding 13 Platoon, organised their evacuation to the General Hospital. It was a demoralising start for the Marines of C Company. Sgt Jock King took over Locklin's command. Marine Maurice Edwards was No.2 on a bren gun. His No.1 was injured in the back by shrapnel. Fortunately there were ambulances close by.

Some heavy dive-bombing followed and Hurricane fighters were seen taking on the Japanese aircraft. Light evening drizzle gave way to torrential rain. Captain Mike Blackwood, scouting ahead up the road, found an Australian Gunners' Command Post that had received a direct hit from the Japanese bombing. He called up Angus Rose to help him deal with the dead and wounded Australians. Rose later recalled Blackwood's sensitive nature and distress as they straightened out the dead Australians and collected their tags and valuables. Rose advised him to steel himself in such situations and only regretted that he knew so little about first aid. "If ever I get out of this," commented Mike Blackwood, "I shall never take anything for granted again. One didn't realise how damned lucky one was, and half the good things in life one never appreciated."

Tengah airfield was abandoned by the defending Jind Infantry, and Australian units in the area were pulled back. The Johore Volunteer Engineers under Major Jack Crosse were on the edge of the airfield and supposedly under Australian command. Left behind by the Australians, some of whom stole vehicles from their own front line units, Crosse put himself under the command of "Stewart of the Argylls". By this time the artillery fire on Tengah was coming from the British guns and front line Australians were cursing the Volunteers, thinking they were spotters for the offending artillery.

L.Cpl Joe Lonsdale of the Argylls encountered a Gunner who was particularly angry that he hadn't been allowed to shoot at the Japanese observation balloon that was flying above the Sultan of Johore's Palace across the Straits of Johore. Both balloon and Palace tower allowed the Japanese to watch the Allied positions on the north of the island. There is little doubt that the decision not to fire on the palace was because of the Sultan's friendship with senior Allied officers and officials, particularly the Australian divisional commander Gordon Bennett, and the

Governor of Singapore, Sir Shenton Thomas. The Artillery was also severely rationed in the number of shells it was allowed to fire as policy was that Singapore should be prepared to withstand a three-month siege.

The Plymouth Argylls were ordered to hold a position in marshy land west of Keat Hong village and north of Bulim village around 'Point 156' (a low hill clearly visible today on the edge of Sungei Tengah Agrotechnology Park) overlooking Tengah airfield. Ian Stewart's orders were to take up defensive positions through which the Australians could withdraw and prevent Japanese encirclement from the north. Australian units were on the Argylls left and an artillery unit on the right. The Japanese prepared for a thrust in force towards their second objective – Bukit Timah Village and the nearby Bukit Timah Hill, east of the main road and dominating the area.

Point 156 was defended by A Company with B Company on the right, D Company between Point 156 and the road, and C Company in reserve defending the road half a mile behind. Battalion HQ was in a Chinese house 500 yards behind the frontline positions. The armoured cars and carriers were at various points down the narrow Tengah Road. Trenches were dug amongst the rubber plantations and thick undergrowth close to the airfield perimeter. Patrols were sent out. The order was to hold these positions until 9.00 a.m.

It rained heavily that night. Early February is towards the end of Singapore's 'cool' rainy season. The Jocks donned their capes while the Marines, never issued with capes, found what shelter they could under the trees. Freshly dug trenches quickly filled up with water as B Company guarded the right flank of the Plymouth Argyll position, carefully watching for Japanese infiltration through the creeks and mangrove swamps. Badly shaken Australian stragglers from Kranji, mostly unarmed and demoralised, and Chinese survivors from the valiant Dalforce were coming through the lines from Kranji creek. This created problems of identification particularly as the Argylls were already very familiar with the Japanese subterfuge of fighting in various assortments of clothing including native sarongs and singlets.

Captain Lang noted the demoralising effect some of the Australian stragglers had on the younger Marines: "Nearly all were asking the way to Singapore and many were openly saying that if we had any sense we would 'get back out before the Japs came' and other remarks liable to spread alarm, apprehension and panic." Lang also noted "the incessant and loud noise from the bullfrogs which made it so difficult to hear anyone approaching the position."[29]

It was a dark night and the rain was black with carbonised oil from the blazing Kranji oil tanks. "I have never in my life seen such a terrible looking lot of tramps," said David Wilson.[30] The men became so thickly coated with oil it became virtually impossible to distinguish friend from foe. When Padre Beattie later collected the wounded Captain Aylwin and Corporal Warn in his car, the two RMs failed to recognise each other.

During the night Marine Maurice Edwards observed an Indian Army unit, probably Lt Colonel Garbuk 'Gearbox' Singh's Jind Infantry who were moving from Tengah to defend the area around Bukit Gombak Hill, marching in good order down the road. Sgt Nunn RM (CQMS B Company) and Colour Sgt Stokes brought up hot sweet tea, bread and stew in a bren gun carrier.[31] Hot food was transported in boxes packed with hay into which were placed big camp kettles with the lids clamped on then a mat over the top. Ian Stewart evacuated the Johore Volunteer Engineers from the Tengah area in a local bus. It collided wing to wing with an Argyll armoured car coming up to act as a rearguard for anyone left at Tengah. The armoured car escorted them towards the Upper Bukit Timah Road.

At dawn on Tuesday February 10th the Japanese attacked the Plymouth Argyll positions, predictably carrying out their usual wide flanking movements. Large numbers of dive-bombers supported them. B and C Companies (RM) were engaged at a distance of about 150 yards. C Company, returning fire, wiped out a Japanese mortar section. A very efficient and courageous Australian 3 inch mortar crew did some very good work lobbing bombs "at a rate of knots" into the advancing Japanese while Cpl Glover RM's armoured car fired into the rubber and undergrowth to the right hand side of the road. Sgt Terry Brooks RM later remembered seeing this armoured car wrecked on the road but still facing towards the enemy.

This was when Captain Aylwin and Cpl Reg Warn RM were wounded. Marine Peers Crompton recalls his section was positioned on a rise looking down onto the road when the Japs opened fire: "We retaliated and all hell let loose. We were ordered to withdraw, as the firing was thick and heavy. It was a crawling job. Cpl Warn on my left cried out that he was wounded. I crawled across to him, blood was streaming down his face, and there was a jagged hole in his helmet. By now the rest of the platoon had withdrawn and the position was serious. I was trying to drag him to a safer place when Lt Davis appeared, slung Corps over his shoulder and carried him to safety leaving me free to wriggle back unhindered. It was a brave act Lt Davis performed that morning."

Marine Smart, formerly a Fleet Air Arm pilot who still proudly wore his pilot wings, was shot in the head by rifle fire and killed instantly. Marine Arthur Campion, who had been in Lt Jim Davis' up country party, was slightly wounded. Maurice Edwards was only yards away, as was David Wilson of the Argylls, when Aylwin "the very best of officers" was shot through the right wrist by Japanese sniper fire. At the time Aylwin had been trying to destroy C Company's abandoned supply truck. It was Aylwin's 27th birthday and he was not enjoying it. He dug out the bullet and used a map to bandage his heavily bleeding wrist, remaining at his post for some hours until ordered back by Ian Stewart for medical attention. 32 Aylwin was sent to the General Hospital where he found himself in a ward with a wounded Argyll officer, Lt C.R. McArthur. Warn went to Alexandra hospital where days later he witnessed and survived the notorious massacre, as did the Argylls medical officer Captain Bartlett RAMC. One Argyll was among the 323 victims of the Alexandra Hospital Massacre (see on).33

By 8.15 a.m. the Japanese were very close and at 9.00 Stewart ordered a successful withdrawal of about a mile towards the Upper Bukit Timah Road. This withdrawal, led by Bardwell's A Company, was covered by the armoured cars. Cpl Francis Murfin's RM section covered B Company's withdrawal (for which he was posthumously mentioned in dispatches 13.8.46 – he died of cholera in captivity).34 The morning haze assisted them, with small groups dashing across the road into the cover of jungle clearances. However men were still getting separated from their units. Cpl Murfin ended up with an Australian unit.

From a better position on high ground west of the Choa Chu Kang Road junction the Plymouth Argylls held the Japanese without difficulty till 11.00 a.m. before being ordered onto higher ground south of Bukit Panjang village on the west side of Upper Bukit Timah Road. From here they observed large numbers of frightened, unarmed Australians heading south towards Singapore City. This was a demoralising sight that angered many who witnessed it. Duncan Ferguson saw men throwing away their rifles, ditching their chestnut brown boots and putting on gym shoes. He never felt very good about the Australians after this. Eric Moss had his own view about who these men were: "It was a couple of Sydney units that were quite different from the ordinary Australian – the Australian from the Outback is a tough, good humoured, good chap, intelligent. But the people who were sent from Sydney were often wee weeds – the horse jockeys all came from Sydney – wee skinny men, and it was these people from Sydney that ran away in Singapore and filled the ditches – they wore red boots, so you knew they were Australian, so when they were deserting they took to taking their boots off, and the monsoon ditches were full of rifles and red boots!" ('Red' boots = chestnut coloured boots.)

This may at first seem a highly prejudicial statement but Australians will confirm this and relate the stature of some of these Sydney men and their 'look after No.1' mentality to social deprivation in the years after the First World War. Certainly these were not men who would show loyalty to their officers, especially when the going got tough. Nor had all the Australian reinforcements received adequate training.

Some Marines had the opportunity to snatch a rest. Each platoon had a small house within its area. Peter Dunstan found a Chinese China pillow to rest his neck in and grabbed a few hours sleep.[35] There were no civilians in the area for all of them had been evacuated to the south of the island and into the City on February 4th.

That day, Cpl Norman Overington RM led a B Company patrol forward to engage the Japanese then successfully withdrew through inaccurate Japanese machine-gun fire. Cpl R. McKillen RM was equally successful with his men wiping out a Japanese patrol armed with tommy guns. That afternoon three companies of the Australian 2/29th battalion were defending the Plymouth Argylls' left flank at Bukit Panjang. They would withdraw down the Pipeline that night at about 10.30 p.m. without letting Brigadier Paris know, just as a Japanese tank attack was developing. Paris' HQ was in the Public Works Department granite quarries, just south of St Joseph's Church off the main road. By nightfall Japanese tanks and infantry were moving south down the main road from Mandai village towards Bukit Panjang.[36] Lt General Yamashita had moved his HQ from the Sultan's palace in Johore Bahru to a rubber plantation near Tengah airfield.

That night A and D Companies were dug in among the rubber trees on the east side of the main road, 3/4 mile south of Bukit Panjang village and just north of Brigade HQ. Ian Stewart's Battalion HQ with Royal Marines B and C Companies were also on the east side of the road but 600 yards further back near the PWD quarries. They were in fact two miles in front of the British frontline. Japanese advance patrols crawled down the ditches at the sides of the road. Marine Tom Webber remembers: "During the second night a mixture of Marines and soldiers were sheltering in a monsoon drain when a party of Japanese soldiers crawled along the drain on the opposite side of the road. They shouted across to us in broken English that we should lay down our arms as the war was over for us. We replied rudely but effectively with a volley of small arms fire."[37]

Japanese troops were aware of the Argyll and Marine rifle companies in the plantation but were reluctant to enter the area. Japanese light tanks twice came down the road, firing then withdrawing. Two Argyll armoured cars were hit including that of Cpl William 'Billy' Doherty, twenty-year-old half-brother of the

Argylls' Quartermaster and like his half-brother a former Boy Soldier. Billy Doherty had his legs crushed as the armoured car overturned.[38] Joe Russell and the others present wanted to keep him with them but he couldn't walk and insisted on going to hospital – a fateful decision – so Joe later drove him to Alexandra Hospital.

Captain Mike Blackwood had a narrow escape when a splinter from one of the armoured cars grazed his forehead. David Wilson got a bullet through the barrel of his tommy gun. He said of Blackwood, "Mike was an absolute Jonah for attracting bombs. Everywhere he was you could be quite sure that something in the explosive line would descend sooner or later, so we always used to try to send him out of the camp whenever we thought that there was a Jap raid on the way."

At 8.00 p.m. a lone Japanese tank moved off the main road and smashed through the flimsy gate to Paris' Brigade HQ in the PWD buildings (still today PWD property on the Dairy Farm housing estate) at the entrance to the quarries, and fired on the ever-unruffled Paris who at the time was wining and dining in some style. This he was accustomed to doing even under the severest battle conditions. David Wilson recollects: "We heard some shooting come from Brigade HQ, and soon after Brigadier Paris turned up to say that he had been shot at by a Japanese tank as he was having his dinner, that he had replied with his revolver and the tank had drawn off, but he added 'It'll be back again soon'."[39] According to one account Paris actually ran and leapt on the tank, mounting the turret and firing his revolver through the slits in its side.

Wilson went out to lay his six anti-tank mines on the road. Blackwood accompanied him on this pitch-black night to locate one of his armoured cars. It was about 10.00 p.m. Wilson says, "There were still supposed to be troops in front of us, so we walked up the centre of the road chatting merrily, when we heard a rumbling noise coming round the corner. I put up my hand to stop it and really thought it was one of our Lanchesters. It was a large Jap tank and it opened up on us with everything it had." Blackwood lobbed a couple of grenades at the tank, which disappeared into the darkness but returned with others a half hour later to attack the Argylls' roadblock. The roadblock of five transport vehicles had been thrown up across the wide Upper Bukit Timah Road. As Wilson completed laying his mines a column of medium Japanese tanks arrived. In the firefight that followed Sgt Harry Nuttall's *Stirling Castle* Lanchester – last survivor of the mainland campaign – engaged the Japanese tanks but was knocked out. Nuttall was wounded. The two Royal Marine armoured cars were lost, one to air attack and the other crashing into a ditch.

Lt Edward Bremner of the Argylls, commanding a second roadblock, was killed. Mike Blackwood sheltered behind a culvert and for some time engaged the leading Japanese tank and its enraged crew at twenty yards with a Boys anti-tank rifle, firing off five rounds from its savagely recoiling long-barrel. One tank hit a mine. Lt Jim Davis RM also participated in this action.

Meanwhile 29 year old Major Angus MacDonald, Paris' Brigade Major, sped two miles down the road in his little Fiat, under the railway bridge, past the Ford Factory and the fire station to prepare a third roadblock at Bukit Timah village. MacDonald was fired on by the leading Japanese tank as he drove the last vehicle in to complete the roadblock This tank had pursued him down the road but was knocked out at the roadblock at about midnight. The roadblock, supported by two anti-tank guns, held and prevented the Japanese tanks ploughing on into Singapore City that very night.

The Argyll and Marine companies were still in the rubber 100 yards east of the road. They lay in a circle facing outwards with patrols creeping forward to the roadside. The Japanese, having successfully split the Plymouth Argylls, were shouting in English and Hindustani: "Come on over! Bring chocolate or cigarettes". Some of these attempts to draw men out were successful. At about 3.00 a.m. 2nd Lt John O'Callaghan, an Irish planter from the Harvard Estate near Bedong in the state of Kedah who had joined the Argylls from the FMSVF, was angered by these shouts and told his friends that he was going out to 'sort them out'. He was never seen again. [40]

Stewart estimated that there were 50 to 75 Japanese tanks and carriers along the road with no anti-tank defences to stop their progress. He ordered the companies to remain silent and unobserved until dawn. The password for the night was 'Argyll'. [41] Certainly the enemy were very close: Angus Rose, flattened against a tree, was bumped into by a Japanese officer who muttered what he took to be an apology then disappeared into the darkness.

Some hand-to-hand fighting took place on the edges of the Plymouth Argyll positions. Among those killed were 22-year-old Argyll 2nd Lt John Leahy. At 4.00 a.m. a large Japanese patrol found Lt Albert Gispert's mortar trench and killed him and his three companions. Sgt J. Skinner of the RM Signals section was captured, used by the Japanese to carry ammunition, then executed. Two other captured Marines, Cpl A. Brown and Marine McKirley were threatened three times with being shot but were later allowed by the Japanese to return to Tyersall.

Before dawn on Wednesday February 11th Stewart decided on a withdrawal to the agreed Dairy Farm rendezvous. The government Dairy Farm, today a housing estate, was an expanse of hilly grassland north of Bukit Timah Hill. It had been set up in the early 1930s as an experimental dairy farm.

The withdrawal began with Battalion HQ, B and C Companies led by Brigadier Paris, moving off in the early morning darkness. It was at this stage that Cpl Charles 'Dusty' Miller arrived with ten other Marines at Brigadier Paris' PWD headquarters. They had spent the previous week guarding the Naval Base that had officially been evacuated on February 2nd. Here they had been stranded by the Japanese attack, then evacuated by truck. At Dairy Farm all was confusion.[42]

As the Marines withdrew Captain Lang heard a voice calling to him from a small shack. It was 25-year-old Lt Douglas Weir of the Argylls. Weir, an FMS Police officer who had recently volunteered for the battalion, had a few hours earlier been ordered by Ian Stewart to take his heavily armed Tiger patrol down to the road to see what was happening. They had come down through the rubber and seen Japanese tanks moving along the road, dropping off sections of troops. The patrol came under fire from Japanese infantry and Weir was shot in the stomach at a range of 22 yards, a distance which as a keen cricketer he could estimate. He couldn't walk and was in great pain so was left behind by his three companions to be found by the Marines "to whom I am eternally grateful."[43]

The Marines, who included Charles Miller and Tom Webber, hastily improvised a stretcher and rescued Weir. They carried him across Dairy Farm and all the way along the Pipeline to Adam Road. Maurice Edwards, carrying his bren gun, was in a group nearby, escorting Brigadier Paris who led the way down the Pipeline.[44] Charles Miller remembers a family sitting on their verandah calmly having breakfast, oblivious to the noise of battle and without a care in the world. They also saw men of the 18th Division "in nice clean uniforms and looking very fresh" moving from the Golf Course towards Bukit Timah. These were presumably members of Tomforce.[45]

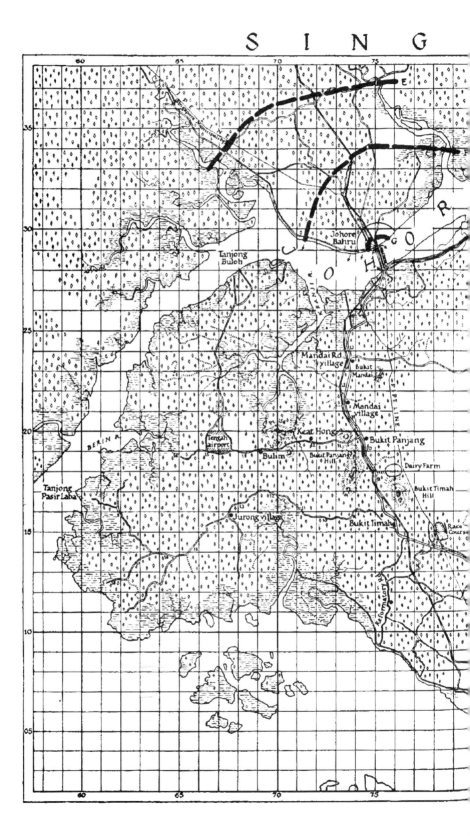

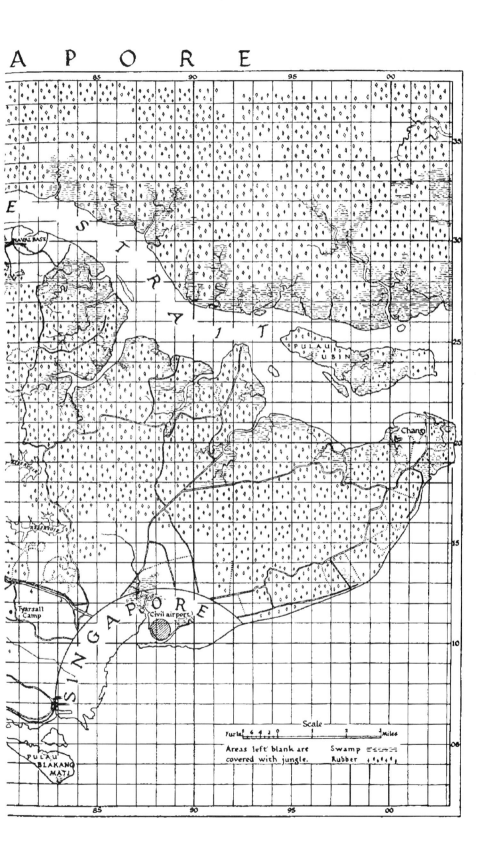

Lt Sheridan found an abandoned ambulance to take the wounded Argyll to hospital.[46] They intended delivering him to Alexandra Hospital but he asked to go to the General Hospital instead. Two mortally wounded Marines, Cyril Brown and Arnold Holland, both with bomb blast wounds, were also taken there. Douglas Weir's choice of hospital probably saved his life, otherwise he would have been caught up in the Alexandra Hospital Massacre. Why had he insisted on going to the General Hospital? Some time before he had received a bad head injury playing cricket. He was carried from the pitch and an RAMC man had treated his torn ear in a rather callous manner, patching it up and saying it wouldn't really matter if he had a cauliflower ear. The captain of the cricket team had intervened and taken him to the General Hospital on the edge of Chinatown. Weir was particularly concerned that he would be able to play cricket and rugby again. At the General Hospital a surgeon from Penang called Sam Campbell operated on him: "He told me I was damn lucky. I had twenty-one stitches, but the bullet had missed my bowel and liver. The next night the Japs came into the hospital and told us we had to get out by the Tuesday morning. So on the 17th I was carried to the Fullerton building and put on a desk. There was a great shortage of lavatories and of water but we were looked after by a First Aid unit. I couldn't eat in any event."[47]

East of the Upper Bukit Timah Road, A and D Companies were in a far more precarious position than the Marines had been – unable to move because the Japanese were between them and the Battalion HQ. They prepared for a fighting withdrawal at dawn through an area already heavily infiltrated with Japanese.

Duncan Ferguson remembers the order coming through "Every man for himself." While most men headed south eastward towards the Pipeline, he somehow managed to make his way with Pte Jimmy Robertson, also from Falkirk and in D Company, back to the Transport at the Bukit Timah Road/Reformatory Road junction. A battery of 25 pounders was nearby. When Ferguson told Robertson to come along with him, Robertson insisted on going to find his mucker, Pte David Gibson. Both Gibson and Robertson were caught and killed by the Japanese.[48] Ferguson began driving back to Singapore city via Holland Road: "You couldn't get moving for lorries nose to tail, and the wee chap I had as escort jumped out of the truck and away." The Japanese gunners were targeting a particular crossroads and Sgt 'Smudger' Smith, the Transport Sergeant, was timing the salvoes and saying to the drivers 'Right. Start up! Rev up! In gear – Go!' Eventually, Duncan pulled out of the convoy and abandoned the truck, walking the last two miles to Tyersall.

Lt Colonel Stewart stayed on the edge of Dairy Farm with a few of the newly appointed officers of the battalion whom he sent out on Tiger patrols to harass the Japanese pursuit, while Stewart waited for his missing companies. He also continued trying to send the only surviving armoured car up the road. Duncan Ferguson tells the story of its driver, Pte Joe Russell: "The CO said to him 'Go down the road and give these men support!' And he says 'There's nae men down there to give support to, Sir.' The CO says 'Down the road and give these men support!' 'But that's the Japanese, Sir!' He made Joe Russell go down and Ping! Ping! Ping! So he reversed back and the CO says 'I thought I told you go there and give these men support!' Joe says 'That's Japanese, Sir!' 'Don't be stupid. Away, back down!' He went again and the same thing. So Joe came back again, and the CO – it was Busty – took his revolver and said 'Now I'm telling you Russell for the third time – Go down there and give these men support!' And Joe says 'I'm telling you, Sir, there's none of our men down there! That's Japanese!' And just then a bullet hit the armoured car and ricocheted off and hit this Lieutenant that was beside Busty – just glancing off. The CO says 'What's that?' And Joe: 'I've been trying to tell you, Sir – that's Japanese!'."

L.Cpl Joe Lonsdale says, "We'd come back through Bukit Timah Road getting dive bombed. One of the Marines I remember got shrapnel in his head at this time. They were pretty good lads, those Marines. Then the Japs came through us on one stretch of the road. I was in a slit trench in the Dairy Farm area with three or four others, with a tommy gun."

RSM Sandy Munnoch came to warn Lonsdale and his companions to be careful as the Japanese were all around. Munnoch said he would return to see that they were OK. Shortly afterwards Munnoch returned and announced that every man would have to look after himself. The RSM led this party eastward towards McRitchie Reservoir, passing through the Japanese in the early morning at about 5.00 a.m. then escaping southwards.

By first light at 7.00 a.m. there was no sign of the missing companies. Stewart returned to Dairy Farm to find that Brigadier Paris had already taken the Royal Marine companies onto the Sime Road Golf Course, the agreed Battalion Rendezvous, where they remained for three hours under heavy artillery fire. Several Marines, including Sgt Thomas who was blown over a hedge by the force of an explosion, were wounded or concussed. Eventually transport arrived under C.Sgt Stokes' direction to take them back to Tyersall. Marine Peter Dunstan recalled angry Golf Club members even at this stage complaining as the Marines dug trenches for their very survival across the immaculate golf course. Dunstan was later evacuated to the General Hospital when light mortar fragment injuries sustained that night became infected and his left hand swelled up badly.

Arriving back at Tyersall, Cpl Charles Miller, Marine Maurice Edwards and friends, three days without a decent meal, approached Argylls' Rations Sgt Percy Evans requesting food. They eventually received some tinned corned mutton, something of a wartime delicacy. Maurice Edwards was less than impressed by the cuisine at Tyersall: "My impression of the Argyll messing was that it was deplorable! The first meal that I had at Tyersall was a tin of bacon on a table and a loaf of bread – we were used to feeding better than that. Their trouble was obviously some crooks in the QM's Department."

Meanwhile the Argyll companies had begun their fighting withdrawal in small groups. Some got through although Lt Donald Napier, a Slim River survivor, was killed as he led his men forward in hand-to-hand fighting. He was shot and fell into a monsoon drain. Sgt 'Bluff' Wallace of D Company and Lt John Love were also in this party. Love was nearly strangled with his own pistol lanyard but an Argyll shot his assailant in the backside. Lt Hubert Strathairn, like Weir a police volunteer, was captured and owed his life to an American educated Japanese interpreter.

Other Argylls were not so lucky – a section of 12 men were captured trying to break out near Bukit Timah Village. Somewhere in the area of Dairy Farm, they were tied up with barbed wire and bayoneted. Only two survived: Pte '298' Jimmy Robertson and Pte Jimmy Anderson with six bayonet wounds. They lay on the ground moaning. Anderson told Robertson to keep quiet and they would have a chance of getting out of it. Robertson died shortly afterwards but Anderson was rescued by local Chinese, his wounds treated and he was later smuggled into Changi POW Camp.

The story of this massacre had to be kept secret in Changi for to even mention such an atrocity might bring instant Japanese retribution. Pte Anderson, believing that he was dying, did tell a friend and certainly a number of Argyll officers in Changi got to know about this incident. Even some civilians in Changi jail heard about it. Given the dangerous position of Pte Anderson, both as survivor of the massacre and as having had contact with a Chinese resistance group, he was sent away on one of the first 'Japan' parties. He died at Haito Camp in Formosa. Today former members of the battalion would still like to know which Chinese rescued and helped Pte Anderson, and see if they can shed any light on the last resting place of the other victims of this massacre, who have no known grave.

They were not the only Argylls to die in a massacre. Twenty year old Cpl Billy Doherty, wounded in the legs during the Upper Bukit Timah Road fighting, was in one of the upstairs wards in Alexandra Hospital when on February 14th the Japanese stormed in. Some of the patients with him saw from an upstairs veranda the Japanese coming and headed down a back staircase and into the hospital grounds. Billy Doherty couldn't walk and was presumably among the wounded men bayoneted, as they lay helpless on their beds. His body was never found.

The well-camouflaged Japanese, led by a man carrying a Japanese flag, approached in single file down the Ayer Rajah Road, entered the hospital grounds and approached the Sisters' Quarters. Others saw the Japanese moving through the grounds in company strength. Dick Lee, a Royal Artillery Den-R, was one of the survivors of the massacre and describes his experience: "I got wounded – blown off the motor bike – in Johore Bahru and was in Alexandra when the Japs came in and they did some terrible things in there. Killing patients, doctors and orderlies. I was lucky. I was lying in the corridor, the wounded being congregated in here from several hospitals in Singapore. It was chock-a-bloc, so I was on a palliasse on the floor. The British medical officers came round – because it was only a day or so before the surrender – and said the Japs would soon be arriving at the hospital. Everyone, even walking wounded, was to stay on their beds, stay where you are. If the Japanese come in all you do is raise your hands, because of the language problem, and let them see you aren't offering any resistance to them.

"I was near the door in an open area," Dick continues. "It all went quiet. The machine-gun fire outside died down as our troops fell back further from the hospital. Some sense told me to look up, and I saw two of the biggest Japs you have ever seen standing there. I had one leg in plaster and one up in a cradle. As one Jap grinned down at me I could see gold filling, and I can see his face now, and his mouth with this filling. He had a rifle in his hand, and they had big long bayonets – 18 inch – and the bayonet was just about touching me, and as he looked down and grinned at me there was an Australian, wounded in the arm, on the staircase walking down.

"Everyone had been told to stay where they were but with all the excitement he decided to come down. He had his arm in a sling and no pyjama jacket, all he had on was these striped pyjama trousers, and as he came to the bottom of the stairs he leaned against the concrete pillar as these two Japs came in. One stopped and looked at me and with his bayonet he lifted up the sheet that was covering me to have a look underneath it. The other one walked over to the Aussie and just put his bayonet right in. As the fellow slumped down to the floor, the Jap stood back, the Aussie's other hand went up to his stomach and the blood was welling up between his fingers. Then they both just turned round and walked out of the door the way they came in. After that the Japanese were coming in looking for rings, watches and taking them off you. The first lot through the hospital got all the plunder, then they moved on, and the next lot came in looking for the same things and you're trying to explain. They were tipping men off the mattresses, off the beds, looking underneath trying to find things, and shooting and bayoneting going on. No, they were not just bayoneting the able-bodied, but the wounded.

"The operating theatre was just down the corridor where I was lying and there were a lot of terribly wounded people, legs off, arms off, faces, backs – we had our own Army doctors – they were actually operating, had a man in the theatre and a bunch of Japs were in there and bayoneted the man on the table (one of the FMSVF Volunteers) and shot two or three of the people doing the operations. Captain Smiley, who was my surgeon, was an Irishman, and they shot some of his colleagues in the theatre and he got bayoneted through the hand and the leg, and he just fell down. But when it was all over he was limping about still attending to the wound. He wasn't one of those taken to be massacred and he survived it. In another incident when they were looking for plunder, they took out the RAMC orderlies – the orderlies were wearing Red Cross bands – as far as I know there were no nurses there then, they'd been evacuated out of the hospital – and I saw them crying when they left and then they were sunk on the ships – but the Japs took 8 or 9 of the orderlies outside past me where I was lying, although the men were pointing to their armbands, and they took a British medical officer out and made him watch as they machine-gunned the orderlies."

On one of the top floor wards was the wounded John Wyatt of the East Surreys. When the Japanese arrived in his ward two patients were killed and only the arrival of a Japanese officer saved the lives of the others. Nick Carter of the Argylls had been badly wounded in the side and thigh during the fighting in the north of Malaya and had been sent to a hospital in Johore Bahru. There he remembers an Australian nurse who would pick him out of bed when the bombing was going on, put him under the bed and lie there beside him. With the general evacuation he was transferred to a ground floor ward in Alexandra Hospital. On February 14th he saw retreating untrained Sikh troops running into the hospital and thought they were going up to the roof. These Sikhs had been retreating along the railway line and many of their number lay dead between the hospital and the railway line. Certainly the Japanese were later to claim that they came under machine gun fire from the hospital grounds. Some have attributed blame for the massacre to the Imperial Guards Division because the Japanese involved were tall men. In fact they were men from the 18th Division who came from the island of Kyushu and were taller than the average Japanese soldier.

Nick Carter's instincts warned him to get out: "When you're unarmed you're taught to dodge as much as you can – self preservation. The Jap frontline troops were closing in and I knew what was going to happen." The Japanese were still on the opposite side of the hospital. Carter ran from his bed wearing only his pyjama bottoms and no shoes. He raced out of the hospital grounds with a companion and down the road to an empty schoolhouse. By the time he reached there his stitches had opened and he was bleeding heavily as he made his way to a temporary auxiliary hospital in the Fullerton Post Office building near Clifford Quay. "I could barely crawl! Went to Changi from there and the Sikhs were lining some of the road and they battered us with rifle butts. I ended up in Roberts Hospital."

Nick was unaware that Billy Doherty had been in Alexandra Hospital. The Argyll medical officer, Captain Bartlett, witnessed the Japanese arrival at the hospital. He saw a Japanese soldier coming through the gap between the overlapping blast walls.

Bartlett approached him with arms raised saying "Hospital" and pointing to his Red Cross brassard. The Japanese soldier looked at him, saw his camouflaged steel helmet and fired at him at point blank range. Luckily he missed and Bartlett ran back into the adjacent ward and threw himself on the floor. A hand grenade came through the window but exploded harmlessly. Bartlett survived to tell the tale.

When it was all over, 323 men including 90 RAMC staff were dead. Those murdered included a Padre, the CO of the 6th Norfolks, a wounded RAF Hurricane pilot, the wife of an RAMC man, and a Japanese POW. The hospital had been camouflaged with blast walls built around the outside but was clearly marked with Red Cross markings on the roof, Red Cross flags hanging out of windows, and red crosses made of white sheets and red blankets on the lawns. In fact two massacres had taken place: some sixty men murdered in the initial assault on the wards which contained some 800 patients, and the rest taken out and killed six at a time on February 15th, after 24 hours' incarceration in the nearby servants quarters. A few of this last group escaped and lived to tell the tale though at first they were not believed by British officers in the area.

Others disappeared on the battlefield. Lt Neil Stewart, one of the FMS Police officers and the son of a senior colonial police officer, had been wounded earlier in the Upper Bukit Timah Road fighting. Two young Argyll bandsmen, carrying him on a stretcher, came under fire, panicked and left him behind. Lt Stewart was never seen again. Lt Guy Hutchinson of the Johore Volunteer Engineers remembers encountering a solitary small and dirty Argyll marching up the Bukit Timah Road all on his own. He asked Hutchinson if he'd seen the Argylls, and went off muttering "I must find the Argylls, where's the Argylls?"

Some Argylls approached the Dairy Farm along the water pipeline east of Bukit Timah Road. A story of this retreat reached the British press shortly after the fall of Singapore and was repeated in the Stirling Observer of June 18th 1942. It was the story of a ragged, sun-scorched and oil-stained Argyll corporal and his two companions who made their way through a British position where they were told that the Argylls had been wiped out and that they should get some rest. The Argyll corporal replied: "If we're the last of the Battalion then I'm the senior NCO. My last order was to hold the Pipeline. If the CO is alive he'll be expecting us. If he isn't he'll expect us to be at the Pipeline, so we'll be moving off, sir." With a thumbs-up sign the corporal and his companions passed through the British position in the direction of the advancing enemy. Sustained firing came from the area shortly afterwards, then silence.[49]

This oft-repeated story may be propaganda for Home Front consumption, but it certainly captures the fighting spirit of the Argylls in Malaya and Singapore, and their rare devotion and respect for their commanding officer.[50]

Marine Peers Crompton was a late escaper from the Bukit Panjang area: "My oppo and I were separated from our unit, no map, completely lost. The main road was our only guide and the Japs were in control of that. We decided to head for Tyersall following the road. All day we plodded through rubber and various fruit plantations. Nearing dark it was time to cross the road. We thought we must have been in the vicinity of Tyersall. It was now darkish; there was the sound of marching. Dropping into the ditch we held our breath, was it theirs or ours? As they drew level we heard English voices. We could not believe our luck when they turned out to be Royals, about twenty in all detailed to Naval HQ, Oranji Hotel, Singapore. On arrival we were under Naval Command. The 12th and 13th were spent at Keppel Harbour, evacuating hospital patients and civilians."

Marine Arthur Campion, lightly wounded on the Choa Chu Kang Road, was sent to Alexandra Hospital. He was lucky enough to be discharged the following day – February 12th – and was told to report to the Union Jack Club. From there he was directed to Fort Canning and only returned to Tyersall Camp after the surrender of Singapore.

At 1.00 p.m. on February 12th what remained of A and D Companies were still fighting in the Race Course area. Transport eventually arrived to take the blackened, exhausted survivors back to Tyersall. Among the wounded that day was Sgt J. Burke, wounded in the left foot. He had come out of hospital to rejoin the battalion after being wounded in the buttocks on December 23rd 1941 in the north of Malaya.

No sooner had they arrived at Tyersall at about 3.00 p.m. than the Plymouth Argyll survivors found themselves involved in a major rescue operation. The neighbouring Indian military hospital had now spilled over into the Argylls' barracks area and was heavily bombed by Japanese medium bombers. It is estimated that as many as 700 patients and staff died in the fires that followed, some unable to get out of the attap thatched huts, others having taken cover under them. The huts burned furiously, flames rising 30 feet in the air. Argylls, Royal Marines and Gordons worked to save lives. CSM Arthur Bing, a renowned fighter, treated casualties and organised stretcher parties.[51] David Wilson said, "The fire engine turned up, but the water mains were all broken by then and so there was no means of putting it all out. A lot of the hospital staff ratted and we had to pull these wretched fellows out of their beds. Some of them had no legs and arms and some were very badly hit about, but it was better to take that chance than leaving them to roast alive."

The hospital buildings were clearly marked with red crosses. The attack, however, may not have been an act of deliberate bestiality but provoked by the presence of carriers and transport parked by the Gordons in the hospital grounds. Ian Stewart had retired to rest on his return to the camp. He was awoken by the air raid. Together with Sgt Percy Evans he dragged out and rescued the battalion stores. Rescuers in the hospital area vomited at the dreadful smell of burning flesh.[52]

RSM Munnoch's escape party, which included Joe Lonsdale, arrived back at Tyersall soon after this: "There wasn't anything there. It was all burned down as far as I could see, and where our clothes were stored. We didn't have time to go and look around as we were all getting dive bombed, so we went into slit trenches. Ours were already dug and had been occupied before. Our food? Well, we didn't get much."

Marine Maurice Edwards got a lift out of the burnt out camp in a lorry taking several wounded Indian survivors to another hospital: "I remember one of the Indians being prepared to act as No. 2 on the bren. We were eventually stopped at an Aussie roadblock, which was under continual sniper fire, and were forced by the officer in charge to join his little force. After a few hours he managed to check our credentials and we were taken back to Tyersall Park."

Meanwhile at 3.00 p.m. Stewart received an order that the Plymouth Argylls were to rejoin the battle which was now raging in the Reformatory Road (today Clementi Road) area. Of the Argylls there were four officers and fifty very tired and dirty men left – all that remained here of the 860 men of Stewart's original battalion. Because of the bombing, twenty-one year old Lt Geoffrey Hulton RM, apparently on his own initiative, had ordered the Royal Marine survivors to move till nightfall from the burnt out hutments to higher ground on the northern edge of the camp, probably Cluny Hill, where they settled into slit trenches. Sgt Terry Brooks, the youngest regular sergeant in the Corps, remembers Hulton saying that the position was being evacuated and that they should join other units. Led by Sgt Brooks, some of these Marines including Cpl Glover and Marines Mills and Webber located an AIF field gun position deserted by the gunners except for a despondent Australian major. The Marines, trained gunners as well as infantrymen, brought the guns into action against the Japanese advancing from Bukit Timah Village down Dunearn/Bukit Timah Road to the north of Tyersall, and fired away until the ammunition was exhausted. These Marines were later attached to an RASC Supply Depot and only returned to Tyersall on February 17th.

This was a time of confusing messages. Cpl Jones RM believed he had received an order to leave Tyersall and after various adventures ended up at Fort Canning. Others, like Sgt Edmunds with two Marines suffering from "nervous strain" simply took off from Tyersall in those final days. They were later lost at sea aboard the destroyer *Stronghold*. The dispersal from Tyersall was such that on February 15th there were only seventeen *Prince of Wales* Marines left in the camp.

Captain Lang in his report states that "a number of men, both Argylls and Marines, who had become separated from the battalion earlier in the day were trying to rejoin the unit and were informed erroneously, that Tyersall had been evacuated. Most of these men reported to the nearest military unit and in some cases the Naval authorities. They were largely from the Signals and Mortar Sections that had been cut off after expending all their ammunition and from the armoured cars."

Ian Stewart, unable to contact the Marines, gathered the remaining Argylls and for the first time asked them, not ordered them, to march one more time against the Japanese. They marched in open order through the burnt out camp, through Argyll gate and up Holland Road. Angus Rose, David Wilson and Mike Blackwood led the way, discussing Singapore escape plans as they marched. Stewart remained at Tyersall and made final arrangements to transport ammunition and supplies.

They had marched nearly a mile down the road to Holland Village when Angus MacDonald drew up in his Fiat with a message from the commander of Singapore Fortress, Major-General Frank Keith-Simmons CBE MC, that they were to return to Tyersall. They had done more than their share of the fighting. Brigadier Paris was determined that the Plymouth Argylls would not get involved in street fighting which he regarded as "just plain murder", but if necessary would make their last stand defending Tyersall Park.

Returning to camp the Argylls and the returning Marines moved into the few surviving huts vacated by Indian troops. All the Plymouth Argylls' personal belongings and kit had been destroyed along with the Argylls' pipes, drums and band equipment. Ian Stewart had lost all his personal and family possessions when the married quarters went up. David Wilson remembers: "I was sitting on the lawn at 4.00 in the afternoon drinking copious draughts of champagne from a bottle that I had got hold of somehow. It was as well I did, as Angus Rose and I came across one of our warriors who had gone a bit crackers and was walking about the camp with a grenade in his hand with the pin out, that he said he was going to throw into the fire to try and put it out! We relieved him of his somewhat dangerous toy."

That evening the Argyll officers headed for the surviving Brigade Mess where they dined on cottage pie with whisky and soda. At 8.00 p.m., as more Argylls returned, Stewart received an order that had come direct from General Wavell. He was to be evacuated from Singapore so that his specialist knowledge of jungle fighting against the Japanese would not be lost. Stewart was instructed to select two officers and one NCO with similar experience to accompany him. Similar escape parties were sent from other battalions including the Sherwood Foresters and the British Battalion. The idea was that they would form cadres for the reforming of the battalions in India or the UK. The evacuated Argylls were Ian Stewart, Angus Rose, David Wilson and the mild-mannered, but in battle extremely ferocious, CSM Arthur Bing. In fact none of these four would be involved in creating the reconstituted 2nd Argylls. A new battalion came into existence on May 28th 1942, created from the 15th Battalion.

David Wilson describes how he came to hear of his good fortune: "When I was just about to get to bed I was suddenly told to report to Fort Canning (Command HQ). I thought of course that it was for some sort of orders that would keep me up half the night, and went off cursing and swearing. When I got inside, after a hectic drive through the burning town, a friend came up and shook me warmly by the hand, wishing me the best of luck. I was quite staggered as to what all this was about, until he said 'Don't you know? You're off to Java'. This was like the feeling a condemned prisoner must get when he is told that he's going to be released."[53]

At Fort Canning's 'Battlebox' bunker Stewart agreed to obey the evacuation order only on condition that the Plymouth Argylls would not again be used in the Singapore fighting. This was agreed by Malaya Command and Stewart and his three companions departed for Keppel Harbour where they arrived about 8.00 p.m. *Durban* came in about midnight, and the cruiser departed early the next morning. Command of the Plymouth Argylls passed to Captain Bob Lang RM with Argylls Captain Tom Slessor as 2 i/c and Lt Robert or Rab Mundie as Adjutant. Mundie, formerly a platoon commander in A Company, had in recent weeks been serving as Adjutant on the Brigade staff.[54]

In the last days of the fighting Tyersall camp was under constant heavy artillery, mortar and sniper fire. The one surviving armoured car patrolled and, according to Captain Lang's post-war report, Molotov cocktail parties led by Lt Jim Davis went out to deal with any Japanese tank that approached.[55] One Marine remembers that volunteers were asked for and he didn't volunteer; another disputes that these anti-tank parties actually went out. Under heavy fire an Argyll Lance Corporal calmly climbed a telegraph pole to repair the wire that provided the only link with Brigade HQ. One platoon of Marines was dispatched to Keppel Harbour to guard the gates in a rapidly deteriorating situation – many Royal Marine escapers were to be from this group.

The heavy bombardment had angered the Tyersall Park hornets. Some days earlier Ian Stewart had been stung by a hornet much to the amusement of the Jocks. This was all the funnier because he had come out to reprimand them for running away from the creatures and jumping into the slit trenches. The enterprising Marine Cyril Tiddy of *Prince of Wales* detachment decided to take action. At a time when there had been a gas attack scare and gas masks were worn for a short time, Tiddy in full anti-gas gear with tin helmet, gauntlets and gasmask, shinned up a tree to cut down the offending hornets' nest, a giant one measuring some four feet high by two feet wide, with his bayonet. Of course, the hornets found their way through his 'armour' and he was badly stung. However it was not all misfortune for Marine Tiddy – he was in such a bad way that the doctors evacuated him to India with the seriously wounded only hours before Singapore fell.[56]

Cpl Charles Miller remembered the mortaring of Tyersall Park as the most terrifying experience of his war, with large fragments of metal flying everywhere. A young *Repulse* Marine was killed in his slit trench when a mortar bomb hit a tree above the trench.[57] At nightfall, he was buried where he fell, some officers, knowing the end was near, disposing of dum-dum revolver ammunition in his grave. The reason for the existence of these bullets should be explained: their Smith and Wesson .38 revolvers had flat nosed rounds with little stopping power. With judicious use of a file or brick the bullets were sharpened to prove much more lethal. Servicemen found in possession of such bullets could expect little mercy from the enemy.

Sgt H. Tranter of *Prince of Wales* was also killed in his trench by the mortar attacks, and six Marines were wounded. Maurice Edwards, sheltering under a hut, saw Sgt Reg Nunn running down the road "yelling blue murder" with a very bad head wound from which he was very lucky to survive. Mortar shells also rained down on the neighbouring Botanic Gardens, many failing to explode and causing a serious hazard in the weeks that followed.

Maurice Edwards also recalls another incident in these final days: "There was one idiotic thing I can remember doing; getting an Indian driver to move a lorry load of mines to a position beyond the mortaring area. Not the easiest thing to do when the Japs were mortaring very heavily that day. We did it nevertheless. I don't know who was more relieved, me or the driver who had to be coerced with Lt Davis' pistol."

On Saturday February 14th, Brigadier Paris was ordered to escape Singapore. This was much against his wishes as he wanted to stay with the remnants of his Brigade. Major Angus MacDonald, Captain Mike Blackwood, Sgt Willie MacDonald (who Paris particularly admired), and Stewart's batman/bugler Drummer Albert Hardie were to accompany him on the motor launch the *Cecilia*. All five died following the sinking of the *SS Rosenbaum* off Ceylon in March 1942.[58]

Did the departure of this group, following close on the departure of Ian Stewart's party, have a demoralising effect on those who left at Tyersall? Captain Lang considered this the biggest shock to the survivors of the battalion because it made clear to them all that the end was approaching. Maurice Edwards, however, was left cold by their departure as it was the presence of his own officers that really mattered.

There was still no let-up in the fighting around Tyersall as the Japanese probed the Tanglin defences. Captain James Doherty, the Argylls' quartermaster, was wounded in the left arm and side on February 14th. Everything seemed to indicate that the Japanese would make an all-out assault on the camp. The men fortified themselves with swigs of whisky. By this time only 14 *Prince of Wales* Marines and 19 *Repulse* Marines and their six officers remained at Tyersall. Cpl Charles Miller remembers Captain Aylwin coming to his slit trench and offering him a bottle of near empty Johnny Walker whisky. Food was delivered from Tanglin barracks, driven across Napier Road under cover of darkness early each morning and in the evenings. Marine Percy Back was later commended by Captain Lang: "He showed exceptional courage and devotion to duty when, as battalion cook, he carried on alone preparing the food during heavy shell fire when casualties were being suffered and everyone else had taken cover. It was a prolonged shelling and it was due entirely to his efforts that the battalion got their meal." His name was forwarded for recognition but Percy Back later died of dysentery as a prisoner of war.

At night it seemed the whole of Singapore was on fire as areas of the town and ammunition dumps blazed. Thoughts turned to escape. Some seventy Marines escaped Singapore, mostly 'officially' on naval launches or escorting Japanese prisoners; a few 'unofficially'. Some of men had been in the platoon guarding the gates to Keppel Harbour and some on *HMS Grasshopper* were ordered to take out Japanese POWs. Others, including Sgt Edward Hornby, Marines Terence Sully, James Sneddon, William Smith and Charles Davy of *Repulse*, escorted Admiral Spooner on motor launch ML 310 and two of them, Hornby and Sully, perished with him on the island of Tjebia in March 1942.

Sgt Jack Reynolds, the RM Gunnery Instructor on *Prince of Wales*, transferred to the cruiser *Exeter*, later sunk in the Java Sea. Rescued by the Japanese, Reynolds was landed on Macassa Island and died in captivity at Ambon in the Moluccas (Spice Islands) on April 4th 1945.

Sgt Jack King RM, the physical training instructor on *Prince of Wales*, had become separated from his platoon on the night of February 11th when the Japanese tanks broke through on the Upper Bukit Timah Road. He made his way to Keppel Harbour where he met up with Pte Tom Wardrope of the Argylls who had come from the hospital. They were among forty-four passengers on the minesweeper *HMS Tapah*, a converted Straits Steamship and coastal cargo vessel acquired by the Royal Navy in September 1939. After the war Sgt King encountered Captain Aylwin at Plymouth and received a severe reprimand for not returning to Tyersall.

Marine Harold Leadbetter escaped from Singapore on the *Mata Hari* but was captured at Muntok and spent the rest of the war as a POW at Palembang. On the *Tapah* with Sgt King was Marine Peers Crompton who takes up their story: "Sitting on a bollard on the quayside at Keppel Harbour I was contemplating the events of the last few days. All around me chaos raged. My duty at that particular moment was to assist in the evacuation of all civilians, hospital patients, staff, in fact anyone who could prove that they had a right to leave, which seemed to be everybody. Civilians whose lives had been one long round of luxury over the years and had not been too pleased to welcome the troops, were the ones now pleading for priority. They arrived in huge cars packed with huge suitcases and trunks, none of which they were allowed to take with them, only hand luggage. This ruling led to several bribes being offered. I was given the keys of a large American Oldsmobile to use as I wished... It was Black Friday, 13th February 1942. My Oppo was sat on the other bollard; we had been together since the *Prince of Wales* sailed from Blighty in October 1941.

"Another boat came alongside. We tied it up, loaded it with scrambling passengers, then it pushed off to unload on one of the ships waiting in the bay. The ack-ack guns behind the Docks spat out their shells as three Nip planes dived into the attack. I saw the bombs spiralling towards their target. My opposite number and I knew what our next move was: off the quayside into the drink, we jumped as one. The water was about twelve feet below, but better a soaking than being exposed to the blast and shrapnel... Dragging our sodden bodies up the harbour steps we saw the devastation left by the raiders. The anti-aircraft battery had taken a direct hit, the guns were tilted at a crazy angle, the crew was probably wiped out. Nearer to us the evacuees seemed to have escaped serious injuries and prepared again for evacuation.

"By now the time was mid-afternoon, we were feeling hungry, so I went on the scrounge for food. I wandered into a godown that was stacked with boxes of tinned pineapples. I suppose having no success at finding more substantial grub I took two tins of chunks then made my way back to the quayside. I saw a section of Royal Marines were lined up, among them my mate who was beckoning me to get a move on. I rushed to fall in at the end of the line but the Sergeant told me in no uncertain terms that he had enough volunteers. A naval launch glided alongside, two seamen, one fore one aft, pulled the craft in, keeping it steady as the Marines climbed aboard, then pushed off, showing their skill as they went through the Boat Drill routine, as they sped across the harbour to *Grasshopper.*" (A Yangtse River patrol boat).

Royal Marines known to have boarded *Grasshopper* were Marines Barnes, Faint, Gibbons, McNamara and Bugler Leavers. It is likely there were others whose names appear as "missing" on the Roll of Honour, for some 30 Marines and 6 Argylls were put on board *Mata Hari* and 26 Marines on *Tapah*. *Grasshopper* was sunk later that day and Tom Barnes and a wounded Marine Faint, the only known surviving Marines, were captured.

Peers Crompton continues his story: "I cursed my luck, there was my golden chance of getting away from this island of death and misery. A Sister from the Queen Alexandra Nursing Service asked me to open a tin of cigarettes. She asked me where the ships were bound for; a question I couldn't answer. Information of that nature didn't come down to my level. Another boat pulled in and the Sister joined the others filing onto the boat which when full chugged its way across the harbour to one of the passenger liners.

"A bellow from the Sergeant ordering us to fall in made me jump to it. There were ten Marines left. A water boat tied up and we were ordered aboard. We had steamed in with flags flying on the battleship *Prince of Wales,* Flagship of the Far Eastern Fleet, and we were leaving in a water boat! How far we would get I shuddered to think. Darkness came quickly... The silhouette of a ship loomed out of the darkness; the water boat pulled alongside, it was a naval ship, exactly what kind was hard to discern in the gloom. Clambering aboard we were mustered on the Quarterdeck for further instructions. The ship we had boarded was the *Tapah,* an elderly Straits Steamship vessel. Our duties were to man the twin Lewis guns mounted on the bridge and the Twelve Pounder on the Foc's'le."[59]

The crowded *Tapah* set off down the swept channel, through the minefield, out among the southern islands and on to the coast of Sumatra, hiding by day and travelling by night hugging the coastline.

Twenty Marines reached Ceylon. From *Prince of Wales:* Jack McPherson DSM who arrived at Trincomalee in a motorised junk, probably in the company of O'Shaughnessy. Also Marines Alexander, Gleave, Hitchin, James, McKinley, Palin, Porter, Seddon[60] and Willey. From *Repulse:* Sgt Morris, Cpls R. Bassett and J. McCarrol, Marines Brighton, Garner, Hughes, Powell, Rundle and Withers. Some fifty others were either captured in the Banka Straits or perished at sea or on remote islands.

Marine John Garner of the Signals Section escaped during the night of February 14th just hours before the surrender. He had been cut off in the Bukit Timah fighting and was the only marine in a party of thirteen led by an Australian lieutenant. They found a small motor boat in the docks and with Chinese help reached the island of Pula-Pula where they found a tug. They reached the Indragiri River and the town of Rengat, where they split up. Garner palled up with a Norfolk later killed in Burma and spent three weeks with the Chinese guerrillas before, practically starving, they reached Padang where they were put into the Dutch army. On the night of March 1st they left on the British destroyer *Scout,* bound for Colombo.[61]

Seddon and another escaping Marine were transferred to *HMS Warspite*. On their return to the UK, Marines Garner, McPherson and Palin were later sent on the same NCO course at Deal. Opinion is divided among Plymouth Argylls on the subject of 'unofficial' escapers. One Marine said: "Those of us who stayed behind did so either because we were too scared to escape or never had the opportunity." However, another disagreed: "There is a point that if everyone had left their posts and escaped, the Japs could have moved through to Singapore city much earlier than they did." Certainly the opportunity to escape was only a remote possibility after February 15th though a few daring individuals made it. Two officers of the Malay Regiment, E.H.S. 'Jonah' Bretherton MC and Gussy Richards, were to escape three days after the surrender while held captive at Gillman barracks. They slipped away in a sampan from the west coast of Singapore. Five days later, two SSVF Volunteers coolly walked out of Kitchener barracks: Pte Geoffrey Mowat MCS and L.Cpl Bob Elliott, both of the Malacca SSVF, got to Johore and jungle-walked north in Malaya for six weeks, but were caught and sent to Pudu jail. However, Charles McCormack DCM, RAF HQ, with several others broke out of Pasir Panjang Camp nearly seven weeks after the surrender. He and an Australian, R.G. Donaldson, got to Darwin five months later.

Argyll escapers included the seriously wounded Pte G. Face, Cpl H. 'Chocolate' Farquhar, L.Cpl M. Friel and Sgt James Wailes, all evacuated to India. Forty-three year old Colour Sgt Jimmy Wailes, a big man and a well-known middleweight boxer, had been shot in the back in the fighting before Slim River. He telegraphed his family in Stirling while a patient at the British General Hospital, Karachi. Sadly, he was killed shortly after the war when his bicycle collided with a vehicle as he went to work at the Forthside Army Depot at Stirling.[62]

Padre Hartley Beattie and Sgt C. 'Bluff' Wallace of D Company escaped to Ceylon. Sgt Frank McDermott, Cpl Robert Laird, L.Cpl J. Masterton, Ptes George Burns, Joseph Black, George Dickinson, A. Drysdale, Peter Glen, William Greer, Malcolm MacDonald, Fergus McWhirter, James Priestley, William Sutherland and William Thomson and a battalion cook Pte James Queen were evacuated wounded or escaped to India. Most of them were later transferred to the Seaforth Highlanders and served in Burma.

Ptes John Andrew, William Burnside, R. Campbell, James Dawson and Michael Morley arrived at Fremantle, Western Australia in March 1942 and also later served with other units. Curiously, the names of twenty escapers and evacuees mistakenly found themselves on Brigadier Stewart's 1946 Battalion Roll of Honour as missing in action, a fact discovered and rectified during the research for this book.

Others, like Eric Moss, and Duncan Ferguson and his driver friend, Fred Murray, had the opportunity to escape but didn't take it. "I was escorting a party of women and children to the docks," Duncan said. "Fred and I found drunken Australians actually pushing these women and children off, and we had to get them onto the deck, and an officer said to us: 'Come on, boys, I'll show you where to kip down'. And Fred said: 'What? We're not staying with you. We're going back to the battalion'. 'Oh,' he said, 'don't be stupid. Singapore's finished'. Fred said 'Don't bother. We're going back to our battalion'."[63]

Captain Eric Moss was also at Keppel Harbour. Here he encountered Padre Beattie who commented that "The game was up". Moss explains his own presence at the docks: "I had been sent down to clear a ship of Australians who had already hijacked it. It was due to take off technicians and there was another ship leaving taking the rest of the women and children. I went round this ship and with the point of my revolver I hope I cleared every one of the Australians off. I met a lot of nurses I knew, and they tried to persuade me to sail with them. Even the Captain said 'You are surely not going back again'. I said I had to, otherwise it was desertion. He gave me lunch up on the bridge and tried to persuade me, but I couldn't do it. Now, looking back, I wonder if I wasn't sent down there to take the opportunity to try and get away. But anyway, I didn't. There were a lot of chaps on the quayside and I waited at the head of the gangway as the gangway ropes were cast off, and then I ran for it as the last was going. But there was still one rope holding the ship to the quay and there was an Australian sergeant trying to shimmy up it. I called to him to come down but he took no notice, so I drew my revolver and fired. I don't know if he was hit, but he fell off. The ship got away but was heavily bombed. I heard from one of the nurses after the war. Her father was Secretary of the Football Association of Singapore."[64]

Standing on the quayside, Moss waved his bonnet to the departing ship.

George Patterson, an MCS official commissioned into the Royal Artillery, had succeeded Ian Stonor as Percival's ADC. He went to Keppel Harbour to deliver documents to an American ship: "Boarding permits had been issued to women and children but the dockside was a milling throng, fighting to get on the ships. From my personal observation, the vast majority of the troops were Australians who should have still been in the front line. I remember threatening one with my revolver as he stood between me and the gang-plank. The majority were very drunk of liquor they had looted from shops and bars as they streamed through Singapore."[65]

Padre Hartley Beattie had left Tyersall on February 14th and driven in his old Morris down to Keppel Harbour. He was not only Chaplain to the Argylls but also to various small artillery units in the area of the Harbour and on Blakang Mati island (today Sentosa). After his conversation on the quayside with Eric Moss he took the military ferry to Blakang Mati. While he was on the artillery island there were several heavy air-raids, one of which brought the roof down on the officers' mess.

Towards evening, Beattie telephoned Tam Slessor at Tyersall to say that he was returning. The line went dead. Beattie made his way to the ferry but there was no ferry, so he was spent the night on Blakang Mati. Next day an officer from a passing ship hailed the Gunners on the shore: "The game is up!" Together with an RC Padre Joe Lombardi and the IAMC MO Captain Pat Kirkwood, Beattie got rounded up some wounded Gunners and boarded an RAMC launch, the *Florence Nightingale,* an open boat with an in-board motor. They headed for the nearby island of Bintan.[66]

At 6.10 p.m. on February 15th 1942 Lt General Percival drove to the Bukit Timah Ford Factory which for the last two days had served as Yamashita's headquarters. The factory, opened in October 1941, was the first motor car assembly plant in Southeast Asia. It had been used in the Campaign to assemble newly arrived Hurricane aircraft, which had been destroyed in a heavy Japanese raid on the factory. Here, after brief negotiations, Percival signed the unconditional surrender of Singapore. At 8.30 p.m. the cease-fire took effect. The guns fell silent. Marine Tom Webber comments: "I often wondered later whether the initials of the *Prince of Wales* were a foreboding of the fate awaiting us."[67]

Sgt Terry Brooks RM felt and still feels the shamefulness of what happened: "My opinion of what happened at Singapore is still that the whole period was shameful and in some cases some Royal Marines gave a little less than was expected of them.

But I think with the exception of one or two they did a darn good job under extenuating circumstances not greatly enhanced by the activities or rather non-activities of certain senior Army officers. There was a singular lack of information. I don't think Captain Lang and Captain Aylwin knew what really was going on, no information, no maps, no real orders! Not the ideal treatment to be meted out to two such good officers."

Of the 220 Argylls including 17 officers who lost their lives in the Malayan campaign, 7 officers and 39 men fell in the Singapore fighting. Wounded were 162 Argylls, including 12 officers, while 31 Plymouth Argyll Royal Marines died in the battle for Singapore. The vast majority of these men have no known grave.[68]

The Argylls were subsequently awarded six battle honours for their actions during the seventy days of the Malayan Campaign: North Malaya, Grik Road, Central Malaya, Slim River, Singapore Island and Malaya 1941-2.[69]

NOTES

1. The best published account of the loss of the warships is 'Battleship' by Martin Middlebrook and Patrick Mahoney (London 1997). Many Plymouth Argyll Royal Marines contributed to this book. Royal Marine casualties December 10th 1941 from Peter Dunstan whose fine documentations of the two RM detachments can be found in the RM Museum Library, Eastney. Extract from Singapore National Archives interview with fromer A\S Fred Hodgson of *Prince of Wales*.

2. Captain RGS Lang RM's official report 19.11.45 (RM Museum). Lang also wrote a less detailed but similar account in 'Globe and Laurel' 12.45 entitled 'A Tale of Two Regiments'

3. Charles Miller interview 5.96

4. The Lang Report

5. Dunstan

6. Lang Report

7. See memoirs of Admiral Sir John Hayes, a *Repulse* survivor: Face the Music (Pentland Press) Also interesting on Colonel Stewart.

8. Rose

9. Information on Roseforce from Rose, Dr Jim Davis 1.98 and War Diary on No. 1 Independent Infantry Company

10. Dunstan

11. Lang

12. Stewart

13. Information on the fight form Dunstan and Duncan Ferguson of the Argylls. Communication with the Argylls from Tom Webber letter 1994 and observations of the authors.

14. Maurice Edwards letter 1994

15. Brigadier David Wilson 1995 and 1998. Letters and two unpublished manuscripts. Wilson subsequently served in Burma and Korea. In September 1942 while at a restcamp in Dimapur he wrote 'The Causeway and Singapore Island' and in 1995 he wrote for the authors 'The Bridge at Seremban'. Recollections of Hoostie McNaught by Duncan Ferguson/Jockie Bell.

16. Walter Green letters 3.97 and 12.97. Maurice Edwards letter 10.97

17. Rose and 'Thin Red Line' obituary to Bardwell. Bardwell's brother had also served with the 93rd in India.

18. Details of RM officers from M. Edwards

19. J.W. McPherson

20. Dunstan: The forming of the Plymouth Argylls and M. Edwards 1997

21. Dunstan

22. Rose

23. Kinvig: Scapegoat p.205

24. Dalforce, or the Volunteer Army, was formed by Colonel John Dalley, an FMS Special Branch officer from Kuala Lumpur. The Chinese volunteers, some of whom were Communists released from prison though poorly armed, fought to the last round and often the last man both at

Kranji and Bukit Timah village. Dalley disbanded what was left of his unit on February 13th 1942. Estimates of the numbers in Dalforce range from 2000 to 4000.

25. 2/20th Battalion AIF suffered very heavy casualties including its CO Lt Colonel Charles Assheton killed in action.

26. Finlay McLachlan, 2nd Argylls

27. Wilson

28. The co-author lived on what had been Dairy Farm and worked in Choa Chu Kang while researching for this book.

29. Lang/Rose/Dunstan/Hutchinson

30. Wilson

31. Lang's report

32. The wounding of Aylwin was witnessed by Wilson, Edwards and Webber. Charles Miller who had worked together with Aylwin on *Prince of Wales*, arrived in the chaotic frontline that night and was unaware of his wound.

33. Information on the Massacre from Peter Bruton's research paper 'The Matter of a Massacre' and three survivors: Nick Carter, Dick Lee and John Wyatt. See also 'The Epic of Alexandra Military Hospital' by Cpl R.T. Warn (RM Museum archive). Today a small memorial in the hospital garden commemorates the victims.

34. Lang/Dunstan

35. Dunstan letter 6.96

36. When the British 18th Division counter-attacked Mandai that evening it was deserted, the tanks having moved south down Bukit Timah Road.

37. QM Sgt Tom Webber: Last of the Plymouth Argylls 'Globe and Laurel'

38. QM Captain James 'Doc' Doherty MBE died in 1996 aged 96. His 20 year old brother died in the Alexandra Hospital massacre.

39. Wilson/Rose

40. Weir interview. Somewhat different to Rose's interpretation.

41. Details of that night from Rose, Wilson, Dunstan, Edwards and Weir

42. C. Miller

43. Weir interview. Rose wrongly suggested that Weir was shot by an Indian soldier discharging his weapon. He was in fact close to the road with his Tiger patrol including Cpl Jennings MM and was shot at about 22 yards range by Japanese

infantry mounted on tanks.

44. Details of Weir's rescue from Lang, Webber, Miller. The two mortally wounded Marines were later buried in a mass grave in the General Hospital grounds and remain there till this day – the only Plymouth Argylls killed in the Singapore fighting who have a known grave. The grave at the Singapore General Hospital contains the remains of 117 British servicemen and 300 civilians. It is marked by a small wooden cross.

45. Dunstan

46. Miller

47. Weir. Like Weir and Calderwood he became a senior Malayan Police officer after the war. 'Strath' lives today in the Highlands of Scotland.

48. Changi diary of TP Lewis published by the Malaysian Historical Society 1984. Entry for 19.7.42. The massacre was also confirmed 10.97 by an Argyll who was a friend of some of the victims and after the war faced the agony of enquiring relatives. Lewis' diary names the officer as Lt JDG McPherson. Lewis also states that Pte Anderson's rescuers delivered him to Miyako (Woodbridge) Hospital.

49. Stirling Observer

50. Stewart was also greatly feared, especially by junior officers. They secretly nicknamed him 'Busty' on account of his extreme thinness, but were amazed at his fitness and that he never sweated. (Wilson)

51. See Stewart and Rose's accounts of Bing's exploits.

52. Accounts of the Tyersall bombing from Lang, Rose, Stewart, Edwards and Wilson.

53. Wilson/Rose

54/55 Lang

56. Verdon fragment in RM Museum archive. Confirmed by C. Miller and P. Dunstan. Date of incident disputed by M. Edwards who places it earlier. Cyril Tiddy lives today in Cornwall. Hornet information also from Stewart and Ferguson.

57. Dunstan/Miller/ Edwards

58. See 'The Boat' by Walter Gibson (WH Allen, London 1974). Cpl Gibson of the Argylls was the only surviving passenger. For the fate of RM Sgt Edward Hornby and Marine Sully see Richard Pool's 'Course for Disaster' (London 1987). The

best overall picture of these events is 'The Escape from Singapore' (Revised edition) by Richard Gough (Mandarin 1994).

59. Peers Crompton 1997. List of Marines on Tapah to be found on ADM 199/622A PRO).

60. Seddon's story is in a wartime Admiralty publication 'The Royal Marines were here'. He was also photographed with another escaped Marine aboard *HMS Warspite*

61. J.W. McPherson 1997. Garner ended the war with 42 Commando and retired from the Royal Marines as a Sergeant. He later became a Major in the Territorial Army.

62/63.D. Ferguson 1997

64. Eric Moss 1997

65. George Patterson: A Spoonful of Rice with Salt

66. Hartley Beattie 1998 and Pte Hey RAMC (ADM 199/622A PRO)

67. Webber 'The last of the Plymouth Argylls' and Brooks letter 1998

68. Kranji war memorial/Argyll Roll of Honour (Stewart)/Argyll Record Book (QMS Aitken)/Commonwealth War Graves Register/P. Dunstan's *Prince of Wales* and *Repulse* RM Roll of Honour. Correspondence with Lt Colonel Alastair Scott Elliot (Regimental Secretary) regarding Argylls listed as missing 15.2.42). Stewart's Roll of Honour contains a number of inaccuracies. His figure of 244 dead is not correct. About twenty of these 'missing' men returned home and some are still living! Two men listed as killed in action died in captivity and another was killed-in-action in Europe in 1945.

69. Lt Colonel Alistair Scott Elliot.

Nick Carter before the war and as a prisoner of war (X).

X

"INTREPID AGAINST ALL ADVERSITY" - JAPANESE CAPTIVITY

ESCAPE

At dawn on Thursday February 12th, after many delays, the light cruiser *Durban* (Captain Peter Cazalet RN) left the man-of-war anchorage east of Keppel Harbour to lead the naval escort to five ships including the cargo liner *Empire Star* and the liner Gorgon. *HMS Kedah* (another Straits Steamship later sunk) also escorted the convoy. The ships were packed with civilians; selected army and RAF technicians, specialists and a party of Naval Base police officers led by an officer later to distinguish himself in the Malayan Emergency. The presence of these police officers on the vessel was to remain a matter of controversy that was to divide the leadership of the Malayan Police Force long after the war.

The convoy's destination was Batavia, today Jakarta, then on to Sydney, Australia. Among sixty key personnel aboard *Durban* were Ian Stewart, Angus Rose, David Wilson and CSM Bing – all ordered out in the "specialist" category. Also on board were a party of British Army Japanese interpreters, all of Japanese descent, and two Royal Marines, Bellwood and Wooding of *Prince of Wales*, who had been transferred to *Durban* prior to the Singapore fighting. The Argylls were already well known to the ship's crew, having acted as their hosts then. She had returned as escort to the January convoy bringing part of the 18th Division to Singapore.

David Wilson slept in a cabin until awoken by gunfire at 8.00 a.m. Some eighty Japanese aircraft had appeared overhead and had started dive-bombing and machine gunning the convoy, which was now in the Banka Straits. Attacks continued until 1.00 p.m. The *Durban* was attacked eleven times, hit three times, with five near misses as it circled at 30 knots. A gun crew was killed. Rose and Stewart sheltered under a wardroom table. Rose attempted to take his mind off things by reading a copy of "Riddle of the Sands" until a nearby hit sent splinters flying across the wardroom and started a fire close by. Wilson joined his two comrades, lying flat on their faces in their tin hats. There they remained for over four hours.[1]

Durban was in fact so damaged she never fought again but was used as a Blockship for Mulberry Harbour during the D-Day landings on the Normandy beaches. Amazingly, however, no ships were sunk and casualties were light. The Empire Star, the main target, received two direct hits setting the deck on fire but succeeded in shooting down two Japanese aircraft and remained seaworthy with only fourteen killed. The dead were buried at sea to the emotional strains of 'Abide with Me.'[2]

On February 13th there were mercifully no air-attacks on the convoy. Japanese aircraft were too busy bombing Palembang in Sumatra. A day later they were to return to the Banka Straits and together with their warships decimate the last convoy to leave Singapore. Ships such as the *Kuala, Giang Bee*, the *Aquarius* and *Vyner Brooke* went down with large loss of life. Thousands died: civilians, nurses, and military personnel. Many were murdered by the Japanese as they came ashore. L.Cpl Robert Seddon RM of Repulse, after swimming ashore at Banka island stumbled upon the bodies of murdered nurses and was himself kicked and bayoneted by the Japanese. Left for dead, he survived to join fifteen other *Repulse* Marines interned at Palembang.

Some 862 British civilians including 200 women who left Singapore between 10th and 15th February 1942 remained unaccounted for among Japanese internees or successful escapers.[3] They were victims of both the Japanese and a voluntary civilian evacuation policy.

For two days the *Durban* convoy waited at Batavia where the gloomy news of Singapore's surrender was heard over the radio. The four Argylls came ashore leaving the convoy to proceed to Sydney. After the removal of a group of AIF deserters from the *Empire Star*, most RAF personnel were ordered off to help defend Java – few of them survived subsequent Japanese captivity. The fate of the Australian deserters remains a mystery. Walter Green RAF remembers seeing them lined up along the quayside under heavy guard and heard a rumour that they were later shot.

The Argyll officers spent the night in the corridor of the crowded Hotel des Indes, Batavia. Ian Stewart was ordered to report to General Wavell at GHQ Pacific Command, Bandoeng. Rose and Wilson were instructed to take a ship to Ceylon. They boarded a bomb-damaged coastal steamer *HMS Pangkor*, arriving in Ceylon on March 2nd where they met Padre Beattie who escaped Singapore on February 15th and was staying at the Galle Face Hotel in Colombo.

Beattie takes up the story of his escape with Dr (Captain) Kirkwood's party of wounded Gunners and R.C Padre, Joe Lombardi: "At Bintan, I remember the large Petroleum farm with all the storage tanks intact. We went ashore on this Dutch island and hunted around some of the vacated bungalows. I found an atlas and this became our guide until we got to Sumatra. The local inhabitants paid no attention to us. After a while we decided to hunt down some gasoline of which there was plenty. We set off for another island about 4 or 5 miles distant. The modus operandi of the excursion was as follows: the patients lay in the bottom of the boat; Captain Kirkwood sat in the stern and steered; I sat in the bow and navigated. The others sat in the middle of the boat and we all kept a weather eye open for hostile aircraft or motor boats. Our next island was somewhat more exciting than the last. At the fairly large Dock there was a steamship filled with soldiers and other assorted people. It was about to set off and we were invited to come aboard but decided to stick together. Later a Zero came over flying low. The two men with me jumped into the water. I quickly bound my head in a white cloth and walked bow-legged trying to look like a native workman. The Zero flew off after circling a few times. I am sure the pilot thought we were not worth a bullet.

"We set off for another island not far away. Our reception from the natives was one of complete iciness but we managed to buy some food with the little money we had. The next island, Singkep, was a different story. Here we found a group of about fifteen British nurses and some Naval personnel, survivors of one of the ships sunk on its way from Singapore. The villagers, especially the Headman, had been most kind to these survivors providing them with food and a few huts. I remember great big buckets of rice being brought to the little encampment. We joined them and shared some tins of bully we had which, with the rice, was quite a good meal. One young man was sitting at the foot of a palm tree. He would not move or speak. I don't know whether he was a serviceman or civilian. I was told that he could not be induced to eat or speak."

Dr Kirkwood stayed on Singkep to attend to the wounded evacuees. Beattie and Lombardi continued their journey and eventually made it to the Indragiri River and the town of Rengat in Sumatra. This was the organised and accepted escape route to Padang on Sumatra's west coast, and it was crowded with survivors of ships sunk whilst leaving Singapore. They took the crowded train from Sawalunto to Padang. Beattie remembers one man nearly missing the train: "The train pulled out but had to stop several times to get a head of steam. A soldier jumped out and raced for some nearby scrub to answer nature's call. After a few minutes the train started off. The unfortunate man holding up his pants with one hand, started running and shouting 'Wait for me!' The train stopped and the man was quickly hauled aboard to the merriment of the passengers."

At Padang, Beattie was struck by the hospitality of the Dutch. He encountered Ernest Gordon who had done tremendous work ferrying evacuees along the Sumatra escape route. Gordon told him of his preparations to escape to Ceylon. One day there were rumours of evacuation: "Eventually we were told by the Dutch authorities to go down to the Docks. We streamed there with our possessions, which in my case were nil. A battlecruiser, *HMAS Hobart,* lay at anchor about a mile off shore."

In the harbour were *HMS Tenedos* and *HMS Scout,* looking for oil supplies. They ferried evacuees out to the *Hobart.* "Once alongside we scrambled up the rope netting on the side of the massive ship. As soon as one's head appeared at deck level we were grabbed any old how by Australian sailors and dumped unceremoniously on the deck. Never in the history of mankind were so many hauled aboard by so few."

Hobart sailed from Padang on March 2nd and arrived at Colombo on March 5th. Beattie spent the next two years in the Middle East where he went down with smallpox and diphtheria before returning to Scottish Command.[4]

Stewart arrived in Ceylon shortly afterwards. In Java on February 16th he had been interviewed at length by the CO 7th Australian Division (Major-General A.S. Allen) and Brigadier F.H. Berryman (HQ 1st Australian Corps) particularly with regard to jungle warfare. After one week's rest in very agreeable surroundings, he was despatched from Java to Ceylon. On the voyage to Ceylon he was accompanied by two senior Australian staff officers, Colonel C.M.L. Elliott, chief of staff 7th Australian Division, and Lt Colonel K.A. Wills, an intelligence officer, who interviewed him further. Their extensive note-taking, not the information brought back by the escaped Australian Lt. General H. Gordon-Bennett, would form the basis of successful Australian tactics manuals, and tactics in the retreat along the Kokoda Trail and subsequent offensives.[5]

Quite by chance, Stewart encountered his wife Ursula and daughter Cherry Linnhe outside a Colombo hotel. They had been evacuated from Singapore on February 12th in a Royal Navy intelligence ship. After a week-long lecture tour of Ceylon, Stewart was sent to Delhi where he stayed with General Wavell. Three more weeks of lecturing followed then he went to Bombay to make a BBC radio broadcast about the Argylls in the Malayan Campaign.[6]

Wounded men were also getting out of Singapore. Pte Tom Wardrope of the Argylls, wounded in the head during the Grik Road fighting, was in transit from a Singapore hospital when he found his ambulance abandoned at Keppel Harbour on the night of February 12th. Together with a Pte F. Brown of the Argylls and fellow Scot, Sgt Jack King RM of the Prince of Wales Company, Wardrope boarded the *Tapah.*[7] There were 25 Marines on board, put there by Commander Alexander RN on the authority of RAMY (Admiral Spooner). *Tapah* on her journey down the Banka Straits picked up 13 survivors from the steamers *Giang Bee* and the *Redang,* both sunk by Japanese Navy gunfire on February 13th with heavy loss of life.

Tapah was a 75 tonner built for coastal waters in 1925 by the Straits Steamship Company at their shipyard at Sungei Nyok near Butterworth. She was steam driven but converted like most of their vessels to minesweeping for the Navy. Marine Peers Crompton describes the events leading to their capture: "The Skipper resumed his original plan to steam at night, sheltering at daylight, and on Tuesday 17th February we dropped anchor in an inlet off the coast of Sumatra. Here there was frantic signalling from the shore about half a mile away. A boat was lowered and I was detailed as one of the crew, the Skipper giving instructions that we could not bring anyone back with us as the ship was overcrowded, but we took supplies of food and water.

"On arrival at the spot we were astonished to find that the group were all women. This of course altered the situation. Here again was the story of their ship being bombed and sunk by Japanese aircraft. They had managed to fill a lifeboat but as the boat was overcrowded it was decided that the men would row along the coast to seek help, convinced that it was not far away, leaving the women to fend for themselves until they returned. There were nineteen women altogether and with the exception of two they insisted on remaining here until the men returned with help. All they needed were supplies of food and water to tide them over. We unloaded what we had brought and two Marines, A. Wynn and G. Hayes, volunteered to stay ashore while the two who wished to be rescued were taken to the ship with us.

"During the afternoon there was considerable air activity. Twice two formations of enemy bombers passed high overhead, flying in a southerly direction, formations of twenty seven like the ones that had devastated Singapore. Fortunately they were not interested in us – they had bigger targets in mind as we were to find out later. As night fell we were on our way again. This, said the Skipper, was the most dangerous run to date, through the Banka Straits between the island of Banka and Sumatra, now known as Bomb Alley. It was intended we proceed full speed ahead, clearing the Straits by daylight. The night was pitch black, no moon, no stars. I had the middle watch manning the twin Lewis guns on the bridge. As I passed the door leading to the engine room, the Engineer was sitting on the steps counting the revs. 'This is the fastest this old tub has ever been; must be doing all of eighteen knots!' he said proudly.

"Suddenly out of the blackness the blinding beam of a searchlight lit up the ship and the brightness of light prevented an identification of the vessel carrying it. The bridge of the *Tapah* was an open structure, so I was only a few feet from the centre of activity and could hear all the comments and instructions passed from mouth to mouth. The first words uttered were by the Skipper: 'What the hell?' Then the Signalman: 'Aldis Lamp sending a message, Sir. It's an international code: Heave to for Identification.' The Captain gave the orders down the voice-pipe to the engine room. The vessel with the searchlight was circling us from a distance of about five hundred yards. Next came another signal. 'Put your steaming lights on and follow me.' The Captain seemed relieved. 'Must be a Javanese patrol vessel,' he said. 'Probably going to escort us through the Straits.' So once again we steamed on following the light of the mystery ship ahead.

"Everyone accepted the escort theory but the hope was soon to be shattered. About 2.00 am there was another signal: 'Heave to, drop anchor.' This order was carried out without question, the searchlight once again illuminating *Tapah* in a silvery light, also making a silvery path across the calm sea between the two ships. Then into the beam appeared a boat manned by sailors in white uniforms, not unlike our own duck suits. As they pulled alongside, the Skipper who was looking over the Bridge guard rail gave a gasp, shouting 'My God, they are bloody Japs!' My blood ran cold; this was the unforeseen, the thought of capture had never entered my head. I moved back into the dark side of the funnel, out of the glare of the searchlight as if it would give me some protection. There was some activity on the Bridge as the ship's papers were ditched over the port side, the opposite side to the landing party.

"The Japs clambered aboard fanning out to stern and bow as they did so. The officer coming up the ladder to the Bridge. This was the first time I had seen a Japanese officer in full uniform. I was impressed by his smart appearance as he stepped onto the Bridge. As he confronted the Skipper he spoke in clear English: 'You are my prisoners, you will obey orders. Where were you heading?' I was then surprised at the Skipper's reply: 'As far away from you as I could get.' It was at this point that a Jap urged me at the point of a bayonet to join the others in the stern."

The passengers and crew of the *Tapah* were interned at Palembang. On the advice of an Argyll officer, Tom Wardrope pretended to be a Royal Marine PLY X774 (Sgt King was PLY X775) to escape any fury directed at Argylls for the heavy casualties they had inflicted on the Japanese in the north of Malaya. There were well-substantiated rumours of a Japanese 'hate' against the Argylls. As early as July 18th 1942 eight Argylls (Ptes E. Brown, R. Cain, A. Fergus, J. Murray, G. Ramshaw, D.Simpson, J.Spence and J. Ure) and one Marine (J.Kent) were in a draft of prisoners sent from Palembang to Japan. The remaining Marines occupied a hut where, under Sgt King, it was noted by fellow prisoner Jack Stubbs RN that they kept up their smart appearance and military bearing longer than most.

Captain Bal Hendry, badly wounded at Telok Anson in early January, had been sent to Singapore's Alexandra Hospital. From here he was evacuated to Poona in India only days before the hospital massacre which began at 1.40 p.m. on February 14th and continued into the morning of the 15th. The seriously wounded Captain Robert Kennard, formerly OC of C Company of the Argylls, who was shot in the thigh at Kota Tampan, was still attending a Singapore hospital when the battle for the island began. Unfit to fight, he obtained permission from Brigadier Paris to escape on February 15th and made his way to Sumatra on the launch *Joan* taking a battery of gunners with him (30th Battery HAA Regiment). The vessel ran aground on St. John's Island off Singapore but was successfully refloated.[8]

Lt Montgomery-Campbell who had escaped from Slim River and crossed to Sumatra continues his story: "We got to a big Chinese fishing place in Sumatra called Bagan Siapiapi and it was there that we got in touch with the Dutch and they were very good to us. I had malaria at this time and they also fixed up my foot. Then we got passed on to Pekan Baroe where the RAF had an emergency landing spot and we got attached to them. We did odd jobs like replenishing the planes and doing aircraft spotting for them. Then one morning a Japanese reconnaissance plane came over and that afternoon about 300 Japanese paratroopers arrived and surrounded the airfield, but we, the Argylls, had enough jungle lore to get through to a place called Fort de Kok, getting a lift there by 'piggy' bus. It was in the hands of the Dutch and then we got to Padang."[9]

In Padang the British Consul sent Montgomery-Campbell and his six Argylls, who included Bertie King and PSM Colvin, to the Docks where they helped women and children board a British warship. They themselves were not allowed to escape with the Royal Navy but boarded a prahu, which sailed with some forty men on the same day as the ill-fated *Rosenbaum,* which they spotted in the harbour. Deciding on the impossibility of crossing the Indian Ocean in the sampan they changed course for Batavia. Here they were attached for aerodrome anti-paratrooper guard duties to 6th Heavy Anti-Aircraft Regiment. which had already lost its guns.

About forty Argylls in all were captured in Sumatra or in Java. They included Lt Montgomery-Campbell; Lt W. Bruce; Plt Sgt F. Colvin; Cpls R. King; J. McCall; A. McGowan; Robertson; L.Cpl Joe Lonsdale from Singapore; P. Neanse and Ptes A. Bolton; Campbell; F. Chapman; A. Fergus; J. Hynds; J. Kirk; W. 'Spud' Thompson; W.Willison, and two Geordie Argylls from County Durham, Ptes A. Metcalfe and G. Morley.

Montgomery-Campbell met both the Australian Major-General Gordon Bennett and Ian Stewart at Bandoeng, Java. He got malaria badly and was put in Bandoeng Hospital in the next bed to Gordon Bennett. On the first day, he explains: "I got into a conversation with Bennett thinking I might get taken out with him, but no way in the world – he left very early in the morning. Stewart was there as a jumping off point for India. I saw him some years ago in his home in Appin, and he told me then he was very sorry to give me the orders that I'd have to stay with the men. He was ordered to leave but the officers must stay with the men. I said, 'Right, no worries about that, I don't want any apologies, Sir'."[10]

Two days later the Japanese arrived at the hospital. Montgomery-Campbell joined others captured in Java in Tanjong Priok POW camp which was in the coolie lines in the Dock area of Batavia. Here he narrowly escaped Japanese retribution: "One day about thirty Japs barged into the camp without any warning. They had rifles and fixed bayonets – and they certainly meant business the way they pushed us around. The officers were segregated from the men, and at this point there was anxiety in more ways than one. You see, there was a wireless set hidden underneath a concrete slab in the toilets, and then there was a daily news sheet floating about somewhere in the camp when the Japs arrived.

"It was later ascertained that a search would be made. An officer had to accompany a Jap with the view to the turning out of the few belongings of a POW for a kit inspection. As a result several knives and daggers were confiscated. I accompanied one of the Japs and we duly entered one of the small cubicles. It was furnished with a bunk, a bed and a chair, crudely made from bits and pieces. On the table was a typewriter, and as I glanced down at the typing I simply froze – the news sheet was in the process of being typed 'BBC NEWS,' 'NORTH AFRICA' and so on. I broke out in a cold sweat. I immediately thrust myself forward between the Jap and the typewriter. There was that ugly silence before a storm. I followed his gaze and to my amazement I realised that he was most intrigued with the letters of the keyboard rather than what had been typed out. It was at this point I thought to humour the Jap. I showed him my index finger and gave a quivering sort of laugh and said very sheepishly 'I one finger ka!' He gave a broad grin showing his gold fangs and replied, 'Ah so desu ka! I also von binger ka!'

"We both walked out and I gave a huge sigh of relief. At the other end of the camp a colleague of mine Dennis Glasgow accompanied a Jap who paused to admire a photograph of either a wife or a sweetheart of a POW. In so doing the Jap picked up the photograph to have a closer look and two Army ordnance maps fell out of the frame. The maps were of Java! Dennis Glasgow immediately laid out the maps on a bunk and in a flash said to the Jap 'England ko Mooto ka!' And with this he demonstrated driving a car. 'Ah so ka! England ka,' nodding his head several times. Tanjong Priok and Batavia were right under his nose. It was a miracle and to this day I say 'Thank God these two Japs could not read English!'.".

Montgomery-Campbell was among 1846 prisoners sent back from Java to Singapore and Changi POW camp early in 1943. While in a work party at the Docks another Argyll who had been working at HQ Malaya Command Fort Canning before the surrender handed him for safekeeping two important documents which in Japanese hands would have been valuable propaganda material: a telegram from Wavell dated February 10th 1942 urging Percival to fight to the end, and Percival's letter to all Officers and Men of February 15th 1942. Throughout his captivity Montgomery-Campbell kept these and a typed copy of "The Malayan Campaign," a lecture given at Changi by Lt General Heath.

Six weeks after arriving in Singapore, the Java prisoners were shipped out to Borneo on March 28th 1943. Montgomery-Campbell and about a thousand others disembarked at Kuching and were put to work on lengthening the aerodrome. The remainder were sent to Jesselton, today Koto Kinabalu. The Japanese had decided that these prisoners would be used as labour to construct airfields in Borneo. They were known as 'E' Force.

CSM Alexander Porter, a very fine NCO, was also in this party but in June 1944 was among 200 British Kuching prisoners sent north first to Miri in Sarawak then to Jesselton and eventually to Labuan to build an airfield. None of these men survived. The situation for the Kuching prisoners deteriorated drastically from October 1944 when US bombing and Blockade cut food supplies. Japanese 'death marches' followed and fourteen Argylls, including CSM Porter, were to be among the victims of this horror. Montgomery-Campbell later heard that they had been murdered after making contact with a local resistance group.

At Kuching, Montgomery-Campbell looked after Argyll and Gordon Highlander POWs and kept a careful record of the names of his fellow prisoners. He made a colourful embroidery on which can be seen the names of himself and his fellow prisoners. The embroidery is today in the possession of the Regimental Museum, Stirling Castle. Montgomery-Campbell first got the idea of making the embroidery when in charge of a work party at Kuching in Borneo. They were using former British Army trucks. Montgomery-Campbell found some waste material, basically coloured rags, in a glove compartment. This served as thread. As cloth he used the top part of a mosquito net and calico which the Japanese had supplied to cover up the prisoners' food. He was taught to stitch by a fellow POW who had been in an embroidery firm in London. Montgomery-Campbell's original idea was to try and make a copy of the Argyll badge and to use the colours to differentiate rank: Captains in blue, Majors in green etc. Each man pencilled his signature on the calico and the embroidery began to take shape. It survived confiscation and tearing following a Japanese search.

Kuching POW Camp, under the guidance of the British CO, Lt Colonel T.C. Whimster RAOC, a persevering but not particularly forceful man, became a place where art and learning thrived. Some officers set up a secret 'University' directed by Lt Frank E. Bell BA, Royal Artillery. Books were made of tobacco paper, brightly covered with sarong cloth. Others painted and drew, keeping a record of camp life. There was a secret radio in the camp concealed in a cavity in a brick oven and run on a hand-powered generator. At great risk Montgomery-Campbell collected news, "getting in the ice creams" it was called, and passed it on to adjoining camps. Often he would go under the wire, sometimes accompanied by his friend Lt Neil

McArthur, an Indian Army officer from Dundee. He also obtained some bagpipes and played them at monthly concerts including New Year concerts in which he directed the singing of 'Auld Lang Syne.' If he played a dirge the prisoners knew the news was bad. A lively march indicated good news.

Montgomery-Campbell explains the need to keep up morale among the prisoners: "Life itself was a struggle, something that had continually to be fought for. One very vital factor in survival was the framework of a unit organisation, and this was particularly so with the Argylls who had a proud record and a lot of Esprit de Corps. This cohesive military discipline managed to withstand the worst shocks which the Japs could inflict. The mind just had to be exercised and the will to live and to help one's friends followed."

A fellow prisoner said, "Monty was a great chap who did some excellent and hazardous work in Kuching to obtain BBC news for the officers. He took many risks and had he been caught I'm sure that he would not be alive today."

Was resistance to the Japanese possible at Kuching? Captain John Mackie of the FMS Volunteers reflects, "Any attempt to avoid blows or even to flinch before being struck resulted in extra whacks. As to any resistance! Almost a case of 'off with his head' – very severe punishment for striking a Jap or guard of any sort. Possibly the only use of unarmed combat skills was the art of falling properly i.e. with a shoulder tuck and a roll – if you had time when suddenly tripped up. I can't imagine our Senior British Officer in Kuching, Lt Colonel Whimster leading any aggressive action against the Japs. He was an Ordnance Corps man with little training, I should think, for offensive action. There were probably few in our Officers' section who would have been happy to have a go at the Japs in favourable circumstances. One was Montgomery-Campbell of the Argylls. Conditions for escaping or taking on the Japs were practically non-existent. I suppose it might have been possible to communicate with the Mens' camp to organise a rebellion, but many of them were in a parlous state physically, and while the spirit may have been willing, the flesh was too weak. I gather there was a permanent Jap garrison of 5000 in Kuching, anyway."

Six Argylls and three Royal Marines interned at Padang were among 500 men sent in May 1942 to Burma then Thailand in the 'Sumatra Battalion' under Captain Dudley Apthorp of the Royal Norfolks. Sgt Robert Kerr joined this group in Thailand and departed for Saigon with them in April 1944. Apthorp described him as "an NCO of outstanding conscientiousness and ability."

Lt Ian Stonor of the Argylls had been Percival's ADC throughout the campaign. He was personally told by Percival to escape at the last minute. It should be recorded at this point, that Percival himself had been ordered out, but he was determined, unlike Wavell or the AIF 8th Division commander Major-General Gordon-Bennett, to stay with his soldiers. Percival behaved with courage and dignity in captivity and championed the cause of the Far East Prisoners of War and local units such as Dalforce in the post-war years.

Stonor boarded the RN Motor Launch ML 310 with eight other officers and thirty-five men. The escapers included Rear-Admiral Ernest 'Jackie' Spooner, Air-Vice Marshal Conway Pulford and Commander P.L. Frampton. These three officers were among nineteen who died in March 1942 after the wrecked launch beached on the malaria-infested island of Tjebia. Eventually Stonor, together with Lt Richard Pool RN of *Repulse,* chose captivity rather than death on the island. They soon found themselves back in Singapore and were taken to Changi POW Camp.

Tiny Gordon had left Tyersall camp on February 11th to lead thirty Argylls in keeping Keppel Harbour open and the flow of refugees moving to the evacuation ships. He spent the final days before the surrender with Sgt Major MacLaren RASC operating a ferry the *Sir Theodore Fraser,* off Changi. They rescued an Argyll raiding party from Pulau Ubin Island, then on Black Friday February 13th, Gordon was ordered to take Indian Army gunners off another island and drop them behind Japanese lines. This operation was then called off and Gordon was still on the ferry off Keppel Harbour when the surrender came on February 15th.

Gordon proceeded to Moro Island where he met Captain Ivan Lyon of the Gordon Highlanders and took on eighty escapees. He headed for Rengat in Sumatra then made his way by land to Padang to assist Major Jock Campbell (later of SOE) evacuate escapees along the organised route across Sumatra: Tembilahan to Rengat then on to Ayer Molek by boat; Ayer Molek to Taluk, then to Sawahloento by bus and from there to Padang by train. Lyon and Campbell were later to mastermind the successful Operation Jaywick, an April 1943 attack on Singapore shipping, followed by the disastrous Operation Rimau of October 1944 in which Lyon and his entire unit lost their lives.

At one stage, as a former RAF pilot, Tiny Gordon contemplated taking a Dutch aircraft and escaping but the Dutch Air Force proved uncooperative. Relations with the Dutch at this time and in captivity were not good. Prisoners of war were later to call them "the Cheese Eaters" and when the cheese ran out, "the Dog Eaters."

In March 1942, with the Japanese closing in, Gordon was selected as one of ten escapers to try to reach Ceylon on a 50 ft. fishing prahu called the *Setia Berganti.* The crew included Colonel Francis Dillon MC IASC and Edward Hooper RMNVR Harbour Master, Singapore and a former chief officer of the Kedah. Dillon had escaped Singapore under orders on February 13th and stayed in Sumatra to organise escapes until Lt Colonel Alan Warren RM arrived and took over from him. He gave Dillon the money to purchase the prahu, and wished him 'God Speed' while he himself remained behind, particularly at risk from the Kempetei (Japanese secret police) because of his guerilla party activities. He passed himself off later as a different Warren, and as soon as the opportunity came he left on a work party to the Burma railway.

The voyage began on March 16th with a compass, a small-scale chart and a school atlas to assist navigation. On April 4th, a thousand miles into their journey across the Indian Ocean they had the misfortune to run into three Japanese naval tankers full of Japanese marines. These tankers were accompanying Admiral Nagumo's carrier group whose aircraft attacked Colombo the following day. Gordon and his friends were returned to Singapore where he joined 256 other Argylls in Changi POW camp. Sgt Percy Evans was at hand to conjure up a pair of boots and socks for the barefooted Tiny Gordon.[11] Dillon's future role would be to save many a man's life on the Burma Railway by his patient persistence.

Mike Blackwood, a keen yachtsman, escaped from Singapore taking with him 43 passengers including Brigadier Archie Paris and Major Angus MacDonald. On the motor launch the *Cecelia* they reached Rengat in Sumatra and met other Argylls. Also in this group was Sgt Willie 'Mac' MacDonald who had been severely wounded at Dipang and was described by a fellow Argyll as "a real Highland gentleman." Others in Sumatra included Slim River escapers Cpl Walter Gibson, L.Cpl Jock Gray and Captain Dougie Broadhurst. Broadhurst explains: "At Padang, I met Brigadier Paris who had commanded the 12th Indian Brigade. He told me that he was going to India and said he would take along Gibson and Gray with him. And he said as I was a Cantonese/Malay speaker, I would be much more useful if I went to Java where there was still resistance and I might be of some help there. So Gibson, Gray and I separated." [12]

Paris boarded the ill-fated 1035 tons Dutch KPM island steamer *Rosenbaum* with eight Argylls who set up bren guns on the deck to combat air-attack. The ship left Padang on February 26th. Crowded with over five hundred evacuees including most of the Cecelia party and many Army colonels and majors, the *Rosenbaum* was torpedoed on March 2nd within reach of Ceylon. Sgt Willie MacDonald was killed instantly in the explosion as he slept on the deck next to Gibson. The other Argylls found themselves amongst struggling survivors in the water. Major Angus MacDonald, from a wealthy Argyllshire family, died on a raft the following day, supposedly after drinking from a bottle of brandy and going mad. Gray also died on another raft.

According to Gibson, Brigadier Paris, weak from internal injuries after being dragged down by the sinking ship, and clothed only in a borrowed shirt, organised 135 survivors in and around a lifeboat 28 feet long by 8 feet beam at its widest point and built to hold only 28 persons. Paris soon died and the brave Blackwood slipped into unconsciousness the following morning and drowned. Blackwood had swum around in the sea for a whole day before joining "the Boat" and had been terribly sunburned.

Many days went by; some went mad and others contemplated cannibalism. Drummer Hardie was killed assisting Gibson to quieten some apparently murderous British survivors. Some Javanese sailors did resort to cannibalism. After twenty-six days and a thousand miles adrift, an emaciated Gibson, a Chinese girl, Doris Lim and three mad Javanese sailors ended up on the coral island of Sipora, a hundred miles from Padang. They were thought to be the only survivors of the *Rosenbaum* though in fact two other Javanese sailors were picked up by an Allied ship and taken for questioning in Bombay.

Gibson became a prisoner-of-war in Sumatra and tells how he survived a further sinking in 1944 – that of the cargo liner *Van Waerwijck*, an old KPM vessel scuttled at Tanjong Priok in March 1942 but salvaged by the Japanese under the name *Harrikiku Maru*. This vessel was sunk on June 26th 1944 by the British submarine *HMS Truculent* in the Straits of Malacca en route from Belawan Deli (the port of Medan) to Singapore where Gibson ended the war. Doris Lim was murdered near Padang in early 1945 by her Chinese husband, a peasant farmer she had married to get away from a clinic where she was nursing. [13]

Some Argylls who knew Gibson well are sceptical about the full truth of his story which first received newspaper publicity when he appeared as a witness at a post-war court hearing to determine if Major Angus MacDonald, the heir to a large fortune through a wealthy aunt, was in fact deceased. In 1954 Gibson wrote his memoirs 'Highland Laddie.' His story received much attention from the Sunday Express and he subsequently had a second book published using a ghostwriter.

The first doubt about Gibson was concerning his rank. He was a Corporal but he told the Press he was a Sergeant, and later claimed to have been commissioned Lieutenant and even Captain. Surviving Argylls say this is nonsense. They say that Gibson was a little man, a former Mossbank borstal boy from Glasgow who liked to stroll around the barracks and model himself on the Argylls energetic 2 i/c Major Lindsay Robertson. Gibson was certainly intelligent and had been in the Brigade

Intelligence Section until a misdemeanour put him back with the battalion. The battalion record book shows that he was demoted from Lance Sergeant to Corporal at this time and was never reinstated. One Argyll says: "Do you know what most of us think happened to that wee Chinese girl who was in the boat with Gibson? We think he ate her!"

In September 1945, from a hospital bed in Rangoon, Major Mali Gairdner, recovering from malnutrition and jungle sores, told a visiting friend: "If you see Cpl W.G. Gibson, Cpl 'Bloody Hoot' Gibson, wearing two pips on his shoulders, get them off him!" (Appropriately a 'Hoot Gibson' was a cowboy character in the silent movies)

After the war, Gibson posed as an officer and was believed to have worn an MC ribbon on a blue Argyll patrol jacket. It was said that each time he promoted himself, he added another 'G' to his initials. Although he lived in Paisley after the war he avoided contact with former Argylls. These doubts about Gibson are shared by John Hedley, a rubber planter in the Johore Volunteer Engineers, who had been commissioned into the General List on December 18th 1941 and attached to the 1st Mysore Infantry (State Force). Hedley was taken prisoner in Padang on March 17th 1942 and imprisoned at first in the old Dutch barracks. Sometime in April, Gibson arrived at the camp looking no more emaciated than the other prisoners. He claimed to be a 2nd Lieutenant "commissioned in the field" and had stories of Javanese cannabilism. He wasn't taken seriously but stayed with the officers and claimed to often join in rough games with the Australian officers. There were only two Australian officers in the camp. Later Gibson was in a party sent to Glugor camp in Medan.

Hedley also witnessed the activities of a group of Argylls in the camp who showed none of Jockie Bell's inhibition after Slim River about killing and skinning a goat. Imprisoned in a room with a high, iron-barred window this group of Argylls looked out onto a large open space where various animals wandered at will. They put together a rope lassoo and practiced catching any passing animal, whether chicken or goat, by the leg. There were two loose bars in the cookhouse window, and two of the Jocks would nip out between these, grab the beast and fetch it back in. All in the space of a few minutes "almost before we'd become hungry," they had it skinned and in the cooking pot with not a trace of feather or fur to be seen.

Douglas Broadhurst, the Straits Police officer who had parted company with Gray and Gibson at Padang, boarded a Dutch tramp steamer, the *Van Twist,* which took him to Tjilatjap on the south coast of Java. There he immediately picked up another ship, the *Zaandam* to Fremantle. After arriving in Australia he had many adventures in Timor and the Philippines with Australia's SRD (Services Reconnaissance Detachment) before joining SOE's Force 136 and parachuting back into Malaya in May 1945 to link up with MPAJA units.

CAPTIVITY

In Singapore on the night of February 15th, the surviving Plymouth Argylls experienced the relief of still being alive, together with the shame and uncertainty of impending captivity. Civvy Cameron was on a hillside to the rear of Tyersall Camp, overlooking the Bukit Timah Road. When he saw a white flag appearing on the road he and his companions took out the firing pins of their rifles and machine gun and dumped them. They headed for the centre of town where they met Cpl Budd and some other Argylls near Anderson Bridge. In a nearby hall they got something to eat.

According to Brigadier Stewart's history of the campaign, the Plymouth Argylls on February 17th did not, like other battalions, march the 15 miles from Tyersall to Changi. In defiance of Japanese instructions, they embussed in their few surviving vehicles, and with Captain Lang RM and others ahead of them in a staff car and Piper Stuart piping them on the way, most made their journey into captivity with a degree of comfort, passing the foot-slogging Gordons and Manchesters on the way. Passing comments are not recorded. The Japanese, mightily impressed by the striking red and white hats of the Royal Marine officers, did nothing to stop Captain Lang's stately progress.

However, survivors who were there dispute this. If Stewart's version is correct then Cpl Charles Miller clearly 'missed the bus'. Captain Aylwin, who had helped himself to a few shirts and other items in Percy Evans' store, advised Miller to look around Tyersall's remaining huts for anything that might be useful later. In a deserted IAMC officers' hut he found a good pair of shoes before joining the marching columns to Changi.[14] Maurice Edwards also remembers finding "rich pickings" in these huts. He was with Piper Charles Stuart who retrieved his bagpipes, probably the only ones to survive the fire, and opened a tin of treacle, using the contents to lubricate the bag. Eric Moss, a former Pipe Major, explains this practice: "You use syrup, or sugar and water, to season the pipe bag which is made of sheepskin and kept soft by treating it with syrup. There are various concoctions, but Lyles Golden Syrup is the best. Otherwise the bag gets dry and fails to be airtight. The syrup is applied to the inside of the bag, pushing the bottom of the bag forward towards the top and working it with your hand. You kept your pipes in a box, but in the very hot weather in India you put a wet towel around them which you had to keep wet. In India we got a regimental bootmaker to make bags of leather, thinking to save some money, but it wasn't as good as sheepskin."[15]

It is clear that the main body of surviving Plymouth Argylls led by Captain Aylwin actually marched out of Tyersall Park, piped on the way by Piper Stuart. They had gone less than a mile when twelve lorries laid on by Captains Lang and Slessor drew up and many were able to make use of this transport to Changi. However, Duncan Ferguson, who was an Argyll driver, is adamant that he marched all the way to Changi with his friends Ptes Willie Eckford and Spud Thomson.

What is certain is that as the Argylls and Marines marched out of Tyersall they passed hundreds of disarmed soldiers from other British and Australian units who were called to attention and cheered them as a mark of respect. Lee Kuan Yew, the first Prime Minister of Singapore, recalled in his recent memoirs 'The Singapore Story' how much he admired the style of the Argylls when, even in defeat, "they held themselves erect and marched in time."

Eric Moss was still at Keppel Harbour on February 17th: "I had ended up at the Docks and there were quite a number of troops around the railway station. I got all of these people organised and decided I wasn't going to march to Changi. We managed to get hold of two or three trucks and we roared off up the road. It was heart breaking to see those thousands of troops marching along the road. The Japs didn't stop us."

The Japanese were ill prepared for managing so many prisoners. Eric Moss says: "When we assembled in Changi village the Japs weren't prepared for it, it happened so quickly, nor did they expect to take so many prisoners, so our General Staff from Fort Canning remained intact and the Japs merely gave them orders. We were in the village and we were sharing with the Marines at this time, so we were in Changi School and so were all six Marine officers."

Changi POW camp, not to be confused with the nearby Changi jail where civilian internees were incarcerated, was a large area of some 6.5 square miles on the eastern tip of Singapore Island centering on a 4-barracks complex. Some 53,000 British and Australians were crowded into an area designed to accommodate 3,600 men. At first there was no running water or electricity. Each unit was confined to a tiny area of living accommodation. The Argylls and Marines with other naval personnel were briefly in the school in Changi village before being shifted into the Changi village shops area.[16] Duncan Ferguson and Civvy Cameron found some hens left in coops by the evacuated villagers. In the school Eric Moss found a Bible which he keeps to this day though it could have been used in captivity for cigarette paper. Cigarette smoking helped lessen the pangs of hunger and Bibles were a valuable source of paper but it had a bitter taste – some said this was the arsenic in the paper. Boredom, hunger and intense discomfort were the common feelings in Changi POW camp.

Marine Peter Dunstan's billet was in a Chinese shop house right opposite where the Changi Meridian Hotel now stands. He shared a room with Cpl Norman Overington RM and Cpl W. Farrell of the Argylls.[17] The officers, including a recuperating Lt Douglas Weir, were in the next two shops. Douglas Weir had spent the two weeks after the surrender among the wounded in the Fullerton Building before being transported to Changi's Roberts Hospital in an ambulance. At the time he was among hundreds of prisoners who went down in a severe outbreak of dysentery. Once thought to be out of danger he was discharged and his friend Hubert Strathairn took him to join the Argyll officers in the shophouses and took care of him. Peter Dunstan acting as a medical orderly gave Douglas a very powerful enema for which he was not to be forgiven!

Sgt Percy Evans brought two lorry loads of food from Tyersall to Changi but some Argylls did not feel too grateful: "He put them into this shop they took over in Changi village, and he slept in the storeroom. He'd dish out a tin of pilchards between sixteen men – but he'd be keeping his friends sweet. Joe Russell reported him. He and I had been keeping a note. Joe handed it to the HQ Sergeant Major but we never heard a word more."

Also in Roberts Hospital in the care of Captain Meldrum RAMC was Alexandra Hospital survivor Nick Carter. On his arrival at Changi he had gone down with cerebral malaria and encephalitis. On his recovery he returned to being a cook for the officers: "I've made a five course meal from rice alone. I used to bake bread from rice. We used either some sugar or red palm oil and mixed it with ground rice and let it ferment just with the natural yeast, then take some out and mix it with more ground rice and that makes a dough you put in a little tin to rise and then into hot embers. Rice cooking, for those who knew how to cook it dry and preferred it that way, was done in the big kuali pots, round, heavy cast iron cooking pots about 30 inches in diameter and 12 inches deep in the centre. To cook rice you built up a fireplace of stones on which to place the kuali, lit the fire underneath, washed the rice, put it in the kuali, added water to just above the rice and boiled it. Then you covered it with sacking and allowed it to steam.

"Rice has a red skin – the husk, the polishings as it's called, left over from making the white rice. You mixed this with the dough to make the bread because that was the vitamins. After using eggs we would break and grind up the shells and send that to the hospitals for the calcium. And when you cook rice in the kuali it leaves a burned crust round the pot. We scraped that up, rolled it up like parchment, and sent it to the hospitals. It was good for dysentery."

Maurice Edwards, who was clerk of the battalion office in Changi camp, remembers: "The village cinema was just at the rear of the shop in which I was situated which was the Detachment Office. Here very soon after we arrived a concert party was rehearsing a show. I distinctly remember a tenor who was constantly rehearsing the prelude to 'Il Pagliachi." Over the road at the last shop the officers were situated. I did not know it at the time, but two new arrivals from Padang were a Naval Commander and a mysterious Lieutenant Colonel of Marines. They were Commander C.C. Alexander and Colonel A.F. Warren. They were lying very low."[18]

In the early weeks in Changi many Argylls and Royal Marines separated from their unit in the fighting, returned. Marine Lenny of *Prince of Wales,* after being discharged from a Singapore hospital found himself with the civilian internees in Changi jail, but was returned after some weeks without too much trouble. Pte Jimmy Anderson, the sole survivor of the Dairy Farm massacre, also arrived. He had been rescued, nursed and smuggled into Changi by some unknown brave Chinese.

For some those early weeks in Changi POW camp were a time of reflection on the causes of defeat. One Argyll lieutenant commented to a fellow POW in the Volunteers that he believed the defeat was caused by officers of many units spending too much time in clubs and gaining no knowledge of Malaya. He also believed that many officers refused to leave HQ and tried to be posted away. He bitterly commented that in the Argylls they shot officers who refused to lead them.[19] "Too many army people away at the dancing and that. Cock ups!" said another Argyll in later years.

Food and medicine shortages quickly became acute in spite of widespread scavenging across the Changi area and by outside work-parties sent out to clean up Singapore, disposing of the bodies, the wrecked vehicles, handling live ammunition and clearing mine fields, and building the road across the Golf Course to the Japanese victory shrine.

'Scavengers' were to witness some of the atrocities committed against the Chinese population, particularly the terrible *Sook Ching* massacres of thousands of Chinese along Changi Spit and elsewhere. They were able to rescue several young men left for dead by the Japanese, and give them new identities as POWs.

In Changi men began to die – first the badly wounded then the victims of dysentery, beriberi and diphtheria. In the first seven months over four hundred died including 25 year old Marine David Mills who "put up a long and great fight and weighed only 49lbs when we buried him." Many of the Royal Marines like Peter Dunstan and Charles Miller were big men and well over six foot tall. There was little food to sustain them. Lt C.R. McArthur, was put in charge of making "the battalion brew" for the Men. This was a heavily diluted Vitamin B drink made in large tiger beer bottles: 4oz. of the brew was issued to each man daily. This recipe required 30 gallons of water into which went 14 heaped teaspoonfuls of coarse ground rice, 11 teaspoonfuls of sugar, 2 of salt and 2 of ground peanuts. Yeast came from the hospital, and wild berries could be added. The mixture was then boiled for 5 hours, added to the bottom third of the previous day's brew, and two-thirds of it was issued.

In Changi there was also a very unpleasant infection called scrotal dermatitis, more popularly known as "Red Balls" or "Changi Goolies." In his recent memoirs

Keith Mitchell recollects an incident in Robert's Hospital: "One hilarious incident nearly caught our dour MO off guard and he had to turn away rather than be seen to smile. A large Scot with an accent almost thick enough to need an interpreter, was brought into the ward and told to get into bed. Next morning the MO arrived at the chap's bed, and the poor laddie, lying rigidly to attention, answered the Doctor's question in a loud voice, 'Hit's no me guts, Sor! Hit 's me bollicks! They're giving me Hell! Sor!' In other words this extremely regimental Scottish soldier had scrotal dermatitis, another very nasty vitamin deficiency disease, and he was possibly in the wrong ward."

The MO made no comment to the patient but turned aside to the medic sergeant, telling him to put this man on an ounce of Marmite a day, and moved on to the next patient.

"The next day Jock was obviously suffering discomfort and complained that the offending 'bollicks' were 'much worrse, Sor!' The MO said 'Let me have a look at them' and the poor fellow's raw scrotum was revealed, liberally anointed with brown, salty Marmite. To his way of thinking sore testicles needed ointment, and no one had told him to eat the stuff!"

Meanwhile, at Pudu jail, the Kuala Lumpur civilian prison built in the 1890s, conditions were far worse with a terrible death-rate among Argylls already weakened by jungle fevers and dysentery after the Slim River debacle. The Pudu prisoners were segregated: Indian, British, Australian, and put three to a cell. The Argylls were in C Block; the Australians in A Block. Of a thousand prisoners in Pudu about a hundred died within six months including thirty-seven of just over two hundred Argyll captives.

Many had been very fit men before their jungle ordeal. They included Battalion boxing champion Patrick 'Sophie' Stewart, the last of the Slim River escapers brought in. They are buried today at Cheras Military War Cemetery, Kuala Lumpur.

Captain David Boyle, 2 i/c the Pudu Argylls, occupied his mind learning Japanese. Major Gairdner attempted to get some control of a situation in which military discipline was rapidly deteriorating. Gairdner, who was approaching fifty, was a typical pre-war regular officer, used to an afternoon nap and a few chota-pegs, he was unprepared for war and lacked authority and energy. The surviving Argylls became increasingly "hard to control." Jockie Bell was still angry with David Boyle. He felt that Boyle had not helped him and had left him behind after the Slim River breakout. Jockie decided not to talk to him or respond to him until an old soldier, Harry Paton, took him to one side and warned him: "If the Captain wants you to go and see him, you go! Otherwise you lose your credits after the war."

Captured near Klang, Jockie was one of three men who collapsed with malaria on arrival at Pudu. They were put in an isolation hut in the charge of an Indian Army colonel who possessed a bottle of quinine. Jockie survived but the other two – an old soldier, Dinky Day, and Lee Cobb, a Cockney – died as they lay on either side of him. John Crone of the Regimental police also died. Jockie remembers the death in Pudu of Peter Corr, an orphan from Glasgow and a "wee chap, thin, real pigeon-chested type," but a man who under fire in the north of Malaya had carried the wounded Sgt James Wailes, a very big fellow, on his back to safety. "Peter was one of the first of our lads to die in Pudu jail. Some boys just lay down and died. They said the Japs were just savages and they'd kill us all anyway. They wouldn't eat the rice and they died, and this wee man was one of them. They wouldn't let us bury them anywhere outside, just in the garden there, wrapped in a blanket."

Also in Pudu was the oldest soldier in the battalion, Old "Crasher" Private Christie who at Tyersall Camp had been the equipment repairer and didn't leave the barracks much. He had a long reputation for good behaviour and "had good conduct stripes from his wrist right up to his elbows." Jockie Bell remembers: "He was that old when he was in Pudu, the Japs used to say 'Papa soldier, you sit in the shade and the young ones will do the work!' We buried a boy of 17 in Kuala Lumpur, a boy called Gibson, and the Japs used to say 'You baby soldier,' and they put him in the shade. That boy died – all overcome with emotion and depression."

Sometimes they were able to scrounge food while in work parties or unloading Japanese lorries. An officer prisoner, in civilian life the owner of a Glasgow timber mill, advised the Jocks to look particularly for books and blankets. They even managed to obtain a piano from a house near the prison and hold some early morning sing-songs and later evening concerts. Jockie "Ting-a-ling" Bell felt too depressed to sing, but he remembers the perfect voice of Peter Holmes: "I just wasn't happy, so I didn't sing in Pudu concerts, but I sang up in the jungle with a few other lads, Stan Roberts, Adam Baxter and John McFadyen. Hymns, 'Abide With Me' and all that, just lying there in the dark, no lights. We got hymn singing at Sunday School. My father was a great singer and a good musician too, but we thought that if we learned to play an instrument we'd be called sissies, but I was singing ever since school. At Pudu there was a chap from Greenock, Pte Holmes. He sang at a concert there, no musical instruments. His turn was a Gracie Fields song 'As You Go' and he would go way up like her. It was announced that he was going into the so-called hospital next day, and he died, poor boy."

Geoff Mowat of the MCS, one of the Volunteers, remembers a real morale raiser as POWs sang the charming "Moon Over Malaya" and other popular songs.

CSM Sandy McTavish went down with dysentery and was "on his way out." His life was saved by Hoostie McNaught who somehow acquired the necessary drugs. Big Jimmy Anderson, who had done such useful bayonet work in Bal Hendry's attack on the railway station, was also in Pudu. Bell explains: "Him and Big Dolly Grey, and Geordie Russell and Mackinlay, and two Irish boys, they had a great job with the Japs – it was hard work carrying 2 cwt. bags of rice but they got well rewarded, thieving coffee, beans, jam, cheese and MacConnochies (tinned meat) and they gave us part of the loot."[20]

Sgt Alex McDougall of B Company took food and comfort to a lone woman prisoner whose husband had been killed as they tried to escape the Japanese advance.

With the agreement of the Japanese commandant, Alex was positioned in a cell nearby to act as a guard for her. The woman was in a very bad way and was eventually taken away by some nuns. He doubted that she survived.

Pte Stan Roberts remembers: "In Pudu they beat an Argyll to death when they were searching us for anything we were trying to smuggle in. My mucker was Smudger Smith (Pte W. Smith) from Dundee. He was in Pudu but when we left we got separated and I never saw him again. We had a great padre in Pudu, from Cambridge, Padre Noel Duckworth – he helped us a lot, he could stick up for you against the Japs. He wore a blue surplice and took the burials so they knew he was a padre. They slapped him around a bit, but he called them every name under the sun."

Another outstanding Padre during the Captivity was Henry Babb MBE of the East Surreys/British Battalion. Babb was a terrific footballer who had played for

Corinthians. Civvy Cameron says, "He was an exceptionally good Padre too. He tried to stop a lot of beatings going on and took a lot of punishment."

In April 1942 the surviving Taiping jail prisoners captured in the fighting in the north of Malaya were moved south to Pudu. Some of these were Slim River captives taken north of the river. They included Ian Primrose.

Eric Moss explains how units gradually thinned out, a process that was to continue in Thailand: "Then the Japs decided that we'd start work in Singapore and they would tell British Command, 'We want 450 men tomorrow to move into Singapore,' so they would get their heads together, so many from the Gunners, so many from the RASC and so many from wherever. Well, you'd find yourself with a mixed bunch by the time you got to Singapore. Then you'd move from there to somewhere else and you'd be another mixed bunch so gradually you got thinned out."

In Singapore, Cpl Charles Miller RM was among several Plymouth Argylls transferred to Kranji POW camp on the north coast of Singapore near to where the Commonwealth War Cemetery and Kranji Memorial now stand. From here the prisoners were marched each day to the four hundred feet Bukit Batok Hill, north west of Bukit Timah village. Here, together with Australian prisoners, they constructed the road and 121 steps to the Japanese shrine overlooking the Plymouth Argylls battlefield. The prisoners also erected a ten-foot wooden cross to commemorate their own dead. This work was completed in September 1942. En route to Bukit Batok Hill, through Bukit Panjang village, the POWs regularly saw decapitated heads on poles in the Bukit Timah area. They averted their eyes so never really knew if they were the same heads each day.[21]

The Syonan Times (the name given to the Straits Times newspaper during the Japanese Occupation, and pronounced 'Shunan') of September 11th 1942, reported the official opening of the shrine known as the Syonan Chureito. It also reported the erection of a large cross behind the main shrine to commemorate the Allied war dead: "Memorial erected to fallen enemy soldiers. Spirit of Bushido reflected in our Army's gesture." Such gestures of the spirit of Bushido did not extend to the prisoners of war and civilian population of Singapore.

Other Argylls and Marines were detailed to move to Havelock Road Camp which briefly had the unusual distinction of having its own Masonic Lodge until the Japanese dispersal of POWs to Thailand put a stop to it. Separated from Havelock Road by a stretch of open ground was River Valley Camp. The POWs were in these camps to clear up and repair the damaged city, particularly the badly bombed China Town area. Although contact between the two camps was forbidden there was communication. Captain Eric Moss, then in Havelock Road Camp, tells the story of how he was able to recover some of the Argyll Silver including the Communion Silver that had been first used by the 93rd in the 1812 Cape of Good Hope campaign: "I was called to meet Pte Finlay McLachlan (Moss's batman, also a battalion drummer) who had made his way across from River Valley Camp.

"He told me that some of the men who had been working the day before in Singapore City, had looted some boxes in the godown and come in with some silver which belonged to the 93rd. McLachlan said that he had been round collecting most of the stuff but there was one chap who wouldn't hand it over. So we got past the Japs and went over to River Valley Road to see this man. He had quite a bit of silver including the Regimental Communion Cup. So I sent for his officer who happened to have been in peacetime an Episcopal Minister in Edinburgh, Major McNeill (Padre George McNeill) was his name. Well, when this man refused to give it back even when McNeill had spoken to him, McNeill grabbed it from him. I kept it and carried it with me for the next three years and when I came home I handed it back. Unfortunately the flagon had to be buried under the airfield at Kanchanaburi, but it was less important. It's still there."[22]

When he was sent north to Thailand, Eric Moss hid the silver in the tight sleeve of a large raincoat he had found in Singapore. He distributed some for safekeeping among fellow officers at Kanchanaburi and buried some items. Also in Thailand he was to save the life of Pte Finlay McLachlan in a very simple way: when McLachlan went down with cerebral malaria and the Doctors said he was going to die, Moss produced a small tin of condensed milk which was spoonfed to McLachlan. Amazingly it did the trick and McLachlan recovered.

At Changi, senior officers above the rank of Lt Colonel were in a party to depart for Formosa. Lt Ian Stonor accompanied Percival in this group but was not to remain with him for long. Stonor was a POW in Formosa, Kyushu in Japan then Mukden in Manchuria where he was eventually liberated by the Russians in August 1945. Another party, 'A' Force under Brigadier Arthur Varley AIF, was sent to Burma on May 14th 1942.

In June 1942 rumours began to circulate of a large-scale movement of prisoners-of-war up-country, most believed to new camps around Penang or Kota Bahru. Some sick men decided to go, for the prospects seemed brighter than staying at Changi. Others, like Cpl Reg Warn RM were too injured to go. He was paralysed from the waist down as a result of wounds and had to drag himself around on his elbows. Before the departure north, Captain Aylwin instructed Warn to draw up a detailed record for him of *Prince of Wales* Marines. Few expected Warn to survive but some twenty years later, a much recovered, indeed sprightly Warn surprised all present when he delivered the required Documents to Aylwin at a FEPOW reunion at the Festival Hall, London.

On June 18th 1942, 600 men known as B Battalion left Changi under Major Paddy Sykes RASC. Four groups of similar size followed at two-day intervals. On June 22nd the first party of 100 Argylls left for Thailand in a work party of 600 men led by Major Jack Hyslop of the Argylls. The party included Tiny Gordon, weakened by a recent appendix operation, Captain Tam Slessor and Captain Aylwin. In the words of Gordon "packing was a simple business; I had only to wrap up my blanket, a pair of shorts; two tin cans and a toothbrush."[23]

Some of the Marines including Tom Webber were in this party. One survivor comments that they "fell hook, line and sinker" for the Japanese interpreter's flowery description of the holiday camp living conditions and plentiful food awaiting them in Thailand. They marched to Singapore railway station, relieved to be leaving the over-crowded deteriorating conditions in Changi. Each man was issued with two balls of cooked rice for the first stage of the journey.

A shock awaited the party at Singapore railway station: they were herded into metal rice wagons – sometimes called salt wagons – measuring 30 ft by 8 ft with 30 men and their baggage to a wagon. Fortunately the sliding door was not barred.

The journey lasted four terrible days and nights with the temperature and the stink unbelievable. Men shuffled round the wagons to take turns to get a breath of fresh air at the doorway. At a few stops they were allowed out to relieve themselves and were able to make some contact with the local population. They crossed the Thai border at Padang Besar. Eventually they arrived at a little Thai town called Ban Pong. Half a mile from the town they found not the "holiday camp" they had been sold at Changi but a jungle clearing stocked with bamboo for them to build their own camp of attap huts for 3,000 prisoners with a high surrounding bamboo fence.

Back at Changi the Japanese decided to put an end to escape attempts. There seems to have been a definite change of tone towards the POWs since the departure of Lt. General Yamashita from Singapore. On September 1st 1942 four prisoners recaptured after an escape attempt were taken from Roberts hospital still wearing their red dressing gowns. One died in the truck; the others were shot in a botched execution in front of senior British and AIF officers.

Two days later, following the refusal of POWs to sign 'no escape' pledges, the 15,204 prisoners including 3000 hospital cases, were herded with all their belongings into Selerang barracks square, an area of 150 x 250 yards perimeter. There were no toilet facilities and bore holes were dug. There was a certain novelty and daring about relieving yourself on the sacred parade ground. "We claim to be the only Marines who used the middle of the parade ground and never got on a charge," says Peter Dunstan.

The ordeal eventually ended at mid-day on September 5th when, faced with a deteriorating health and hygiene situation, the POWs signed the 'no escape' pledges under duress, many with unmentionable or comic signatures such as 'U Bastard' and 'Mickey Mouse of the Argyll and Sutherland Highlanders.'

In October 1942, following the Selerang barracks incident, more Argylls and Royal Marines went north on the terrible journey to Ban Pong. Marine Maurice Edwards in Group 4, W Battalion, commenced his journey on October 26th 1942 together with Captain Lang, Lts Sheridan and Davis, Cpl Norman Overington and Marine Peter Dunstan. Colonel Warren, Commander Alexander and Lt Poole RN were also in this party. They found Ban Pong camp heavily flooded with men liable to fall into the hidden latrine pits. Excrement and flies were everywhere. The bamboo bedboards on which the men slept were only two or three inches above the water. Captain Eric Moss found Ban Pong particularly awful: "I was appalled at how filthy Ban Pong Camp was. I went to the latrine, and I said to myself, 'What the hell are they throwing rice away for?' But then I noticed this 'rice' was crawling all over my boots. It was maggots."

Sgt Terry Brooks RM remembers running away from a large python in his hut at Ban Pong. A few months later he would have killed and eaten it.

From Ban Pong each party proceeded 46 miles northwards, night marching. Many men were sick with dysentery and malaria. All were short of safe drinking water. Eric Moss describes their journey: "On the way we stayed one night at Tamuan. But it was an awfully long walk. It was hot weather and it was dry. A long, long column. The Chinese would come out and offer you water and fruit. The Chinese, not the Siamese."

Exhausted and beaten by their guards, they passed the village of Kanchanaburi and came down the banks of the River Kwai (more correctly Kwae Yai River). Here they were crammed aboard rice barges and towed up-river to Chungkai on the Kwae Noi River. At Chungkai, the first June party of POWs had built their own bamboo and attap huts with split bamboo sleeping platforms. Each hut had 200 Occupants with an area 6ft by 2ft for each man to sleep on.

Eric Moss describes the local boatmen and his arrival at Tarsao camp: "The Thai in the barge, the chap who drove the motor had a cigarette lighter that was like a piece of kapok in a tiny bamboo. There was a flint inside it and the sparks lit the kapok and you blew on it. Anyway, we marched on and eventually ended up in

Tarsao. That's where I saw the Japanese major come out of his tent to take Tenko. He was still in his pyjamas, with his suspenders holding his socks up, and over all that he had his sword. Oh! They were comical at times."

The main Royal Marine group eventually arrived at Konyu River camp. Lt Jim Davis, Sgts Gannon and Stokes of *Repulse* and Marine Maurice Edwards were among those here. Their first task was the building of the roadtrace and eventually the road further up the hillside. From here they were dispersed to other camps along the line. In such terrible camps men worked and died building a railway that was completed on October 17th 1943 – 260 miles of track linking Ban Pong to Thambyuzayat in Burma. The NCOs and Other Rank POWs were organised into battalions of 600 men with one officer per hundred men for command and administration purposes. Surplus officers were formed into two officer working battalions.

In October 1942 four hundred Pudu prisoners including 150 Argylls under Captain Boyle came north, arriving on October 20th at Tamarkan where they built a bamboo fenced camp consisting of five long attap huts, each of which contained three hundred men. (Most camps were not fenced. There was nowhere to escape to, for most.) With the Argylls were men of the 80th Anti-Tank Regiment. Their rail journey from Kuala Lumpur was particularly unpleasant as Kenneth McLeod remembers: "The metal cars were unbearably hot, and they only had the door open six inches. We had to take it in turn to stand beside the door to get some air and some died on that journey."

The Japanese appeared not to have heard that wagons coming up from Singapore had the doors open following the first diabolical journey north. A handful of the Pudu Argylls sick and wounded, including Captain Drummond Hay, were sent south to Changi.

The British commanding officer at Tamarkan – or more correctly *Tha Makham* – camp, was the immaculate 18th Division Territorial Lt Colonel Philip 'Champagne' Toosey, CO 135th Field Regiment RA, who was said to exercise some influence over the Japanese. Boyle was appointed Toosey's adjutant and acted as interpreter curiously replacing a fluent Japanese speaking officer who was also an Argyll with a sound reputation for standing up to the Japanese. This was Captain Gordon Skinner, a former businessman in Japan who had served at Fortress Singapore HQ during the Campaign. As misunderstandings resulting from the language barrier were one of the greatest causes of trouble for the prisoners, Toosey's replacement of Skinner by Boyle as his interpreter, was a curious decision.

Toosey and Boyle believed that the best way to save lives was to 'win over' their captors, but this didn't always go down well with all fellow prisoners. Some regarded them as 'Jap Happy' and disliked Boyle not only talking to guards in Japanese, but at Nong Pladuk camp spending much of his time working with his captors in the guardroom. Maurice Edwards comments: "This appellation of being 'Jap Happy' fell frequently on those who had to take charge and had to make decisions for the common good. The highly principled officer would be useless as a Camp Senior Officer. There was no black or white as in normal life, always shades of grey."

It was perhaps easy for officers who stood on their dignity and avoided unpleasant contact with the Japanese to criticise men like Boyle and Toosey, but critics are correct when they point out that Toosey was never in one of the more terrible camps. He was always in areas where contact could be made with the local population and limited food and medicines could be obtained. One Argyll officer comments: "Toosey was a difficult person and very pompous. He took on Boyle as interpreter. Boyle did a really great job after the war on Erskine Hospital but I didn't rate him in captivity."

Certainly David Boyle did face animosity in captivity some of which was to linger on after the war. Some regarded him as egocentric and selfish. Another officer who did rate Boyle's performance in captivity nevertheless comments: "He was a selfish chap, a lot of one-upmanship about him..." However it was for his POW work that Boyle received an MBE, which perhaps illustrates the difficulty of POW leadership and relations with the captors.

Tamarkan (in Thai the name means 'Ferry of the Tamarin') is on the east bank of the Mae Klaung River, two miles north of its confluence with the Kwai and should not be confused with Tamuang Camp ten miles downstream. The railway ran along the north bank of the Kwai. The prisoners' first task was to bridge the Mae Klaung River with a 220 metre wooden bridge then a concrete and steel bridge. Lt Ian Primrose acted as foreman to the construction team.

Certainly compared with other camps such as Songkrai, where 1200 of 1600 prisoners died in three months, Tamarkan was a 'good' camp with only nine deaths among the 3500 prisoners between October 1942 and May 1943. "It was one of the better camps," explains Kenneth McLeod, "as the river boats could get up to it and you could get vegetables and sometimes cow, very lean, but we'd only been able to get rice further up-river."

However Tamarkan camp had its share of sadistic guards and beatings. In January 1943 two officers, Lt Eric Howard of 80th Anti-Tank Regiment and Captain Eugene Pomeroy of 2/12th Frontier Force Rifles, escaped from Tamarkan. They asked Kenneth McLeod's advice on how to travel through the jungle. He advised "travel light in order to travel as fast as possible, take a little rice and a container and live off the country."

The POWs waited for three weeks, hoping against hope that the two would make good their escape. Three weeks later they were returned to the camp, made to dig their own graves and 'executed', actually bayoneted to death. In January 1943 Captain Boyle had his arm broken and ribs crushed by a guard's rifle butt. This incident led to a POWs strike that was resolved when the Japanese commandant beat the offending guard.

Stephen Alexander, a subaltern in 135th Field Regiment RA, remembers the Argylls at Tamarkan: "Two subalterns, Kenny McLeod and Ian Primrose, were extrovert types who were viewed with wonder by the more uptight Territorials for their disdain of rank and for their chumminess with their men. They perfected a cabaret act of wrestling in mud to enliven the odd camp concert, and this provoked a mixture of hilarious laughter and misgivings of 'lese majeste'. As for their men, they too were not quite what we were used to. When I addressed one on a working party, he stared blankly at me as though I were speaking a foreign language; at my third repetition he was good enough to say in a pitying voice, 'We only take orders from our own officers'."

Other prisoners did not always welcome the arrival of Argylls at camps in Thailand. The Jocks' reputation for scrapping went before them. Jockie Bell, who is a slight man and was no scrapper, says, "As soon as you arrived at a new prison camp: 'Oh, hello lads. How's it gaeing?' See as soon as you spoke they were saying:

'Hello. Who are you? Where are you from?' 'We're Argylls.' Half the hut disappeared and you got plenty of space! OK, we got a bad name, supposed to be fighting, looting and thieving, but that's how we stuck together, because we mucked in and all helped one another and the only thieving was from the Japs."

A young Northumberland Fusilier, Harry Howarth, shared a Tamarkan hut with eighty Argylls including Robbie Burns enthusiast Drum Major 'Busty' Simpson from Bishopton, Glasgow. Jack Simpson, whose real name was Docherty, had entered the Argylls under age, lying about his age and name, changing his name to avoid his family tracing him and getting him out. His nickname, the same as Ian Stewart's, was acquired when he was a scrawny youth, but by the 1940s Simpson was "a fine, big chap, over six feet tall with broad shoulders."

Howarth comments that when others despaired the Argylls "never gave up." This was particularly apparent when it came to Christmas and Hogmanay celebrations when Thai whisky flowed freely. On the night of December 31st 1942 to the swirl of the pipes Argylls ran and reeled through the camp even entering the guardroom. Unfortunately a guard was assaulted and punched by three returning Jock revellers. Retribution was to follow. On New Year's morning all the prisoners were made to stand to attention in the sun until the culprits gave themselves up. Unfortunately few of the Argylls could remember their activities of the previous night! At first the Argylls and Gordons agreed to take the blame collectively. This wasn't accepted. Then an Argyll 'owned-up' – this wasn't accepted. Eventually, after five hours in the sun, three Argylls volunteered to 'own up.' It cost them the usual guardroom bashing and twelve hours standing in the sun the following day.

Eric Moss describes how he was able to repair his bagpipes so the Argyll officers could perform a foursome reel: "I had a set of pipes, but during the monsoon the bag had completely rotted away. I went to the cookhouse and asked if they were slaughtering a calf could I have the skin. Well, they had a calf and I got the skin. I had no idea how to take the hair off but I managed to get some alum, which is an astringent. God knows where I got it from, and some salt, and some people told me what to do. There was a lot of talent around among all those men you know, especially with the engineers and the Malayan civilians – the Volunteers. Anyway, the skin had to be dried in the sun, pegged out, and you scrape off the flesh then soak the skin in the water, alum and salt for three days, and dry it again, pinned down on a flat surface. You rub it with a stone to get the hair off, and manipulate it in your hands to soften it. Then I had to cut and sew it.

"You normally use some yards of hemp, fine hemp which is on a bobbin, so that you secure one end, and walk to and fro until you have sixteen strands. Then you have to twist it, and wax it until it's quite smooth. I had seen a bee or wasps' nest up in the roof of the hut, perhaps it was an old one because I didn't get stung, so I got wax from that. I took an old Indian prayer rug and picked the hemp out of that and stretched out the thread and waxed it. I found a Dutch shoemaker who sewed along the seam to make it airtight. Then I made the holes in the bag to fit in the five socks – the drones, chanter and blowstick – and bound the calfskin tight around these... I seasoned it with gula Malacca and yes, we did have a Foursome Reel."

One day, while at Kinsaiyok Camp, far north of Chungkai, Eric Moss had a surprise visit from Captain QM James Doherty who he hadn't seen since leaving Changi: "Doc had come up-river by barge on some errand or other. He had with him the remains of a letter from a girl I knew in Singapore. Its single sheet was broken into four pieces during its travels up and down the river in search of me, no doubt being read on its journeys by many eyes hungry for news."

The Japanese senior NCO at Tamarkan, described as "strict but fair" by Colonel Toosey, was Sgt. Saito. One FEPOW had quite a different view of him: "We, the ordinary squaddies, referred to him as 'the ball-breaking bastard.' He had a wooden cross built beside the bridge and men were tied to this for any misdemeanour. Sounds simple, but in reality it was vile torture. Men would be tied firmly by the wrists to the cross, leaving the hands free. The unfortunate victim was then made to hold a bucket of sand or water in each hand for anything up to twelve hours a day in the blazing hot sun."

From May 1943 Tamarkan became a base hospital and most fit Argylls were moved up into the jungle to further work. Even the sick men worked twelve to fourteen hours a day: carried out on their stretchers they broke rocks with their 4-lb. hammers to make egg-shaped ballast. The men worked bare-footed, wearing only loincloths. At times they worked eighteen hours a day.

Some Argylls faced unusual employment in captivity. Pte Jim McCutcheon, an India veteran in D Company who had been in the jungle after Slim River with Lt Colonel Robertson, had spent only a few days at Kanchanaburi when his captors asked for volunteers for diving. McCutcheon was a keen swimmer, had some experience of diving and had worked in Tiny Gordon's Dock party in Singapore. He volunteered and soon found himself diving down to Japanese ships sunk in and around Rangoon and working on the wharves. He was based with the Australians at Thambyuzyat camp in Burma.

As part of the Sumatra Battalion, L.Cpl Joe Lonsdale was with six other Argylls at the Burma end of the Death Railway. His companions were Cpl Alex McGowan, L.Cpl Jimmy McCall and Pte Derek Neame, all from HQ Company; also Ptes Jimmy Hynds, W.'Spud' Thompson and S.J Fitzpatrick, a bandsman and stretcher-bearer who distinguished himself as a medical orderly in the camps. They were sent by sea to Moulmein and then to Thambyuzayat in a party sent to replace the survivors of Brigadier Varley's 'A' Force who had left Singapore in May 1942.

The chance of obtaining a relatively easy job on the Railway was rare but for a short time Jockie Bell was employed as a Jap runner lower down the railway where there were engineers from Hashi Motors and they actually had electric lighting. He loaded and unloaded rails for the railway and carried phone messages and meals for the Japanese. Jockie was furious when an Argyll lieutenant came along one day, "shanghai-ed" him out of the job and sent him up-river. Jockie suffered Hellfire Pass and witnessed the linking of the railway on the Burma side. He was in a party led by Major Reggie Lees of the Gordon Highlanders, later the inspiration for the Colonel in George MacDonald Fraser's 'McAuslan' stories.

One Argyll, Joe Russell, enjoyed the distinction of three times being locked in a bamboo cage by his own side for refusing to cooperate with the Japanese. Duncan tells the story. "Wee Joe Russell was put in a cage but not by the Japs – by the British! Old Doc (QM Captain James Doherty MBE) sent for him. He was to go to the Jap camp as barber. He was a barber in Civvy Street. Joe said 'That'll be right! I'll go over there and I'll slit their effing throats, not shave them.' He was ordered to go but he refused. You want to hear the language of Joe, no matter who he was speaking to, it was eff this and every other word. He could have been speaking to the Queen and he'd have been using that language. 'I'm not going, I'm telling you – I'm not going!' So Old Doc – he wasn't the CO at that camp, it was an English officer – Doc tried. He said 'Come on Joe, keep the peace, on you go.' 'Doc, I'm telling you – I'm not going! I'm not bloody well shaving any Japs or cutting their hair!' So he got put in the cage. And all he was getting was plain rice and water. I think it was seven days he got."

Brought out of the cage, Joe still refused to be a barber for the Japanese and was returned to the cage for several days until Old Doc eventually talked him round. In the end Joe was happy enough with the food he got from his Japanese customers: "I finished up fit as a fiddle, and the extras at night I used to bring them out of camp for my pals! Great grub!"

Moved to another camp later, Joe went on strike again after he had returned from a twelve-hour day shift only to be ordered out immediately on a night shift, to make up the numbers. "I'm not effing going back out!" He was yet again back in the cages, and got a beating from the Japanese. But his protest did result in a change to the system.

Pte Tom 'Skin' McGregor, the wiry battalion flyweight-boxing champion and a fine athlete, at first got some satisfaction from swearing at his guards with a friendly smile on his face. They could not understand his words but soon caught on and bashed him. Some Japanese liked to pretend that they did not speak English. Eric Moss remembers approaching a recently arrived Japanese lieutenant to complain about officers having to work. The officer was known always to use an interpreter but this time he replied without any interpretation: "English, Irish, Scottish, Welsh – you'll bloody well all work!"

Sometimes prisoners were put into two lines and made to bash each other- they called this M and B's, after M and B (May and Baker) 693 sulphonamide pyridine tablets, effective against unpleasant ailments and particularly prized by the Japanese to treat venereal disease. In Kuching POW Camp in Borneo, Montgomery-Campbell remembers a particular Japanese officer with a problem: "We heard about the Jap rations officer, an insignificant little wretch, who did the buying at the local market. However, he frequented the local brothel and the inevitable happened. And rather than get cured at his own medical coverage, he came cap in hand to our medicos at the camp hospital. An agreement was made that provided he supplied the hospital with extra food and protein he would be put on the course of M and B 693 tablets – this was the prelude to Penicillin as we know it today.

"Everything was fine. The dysentery and malnutrition patients were coming along extremely well and we were told that this individual was also picking up. The medicos had a confab and they decided to stop treating the Jap as they had to consider the POWs in the main camp; thereupon this individual was told to contact the main camp for the tablets, as there were no more in the hospital. We needless to say had been warned. Yes! We were contacted for the tablets – but not by the Jap officer. No doubt a stooge to do the scrounging for the tablets. And yes, some of us had them alright: we made the same transaction as the hospital. We duly passed some tablets through the wire after the guard change each night for some time. However, we too realised that these M and B 693 tablets had been a Godsend to us up to now in healing our tropical ulcers developed on work parties.

"We all decided to part with a few grains of rice at each meal. This was duly ground into a powder and mixed with latex from the rubber trees in the compound. 'M and B' on one side and '693' on the other were beautifully inscribed on each tablet by one of our artists – you couldn't tell the difference! Literally hundreds of these so-called tablets were made. At the appointed time we handed these tablets to the stooge through the wire, and in return we were given what we wanted – dried fish, banana, sugar, rice, yams. We certainly fed well with this extra food and it was a very welcome treat compared with what we normally had to survive on.

"But it appeared this Jap must have been getting worse after swallowing our contraption, for after a number of days our food supply suddenly stopped and a hate session started – even our normal rations were cut. The guards certainly gave us a hard time with the beating up we all received from time to time. We later learnt on the grapevine that our tablets were taken down to the local Chinese chemist and analysed. We did not see the ration officer again. I wonder why?"

The Japanese and Korean guards were totally unpredictable. Duncan Ferguson explains: "When you marched into your next camp or where you were going to build a camp, you'd get lined up by the Korean guards and they'd come along and say 'Engalander?' 'Hwe!' (the noise for yes) 'Very good,' or else it would be 'Wham!' And the next one asked 'Engalander?' would say 'No.' 'Hollander?' 'Hwe!' 'Wham!' So the third would be 'Engalander?' No. 'Hollander?' No. 'Scotlando?' 'Scotlando!' 'Scotlando very good!' After that it was all Scotlanders. And at another time you'd go to another camp, and it would be all Australia – Australia very good!"

Eric Moss was receiving a beating one day for "being a very, very bad English soldier." Deciding the beating had gone too far when the Japanese officer was about to introduce the flat of his sword, Moss drew himself up and said stiffly that he was not an English soldier, he was a Scottish officer. The Japanese officer exclaimed and stopped the beating immediately. Moss had a theory about this: "I think he must have belonged to Nagasaki, and Nagasaki is a Scots town, completely. It was founded by a chap from Peterhead, called Foster I think. This chap introduced the Presbyterian religion in Japan."

Some two hundred Japanese civilian engineers, "little chaps", were in a camp opposite Eric's camp. "For the first couple of weeks when they came in we had no trouble at all, we went off to work and there was no trouble with the Japs, but one day there appeared a fellow in the Jap camp who was much taller than the rest, and he had badges of rank. We noticed that his job was sitting on the top of an embankment, watching a plumb line, he didn't do anything else, while we drove these piles in for the bridge building – that's what most of the men were employed on. We sang to this pile-driving, pulling on the ropes to raise the pile and then letting it drop: 'Eee-Chi Ni-Say-Oh, Ni-Say-Oh....boom!'. And as the pile went into the ground so the drop increased, so the song increased and you added another 'Ni-Say-Oh' to it. There were twenty men to a rope and they stood up to the knees or up to the waist in water, driving these piles in, and this chap was sitting on the bank, watching the plumb line. One day there was a beating up and it was this chap that beat him. And then after a while another fellow joined, pretty much the same stamp, didn't do any work, but just a roar of rage and run down and belt somebody.

"One day a Sergeant Bull of the Leicesters was very badly beaten up. I went across to the railway, to the Jap Sergeant Major, and said 'This isn't right.' The Jap came over to the lines in the evening after dark and asked for the man who was beaten up, and I showed him. 'This isn't right. You shouldn't do this.' He said 'Alright. My speak' and he gave the sergeant a packet of Red Bull cigarettes – the best cigarettes we could get then. That's one incident of what a decent bloke this Sergeant Major was. Now we had elephants helping us drag the trees. Elephants were marvellous. And there was a wee chap, Gardiner, of the Johore Volunteer Engineers, and I put him in charge of the elephants. A good wee man, never caused any trouble. One day he got awfully badly beaten up, you wouldn't believe it. So I took him with me... and the Quartermaster in this Jap camp tried to keep me away, but I heard a shower running and I shouted out.... 'Andeska?' ('What is it?') The Sergeant Major came out with a towel round his waist and told me to take Gardiner back to the lines, he would come over later on. He came and told Gardiner to show him his arms, turn round and show him his back. I said to the Sergeant. 'In our book it is cowardly to hit a defenceless man. This man is a very very good worker, never causes any trouble and yet he gets this – he doesn't deserve it. This is terrible.' The Sergeant asked if he got paid. I said yes, he gets so much, so he dug in his pockets and pulled out three days pay and said 'Keep him off for three days.' I used to get criticised by one of the officers for not standing up to the Japs which was very unfair. I pointed out that this Sergeant Major was doing his best – he can't do much about it because he's got these two Kempetei breathing down his neck, and if they reported that he was partial to the prisoners, they would cut his head off."

Men's shirts rotted on their backs and reasonable clothing was often bartered with local Thais for food or medicine. Civvy Cameron lost his clothes early in captivity: "All I had was my Jap Happy loincloth and a couple of rice bags for my bed, no blankets." One day Civvy was stood in front of the Japanese guardroom for seven days for failing to salute a Japanese officer: "I was stood to attention on my own for seven days. None of your own people were allowed to come near. I don't know how I managed, but every third day perhaps a good guard came and saw that you were fed. At night they put me in a little cell, like a cage. You crawled into it. If you were lucky they left you alone, didn't punish you. Other times they mucked you about. I remember another chap, not an Argyll, but he was getting tobacco and bananas from the Thais and he was caught. They made him sit down outside the guardroom, and eat every banana he'd got and smoke every ounce of tobacco before he left. You had to laugh at them sometimes."

Alex McDougall got into an altercation with a Korean guard and floored him. "The Korean got angry with one of my men and slapped him, and I just got him and stiffened him – knocked him out. We'd a Major who'd worked in Japan – he was in an insurance company. Anyway, one of the boys went down and got the Major and they were trailing me down to the guardroom when he came up. After that the man in charge of the camp – a wee guy by the name of Yamagida – was standing on a platform and I was standing here. I was saying in English what happened. This Major was translating it into Japanese to the officer. I said I didn't mind when he was arguing with me at first, but when he kicked me on the knee I lost my rag and I just walloped him one. The Major translated, and then he said to me 'Pull up your trousers.' This was to let him see. There wasn't any skin left on my knee. The wee Yamagida never said a word to anybody. He just let one go and hit this Korean guard – near broke his neck – it was one of those funny punches they do. He was only a wee man. That Korean guard was sentenced to look after me for 14 days, at my beck and call."

This was not the only occasion that Alex McDougall hit a guard and got away with it. Duncan Ferguson remembers: "Alex nearly got me beheaded. He was in charge of our party going north up to Ban Pong. We had a watch. We used to show this watch and ask 'How much? Ten tical? OK.' We'd get the money in one hand and the watch being held by the other, and then we'd pull the watch away – we had a string tied to it. Well, we got to Ban Pong and they were making *ma mee* there – it was good. Ten cents a bowl. And our boys were grabbing a bowl and eating it.

So we got to the hut, but there had been people there before us, and it was rotten with lice. Alex says 'Come on Fergie, we're not going in there. We'll build a wee lean-to outside it, and we started building it with a platform at one side for Alex and a platform on the other for me. It was just about finished when this Jap came up and 'Damme, Damme' that, and Alex K.O'd him, because he was a boxer. The Jap was stretched out and what a schamozzle there was. The Camp Commandant came up, sword trailing on the ground, and by this time the interpreter is there and asking what happened, and Alex is explaining to him. The Jap Commandant listens. A wee grin appears on his face, and he's jabbering to the interpreter who tells us: 'You're not to lift your hands or touch a Japanese again. If a Japanese passes you will bow – don't lift your hand to him!' We got away with it. Stretched out he was and his rifle at his side!"

RSM Sandy McTavish also experienced Japanese guards sometimes favouring the prisoners. At Tenko (roll call) on the parade ground, the prisoners stood with shoulders back and arms behind them. Sometimes the Japanese commander came along the rows, and Sandy would feel something, maybe a cigarette, being placed into his hand behind his back.

Often the prisoners worked with elephants that were also cruelly treated by the Japanese. Duncan Ferguson remembered a particularly vicious Japanese engineer who was always beating a particular elephant. One day, the elephant just leaned on the man and killed him outright. Another elephant simply squirted a trunkful of water at an offending Japanese.

"The elephants were worked to death, actually," remarked Ferguson. "There was one, I used to get it a big bunch of its favourite leaves and give it the leaves as it was passing. You'd think it was actually smiling, and one day I was sawing this tree, and couldn't get it down. I was in for a beating alright. The elephant was passing and it came right over, a couple of shoves and it got it down for me and looked as much as to say 'There you are, pal.' Aye, it's true! It came over on its own. Its mahout could do nothing about it! It wasn't paying any attention to him! As much as to say 'That's my pal and I'm going over to help him'."

Sgt McKay, who retrieved Captain Gordon's kilt while in a work party at Port Dickson, stole a Japanese officer's shirt and gained "a little victory" against their captors. "We used to bathe in the river in the evenings,"says Eric Moss. "McKay was bathing downstream of a Jap officer, who'd left his clothing on the bank. McKay pinched the shirt. When the Jap found the shirt was missing we were called out and there was a hunt for it, but it wasn't found, and we ended up having our faces slapped, that kind of thing. (The Japanese called this face slapping, 'Bintoks'.) In fact McKay had the shirt on all the time, under his own."

There were many ways of getting back at the Japanese but it was always a dangerous game to play. Duncan Ferguson remembers how he got a meal courtesy of the Japanese Colonel: "My pal Spud worked in the Jap cookhouse so he came in this night after I'd got back from working and said to me 'Hurry up and get your wash. Leave your rice here.' I said 'That'll be right – leave it there – you'll have eaten it before I get back!' He said 'No, no. I'll not touch it, honest! Go and get your wash and come back.' So he convinced me.'

"I went to the river, got my wash and came back and says 'What is it?' He says 'Won't be long.' Twenty minutes we waited and then he produced this meat stew. It was really great, it was good.' Then later on that night there was Tenko. We were all lined up. The interpreter says 'The person that took the Colonel's dog step forward and the rest can go.' Take the Colonel's dog? Who the hell's wanting a dog when we canna feed ourselves, never mind a dog?

"We were there all night, and the next day this interpreter kept coming back saying if the man that took the dog steps forward, the rest can go. It never twigged with me! Never twigged! And we were there the whole day and the next night and the interpreter kept saying to the Jap Colonel that the dog could have wandered off into the jungle all on its own. "They threatened to bring the hospital cases out into the sun if the man didn't step forward. And it was just then, when they said that, I thought... the Colonel's dog? And I looked over at Spud... for God's sake! Well they finally accepted that, and the case was dismissed. I said 'What the hell are you doing that for, Spud? You could have got the two of us beheaded there. What were you doing that for?' He said 'Well I was just chopping food and the wee dog came and put his head right on the block so I just went – phit! – and put it in the pot.' Oh what a man he was. That was my pal Spud Thomson."

Jimmy McLean, like Ernest Gordon, was to receive his kilt back in captivity. "It's an extraordinary story. Tyersall having been heavily bombed I thought it had gone. But when I went up country I got to Takanun, and there was a party of officers coming in, and someone came in saying there was someone asking to meet me, saying he had my kilt! It was another officer and he handed it over – he'd carried it all the way there. It had my name tag on it. I wore it quite often before the order came in that all officers must work. Taramoto, the Japanese commander there used to tease me about being idle and getting dressed up each day – he was the chap who said the best treatment for dysentery was hard work! Get them out!"

More and more POWs went down with illness: malaria, dysentery, dengue fever, beriberi, tropical ulcers, pellagra and worst of all, cholera. Cholera was a sudden killer: Lt Douglas Weir was one of sixteen officers sleeping in a tent with Lt Walter 'Dato' Cole. One day Cole was relatively fit and well; the next he had gone. Weir was told he'd died of cholera. [24] Jimmy McLean was also in that tent and believes that Cole died as a result of having a contaminated pipe in his mouth: "He always had a pipe clutched in his mouth, alight or not, and perhaps he had put it down somewhere. We were very saddened by his death. I carried him to the cholera wing."

In September 1943 at Konkuita Camp, an awful place on the Burmese border, Lt Ian Primrose shot a cholera victim with a Japanese rifle to prevent a guard from slowly finishing off the poor man. A fellow officer witnessed the incident: "This fellow had cholera and was separated from the rest of us. The Japs took him out of his tent and he was propped against a tree in a sitting position. The Jap stood about twenty yards away and was going to shoot him, but his rifle was wavering all over the place with nerves. Primrose had been visiting sick men and he came out of a tent, saw this, and demanded what was going on. He learned the Jap was to shoot the comatose man "to stop cholera spreading"! It was an order from the Jap commandant, said to be a nephew of Tojo. The guard was shaking so much he might have taken several shots to kill him. So Primrose took the rifle, walked up behind the tree and from six inches or so shot the man dead. The Japs then accused him of murder."

There was a court martial in Bangkok but Primrose was exonerated and together with Major Roberts, the officer defending him, was given a few ticals and allowed to buy provisions at stores in Bangkok. The Japanese Commandant was charged instead, but whether there was any outcome to that is doubtful. Fellow Argyll

Kenneth McLeod, said later "It was a brave and merciful act". Yes, indeed. But a terrible one. It was learned much later from Ian's widow, her husband had never told her of it.

In a Dutch camp at Kuima, Eric Moss was to bury many POWs. He asked the Japanese to take six of his men, mostly Dutch Javanese who Moss regarded as not very hygienic, off work and the next day realised they had cholera. Moss had seen cholera in India and got a second opinion from a Japanese sergeant. The six men agreed to immediate isolation in a corner of the camp and with Japanese agreement a fence was built to separate them from the uninfected men. All prisoners were warned not to bathe in the stream or put unboiled water in contact with their mouths. Moss also remembered a Kirkcaldy man who went down with cholera and dehydrated so quickly that "I could have lifted him with one hand." Also the story of two brothers, one went into hospital with cholera. The other, much against Moss' advice, insisted on visiting him. "He died, and the first brother lived."

Jockie Bell says, "Lannie Ross and I buried boys like Jim McCuaig and when we were up there they gave us another body and said 'And dump that in the hole and all, so we dug a hole and put two wee bamboo pieces in with the names of the owners scratched on them . And the Japs sprayed us all with a hand pump, took our loin cloths off and sprayed us with a kind of disinfectant stuff and gave us a smoke mask and gum boots – that was at Tonchan Springs."

RSM Sandy Munnoch and Sgt R. Smith, known as 'Sarn't Fixit' within the Transport Section, looked after cholera patients and Munnoch was in charge of burning all the bodies at Takanun. Day after day he built the funeral pyres and burned the bodies. Nick Carter also found himself burning the bodies of cholera victims: "At Waterfall Camp at Kinsayok I was there at the same time as Captain Meldrum RAMC. The Japs wanted three volunteers to burn 150 Tamils who had died of cholera, and he said he'd got the volunteers. And he told me I was one. Joe Leadbetter from the Green Howards was another. And the third was him. After the war I met him again in Scotland. I asked him about this, why he picked us. 'I knew you wouldn't get cholera,' he said. 'How's that?' 'Anybody like us are from a unique group,' he said – 'with more acid in the stomach than normal and that would prevent it'."

Jimmy McLean comments on the cholera deaths: "One of the things that struck me in our camp where seven men died every day for about six weeks was that most of the deaths were ORs. Very few officers died of cholera, and that's perhaps because they obeyed the more intelligent orders they got from MOs whereas the troops didn't. On the march you would see the troops drinking out of a stream when the officers didn't. Repeatedly we told them. But they just said 'Oh, to hell with it, we'll take a chance.' By that time I think they were so worn down by the conditions, some didn't care so much anymore."

Dick Lee supports this view. "Some blokes didn't care. You were told not to drink unboiled water." Duncan Ferguson was able to leave his wood camp in the forest at a time when the pressure was off on the railway construction to visit his sick friend and mucker, Willie Eckford, in another of the camps: "They allowed me to go down to this camp. But oh, God Almighty! I went in and Ecky was lying on his bed, and there was a boy lying beside him. The rest were out working. I spoke to him and stayed with him a while – and it was the time I was quids in with the elephant 'tobacco.' (see on) 'This boy told me that Ecky was daft on that 'nutty-nutty' (Thai peanut brittle or *thua-tad)*. I gave this boy money and told him to get boiled eggs and give them to him. Nothing else! Don't bloody give him 'nutty nutty.' And I lifted Ecky up and said to him 'You do as you're told! He's getting eggs, boiled eggs and he's giving you them. I'll not get back again, but you take those boiled eggs. The war's just about finished and we're getting home shortly. You take these eggs and get built up!' And I said to the other bloke, if I hear you're diddling me and not giving him these boiled eggs, I'll get you! I'll have you! But I soon heard Ecky had died. Joe Russell was there, and he told me he used to sit him up and slap his face, tell him 'Come on!' But it was no use."

Dick Lee describes the agony and discomfort of dysentery: "It did get you down. The week before I went down with amoebic dysentery I was helping to bury other blokes that had died from dysentery, malaria, cholera, whatever. All of a sudden you go down with it yourself so what goes through your mind? That you're going to finish up the same way – although you still fight to get on. You're miles away from home. Your thoughts go for home. You're lying in that stinking, bleeding jungle lying in your own mess because you're so weak it runs out of you the whole time. You're trying to get out to the back, to the latrines. You're weak and it's running down your legs. You're filthy and dirty – and the pain! The bleeding pain! Your knees are up under your chin night and day! You go thirty or forty times during the day or night, it's all water and blood. It was just the luck of the draw who got over it. Emmetine was the thing, an injection of emmetine, because amoebic dysentery gets into the blood stream as well, that was the killer, and if you got emmetine in time and a clean bed or light diet – you couldn't get any of those things – then 99 out of 100 would get clear of it. But you had nothing of these things. You couldn't get a bleeding Aspro. Two or three doses of salts – Epsom salts – they were given me, to try and wash it out. But how can you wash it out if it's in the bloodstream? Don't ask me how I got over it. There were so many hundreds under the turf with the same thing."

Duncan Ferguson used charcoal scooped up out of the fires to treat his own dysentery: "Two or three times a day, a spoonful of charcoal with water. It helped bind you. I'm not ashamed to say I used to cry at night and pray bloody hard to God 'Don't let me die in this God-forsaken hole!'." Duncan also had over forty malaria attacks including three of cerebral malaria. He remembers the first of these: "The first time I got it, there was a wee boy who sneaked back to our camp when they were moving on to another bit of the railway. I was told afterwards it was Boy Booth – that boy did well by me and I could never contact him again, and he looked after me. I was left behind when the rest of the party moved on – left alone without food. Nothing. We had only a flysheet and it was the monsoon season, the rain came through and your blankets were just soaked. I went delirious and they told me about it afterwards. 'You had everyone with their blankets all rolled up ready to follow you.' I was told. Apparently I was saying 'Guess where I was the other day?' 'Where Fergie?' 'I went across the river and over that bloody mountain, doon the other side – and guess what's over the other side? The sea! And there's a big boat. I went aboard to speak to the captain, and the captain said he could take us – but only two of us! He says he cannae take any more than that!' So I says, 'You and I are going! But I've got to go back the morrow and see him to see that everything's all settled!' So in this tent the ears are all cocked.

"So the next night they said I was all on about it again. I was back over and I saw the captain, and he said 'Mind now, only the two of you are going. I havna any room for more o' you, and here's the tickets, two tickets!' And I was going on in my delirium: 'And you don't believe me, divn't ye no? You don't believe me! Well here's the two tickets...' And he tells me that after I came to, they were all ready to follow me! Well, that laddie Boy Booth took his life in his hands. He juked (ducked) into the jungle, and came back and looked after me for a week – Boy Booth, a lovely boxer. But I never saw the laddie again."

Boy Booth was lost at sea en route to Japan. It was surviving these cerebral malaria attacks that convinced Duncan that he would survive to go home. He also believed that the Argylls' rigorous pre-campaign training carried out by Ian Stewart helped many to survive in captivity. Dick Lee says: "I think your constitution did play a part. I was brought up in the East End of London, a family of eight boys – I know what it is to run to school with my arse hanging out of my trousers. Compared to some people who grew up in a more easy going life, they did give up easy, but I've also seen blokes like us, who had plenty of go, and it just got on top of them."

The medical officers were magnificent, working in the most primitive of conditions. Anesthetics were virtually non-existent. Six strong men would hold down amputees. Maggots, spread by flies blown onto dirty bandages, infected wounds but were used by some camp surgeons to clean out wounds. Other medical officers disapproved of this practice as it had a bad effect on the morale of the patient. Safety pins were sometimes used to close wounds. Men with infected feet went down to the river and let the fish nibble away at the rotten flesh. In the words of one Argyll, "Every one of those medical officers deserved the VC."

John Wyatt of the East Surreys remembers the devotion to duty of some medical orderlies and a particular Scottish medical officer: " I witnessed the death of two medical orderlies on a cholera camp at 211 Kilometre camp. They both really sacrificed their lives for their comrades. I don't think anybody knew their names. POWs were dying from cholera at about seven a day in our camp and these two men never stopped caring for them and cleaning them. Tragically for them they both died within 48 hours of each other. They shared a cigarette and forgot to wash their hands. I know that for a fact because I was in the burial party. A wonderful Scottish Doctor, Alfie Roy, was in charge and was very upset. Dr Roy was a wonderful man. Just to see him going by gave you great hope. He must have saved dozens of lives, and we owe him a lot. I ran a red hot bolt through my foot, and he saved it from going gangrenous. I was terribly sad when I heard that he had died recently."

Many FEPOWs also owed their lives to a Thai merchant Mr Boon Pong Siri Vejjabhandu who at great personal risk secretly supplied the POWs with money and medicine from sources in Bangkok. It is widely believed that he was awarded the George Medal.

Curiously, Marine Maurice Edwards had his life saved by a Japanese medical officer: "Early on at Konyu River Camp the Japs had real medical inspectors with obviously well-trained young Doctors. One of these saved my life by taking pity on an obviously dying young man and he rewarded me with a bottle of Virol which I have no doubt saved my life."

Vitamins could also be obtained from the jungle. "We found a tree up there that grew loofahs," explains Kenneth McLeod. "Loofhahs are vegetable, not out of the sea as some people think. They look like a rather thick cucumber. We boiled these 'cog-wheels' as we called them – you couldn't swallow them but we got the juice out and that would have some vitamin."

The Japanese could not understand the cheerful morale of the Argylls amidst such degradation and were entertained by the prisoners singing, particularly "She'll be coming round the Mountain" often with unprintable lyrics. The preference of the Argyll captives were songs such as "To-jo is a baa-stard," "We want leggi doo-vres" (leggi doo-vres " second helpings) and much worse.

In both Thailand and Sumatra Argyll POWs were approached by Japanese 5th Division officers, one of whom commented to RSM Sandy 'Bull' Munnoch "Argyll Scotsmen No.1 fighters." Duncan Ferguson's similar approach from a Japanese officer who had fought on the Grik Road is recorded in Chapter 2. Bertie King of the Lanchesters was supposed to have been "decorated " by a Japanese general, who hearing he was an Argyll and of how he got to Sumatra, was sufficiently moved to pin his personal tiepin on him.

Some Argylls, like Pte 'Honest' John McFadyen of Battle of the Union Jack Club fame, were highly thought of among fellow prisoners for the life-saving work they did for others. McFadyen had a natural talent for using the system and acquiring goods at times when a 4oz. jar of Marmite was literally a life-saver.[25] On Occasions McFadyen risked his life to obtain food and medical supplies for sick prisoners and several owed their lives to him.

Piper Charles 'Boy' Stuart had a similar reputation for his compassion. When a friend was seriously ill he went down to the river and caught fish to feed him. After the railway was completed Charlie Stuart ended up on the Mergui Road in Burma, cutting a path through the jungle to the coast. They were made to carry heavy shells through deep mud for the Japanese artillery. Men were collapsing; even the Japanese were collapsing. Completely exhausted, Stuart threw a shell off his shoulder and he also collapsed into the mud. He later told friends that at that moment his grandmother's face appeared to him and said, 'Come on Charles – you're going home."

Some POWs specialised in 'lifting' items from the Japanese and trading them with the local Thais. This was a dangerous business. In February 1944 a group of Argylls who stole nails from the Japanese ended up in the Ban Pong Kempetei HQ jail and were lucky to be returned alive to their camp for punishment – seven days standing to attention outside the guardhouse with severe beatings each time the Japanese changed guard.

Other Argylls like Cpl John Dickie, later lost at sea, gave blood to save the lives of other prisoners. Sgt Davy Adamson was regarded as "a wonderful man" who did everything for the POWs. In Chungkai, L.Cpl 'Dodger' Green, an orphan and a Geordie Argyll, knew that he himself was slowly dying – he in fact died on the ship home – but did everything he could to help other prisoners, including the cleaning and boiling of ulcer rags so that they could be used again.

Bon Hall, an Australian POW at 55 Kilo Camp, remembers Pte Fitzpatrick, an Argyll with the Sumatra Battalion: "It was to my great fortune that a part-time medical orderly, Pte Fitzpatrick, took an interest in my leg and it was to this one man that I owed so much for his treatment and preventing a serious ulcer developing on the leg. Everyday 'Fitz' would come down to the back room of the kitchen and carefully remove dead skin from my leg and with such tender care he would bathe my leg from knee to ankle. Over the next few weeks 'Fitz' spent many hours carefully treating my leg until new skin had started to grow, the wound cleared and danger of deeper infection passed."[26]

Alex McDougall remembers an Argyll bartering clothes for quinine: "There was a wee bloke in B Company who came from Ranfurley – he couldn't read or write by the way, but that's another story. The man couldn't swim a stroke and here we were at the Mae Klong river, and him and another guy used to go over there with all the surplus clothing we could get – this was the only way we could get quinine for the boys who were dying." This was Pte George Murdoch 'Schnozzle' Murray of "Number One Bridge Building Company," about eighteen of whom were Argylls. Murdoch sold numerous shovels and tools to local Thais in exchange for opium pills which had the appearance of sheep dung pellets. Murray handed these over to the medics. Surprisingly, when the Japanese found out, he escaped with a slapping. It was the same Murray whose last act of defiance against the Japanese at the war's end was to take from his pack a carefully preserved Lion Rampant flag that had been used at funerals along the railway, tear down 'the Poached Egg' and haul up his flag. The flag and Murdoch's medals are today in the possession of the Regimental Museum, Stirling Castle.

"He was a character," says Alex McDougall. "He stole everything from the Japs and sold them to the Thais. He got more beatings up than Duncan Dell. He was a wonderful wee man – he couldna' read or write, this was God's honest truth – before the war he was in my Company – D Company, and he was reading a letter, and he sits laughing. I says 'There must be something good in your letter, Schnozzle.' 'Aye. Read it, Sarn't – read it!' I'm reading it. He says 'Read it out loud!' Well, there was nothing in it to laugh about – that's when I found out he couldna' read! Our Sgt Kerr was a schoolteacher in civvie life, but he used to do a lot of teaching – you know we'd our own school before the war broke out. He and I got wee Schnozzle and we started bringing a wee bit of education into him. In Thailand he'd taken malaria and it went into blackwater fever. And that's when Schnozzle wrote in a book, 'I'm going to live. I'm going to live. I'm going to live!'."

According to another Argyll, young Schnozzle never quite got the best of deals when he bargained with the Thais on the riverbank. He had part of his index finger missing, and when he stuck up two fingers to indicate two baht, the Thais always gave him one and a half. He never quite worked this out.

Maurice Edwards described the sort of blood transfusions carried out in the camps: "A treatment we developed at Chungkai for serious debility was blood transfusions. Not the kind you have today. The donor's blood was checked against the recipient's; if it didn't coagulate it was considered OK. The transfusion was direct, from the donor, through a tube into the recipient. As a muscular injection 200 cc were also administered. My donor was a coloured Dutchman. The rigor that took place afterwards was very much worse than a malarial rigor."[27]

Captain Gordon tells the story of one of his company, Pte Alastair McGillivray, an India veteran, whose mucker became very ill. McGillivray fed the man from his own meagre rations and went out of camp, at the risk of his life, into Thai villages seeking food and medicine for his sick friend. His friend got better but one day at Tamarkan camp McGillivray just collapsed stone dead of malnutrition.

Gordon tells of another Argyll who owned up to stealing a shovel where his comrades were collectively punished. The Argyll was beaten to death. It was found when the Japanese re-counted the shovels, that none was missing! Duncan Ferguson was in this work party and explains the story slightly differently: "We were told there was a shovel missing when we came back to camp. The sergeant was getting a proper beating. A wee Argyll stepped forward – the language he was using: 'Leave him alone, you...!' Well, he got punched to death. They had another count of the tools, and there was nothing missing."

Sometimes money could be obtained in the camps by the most unusual transactions. Duncan Ferguson tells of his initiation into the tobacco trade when he found himself the only Scotsman in a particular camp: "I palled up with two English chaps, Wee Sackie and a corporal in the RAMC, and was there for quite a while. Here we were coming home this night when Wee Sackie says to me, 'Fergie, don't turn your head, but look over to your right. Look beside that palm tree, there's a kati of tobacco!' And I says, 'Christ! So it is! When we're coming back, get to the back. We'll get it.' So we finished work and we were coming back and Sackie and I are at the back. Let them get away a bit. So I go over and start to pick it up. Christ! It's elephant shit! It was all dried and lovely on the top... but! So I got a banana leaf and whipped it over, and said 'We'll get that tomorrow maybe.' So the next day it was dried right through and it looked exactly like a kati of tobacco. So I wrapped it in a banana leaf and said to the RAMC Corporal, 'Snowy, go take that down to the Dutch. It's a kati of tobacco. Fifteen dollars.' He says 'Fifteen? It's more than that!' I says 'No, just gie' them it for fifteen.' So he went away and came back with the fifteen dollars. He says 'Oh, we'll get some eggs, bananas...' I says 'Just a minute,' thinking they'll maybe be up here with a knife and cut our throats. But they never came near! So Sackie and I used to go looking for this dung, dry it and sell it to them. We lived like lords in that camp! We finished up smoking it ourselves! No, I don't think they knew what they were smoking."

Money could even be obtained by selling guards' rifles to local Thais. Duncan Ferguson tells of one Argyll who got away with this when a Japanese sergeant went to visit a prostitute in a local Thai village: "And they used to give you their rifle to carry. So when he gets there he tells the Argyll 'Watch that!' and he goes in. When he comes out, the rifle's away. The Argyll had sold it. Oh, this sergeant was doing his nut. He was in a real panic. The Argyll tells him,'OK, I fix, I fix. You...' And he rubs his fingers together in a money gesture. Well he knew that in the stores there were three rifles. The Jap sergeant there was a pig of a man, but one of us Argylls managed to distract the sergeant, and he got one of these rifles and came out and sold it to the soldier, so he got paid for that as well. The Jap couldn't afford to report him."

In Chungkai camp, where thirteen Argylls and five Royal Marines died, Tiny Gordon survived "the Death Hut" and found his God. Some turned to religion; others turned away from it. Captivity and the closeness of death brought out both the best and worst in men and the Argylls were no exception. The authors are aware of eight Argylls including two officers who behaved badly in captivity, a very small percentage of the battalion, and many of them the same men who behaved selfishly prior to captivity. The offence of the Other ranks concerned was stealing from other prisoners. Such men were court-martialled and punished within the camps. In some cases men, including officers, received corporal punishment. The task of giving this punishment often fell on the highly regarded Royal Marine NCOs.

Probably the worst case was that of an officer who was a Malayan copra producer, planting coconuts. In captivity he first of all made himself unpopular by trying to get a job in the cookhouse at the expense of a man who was ill. He then stole quinine from the hospital and sold it to the Thais to buy himself food. He was court-martialled by fellow officers including Captain Lang and ordered to be either beaten up or caned by two RSMs. He was also beaten up by some other ranks when they learned what he had done.

Another more human category of offender but equally dangerous was the young man who talked too much or wrote too much in diaries, particularly when radio news messages picked up from Radio Delhi were being secretly passed around the camps and men's lives were at stake. An RASC officer was caned for writing pieces of news on scraps of paper. The danger was great. Possession of a radio meant a death sentence. Possession of a diary was forbidden and equally endangered those named in it: or the camp in mass punishment. To others however, it was the only way to remember their humanity.

On October 17th 1943 the 260 miles of railway linking Ban Pong to Thambyzayat in Burma was completed. There was a brief period of comparatively more relaxed captivity with time for camp concert parties. RSM Sandy Munnoch was one of the stars of such shows with his renditions of "The Monk" and "The Pure White Lily." Munnoch was also responsible in 1943 for the erection of a fine 40-ft. wooden cross at the cemetery at Takanun. The cross on which was inscribed the words "In Memory of our Comrades" stood over a stone cairn in which the ashes of the cremated cholera victims were placed. Around it were bamboo crosses with the names of 273 British, 113 Dutch and 5 Australian prisoners. A bamboo fence surrounded the cemetery, grass was planted and paths were cleared. When Padre Henry Babb with a Graves Reconnaissance party located this cemetery two years later it was overgrown, and the names inscribed on the bamboo crosses could barely be read, but Munnoch's cross and cairn still stood.

Many Argyll other ranks did not think Munnoch was the kind of man to make such a gesture as this, to the dead. But he did. Such was the impact of suffering and despair in these camps, the living made what acknowledgement they could.

In late February 1944, Chungkai camp was abandoned and many 'able-bodied' POWs prepared for a further tragic assignment. They were sent by sea via Singapore to Japan to work in the coal and lead mines, factories and shipyards. Crammed below decks in rusting unmarked merchant ships thousands drowned when US submarines and bombers sank the ships.

Particularly notorious sinkings, most within days of each other in September 1944, were those of the *Montivideo Maru* (849 POWs lost); the *Lisbon Maru* (840 POWs lost); the *Kachidoki Maru* (380 POWs lost), the *Jun' Yo Maru* (4897 POWs lost; mostly Dutch and Indonesian), the *Toyofuku Maru* (nearly 1000 POWs lost) and the *Rakuyo Maru* (1030 POWs lost). In all, over 1500 Australian and 2000 British POWs, who had survived the Death Railway, were lost at sea. 29 Argylls and 6 Royal Marines died in this way.[28]

Some Marines from the *Repulse* were sent to Japan in June 1944 on the *Hioki Maru*. Cpl Charles Miller had survived some of the worst camps in Thailand as far north as Takanun near the Burma border. His friend Cpl Lionel Thompson developed jungle ulcers and had his leg amputated.[29] Charles Miller went out to sell Thompson's boots to get his friend more food. He offered them to Captain Lang but they were the wrong size. Thompson didn't make it. He was buried at Kanchanburi war cemetery, as were eight other Plymouth Argyll Marines. Perhaps Miller's most poignant memory of the Railway was a young, unknown Argyll Private who he heard singing beautifully amidst the degredation, "Sweet Mary of Argyll." Miller left Chungkai in late June 1944 heading by train for Singapore.

On arrival at Singapore, Miller was the only marine among 750 men on the 4600 tramp steamer *Osaka* or *Asaka Maru*, formerly the *Glasgow Belle*, commissioned in 1894. This ship left Singapore on July 4th 1944. Prisoners were issued with a list of regulations for the 'very unpleasant' voyage that listed twelve offences that carried an immediate death penalty. These included 'using more than two blankets' and 'talking without permission and raising loud voices.'[30] The *Osaka Maru* was crippled in a typhoon off Formosa on August 13th 1944 and ran aground.[31]

Charles Miller was among survivors picked up from the sea three days later by two destroyers of the Japanese navy. Fifty men had died but the survivors were delivered to Osaka on August 23rd 1944. They found themselves in the same camp but not the same compound as Hong Kong POWs. The ship that had set out with a second batch of Chungkai prisoners, the *Hofoko Maru*, never made it. It was bombed and sunk off Manila by US aircraft with huge loss of life.

Pte S. Edwards of the Argylls was also pulled from the sea. Others who made it to Japan included Marine R.Swain and 78 Argylls including forty-five year old Captain Joseph Allen; Lt J.H. Smith; Sgts Alex McDougall and Albert Skinner; Cpl Bertie King; Ptes Davy Watson; A. Baillie; R. Chisman; William Bannatyne, and the enterprising Rations Sgt Percy Evans, who at great personal risk possessed a camera throughout his captivity.

Alex McDougall, whose brother Hughie was lost in a Maru sinking, explains how he just made it to Japan: "We were shipwrecked. I was on the *Hakasan Maru,* a wee ship built on the other side of the Clyde. Hughie was on this other ship hit by American torpedo bombers. If our Hughie had been on deck... Willie Bannatyne from Clydebank, he was up on the top of the deck, but the torpedo hit the bottom and nearly blew the thing to bits, but Willie survived. We were in a large convoy but our boat got away. We were shipwrecked on Formosa in a storm. I had Albert Skinner round the back of my neck- he was ill – I was carrying him. The Japanese navy put a lifeline aboard us, to get onto this Japanese destroyer which took us to Japan. They nearly drowned us, every time the waves were coming up and letting us down we went under water."

Four Argylls, Cpl James Flynn; Ptes B. McLaughlin; Dan Quinn; W. Robertson, were sent to the notorious Kinkaseki copper mines in Taiwan. They survived but most prisoners died including Marine John Dunn of the *Prince of Wales,* killed in an accident in June 1944. His grave today is at the Sai Wan Commonwealth Cemetery, Hong Kong. A fellow prisoner at Kinkaseki was Arthur Titherington, a Scot who was a Don-R despatch rider in the Royal Signals. In captivity he surreptitiously carved the Argyll and Sutherland cap badge on a piece of Japanese 5"x 4" oak.

Titherington remembers the savage treatment handed out to the Argyll Cpl Flynn. Flynn arrived at Kinkaseki in March 1945 in a party of thirty men from another camp in Taiwan, and was soon transferred with the other Kinkaseki prisoners to yet another camp 30 miles south of what is now Taipei. Here the prisoners had to carry huge heavy stores up into the mountains, clear an area beside an old tea plantation, and plant sweet potatoes and build large huts for Japanese occupation.

James Flynn came from Paisley and had joined the Argylls at the age of 18 in 1934, serving in both the 1st and 2nd Battalions. In India he had served in the Motor Transport Platoon. Now he was working on a 'Garden Party', clearing ground within the camp to grow foodstuffs for the Japanese. The prisoners were starving and reduced to eating a stew made from weeds. One day the Japanese sergeant ordered an absurd increase in the morning work quota from 4 bundles of elephant grass to 15, and ordered the Formosan guards to beat those who didn't work hard enough. Flynn was beaten over the head into unconsciousness with the handle of a sickle. When he came to he was raving and violent and had to be restrained. The American MO declared Flynn insane. He was unaware of his surroundings, he was violent and believed others were plotting against him. The British senior officer and the MO went to the Japanese commandant and demanded that Flynn be admitted to a hospital. They were beaten up and told that Flynn would be shot if he wandered and that they had better tie him up. They refused and allocated two medical orderlies to keep an eye on him. Other prisoners were never quite sure if Flynn had gone mad or was bluffing. Titherington remembers that Flynn wandered about and the Japanese left him alone. Eventually he disappeared from the camp, probably into a hospital somewhere. Flynn did survive and he recovered sufficiently to remain with the Argylls until February 1949, but not seeing out the 21 years service necessary for a Service Pension.[32]

Jockie Bell was on a ship torpedoed by the Americans. He was among the few survivors rescued by the Japanese and sent instead to French Indo-China where the prisoners were used to build a jungle airstrip outside Saigon. Drum Major Busty Simpson and Pte Stan Roberts were also here. When the war ended they were in a camp on the Mekong Delta. Liberated by Gurkhas they were sent to stay with and protect some of the French community until evacuated to Rangoon, then on to a hospital in Ceylon.[33]

In Thailand the POWs were now subject to Allied bombing raids. Nong Pladuk camp was next to a railway marshalling yard. On the night of September 6th/7th 1944 the US Airforce bombed the area killing 98 prisoners and wounding 350. The US Air Force made six unsuccessful attempts to destroy the Tamarkan Bridge that was in the end knocked out in an RAF raid on February 5th 1945.

The Japanese moved anti-aircraft guns into the area of the camp and brought in unhappy Indian INA soldiers to man them. Surviving Argylls remember the trajectory of these guns being so low that shells were whizzing through the attap of their hut roofs. L.Cpl Joe Lonsdale was injured by bomb blast in an air-raid that killed nine prisoners; his chest felt crushed and the monsoon weather exacerbated his discomfort.

Sgt Terry Brooks RM, acting CSM to the British commanding officer Tamarkan camp, was subsequently awarded the British Empire Medal (16.7.46) for his conduct in such an air raid on November 29th 1944. The raid began during evening roll call. Brooks citation reads: " Sgt Brooks, without regard to his own safety, was seen going towards the direction of the falling bombs and the camp hospital where he picked up a sick Marine and having carried him to safety returned to the hospital area and attended to many other prisoners."

Eighteen prisoners were killed in the raid and thirty-four wounded. The sick Marine rescued by Brooks was Sgt Tommy Locklin of *Prince of Wales* detachment. Locklin had been wounded in the Singapore fighting. Peter Dunstan had a further tale to tell of Tommy Locklin as the war neared its end. "He was in Tha Muang POW Base Camp and was semi-conscious; very, very ill and on the last knocking, when the Padre came and told him to get pulling as the war was over. Tommy gave him some of the best RM language about his parents for many generations. With the release by the Japanese of all the Red Cross stores we had been denied for so long he started to improve then a number of days later the RAF dropped supplies to us which included fresh blood on ice which was given to Tommy among others."[34]

Terry Brooks' action during the air-raid clearly impressed the officers in the camp. A few weeks later, when all officers were moved to another camp, Brooks, who was only in his mid-twenties, was approached by a major on the camp staff who told him they wanted him to be senior NCO at Tamarkan in preference to older Army sergeants. It was with some reluctance that Terry took charge of some 8,000 prisoners. Some time later, when the legendary bridge was destroyed, he was actually standing on the bridge when the first of the final bombing runs took place. He and his companions had to run for their lives as the planes came in very low, machine gunning the whole area. Two waves of aircraft came in first to successfully knock out the anti-aircraft guns. Then came eight bombers, each taking several runs at the bridge. The thousand pound bombs exploded, dropping the two centre spans of the bridge into the river. Terry led the prisoners on a 200-mile march south to build airstrips for the Japanese but by this time he was a sick man. Suffering temporary blindness, he had to be carried out on work parties. By September 1945, Terry weighed only 6 st.7 lbs.

Other Royal Marines who distinguished themselves in captivity included Cpl Norman Overington who served as a volunteer medical orderly in some of the worst camps in Thailand. Captain Bob Lang spoke of "his courage, cheerfulness and devotion to duty at all times." A fellow Marine comments: "He was a good man – a credit to the Corps."[35]

Captain Claude Aylwin RM, who was in charge of many small camps in Thailand, was later mentioned in dispatches (4.6.46): "His care and consideration for all the prisoners under his administration was always of the highest priority and many men survived through his efforts."[36]

Sgt W.R Thomas RM received similar recognition for his courage and service in captivity and also for "gallant and distinguished service while fighting in Malaya and Singapore."[37]

Throughout the captivity QMS George Aitken of the Argylls, an Englishman, kept a meticulous record book of the battalion, recording casualties and keeping a record of the dispersal of POWs. The large leather-bound book survived confiscations and bashings. On one Occasion Aitken was made to stand to attention with the book on his head. In early 1945 with the separation of officers and Other ranks, Japanese security tightened. Daily searches were made and possession of paper or even a pencil meant severe punishment. Aitken resorted to burying the book and digging it up when required. In March 1945 he handed his record book to Tam Slessor before Aitken was sent north to a camp in Chiang Mai province. Today this record book can be viewed in the Regimental Museum at Stirling Castle.

A number of FEPOWs kept diaries recording the events of their captivity. No Argyll diaries were traced during the research for this book. Duncan Ferguson explained it was not permitted in the battalion at all. "If we got caught with any piece of paper with writing on it – even just an address – we got a beating. It was extremely strict. Other soldiers buried their diaries in sealed containers and told a friend. If they died the friend got it for them. I don't think any Argylls did that. But our CQMS Aitken kept a nominal roll for the battalion – all those wounded – dead. He kept a very detailed note."

As Allied air activity increased everyone sensed that the end of the war could not be far off. POWs passing through Bangkok were cheered and applauded by friendly Thais giving 'V' for Victory signs and becoming increasingly contemptuous of the Japanese.[38] The Thai Resistance was more active. Operating from caves along the River Kwai they sabotaged the railway, made increasing contact with the POWs and sheltering escapers in the marshland.

In January 1945 came the disturbing order that officers and men were to be separated. Lt Richard Webber of the Argylls explains the reasoning behind this: "The officers were only removed from the troops because the Japs were in full retreat in Burma, not very far away. They were expecting an invasion on the east Malayan and southern Burmese coast, and did not want a repeat of the happenings in the Philippines where American officers were organising breakouts and sabotage behind Jap lines. We had also known for some time that the Japs intended to shoot all POWs, not just officers, in the event of such an invasion."

Sgt Major Sandy McTavish had been senior NCO in Captain Boyle's Pudu group. After Tamarkan, he had been Colonel Toosey's camp RSM at Nong Pladuk. He was highly respected and a survivor of many bashings. Once he was bashed on his birthday when a guard heard his friends singing 'Happy Birthday.' McTavish was chosen by Toosey to take command of the other ranks' camp at Ubon in northeast Thailand, close to the border with Cambodia. The camp at Ubon was to contain some 3200 men: British, Australian and Dutch. McTavish knew only too well from the experience of Toosey, who he admired, and Boyle, that this would mean more beatings as he stood up for the prisoners against the Japanese.

The big officers' camp established in January 1945 was at Kanchanaburi. Eric Moss says, "We put all the majors and all the half colonels together in one big hut, and we called it the Imperial War Museum. We had a Colonel of the East Surreys there. And there was a chap Lewis who was the East Surrey's Quartermaster. We had been confined to huts for some reason and you weren't allowed to smoke, but this chap Lewis who always had a pipe in his hand was walking between the two huts. He may have had the pipe in his mouth but he wasn't smoking. He was hauled in by the Japs and put in front of the guardroom. He stood in front of it for a whole week – Jap military practice. When they let him go he was all black by the sun, he was parched with thirst and dying of hunger. He was staggering back to his hut when this fool of a Colonel came out. 'How are you feeling old boy? Of course it was your own fault, wasn't it?' I'd have flattened him. We used to be confined to our huts for long periods in that camp with nothing to do, so we played dumb charades and so forth. We had a sentry at either end of the hut to warn us if any Japs appeared on walkabout. We weren't supposed to do anything. You weren't allowed to read books, you weren't allowed to play charades, but we were never bored."

In late June 1945 most of the Argyll and Royal Marine officers including Aylwin, Boyle, Moss, Doherty, Slessor, Gordon, Munro and four other Argyll officers, were put on 10 ton trucks at Kanchanaburi. They were driven to Bangkok, where they spent two nights in godowns. Taken across the Chao Phya River by barge because the bridges were knocked out by Allied bombing, they proceeded on foot north-east to Nakhon Nayok on the Cambodian border, about eighty miles north-east of Bangkok. They were in an advance party of 150 officers who, after a forty-mile night march through mud and monsoon, had to clear a site and build a camp to accommodate 3200 British, Australian, Dutch and a few American officer POWs. Other parties of about 500 followed at fortnightly intervals.[39]

In his book, Ernest Gordon tells how in a railway siding they encountered a train full of Japanese wounded who were in the most appalling state and how the prisoners gave the wounded Japanese food and water. Eric Moss remembers an incident that resembles Gordon's account: "We were at the remains of a bridge over the river that had been demolished in an air-raid. We had an officer called the Frog, a Jap who was in charge of us, and we stayed the night there to cross in the morning. Alongside was a green sward with a fairly shallow burn about twelve feet wide. About twelve of us stopped there. Someone rustled up some boiled rice and boiled eggs. I was sitting with my feet almost in the stream and I looked up and here was a small party of Japs, clad in their pyjamas, dead on their feet, their clothes in tatters, and I said 'Good God! What poor souls,' but they'd kept their rifles with them, and the first thing I noticed was their rifles were clean! You know – ex musketry sergeant. Without thinking I lifted my mug of tea and I walked across and signalled to them. One of these Japs came over, jaw hanging, mouth wide open, eyes staring, and he took my tea. I went back and got some rice and handed that to him. All the other chaps followed suit, and there were these Japs munching away. One fellow I went up to I asked, 'Are you not giving anything?' 'No,' he said, 'my batman was killed.' I said 'Don't be a bloody fool. What's your batman got to do with it?' But he eventually came in with us and that was that. In the morning they were gone... We slept happily, thankful in the knowledge that we had done something which the founder of our faith would have approved."

Maurice Edwards remembers a similar incident at a destroyed bridge some ten miles east of Nakhon Pathom but places it before the separation of the officers and the men: "I left Tamuang in a party of about 200 POWs early in 1945. We travelled by rail in open trucks and passed Nakhon Pathom – I remember the big pagoda. Shortly afterwards we arrived at a bombed bridge, impassable for the train. A rope suspension bridge had been organised by the Japs to enable movement to Bangkok. While we waited to cross the rope bridge a further train pulled up behind ours. It contained Jap wounded soldiers in a very pathetic state. They were without water or food. The majority of them were very severely injured. Their pathetic state softened many hearts and prisoners were soon handing water to their wounded captors. This did not please our Korean guards and soon they were handing out beatings. The relief of the wounded was not allowed to continue. We crossed the slender rope suspension bridge which was difficult. How the wounded Jap soldiers crossed over I don't know. I'm sure many of them died in the train at the bridge."

Eventually the officer party arrived at the site for the new camp: "When we started to build the camp at Nakhon Nayok there was no camp there. We camped in the open. We hadn't even got a cookhouse. The troops cooked a meal down at their camp about five or so miles away, then it was trucked along the road, dumped at the side of the road, and myself, Tam Slessor, David Boyle and somebody else would walk every day from the camp, a couple of miles down to the road, load these rations onto bamboo poles and go back to camp, until we built our own cookhouse. Then after the cookhouse we built huts for ourselves, and then we had to build huts for the next party coming in."

Shortly after their arrival at Nakhon Nayok, Lt Colonel 'Gertie' MacKellar, formerly of the 2nd Argylls, CO of the 4th (Pahang) Volunteers and MacForce in Kelantan, lost his battle against stomach cancer. The cancer had been detected the previous December when he was sent from Tamuang to Nong Pladuk for an exploratory operation by Lt Colonel Coates. His condition was considered inoperable. He was unable to eat so was put on a special high calorie diet with gastrostomy feeding.

Gerties' friend, Eric Moss, describes him as "a very mannerly fellow." MacKellar liked to maintain that he had no religious belief. Once when Eric pulled his leg that he was an agnostic MacKellar thumped the table declaring "Once and for all just get it in your head I am an atheist!" Knowing that he was going to die he had actually planned his own funeral which turned out to be a very Christian affair included the Lord's Prayer and the 23rd Psalm, and was conducted by Ernest Gordon and Major Jack Hyslop.

Unknown to these officers they were being concentrated in the one camp to be massacred in the event of an Allied landing in Malaya (Mountbatten's imminent Operation Zipper) – a landing actually scheduled for August 28th with preliminary bombing from August 17th. In Singapore, officers and other ranks had also been separated with the same purpose in mind. Civilians were removed from Changi Jail and taken to the former RAF HQ at Sime Road. The 6000 other ranks from Changi camp were incarcerated in the jail, three to a cell with many sleeping in the corridors. The officers were put in a tented camp around the jail.

News was filtering through to the POWs of momentous events. Then the day came – August 16th 1945 – when Japanese camp commanders across SouthEast Asia sent for the Allied POW commanders. At Nakhon Nayok, Lt Colonel Toosey, the British commanding officer, emerged from the meeting to announce that the war was over. The singing began: "God Save the King," "Waltzing Matilda," "Land of Hope and Glory," "The Lord's My Shepherd." A Lion Rampant flag, preserved for years in an Argyll's sleeping bag, was raised, the Japanese commandant having forbidden Toosey to raise the Union Jack.

One Argyll subaltern smoked the third of three cigars. One cigar he had kept for the Italian surrender of September 1943, one for the German surrender of May 1945 and one for the Japanese surrender. That was the best cigar of all!

David Boyle had the pleasure of going to the Japanese commandant to demand a battery for the POWs no-longer-secret radio. Eric Moss was sent into the neighbourhood to warn locals that promissory notes 'in the name of the British government,' which some cunning Australian FEPOWs were offering shopkeepers, would unfortunately not be honoured. While wandering around local villages to warn villagers about promissory notes he met up with 'Doc' Doherty, who was out and about requisitioning food, mostly vegetables, to take back to camp: "We had a great time. We used to go out in the villages and we'd be given something to eat and drink, and the girls would come out dancing. Doc and I were dancing with them, but you were not allowed to touch ....formal dancing, curling your hands around, copying all the things they did, but not allowed to touch."

Doherty was in his forties, as was Lt Munro who owned a cloth business in Java. Their age had not prevented their full participation in work parties. They had survived when younger men had died. Many survived because it was their good fortune to do so, but the determination not to give up and a sense of humour were also survival factors. It was said that the bigger men died first because the food could not sustain them, but many big men who appear in this story survived: Dunstan, Miller, Gordon, Ferguson, McLeod to name a few.

In the nearby other ranks camp near the garrison town of Ubon there were some 3,035 surviving prisoners, nearly half of them Dutch, under Camp RSM Sandy McTavish. There were also 25 medical officers.

Sandy had heard on the grapevine the news of the dropping of the atomic bombs. The Japanese commandant called to see him, bowed and proffered his sword. He told Sandy that the war was over, but so far no-one else in the camp knew of it. Sandy instructed him to quietly collect together bit by bit all the weapons of the Korean guards and lock them in a shed. The announcement the war had ended should not be made to the camp until this was done. Meantime, the camp would continue normally.

The work parties went out as usual but returned during the late morning. A tenko (roll call) was called and the Japanese commandant stood on his box and announced 'War is over. You go home.' The AIF men started a conga through the camp. Others smashed the gate down but there were no difficult incidents or reprisals. The next day Sandy McTavish arranged with a local Thai for a Monty Banks silent movie show, accompanied by Thai orchestra. Days later, reunified with their officers, a victory parade was held.[40]

Civvy Cameron remembers: "When the surrender came, we wouldn't allow the Dutch to put their flag up because they were considered Jap Happy. We had very little time for the Dutch. Individual Dutch were gentlemen. There was a Captain van der Pol, more like our officers, but otherwise if they could drop you in it with the Jap commandant, Yamagida, they would – they didn't like the British and they would shop you. You know Yamagida at first turned up wearing his British medals from World War 1. Colonel John Rory Williamson of the Artillery was CO of our camp – he was getting near retirement age so he was a bit timid, not like Slessor or Skinner."[41]

An SOE / Force 136 guerilla officer, David Smiley, was in touch with the Ubon prisoners at this time. He wrote: "The camp seemed clean and efficient. The inmates had improvised bamboo pumps to draw water out of the ground. Most of this was thanks to McTavish, a remarkable man who had managed to keep up a surprisingly high morale among the prisoners."

In August 1945, Marine Tom Webber was working in a railway workshop about fifty miles inside the Burmese border.[42] Maurice Edwards was the only Marine in his party at Takali in the Chao province on the railway fifty miles north of Bangkok. He was engaged in re-laying the airfield runway. "Fortunately," he explained, "the first aircraft to land on it were RAF Dakotas."[43] Peter Dunstan was working in a sawmill at a railway repair workshop not far from the Tamarkan Bridge.

Nick Carter went up the Death Railway as far as Moulmein in Burma. He ended the war in a camp in Cambodia where he was among emaciated prisoners in Jap Happies photographed by the liberating forces with newsreel cameras and appearing on Pathe News. He was thirty years old and weighed five stone. A year before in Thailand he was photographed by the Red Cross in a line of emaciated men. The photo, which appears in this book, was sent to his shocked mother who must have doubted he would survive until friends came to see her to say they had seen him on Pathe News at the cinema.

In Singapore, two *Repulse* Marines had spent the Japanese Occupation 'undercover', posing with a little local assistance as Eurasian car mechanics. Hearing that the war was over they handed themselves in to the Japanese and spent the final weeks until Mountbatten's arrival in Changi jail.[44]

Here too was Marine Peers Crompton, shipped back to Singapore by the Japanese in June 1945 after three years as a POW in Sumatra. On release from Changi he was hospitalised at Bangalore, India then transported by hospital ship to Johannesburg where he remained for a year before returning to the UK and discharge in January 1947.

At Batu Lintang camp at Kuching, Borneo, the surviving British prisoners, 116 officers and 684 other ranks awaited liberation. The condition of the other ranks was particularly desperate with two-thirds of them stretcher cases needing urgent hospitalisation . In the final weeks the Kuching prisoners had also faced increasingly threatening behaviour from their guards. These had practised armed manoeuvers through the camp and were awaiting orders to machine-gun the prisoners.

Three four-engined Allied aircraft had flown high over the camp dropping leaflets on August 17th 1945. Aircraft returned on August 28th dropping parachutes with "storpedoes" full of food. Monty Campbell remembers: "For breakfast the next morning there was bread and butter. How delicious it was. We had not tasted bread and butter for over three years."

Liberation finally came on September 12th with the arrival of the Australian General Wooten. For sixteen Argylls it was too late, but they were not forgotten by Monty Campbell: "I was able to procure one of the parachutes, and on being evacuated and hospitalised for a considerable time, I decided to occupy myself embroidering the Regimental badge. I dedicated this to the Argylls who were with me but lost their lives."

Shortly after the official surrender, Lady Mountbatten visited the Kuching prisoners. Monty Campbell was in the camp hospital where Lady Mountbatten asked him what he really wanted. He replied that more than anything else he wanted to get home quickly. Could she provide an aeroplane? Unfortunately not, but a senior Australian medical officer, hearing his remark, was shortly to oblige with a flight out of Borneo.

Derrick Montgomery-Campbell left Kuching on September 14th on a Catalina flying boat bound for Labuan. He was taken out to the Catalina from the POWs tented, down-river hospital, on a very fast American submarine chaser, "The Black Bitch." Monty still had in his possession a small Union Jack flag from the staff car of the Governor of Singapore, Sir Shenton Thomas. During the captivity he had placed this briefly on the body of each prisoner who had died, as they were carried to the pyre. The flag is also at Stirling Castle.

In French Indo-China, today Vietnam, Jockie Bell found himself among a truly cosmopolitan array of prisoners: Dutch, Americans, Australians, two drunken Mexicans, a Spaniard and even a German from Java who kept getting mistaken by the Japanese for a Dutchman. Then one day he heard the best words he ever heard in the whole war: "Senso Awahri – war finished!"

"When we marched through Saigon we knew the Japanese were defeated. We were singing all sorts of rubbish songs. There was a Foreign Legion guy with us. He'd been in hiding but the Vietnam War had started, the French were under curfew and getting shot. We got lost in the town, me and my pal, and finished up in a different camp in Saigon. We saw Rab Kerr at the door and he took us in."

In Japan, Cpl Bertie King DCM was in an altogether unpleasanter situation – the city of Nagasaki. His POW camp was located nearby. Some prisoners were killed and wounded by the Bomb and the survivors found themselves involved in the rescue work in the devastated city. There was little they could do.

In August 1995 HRH Prince Phillip told the story of two RM POWs who swam out to the Fleet in Tokyo Bay in the days before the Japanese surrender ceremony. The author has yet to ascertain if they were members of the *Repulse* detachment from the notorious Mori camp on an island in the Bay.

Duncan Ferguson weighed barely 7 stone when liberation came. He was in the other ranks' camp at Nakhon Pathom, Thailand. "We found a wee Glasgow boy there. He was pouring water to and fro between two cans. He said he was doing this in case the sound would help him, because he couldn't pass water. So Spud and I took over to help him but he died within the week. We were taken out on Tenko and there were no Japs taking us out on working parties, and the Sergeant Major sent out volunteers, two parties of four, to go out and look around the next day, and they reported no sign of the Japs. The natives were telling us the war was finished. Up went the Union Jack and the Sergeant Major sent us out with chits signed that the British government would pay, so that we could get in whatever we needed and these were accepted. Around then a train stopped with Japanese wounded. What a state they were in, and they were gesturing for cigarettes. They had no water, nothing. And our boys were good to them – after what we'd been through. In about ten minutes they had all our bully beef and cigarettes. One of them managed to get out of the wagon onto the embankment, when this Jap officer, immaculate with sword dangling down, came up and hit him such a wallop because he was out of the wagon. What a tanking that Jap officer got from our lads! He was black eyed and bleeding. They took his sword off him."

Duncan remembers the arrival of the first RAPWI (Repatriation of Allied Prisoners of War and Internees) personnel in September 1945, and joining the breadlines that seemed never-ending as FEPOWs went round again and again to pick up bread. For some weeks eating was controlled for there were cases of fatal overeating. In Singapore a man died after drinking a can of evaporated milk. An emaciated Tom Wardrope was taken to Alexandra Hospital and fed on a diet of fruit juice, eggs and liquids.

When Duncan Ferguson's camp RSM paraded the men and asked for volunteers to step forward to serve as officers' batmen, only Duncan did so. Admonished and abused by his comrades, he told them, "And who goes home first? The officers.... And who goes with the officers?" He was "nearly killed" in the stampede of volunteer batmen that followed.

The route home for most Thailand FEPOWs began with a Dakota flight from Bangkok's Don Muang airport to Rangoon, flying over the River Kwai area for a last look at their old camps. Captain Aylwin wrote home from Don Muang on September 3rd: "I shall be leaving here by plane to Rangoon either today or tomorrow. It is going to be a terrific thrill... I get so excited at the thought of the immediate future that on some nights I find great difficulty in sleeping! Other things I look forward to are my first hot bath, eating from a properly laid table with decent plates and cutlery, (I have had every meal from the same old spoon and bowl) a room to myself and so on. One thing I have found irksome and that was lack of any privacy."

Duncan Ferguson went first to a transit camp to await the flight from Bangkok to Rangoon: "Volunteers were asked for to go to the cookhouse to collect the food. So they asked 'What's for it?' And the boy replied 'A chicken a man, a loaf a man and...' He was shouted down. 'What's for the grub?' 'I'm telling you! A chicken a man, a loaf a man – I canna win!' But it was true! It was only a wee chicken but it was a chicken a man. It was a rich Thai millionaire, said he would give a meal to every POW who came there – oh, and cigarettes!"

Eventually Duncan found himself at Don Muang airport. "We were put in batches of twenty eight, and we were told that when it was our turn twenty eight will be there – or else back of the queue. We'd a wee boy with us from Tomintoul, L.Cpl Tom Jarvie of A Company, who used to always wander away. So we tied Wee Tam's hands and feet." They and Wee Tam did not miss the plane. "It was all Dakotas,"

Duncan recalls, "They gave us coffee and someone asked 'Is there a toilet in this place?' So he was told where. He came back and said he certainly wasn't going there – it was a hole in the floor thousands of feet up! He'd rather hold on." [45]

Claude Aylwin flew out on September 3rd with Lt Charles Verdon. They had managed to stick together throughout almost the entire captivity: "I flew in a Dakota crewed by Royal Canadian Airforce to Rangoon and I remember looking down on the dense forests and thinking 'No wonder escape had been out of the question.' But I was to have the biggest surprise of my life, before or since, at Rangoon. The plane arrived in a tropical downpour and we were transferred to a hospital by lorry. We were waiting to debus when someone called out 'Anyone by name of Aylwin there?' I came to the back of the lorry and jumped down into the hands of my younger brother, Peter!"[46]

Aylwin's brother was a naval officer on the aircraft carrier *HMS Searcher* which had arrived at Rangoon four days earlier. The bewildered POWs were taken to a big military hospital in the grounds of Rangoon University. Here their old clothes were burnt and they received such luxuries as toothpaste and soap. Aylwin wrote: "At one time I had weighed only eight stone, which was four stone under my former weight... It took a full two years from then until I resumed 12 stone."

He was to be one of the first home. The following day he and Charles Verdon left on *Searcher* for Madras, then Colombo. Departing Colombo on September 19th they were on the Clyde by October 8th.

In all, 203 Argylls, 189 of whom had served with the battalion in the Malayan Campaign, and 33 Plymouth Argyll Royal Marines, died in captivity.[47]

NOTES

1. Wilson. See also Rose's account of their escape and stay in Batavia.
2. Walter Green in conversation and letter 1995/1997
3. Papers of the British Association of Malaya (Singapore National Archives/ University Library, Cambridge)
4. Rose, Beattie and Royal Army Chaplains Dept. Records. Details of the Sumatra escape route provided by John Hedley
5. See "Guilty or Innocent: The Gordon Bennett Case" by M.Clisby (Allen and Unwin, Sydney 1992)
6. Stewart
7. Tom Wardrope: Sayonara Mine Enemy See Richard Gough: Escape from Singapore
9/10.Montgomery-Campbell 9.97
11. Gordon
12. Broadhurst interview (Singapore National Archives)
13. See Walter Gibson: The Boat. Gibson was a Cpl not a Sgt. Information on him from many Argylls and John Hedley. On Doris Lim see "Sold for Silver" (O.U.P Singapore 1985) by Janet Lim.

14. Miller conversation 1996 and Edwards letter 1997
15. Eric Moss 1997
16/18.Edwards/Dunstan letters 1996-8
19. Diary of an FMSVF officer (Singapore National Archives) and comment by Jockie Bell
20. Details of Pudu captivity: Jockie Bell and Stan Roberts to Audrey McCormick 9.97; Rev.Geoffrey Mowat letter 8.98 and Capt K.J. Archer FMSVF Armoured Car Regiment and Adjutant at Pudu
21. Miller 5.97
22. Eric Moss
23. Gordon/Miller
24. Weir conversation 12.95
25. Ferguson/Alex Bean letter 1995
26. E.R. Hall: 'The Burma-Thailand Railway of Death' Graphic Bks. Australia 1981
27. M. Edwards 1997
28. Aitken/Dunstan/Commonwealth War Graves Register, Kranji War Memorial
29/30.Miller conversations. The authors have a copy of the original Maru Document.
31. Dunstan Documentation

32. Arthur Titherington and Colonel John Lauder 1998. And Paisley Daily Express
33. Jockie Bell and Stan Roberts 1997
34. Dunstan letter 1996
35. Lang report and Edwards letter
36/37. Dunstan.
38/9. Gordon/Aylwin article in 'Globe and Laurel' 1995
40. Details of final days at Ubon from Charles Peat/Smiley/Rose Denny
41. Cameron interview 1.98
42. Webber
43. Edwards
44. Diary of AIF POW James Boyle. A Marine from Prince of Wales had also been in Changi jail in early 1942 posing as a civilian.

45. Ferguson interview. The description of the Dakota's primitive W.C. is hotly denied by a former Dakota engineer known to Audrey McCormick!
46. Aylwin article 1985
47. Stewart/Aitken/Dunstan/Commonwealth War Graves Register. Stewart's original Roll of Honour omitted one man who had died in captivity and placed another as killed-in-action. This is now corrected.

CHAPTER SEVEN

HOMEWARD BOUND AND AFTER

On October 2nd 1945 Marine Peter Dunstan penned a short letter to the Royal Marines magazine the 'Globe and Laurel' to announce that the Plymouth Argyll Royal Marines were on their way home: "Once again after a long silence we are able to say 'Hello'. Although we from Thailand regret to have left quite a few of our comrades behind, the rest of us, under the very able command of Captain R.G.S. Lang, are now on the return to the fold and are looking forward to seeing Guz once again."

In Colombo the returning Marines obtained copies of the 'Globe and Laurel' and berets before continuing their journey home on SS *Worcestershire*. They disembarked on October 16th together with 22 Argylls including Captain Kenneth McLeod. Six Marines including Maurice Edwards were repatriated on the SS *Chitral* which departed from Rangoon on October 1st 1945: "I can remember we were taken off the ship as soon as she docked in Southampton, before everyone else, by the Brigadier commanding Portsmouth Division and welcomed by the Corps."[1]

Maurice, who had joined the Corps in February 1940, took advantage of a discharge scheme for regular Royal Marines and left the service in 1946.

In Scotland telegrams arrived with news of Argyll loved ones 'safe and well'. Local newspapers including the 'Stirling Observer' kept the public well informed on the subject. As early as September 13th 1945 it reported Captain James Doherty, Battalion Quartermaster, telegraphing his wife. The release was announced of Pte William Walker aged 30, blacksmith from Cowie; Pte Thomas Wardrope aged 27; Ptes Jack Gardner and Adam Heslop. Soon there were reports of Japan POWs arriving in Australia: Thomas Goldie, William Robertson, Cpl Robert King of the Lanchester platoon.

A poem written by Tom Wardrope while a POW in Palembang, Sumatra, soon appeared in the Stirling Observer. Tom ended the war "a walking skeleton" weighing only 87 lbs. In the last three months of the war, 276 of the 1350 men in his camp died. He shared his captivity and liberation with Sgt Jack King R.M.[2] Another Argyll who returned, Captain Doherty's batman Pte Geordie McNeil, had the distinction of being the only man never to have had a day's illness during the Captivity.

Typically, RSM Sandy McTavish of the Argylls was on the last RAPWI (Repatriation of Allied Prisoners of War and Internees) ship leaving Rangoon. He refused to leave until all his 3,200 charges from Ubon camp were on their way home. His wife and four daughters, evacuated from Singapore in January 1942 to Durban, South Africa, awaited his return in Stirling.

McTavish together with Captain David Boyle received the MBE for services while in POW camps. Sadly a number of POWs including L.Cpl E. 'Dodger' Green, died on the voyage home. Ernest Gordon mentions one Argyll officer who despite the recuperative sea journey home to the UK, was very soon hospitalised still suffering from malaria, avitaminosis, hepatitis, enlarged heart and ulcerated intestines.

In late October the RAPWI ships began arriving at Liverpool: the *Empress of Austria* brought home 1675 POWs from Hong Kong and Japan; the *Antenor* 2720; the *Empire Pride* and French liner *Boiserain* 1597 between them; the Dutch liner *Tegelberg* carried 1100 servicemen and 600 civilian internees up the Mersey to Liverpool. From Singapore came the troopship SS *Monowa* and from Rangoon the SS *Chittral* and SS *Ormonde*. Together with Peter Dunstan and the Royal Marines from Thailand, 22 Argylls including Major Jack Hyslop disembarked from SS

Worcestershire on October 16th, and 36 Argylls including Major Gairdner arrived three days later on the *Orduna*.

The first FEPOW ships to arrive were greeted by bands and regimental representatives but no bands or crowds of relatives greeted later arrivals. There was no official welcome home, (although King George VI wrote a personal letter to each returning Far East POW.) But in Liverpool crowds gathered to applaud and cheer them on the journey from the docks to the railway station. A dock strike going on at the time did not hamper disembarkation. Jockie Bell remembers: "We were driven in army trucks through Liverpool. We saw women driving the tramcars. We thought it was great. The lassies were all screaming and jumping up on the tailboards and kissing and cuddling the boys."[3] However, POWs were being required to take oaths of secrecy before disembarking.

When he arrived at Glasgow railway station Jockie was met by the Lord Provost and was presented with a book of songs and poems by Robert Burns, a book he keeps to this day. Throughout the captivity no personal mail had reached him. When it was all over, he received a bundle of mail – it was to another John Bell from D Company who'd been killed in the fighting in the north of Malaya.

In spite of greatcoats, it felt bitterly cold after years in the Far East. Tiny Gordon, wearing his grimy kilt, carrying his dirty, bloodstained backpack and kit-bag, took the express train to Glasgow where he was met by his brother.[4]

Pte Finlay McLachlan arrived home to hear that his three brothers had not survived the war. He had thought that only one brother had died.[5] RSM Sandy Munnoch was reunited with his family in Kent.

When Alex McDougall returned from Japan his mother Rubina also took in three other Argyll FEPOWs. Alex explains: "There were four POWs in my house – myself, Albert Skinner, Totty Grant, Spud (Billy) Thomson, and there was also Spud's younger brother, Eric. Why did my mother take them in? Because she lost two sons. Albert Skinner and I were together all the time as prisoners. He had three sisters and a brother and they were all boarded out – a sad story; his mother murdered his father in Edinburgh a long, long time ago. And all the children were boarded out because she wasn't a fit mother, in prison and so on. Albert said he was determined to find all his family and get them together, and he did. I was best man at his wedding."

Billy Thompson, born at Saltcoats and fostered out, was the youngest of these Argylls. He had joined in India as a 15-year old boy soldier and was 17 when he was captured. Alex McDougall had saved his life during a river crossing in Malaya. On his return to Scotland, Billy began a successful search for his younger brother who had also been fostered out. Bill married and Alex was best man. Sadly, Billy died of cancer in November 1997 while this book was being researched.[6]

Montgomery-Campbell was flown from Kuching to Morotai then Western Australia where he spent three weeks before being sent to Brisbane then Sydney and on to the Royal Naval Base at Hearne Bay. Here he was among some five hundred FEPOWs who took passage on the *SS Aquitania* to Southampton. Australia clearly made an impression on Montgomery-Campbell because he returned to settle there in 1950.[7]

Did they return changed men? One Argyll comments: "I think so. I used to be easy-going, carefree, but when I came back I was withdrawn and used to cry at the least thing. It still comes back. I can still cry at anything that brings back memories. I don't think you can get rid of it... Yes, I think it made me a better person. We used to go to the big reunions at Scarborough, and there was a professor who had been studying us over some years. He stood up and told us: 'We know you love your families and your homes, but when you get together there is an unshakeable bond between you'. You never hear any arguing at any of the reunions. If there's any disagreement then it's very quiet. We're very close-knit – no, not just the Regiment – all POWs."

Ernest Gordon wrote on the problems of returning FEPOWs: "We weren't easy to live with; we were tense and taut and could not remain long doing nothing. Rather than sit in a chair we would pace the floor; rather than stay at home we would go out and walk for miles. Our sleeps were of short duration. As soon as we awoke we'd be on the prowl again, looking for something to do or someone to meet.

"We had enormous reserves of nervous energy to be used. Ideas popped up in our mind with amazing rapidity. We hungered for one another's company and for the comradeship we shared. Our friends must have had the impression that our imprisonment was one huge, rollicking party. We fought off a great loneliness – a loneliness that was increased by the fact that so many of our friends had not returned. Old familiar spots were haunted with their faces."[8]

One Argyll officer said: "There isn't a day goes by but I think about that Railway."

Nick Carter, like many FEPOWs, suffers from claustrophobia and has to sleep with his door open: "If I heard a car backfiring I used to get down on the ground – people would think I was mad but it took 15 years for me to get around it. We were trained to take evasive action. My doctor said I should go back, and my first time back I went to sit by the waterfall at Waterfall Camp, Kinsayok. Three of us burned 150 Tamils there – dead of cholera. We had to fish them out of the stream, me and Joe Leadbitter and Captain Meldrum. And I sat there with my feet in the stream. At the side of the waterfall is a road and we used to climb it, steep and slippery and carrying rice bags. The Japs put up a sort of pulley on it – no, not to help us but to help them get it. That's where the pig jumped overboard and swam to the other side – people say pigs can't swim because their forefeet doing the dog paddle would cut their own throats, but that's not true – and that meant short rations for us. But when I sat there, everything was so peaceful."[9]

Some Argylls prospered after the war; others faced unemployment and economic hardship. Tom Wardrope worked as a postman in Stirling and in 1953 emigrated to Canada. Alex McDougall became a postman in Glasgow. Padre Hartley Beattie left the Army in December 1945 and was appointed Church of Scotland minister at Bary Parish Church, Carnoustie, Fife. Later he too went to Canada, first as Minister of Knox Presbyterian Church, St.Catherine's, Ontario then to Alberta. He became Honorary Padre of the Royal Hamilton Military Institute.

Major Peter Farquhar, Lt Montgomery-Campbell, Lt Richard Webber, Sgt Andrew Connelly, Cpl Jock Henderson, Ptes Jim Jardine, 'Big' Jim McCutcheon and much later Finlay McLachlan settled in Australia. PSM F. Colvin and Sgt 'Bluff' Wallace emigrated to New Zealand and Sgt Sammie Moffatt to the USA. Cpl James Flynn worked as a driver for the co-op, then married and went to Canada but later, like Sammie Moffatt, returned to Scotland.

For some, the future held permanent ill health. Pte Archie 'Elmer' Fowler, wounded in the Singapore fighting and a POW in Thailand, spent 51 years as a patient at Bellsdyke hospital in Larbert before his death in January 1997.

Some stories had sad endings: PSM Hoostie McNaught, the popular and outstanding boxer and goalkeeper, remained with the Army. Major Montgomery-

Campbell says, "He came out to Australia with an Army corrective establishment. He used to teach the men bayonet practice." Duncan Ferguson adds: "At a later time he had both his legs off, the result of Japanese captivity, and at a reunion at a hotel in Renfrew, when the Argyll band was playing the Argyll Monarchs he was first up on the floor, marching round on two artificial legs, and the rest of us all got up and followed him. His ambition was to get back and see the war graves in the Far East, but he never had a pension, he never had a halfpenny. He finally saved enough money to go back, and he was about to step on the plane at Glasgow when he dropped dead."

Many Argylls attended the funeral and heard a few weeks later that Hoostie's son, a nightclub bouncer, was stabbed to death in Glasgow. Jockie Bell suffered a similar family tragedy.

Another Argyll attempting to get himself and his comrades back to the Far East was the irrepressible Joe Russell who after his return from captivity returned briefly to his old civilian job as a barber but later worked for British Aluminum in Falkirk.

"We were back home," recalls Duncan Ferguson, "when Joe phoned up George Younger who was Secretary of War at this time. Joe said 'You were in the Argylls same as us, and we're a load of old age pensioners here. We're not asking for much. Our ambition is to go back and visit war graves in Singapore – our dead over there. We're quite willing to rough it, if you've got an aircraft carrier or anything going over there!' He got nothing, but to rub salt in the wound, a fortnight later Joe gets a postcard, and it's from George Younger and he's over in Singapore! He used to call Joe 'Jim'. So as soon as Joe got the postcard, up with the phone calling George Younger's home, and it was his wife. Joe says 'Is that effer in?' She says 'Now, now Jim!' 'Never mind the now, now, Jim! Where is the effing basket?' She says 'He's not home yet, Jim.' 'Tell that effing basket that when he gets home I want to effing well speak to him!' That's the way Joe spoke. He phoned up Margaret Thatcher and all; got a secretary, and that's the way he talked. The Chairman of the POW Association had to phone up and apologise on his behalf!"[10]

Later Joe phoned up the Japanese Consulate in Edinburgh in much the same manner. As a result he got a visit at home in Grangemouth from a bagpipe playing Japanese Consul General, Selichiro Otsuka, who was a great Rabbie Burns enthusiast. They finished up good friends and the Japanese diplomat wrote Joe a poem in the style of Burns and entitled 'To a Golf Ball'. "Oh he wasn't a bad chap for a Jap," remarked Joe.

On hearing the news of the death of the Japanese Emperor in 1987, Tom Wardrope wrote:

"I shed no tears when Hirohito died.
I sorrowed not nor sadly sighed.
Instead I called to mind those friends of yore
Who played and laughed with me in Singapore,
Whose bodies row on row now lie
In graves beside the River Kwai,
Prisoners of the Emperor's Japanese
They died of torture, hunger and disease;
And those who further south did go,
Massacred in Borneo;
Those too who lacking food and clothes
Perished in Hokkaido's snows;

And to round off this sorry tale
Add those who starved and died in Changi gaol.
That list is long and nothing said
About the hordes of Chinese dead,
Some raped, some killed by bayonet thrust
To satisfy the conqueror's lust.
And he who to his lasting shame
Must ultimately bear the blame
Let us forget he ever lived
And pay no tribute to his name."[11]

Cpl Robert 'Bertie' King DCM of the Lanchester armoured cars was employed as a foreman with Singers of Dumbarton then worked for the Clydebank Parks Department. He died on March 30th 1993.

Duncan Ferguson remained with the Argylls until 1949 serving at Redford Barracks, Fort George and Edinburgh Castle, but was "never away from the doctor."

"My doctor said to me the best advice he could give me was to go back on a short term engagement. He said the Army was responsible for the way I was. 'Go back in and let them build you up. They marched you out A1, they can't refuse to take you back on health grounds now.' So I went back and that was me in. I went up to Redford and got put in a hut with a lot of young laddies on their training, and the Sergeant comes round and says 'Ten days Embarkation Leave.' I went back into the hut and the young laddies were saying 'We've two kitbags to pack and got to be all ready' and that. I sat down on my bed and they said 'You'd better hurry up.' I'm saying 'It's alright, you carry on boys.' Then I hear 'Outside the Draft!' and I'm sitting on my bed and the Sergeant is doing the roll call and I hear 'Ferguson, Ferguson!' and a wee laddie saying 'He's sitting on his bed, Sergeant!' The Sergeant comes in and says 'Ferguson!' 'Yes Sir!' 'Outside!' 'No, Sergeant.' 'What d'you mean – No Sergeant? You have ten days Embarkation Leave, don't you? Get out!' I says 'I'm not going on any Embarkation Leave!' 'Fall in!' I was marched in to this officer and I landed dead lucky. He asked what was the reason and I told him. He said 'Were you a prisoner of the Japanese?' 'Yes Sir.' He says 'I've got the job for you.' I was put in the Stores, dead lucky!"

Duncan was spared further service abroad. One day he visited Stirling Castle and encountered the 2nd Argylls' No.1 Singapore practical joker: "I had come up to the Castle to see about getting my driving licence back – all that had vanished with the Japanese – and who should be there scrubbing the guardroom steps but Smudger Smith, that was Davy Smith, the CO's bugler. 'Hi Fergie!' he says, 'How've you been?' And he's making smoking motions with his mouth – I'd have given him a packet of cigarettes but I couldn't. The MPs were watching. 'Have you not learnt yet, Smudger?' I said."

Jockie Bell left the Army in March 1946. He had no pension and applied for Service Disability Pension of 8 shillings and 6 pence a week (20%) for which he had to prove his disability. Following a severe head beating as a POW he became deaf; suffered recurrent malaria and various bowel and intestinal problems common to FEPOWs. Later he became blind in one eye. Jockie says, "I fought them for my disability pension but then after a few weeks they took it away altogether. To get it back and get it increased I had to go to medical boards and I was put in several different hospitals – Edenhall at Musselburgh, a servicemen's hospital outside Edinburgh for four weeks, and in the Eastern General in Leith (Edinburgh) for several weeks. I got the pension up to 40%, then when I heard deafness was going to be taken seriously I got it up to 60% and now its 100%. But I had mates of mine turn blind and never got a pension. One pal of mine who died at 64 never got a disability pension and if you spoke to him he'd say he was not going to bother going to all those hospitals and examinations – I think they are not bad now to Far East prisoners, but then it was old fogies sitting behind a desk and there were times I could have shoved them and their desk through the wall. It was cruel. A lot of fellows said they weren't going to go through this."

Civvy Cameron remained with the Argylls and was trained as a PT instructor then posted to another unit in Korea in the early 1950s. His wife wrote to the War Office to try and get him off this posting but to no avail. Fortunately the Korean War was over when he arrived and after a year in Korea he spent two years in Hong Kong. Subsequently he became 100% war disabled due to his increasing deafness, which he attributes to blasting rocks at Chungkai while a POW in Thailand.

For eighteen months after his return from captivity Kenny McLeod was too ill to return to the battalion. He made a handwritten list of all the illnesses he had suffered in captivity: amoebic dysentery; bacillary dysentery; hook worm; dry beriberi; ptomaine poisoning; ulcerated legs caused by leeches; malaria; dengue fever; jaundice; TB and throat polyps. Throughout his entire captivity he had also been without a shirt and suffered considerably during cold nights in Thailand.

During this period of recuperation, while playing golf at St Andrews, he nearly killed the former Colonel of the Regiment, Major-General Gervais Thorpe, to whom he had written in 1940 requesting to come to the Argylls: "I was out playing at the St Andrews course when I pulled a duck hook – shouted 'Fore!' And the man who ducked as it whizzed over his shoulder proved to be Thorpe, playing along with Field-Marshal Archie Wavell. He ticked me off by name – don't know how he knew who I was."

On his return from Singapore in 1942 Ian Stewart was awarded a DSO and appointed full Colonel and chief instructor at the School of Infantry. He was based at a battle school in Yorkshire. In 1944 he was transferred to SEAC (Southeast Asia Command); appointed Brigadier on the General Staff responsible for 11th Army Group Training. In 1945 he commanded 144th Infantry Brigade. In his final two years of military service he commanded Stirling District and took a special interest in the Polish troops and their families in the area.

On Saturday July 24th 1946 the first post-war Argyll reunion took place at Back o' Hill Camp, Stirling. There were some 300 guests including 205 of those who returned from the Far East. The occasion was presided over by Brigadier Stewart who gave a lecture in the camp gymnasium on the subject of the Malayan campaign. Dinner was then served.

At the principal table sat Brigadier and Mrs. Stewart; Major-General Gordon 'Babe' MacMillan, the Colonel of the Regiment; Mrs. Dor Robertson, the widow of Lt Colonel Lindsay Robertson lost after Slim River; Captain and Mrs. Doherty; Mrs. McTavish; RSM Munnoch; QMS George Aitken and the oldest private soldier in the battalion, Pte J. 'Crasher' Christie of 35 years service.[12]

The Regimental Silver adorned the principal table. Eric Moss had recovered some during the Captivity. Much of the rest was found in September 1945 by Malayan

Civil Servant and War Crimes investigator Mervyn Sheppard, from a Kempetei hoard on the island of Kundur in the Rhio Archipelago, south of Singapore. The silver was returned to Scotland by the aircraft carrier *Emperor* that arrived on the Clyde on December 12th 1945.

The menu was simple: tomato soup; steak pie; plum pudding; strawberries and cream. Stewart commented: "I gave instructions that there was to be no rice on the menu." Toasts were made to "Absent friends," "the Regiment," "Our Fallen Comrades" and "the CO" Pipers Stuart and McLean who had piped the battalion across the Causeway to Singapore were there to listen to the band play the regimental tunes followed by 'Abide with Me' and 'The Desperate Battle'.

Royal Marines Captains Aylwin and Lang both wrote short accounts of their experiences in the Far East and continued their military service into the 1950's. Sadly, Bob Lang died in 1955, well before his time. Aylwin, following his retirement from the Royal Marines, became a probation officer. He made several visits with former comrades to Thailand before his death in 1988.

Geoffrey Hulton retired from the Royal Marines through ill health in 1948 with the rank of Captain. Later Sir Geoffrey Hulton, 4th baronet and owner of Hulton Park Estate, Bolton, he pursued an interest in agriculture, cricket and scouting. He was also a recipient of high Papal decorations. He died in November 1993.[13]

Jim Davis studied medicine after the war and practiced as a GP in the Dover area. He chose to have little contact with FEPOW organisations.[14] Charles Verdon ended his military service as a Lt Colonel and served as a post-war ADC to Mountbatten. He returned to Malaya to command 41 Commando in the early 1960s. On December 10th 1962 he flew over the spot where *Prince of Wales* and *Repulse* went down and he dropped a wreath upon the water. Two days later he was on his way to deal with the Brunei rebellion.[15]

Twenty-nine years later, in December 1991, one hundred survivors from the two warships left Kuantan on *HMS Sheffield* to lay poppy wreaths in the choppy, monsoon blown sea where the two warships had gone down and to hold a memorial service.[16] Cpl Norman Overington returned to Malaya in the late 1940's and served with 45 Commando during the Emergency and on *HMS Belfast* during the Korean War. He ended his 45 years of service with the Corps as a lieutenant in the recruiting service and died in September 1982. General Sir Campbell Hardy said of him: "I find it difficult to picture a more inspiring man for a potential Sailor or Marine to meet." [17]

Charles Miller ended his Royal Marine service as a Sergeant Instructor in 1948. In 1950 he joined the Malayan Police and served throughout the Emergency. He was a police officer at Tapah in Perak State, a hot spot, and 'much bandit' country in 1951–2, and then spent four agreeable years in Songkla, Thailand, in police intelligence liaison work. He also served in Kedah under another former Plymouth Argyll, Hubert Strathairn. In 1958, as an Assistant Superintendent, Charles Miller was awarded the Colonial Police Medal for meritorious service, as was another Plymouth Argyll, Superintendent W.D. McLean. After serving as Head of Special Branch in Pahang Miller retired from the Royal Malaysian Police in 1963 but a few months later was sent to Brunei to assist in the reorganisation of the Royal Brunei Police. When he got there he found the Brunei police in little need of organisation, but what was to be a three-year contract lasted 19 years. He ended his long Police career in 1982 as Deputy Commissioner in Brunei. He received high decorations from both HM the Queen and HM the Sultan of Brunei (Royal Victorian Order and two awards carrying the title *Dato* – Dato Paduka Leila Jasa and Dato Setia Negara Brunei). The sprightly Charles Miller, at 80 years old still a keen golfer, continues to travel the Far East and divides his year between Western Australia and the UK.[18]

Douglas Broadhurst, the Straits Police officer attached to the Argylls, was awarded a DSO and also returned to Malaya. He was appointed Assistant Commissioner Singapore Police. Lts John Love and Stewart Angus continued their service in the MCS and were District Officers in Pahang during the Emergency. Richard Webber, the Argylls Signals officer, also returned to Malaya in the Emergency and was seconded to the Malay Regiment.

After demobilisation Peter Dunstan returned to civil engineering and later worked for Crown Agents. He returned to Thailand to supervise a large engineering project and was reunited with a young Thai called Boonruam who as a 17 year old had 'adopted' him and helped keep him alive in the later days of the Captivity. Peter has done much work assisting relatives of former POWs finding out what became of their loved ones and in leading many pilgrimages to the River Kwai. He lives today in north London and still makes regular trips to Thailand.

On March 27th 1982, 100 former members of the 2nd Argylls and 6 former Plymouth Argyll Royal Marines attended a reception and memorial service held at Stirling Castle to mark the 40th anniversary of the part they played in the Malayan campaign. Among those present were Brigadier Ian Stewart DSO OBE MC, Lt Colonel Charles Verdon, Major Claude Aylwin, *Prince of Wales* detachment survivor JW McPherson DSM, and from *Repulse*, G. Kennedy and R. Struthers.

In November 1985, Maurice Edwards was among a party of *Prince of Wales* survivors and families who returned to Singapore and Malaysia. On the afternoon of November 7th they flew to Kuantan and the following morning proceeded to the local Royal Malaysian Air Force base. Here a Sea King helicopter flew them to a Royal Malay Navy Landing Craft *K.D. Raja Jerom* which was positioned close to the wrecks of the two warships. There a Service of Remembrance took place. Maurice was particularly impressed at the number of Malaysian Naval personnel who turned out for the service. The Naval Prayer was said and the Naval Hymn sung: 'Eternal Father, Strong to Save'.

Maurice recited: "They shall grow not old as we that are left grow old... " then spread 840 Red British Poppies on the sea; one for each man that died that afternoon forty-four years before. "As the wreaths drifted rapidly astern, I sounded the Last Post and, after a sorrowful minute's silence, a bright Naval Reveille. It was so simple, but what an occasion. The sea was running away down the coast and there was a brilliant blue sky just like it was forty-four years before. The only sounds were the sea and the inevitable hum of the engines. I felt privileged to be at such a private Naval occasion, where those who survived, mourned and praised their dead comrades. It was a ceremony more moving than any of the great occasions that I have attended during my years in the Royal Marines."[19]

Brigadier Ian Stewart, 13th Laird of Achnacone, retired from the Army in 1947 to farm his 2500 acre family estate at Achnacone on the Argyllshire coast. He experimented in sheep farming methods and was prominent in local affairs as a deputy Lord Lieutenant and JP. He took on the Forestry Commission over the planting of conifers across the Highlands. Ursula Stewart died in 1969. Her surviving daughter Cherry Linnhe married Henry Steuart Fothringham of Grandtully.

At the age of 89, Ian Stewart was invited to unveil Peter Archer's painting 'Sans Peur' at the Officers Mess, Redford barracks. The impressive, well-researched painting, now at Stirling Castle, depicts the crossing of the Causeway. Ian Stewart gave a marvellous talk about the Malayan campaign and the evacuation of Johore. What was particularly remarkable was that he spoke for some fifty minutes without any notes.

Rena McRobbie at Regimental HQ gives an affectionate portrait of Stewart in his twilight years: "He was a flirt and a terrible kidder – he used to call me Mrs. Thingummy and I called him Brigadier Whatsismame – he was lovely! I don't know what he was like when he was younger but as a very old man I was very fond of him. He took on a tremendous lot with the last 'Save the Argylls' campaign and was always first on the phone each morning. He had a wonderful walled garden at his home which was full of very old species of plants. He said his old gardener had died, it was such a nuisance. So I said I didn't suppose he wanted to die – how old was he? The Brigadier said he was about 85. So I said 'Well, you'll be able to get a younger fellow in now' but he said 'Och no'. He would just get on and do it himself. He only had the one surviving daughter who married later in life, but he had three grandsons."[20]

A neighbour of Ian Stewart's comments that Stewart felt terribly guilty about being removed from his men at Singapore; a feeling worsened by spending the rest of his life among FEPOWs. Ian Stewart died on March 14th 1987 aged 91 Sixteen of the Jocks attended the funeral and were given place of honour on the front row. Ian Stewart's grave is at Portnacroish in Appin, beside Loch Laich, an inlet of Loch Linnhe. Eric Moss played the pipes at the graveside.

Tiny Gordon married in December 1945. He studied Theology and History and became assistant master at Paisley Abbey. David Wilson last saw "this great chap" pursuing his interest in sailing at Gourock Pier. In 1955 Gordon was appointed Dean of the Chapel of Princeton University USA and in 1981 President of CREED (Christian Rescue Effort for the Emancipation of Dissidents) in the USA. He still lives in Princeton.[21]

Bal Hendry returned from India and pursued his interest in rugby and golf as well as running a successful Edinburgh retail business. A real gentleman, he died in June 1994.

Angus Rose returned to the UK in 1943 to command 7th Argylls. Shortly before D-Day he was posted to Burma to command a battalion of the King's Own Scottish Borderers. In 1944 he published a watered down version of his experiences in Malaya entitled "Who Dies Fighting." David Wilson had bashed the original text out for Angus on the ship's typewriter while escaping from Sumatra to Ceylon in 1942. Angus Rose died in February 1981.

David Wilson, evacuated from Singapore with Rose, Stewart and CSM Bing, became chief instructor at 2nd Division's Battle School near Poona in India. The 2nd Division had arrived in India in June 1942 when the country was absolutely defenceless and there was a real danger of India collapsing. One Royal Engineers officer says, "We arrived completely unused to conditions, and David Wilson became our chief source of information about Jap warfare. He was the only one at the time who had battle experience against the Japs. He was invaluable. As other survivors joined us their experience was very much used, and the first action we went into in 1944 was Kohima."[22]

David confessed that for all the training he could give on fighting the Japanese he could not provide knowledge of how they would behave in defeat, burrowing in and hanging on. He later discovered this fighting in Burma. After the war he temporarily commanded the 1st Argylls in Palestine then commanded their A Company in the thick of the fighting in the Korean War. In 1952 he went back to the Seremban bridge to look for evidence of his handywork: "I was sent to Malaya for six weeks from Hong Kong, and one day drove through Seremban. And the bridge was still there, just the same as I thought I remembered it. Had it all been a dream? So I got out of the car and had a good look, and there on the buttresses and brickwork were the marks of restoration, and one or two jagged places which the explosion had made."

In 1957 David Wilson served as Military Assistant to Field Marshal Montgomery. One day at lunch their conversation turned to Scottish generals: "He said that in his opinion our Regiment had never produced any really distinguished high Commanders. He used to call them 'Grand Chefs'. I named one or two like Sir Ian Hamilton of the Gordons, Lord Lynedoch of the Peninsular War, Sir Hector MacDonald of the Boer and Egyptian Wars but all were dismissed as being brave and good leaders, but of no great ability or original thought. I then suggested that perhaps Ian Stewart of Achnacone might qualify. When I said he had served in the Tank Corps and also that he had passed into the Staff College but refused to go, the Field Marshal eagerly took my copy of the Battalion History, read it and wrote the following:

> Human endeavour by Scots.
>
> This is a wonderful story. It shows what the British soldier can do when properly led, and how he responds to a challenge — giving of his best when asked to face up to hard conditions. I know better than most to what heights the soldiers of Britain can aspire. Their greatness is a measure of the greatness of our national character, and I have seen the quality of our race proved again and again on the battlefield. No better example can be found than the story of the 93rd Highlanders unfolded in this book.
>
> Montgomery of Alamein
> F.M.
>
> August 1957

Following his escape from Singapore, Captain Robert Kennard was posted to the 1st Battalion Seaforth Highlanders in Delhi as were several other ranks who had escaped or been evacuated from Singapore. This battalion had been based in Shanghai then briefly in Penang until early 1941. Promoted to Major, Kennard won the MC in Burma commanding C Company of the Seaforths, serving in the Imphal-Shenam area of Assam then in the battles in the Imphal area and advance towards the Chindwin. He left the Seaforths in May 1945. An industrial chemist from the Stirling area, he worked for Allied Ironfounders. On retirement he took over his mother's estate in Gloucestershire and became a farmer. In Scotland Kennard was an enthusiastic member of the Linlithgow and Stirlingshire Hunt. He died in 1979.[23]

'Jock' Hayes of the Royal Navy escaped Singapore on HMS Jupiter and broadcast on BBC London in May 1942. He continued his naval career, was knighted in 1967 and rose to the rank of Vice Admiral. In retirement in Scotland he served as Lord Lieutenant of Ross and Cromarty, Skye and Lochalsh. Forty years after running across the Singapore Causeway with Ian Stewart and Drummer Hardie, he again met Brigadier Stewart, like him the son of an Army medical officer, at the unveiling of the painting 'Sans Peur' on which he too featured. Jock Hayes died in September 1998 at the age of 85.

David Boyle remained in the regular army until 1950, serving as adjutant of the 7th Argylls, then took up farming in Comrie, Perthshire. As a Colonel in the Territorials he later commanded the 7th Argylls. He was appointed Commandant Erskine Hospital near Glasgow and died there of a heart attack in 1983. Erskine hospital was founded in 1916 for disabled and seriously ill former servicemen.[24] Many Argylls who had served in Malaya were to spend their last days there. It was often the case that these men had no family or no relatives to claim their bodies. They were buried in the nearby Bishopton Cemetery. David Boyle made a point of placing a Union Jack on each coffin and attending the funeral. One of the staff at Erskine Hospital says of Boyle: "He had a great affinity with the men who had served in the war because he had been through it himself. He had his finger on the pulse, and we really thought when he died that might mean the end of the hospital. There were three hundred patients in his day, and he knew every one by name and was very well thought of."[25]

Tam Slessor saw post-war service in Hong Kong and the Middle East and continued to serve as a morale-builder. He was Regimental Secretary of the Argylls 1964–1974 and died in 1996, as did his former driver Private Davy Watson.[26] Jimmy McLean says of Slessor: "Tam was a tremendous aid in captivity – he would be sent off to cheer up others who needed it and he did a lot of this. He had a good sense of humour and he was a very sound chap."

Captain (later Major) James Doherty MBE was QM at the Argylls Depot at Stirling after the war. Sadly, the sister of his half-brother Billy Doherty blamed him for not looking after young Billy who died in the Alexandra Hospital massacre, and contact between the two sides of the family was lost. Doherty was widowed and remarried a widow of an officer of the battalion. Retiring in the 1950s he took an office job in Stirling. In retirement 'Old Doc' became a well-known character in the town. He died in 1996 aged 95.[27]

RSM Sandy Munnoch was appointed RSM of the reconstituted 7th Argylls in 1947. He was awarded an MBE and later became military instructor at Bradfield College, Reading. He died suddenly on December 12th 1956.[28]

Lt Colonel, formerly Major, K.D. 'Mali', or 'Molly' Gairdner died on May 15th

1959 in Littlehampton. Like many former FEPOWs his health was damaged by the deprivations of captivity. He had never really been in tune with Ian Stewart's vigorous jungle training but like the others he endured the rigours of the campaign and pains of captivity.[29]

Eric Moss served with the Black Watch immediately after the War but then returned to the Argylls. Promoted Major in 1946, he retired from the Army in 1958. He served for many years in the Glencoe Mountain Rescue Team and one of his bagpipe compositions was named in their honour. He still lives in Glencoe, the oldest surviving officer.

Jimmy McLean stayed on in the Army and received a regular commission. He then transfered to the Colonial Service and served in Uganda until that country's independence.

Kenneth McLeod entered a successful and wide-ranging business career in Glasgow and the West Coast of Scotland. He started off as a specialist salesman with paints and chemicals. "With my golf contacts I found I could sell to anyone." Together with his wife he then bought a family store in Glasgow and opened a quality corsetry business. Kenny still plays golf regularly.

Major Montgomery-Campbell served after the war at the School of Infantry then joined the reconstituted 2nd Argylls in Germany. In 1950 he transferred to the Australian Army, retiring in 1963. He entered the teaching profession, teaching Science and Maths at the Southport School where he was also a housemaster, track and field coach and Officer of Cadets. From 1972–9 he was the school Registrar. He lives today in Queensland, Australia.

After the war Sgt Harry Nuttall worked as a painter on the railways. His health was poor and for many years he lost touch with the Regiment. On February 12th 1992 for the Mountbatten Festival of Music at the Albert Hall, a joint concert by the massed bands of the Royal Marines joined by the pipes and drums of the Argyll and Sutherland Highlanders was attended by former Plymouth Argylls including Peter Dunstan and a rediscovered Sgt Harry Nuttall of the Argylls. Harry died on September 22nd 1992.[30]

Ian Primrose, who showed such initiative and aggression in battle and was such a morale raiser in captivity, suffered greatly in captivity in Pudu gaol and Thailand. In Thailand he developed Blackwater Fever which seriously affected his future health. He died at the age of 65 on Christmas Day 1984.[31]

Another Argyll who died before his time was Captain Mike Bardwell. Formerly a tea planter in Assam he returned to Malaya as a rubber planter through the years of the Emergency. He was manager of Batang Malaka estate in Negri Sembilan State. In 1958 he returned to Scotland to inherit his father's hereditary title as 'Angus Campbell, 21st Captain of Dunstaffnage', the ancient castle at Connel in Argyllshire. He took a keen interest in Scouting and during the 1960s was Scotland's Chief Scout. Mike Bardwell died aged 61 on December 4th 1980.[32]

RSM Sandy McTavish MBE was met by his family at Stirling railway station on his return from the Far East. He left the Army in 1946 and joined the War Department Security Police guarding the Stirling Ordnance Depot. He believed he was living on borrowed time because he felt so very lucky to have come home. His daughter remembers: "When Hoostie McNaught came to visit after the war, they would sit up all night talking. But he would only tell us some of the funnier things that happened. Except for one thing that made him very bitter. It was about a priest taking names down in a book, when he'd been giving masses for the dead. He said that this priest was noting the names down to collect the money due at the end of the war for the masses he'd given. My father was an intelligent man – he'd been offered the opportunity of going home and getting a commission before the campaign, but he preferred to remain where he was with the battalion in Malaya."

Sandy McTavish was still troubled with beriberi and developed angina. After his retirement in 1971 he looked after Forthside police dogs and went out delivering 'Meals on Wheels' to the frail at home. He died in 1975 aged 69.

Piper Charles Stuart continued his service with the Argylls in Germany, Korea and Hong Kong. He died at Erskine Hospital on December 7th 1990. Jockie Bell despite his own health problems, still visits the patients at Erskine and the nearby Argylls' plot at Bishopton Cemetery. On a recent visit to the hospital to see an old comrade who was now "away wi' the fairies," his friend eyed Jockie's regimental tie with tears in his eyes. Jockie left there, minus his tie.

FMS Police officers Hubert Strathairn, Robin Calderwood and Douglas Weir survived captivity and continued their police careers in Malaya. Strathairn was Police Chief in Johore, Pahang then Kedah during the early years of the Emergency. Douglas Weir served as Intelligence Officer at the operational police headquarters Kuala Lumpur, then as Police Chief, Malacca during the Malayan Emergency. He later took up a security appointment in Trinidad with a well-known oil company. [33] He still works actively for the FEPOWs and in 1995 went to Japan with TV cameras to confront one of his former tormenters.

Today the small band of surviving Argylls and Marines continue to meet at reunions. They paraded at the London VJ 50th Commemoration on August 19th, 1995. A 74-year-old Argyll, Hugh Irvine of Kilmarnock, appeared on the front cover of the Times newspaper next day. Nick Carter was eighty years old that day. He had three years, eight months and two days as a FEPOW to remember. The overwhelming emotion brought on a slight heart attack. [34] But he continues, pacemaker fitted, an amputee with enough health problems to overwhelm anyone but the most doughty of spirits...

The survivors from *Prince of Wales* and *Repulse* held a reunion at Scarborough in May 1999. In July 1999 survivors of the 2nd Argylls gather at Edinburgh to meet the Queen, then at Stirling Castle in September to celebrate the bicentenary of the 'Old 93rd'. Each year their numbers grow thinner but the spirit remains.

Such then were the Argylls and Marines. Those who did survive never forgot the immensity of their own and their comrades' experiences.

Those who came home bore emotional baggage which somehow, had to be laid down. These had been years of precarious life; years of facing one's total vulnerability, helpless to any whim and passing barbarity; years without civilised boundaries; years of grief and regret for many terrible deaths among close companions. Some, like Duncan, could not talk to families about the deaths of their loved ones: few were told the unvarnished truth. Some ex-prisoners never, ever, talked freely. For others reunion with other FEPOWS was the only catharsis. The switch from the trauma of starvation and death into ordinary family life, was another dramatic swing on the emotional trapeze, capable of leaving families and men in prolonged confusion. There were the physical results of the worm infestations, tropical fevers, vitamin deprivation, head beatings, broken bones, torture. To provide evidence for pension purposes as Jockie Bell described, ex-prisoners were jumped through medical hoops. Nowadays we know they were inadequately supported. They helped each other – even to Duncan's efforts with

Joe. He spent time trying to calm Joe Russell's language when Joe had important pension medicals to attend. Firmly told to take it easy, stay calm, within two seconds Duncan would hear Joe off again. A doctor may have said he was busy...

They continue to wrap this concern around each other as well as around the widows and families, so far as older age permits.

As for the dead, who dares speak for them? But it is true they live more brightly and longer in the reminiscences of their friends, than any civilian in death. The old soldiers talk of friends' doings as eagerly as their own: even non-friends are tolerantly woven into history.

Does all this come together in Hoostie McNaught? Who marched on two false legs to the battalion music? Or is the illustration of army values in the story of Sgt Alec Carruthers, sent back to the UK on leave when his battalion was in Singapore?

Alec was difficult: tough and quarrelsome, brought up in the hard area that was then Stirling's 'top o' the town'. But Alec found his salvation in the 93rd. He had leadership qualities, from his first, early stripe, although busted from Sergeant six times and from Corporal eight. By 16 he was in India fighting, and became a leading light in boxing and football. He overcame initial moroseness with drink. But he never raised a hand to his later adopted stepson. He sent photographs to his mother, "From your loving son". Much later, he would rely on his wife's presence, hating her to be away from him.

However with Singapore fallen, he was in the 'new' 2nd battalion. His photograph albums no longer reflected his army life. Where they had been full of his comrades in India and the battalion doings, suddenly nothing but a team picture or two, with Alec on the outer edges. But there among the albums was a treasure. Expensively leather-bound it covered the 1954 Balaclava Centenary Celebrations of the 93rd: the invitations, photographs, order of services, with a cover embossed in gold, with the Regimental badge, such an album that even the Castle Museum did not contain. One can guess where his heart remained, this tough old character, undoubtedly a pain to his officers, a local hero nonetheless, and still squaring his shoulders at 80, ready to "sort out" a squabble in a pub.

Tradition, and pride, and belonging, are deep values in a man's heart. He may be praying in fear he will get home again, but he will die for his friends and his pride if needs be. It is his job. Even, such willingness is his entry fee. Pride makes steel bonds of a battalion's unity, and he is bound within them. The further mutuality of devastating experience, makes further ties of deep affection and forbearance. The outsider may not know why such a thing glitters and gleams, unless he looks carefully.

"Those men who did the training march, the 116 miles from Mersing", Duncan said, "had their feet examined each day by the MO. Some of them were red raw. They were walking in agony! But they *pleaded* with the MO – pleaded with him – to let them go on. He would agree in the end. 'On your own head be it' he'd say. And they walked. *That* was esprit de corps.

"As for what we fought for, well it wasn't for King and Country. And it wasn't for the CO. It was for the Regiment. Eric Moss once told the CO that. The CO said he believed that too."

1. 'Globe and Laurel' 11.45 and Maurice Edwards letter 10.97
2. Wardrope: Sayonara Mine Enemy
3. Jockie Bell
4. Gordon
5. Finlay McLachlan
6. Alex McDougall interview
7. Montgomery-Campbell conversations
8. Gordon
9. Nick Carter interview 1.98
10. Duncan Ferguson/Kathy Russell/the Falkirk Advertiser 5.8.92
11. Tom Wardrope
12. 'The Thin Red Line' 1946. To give the Colonel of the Regiment his full name and title: General Sir Gordon HA Macmillan of Macmillan of Knap KCB KCVO CBE DSO MC. His nickname 'Babe' originated from his youthful looks when in 1916 he joined the Argylls.

13. Who's Who/Maurice Edwards
14. Maurice Edwards
15. Captain Derek Oakley MBE RM
16. J. McPherson 1987
17. Obituary in 'Globe and Laurel'
18. Charles Miller/Alex Richards RM
19. Edwards letter 10.97 with article '840 Red Poppies' and Order of Service
20. Rena McRobbie 1997
21. Ernest Gordon / David Wilson
22. Wilson / Major A.M. Fradgley MBE
23/24 'Globe and Laurel' / 'The Thin Red Line' (the Argylls magazine), and Eric Moss who also wrote a splendid obituary to 'Doc' Doherty in TRL 1997.
25. Information on Boyle at Erskine Hospital from Isobel McCartney
26/32 'The Thin Red Line'
33. Weir conversation
34. Nick Carter 1998

LIEUT. J. DOHERTY, M.B.E.

C.S.M. ALEXANDER McTAVISH.

CAPTAIN J. F. ALLAN.

News has reached Mrs Doherty, 10 North End, Cambusbarron, that her husband, Lieut.-Quartermaster James Doherty, M.B.E., A. & S.H., is a prisoner in Japanese hands. An Edinburgh man, he is a regular soldier, and has been abroad with the battalion since it went out to Jamaica in 1927. Like Captain Allan, referred to in another paragraph, Lieut. Doherty was in India when war broke out and was transferred to Singapore. He, too, has now completed considerably more than twenty-one years' service with the Argylls, and was awarded the M.B.E. in 1941.

Mrs McTavish, 14 King Stables Lane, Stirling, daughter of Mr and Mrs John O'Donnell, 12 Weir Street, Stirling, has received intimation that her husband, C.S.M. Alexander McTavish, A. & S.H., is a prisoner of war in Japanese hands. A native of Edinburgh, he was stationed at Stirling Castle from 1927 to 1932. He married Miss Agnes O'Donnell in 1928, and they have a family of four daughters. Mrs McTavish went to India with her husband in 1938, and later accompanied him to Singapore when the Argylls were transferred there. She was evacuated from Singapore before it fell.

Mrs Allan, 8 Alloa Road, Causewayhead, has been informed that her husband, Captain Joseph Fisher Allan, A. & S.H., is a prisoner in Japanese hands. He was attached to the Second British Convalescent Depot in Singapore. Forty-three years of age, Captain Allan has had twenty-four years' service with the Argylls. A native of East Lothian, he came to Stirling early in life with his parents, Mr and Mrs William Allan, of 44 Beatty Avenue, Stirling. For a short time Captain Allan was stationed at Stirling Castle over twenty-one years ago. He was in India when war broke out, just on the eve of the expiry of his twenty-one years' service.

Courtesy of 'Stirling Observer'

Piper Charles Stuart 1939 and 1946

Cpl Charles Miller RM 1941

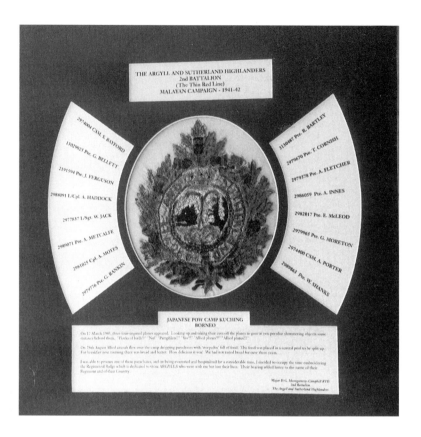

Lt Montgomery-Campbell created an embroidery signed by himself and fellow captives while in captivity at Kuching. A further embroidery commemorates those Argylls who died in captivity in Borneo. Both embroideries can be seen at the A&SH Regimental Museum, Stirling Castle.

Lt Montgomery-Campbell

Battle of Balaclava Commemoration. Brigadier Ian MacAlister Stewart DSO OBE MC, standing full-face to right of centre, smiling and be-medalled, in a gathering of senior Highland officers paying their respects to the 93rd Sutherland Highlanders at the 93rd Memorial Stone (left), at Skially, Strathnaver, Sutherland, where the regiment was first collected in 1799.

Argylls reunion in Stirling 1986 (back row left to right) Stan Roberts, 'Piper' Morrison, Tom Cochrane, Major Doherty, John Hunter, Geordie McNeill, 'Tourie' MacDonald and 'Skin' McGregor. (front row left to right) Hooky Walker, Alex Johnston, Duncan Ferguson, Finlay McLachlan, Jockie Bell and Joe Russell.

At Stirling Castle 1998 (left to right) Johnny Hunter, Duncan Ferguson, Kenneth McLeod, Jockie Bell, Hooky Walker.

Tom Wardrope

Dato Charles Miller RM at the Royal Marines Memorial, Fremantle.

Maurice Edwards RM in Singapore

MARINERS MEMORIAL

1939   1945

THE THOUSANDS OF MEN AND
WOMEN WHO LOST THEIR LIVES
IN THESE WATERS DURING
WORLD WAR II IN THE DEFENCE AND
LIBERATION OF THE TERRITORIES IN
SOUTH EAST ASIA OCCUPIED BY THE JAPANESE.
THEY WERE SAILORS, SUBMARINERS,
NAVAL AIRMEN AND MARINES OF
THE BRITISH AND ALLIED NAVIES
AND MERCHANT SEAMEN OF MANY
NATIONS WHOSE SHIPS WERE
ENGAGED IN THE CONFLICT.
THE 'FORGOTTEN FLEETS'
ARE REMEMBERED HERE
BY THEIR COMRADES.
THEIR SACRIFICES WERE MADE
FOR OUR FREEDOM.
NONE OF US SHOULD FORGET

The Mariners Memorial,
Changi, Singapore

ROLL OF HONOUR

'Tae the braw, brave lads o' the 93rd
Malaya fell at the cost o' your blood,
In rubber plantations and jungle you lie,
Resting in peace 'neath the tropical sky,
Your country called but spoke not in vain,
The Thin Red Line soon answered its name.'

(from a poem by Pte Thomas Wardrope,
written while a POW in Palembang, Sumatra.
229 Argylls have no known grave.)

TO THE EVERLASTING FAME OF THE OFFICERS AND MEN OF
THE 2ND BATTALION THE ARGYLL AND SUTHERLAND HIGH-LANDERS
(THE THIN RED LINE) WHO SERVED IN THE MALAYAN
CAMPAIGN 1941–42

220 GAVE THEIR LIVES IN ACTION
192 DIED AS PRISONERS OF WAR

THEIR BEARING ADDED LUSTRE TO THE NAME OF THEIR
REGIMENT AND OF THEIR COUNTRY

"Still, when a chief dies bravely,
We bind with green one wrist-
Green for the brave, for heroes
One crimson thread we twist.
Say ye, oh gallant Hillmen,
For these, whose life has fled,
Which is the fitting colour,
The green one or the red?"

SIR FRANCIS HASTINGS DOYLE

(memorial tablet in the Presbyterian Church, Orchard Road, Singapore)

Killed in action, died of wounds, missing:

OFFICERS

19305 Lt Colonel Lindsay Robertson
16.2.42 (42) *in the jungle*

74706 Captain Michael Blackwood
9.3.42 (23) *at sea*

74361 Captain Ranald Beckett
16.2.42 *in the jungle*

67451 Captain John Lapsley
24.6.42 *in the jungle*

279562 Lt Richard Armstrong
(from MCS)

20.12.41 (21) Lenggong
Grave at Taiping

204892 Lt Geoffrey Bancroft
20.1.42 (23) *Singapore*
Grave at Kranji

186376 Lt Ernest Bremner
10.2.42 *Singapore*

190254 2nd Lt John Colliston
16.1.42 (19) *in the jungle*

371854 Lt Albert Gispert (from FMSVF)
10.2.42 (38) *Singapore*

274700 2nd Lt John Leahy (from FMS
police) 10.2.42 *Singapore*

193888 2nd Lt Kenneth MacLean
29.12.41 *Gopeng-Dipang*

98583 Lt Donald Napier
11.2.42 (34) *Singapore*

137942 2nd Lt Gordon Schiach
28.1.42 (27) *Singapore*
Grave at Kranji

137943 2nd Lt Alexander Stewart
29.12.41 (23) *Gopeng-Dipang*

67574 2nd Lt Neil Stewart (from FMS
police) 11.2.42 *Singapore*

113423 Lt Arthur Wilkie
14.2.42 (33) *Singapore*
Grave at Kranji

265384 2nd Lt John O'Callaghan
(from the Kedah Volunteers)
11.2.42 *Singapore*

OFFICERS SERVING WITH OTHER UNITS

56135 Major Angus MacDonald
Brigade major 12 Indian Brigade
3.3.42 (29) *at sea*

79398 Lt Maurice Edmonson
former PSM commissioned into
the East Surreys 12.2.42
Singapore

OTHER RANKS

3323207 Pte Thomas Adam
20.1.42 (28) *in the jungle.*
Grave at Taiping.

2979216 Sgt David Adamson
7.1.42 (31) *Slim River*

3322690 Pte Andrew Allan
23.12.41 (27) *Salak.*
Grave at Taiping.

2979594 Cpl Robert Anderson
14.3.42 (25) *in the jungle*

860443 Pte Robert Atkinson
15.2.42 (28) Singapore

2986034 Pte Myles Atkinson
10.2.42 (23) *Singapore*

2979717 Cpl Robert Baird
11.2.42 (25) *Singapore*

3320465 Pte Archibald Ballantyne
13.1.42 (24) *in the jungle.*
Grave at Taiping.

2979910   Pte James Baxter
11- 17.1.42 (23)
in the jungle

2979179   Sgt Robert Beattie
11.2.42 (28) *Singapore*

2982066   Pte John Bell
1 – 7.1.42 (26)

3128486   Pte George Bellis
7.1.42 (30) *Slim River*

3322730   Pte Robert Bellis
13.2.42 (27) *Singapore*

2979605   Pte Hugh Benny
27.3.42 (25) *in the jungle*

2987779   Pte John Bertolini
7.1.42 (27) *Slim River*

2977268   Pte Christopher Betteridge
7.1.42 (27) Slim River.
Grave at Taiping.

2977421   Pte David Birkmyre
23.12.41 (30) *Salak.
Grave at Taiping.*

2979935   Pte James Boyd
15.2.42 (24) *Singapore*

2979488   L.Sgt William Bicker
7.1.42 (26) *Slim River
Grave at Taiping.*

2971522   CSM Alexander Biggarstaff
30.12.41(40) *Bidor.
Grave at Taiping.*

3322731   Pte Henry Booth
13.1.42 (26) *in the jungle*

13044127   Pte George Bolt
Missing 17.12.41
died in the jungle 3.3.42 (28)

2989944   Pte James Bradburn
28.12.41 (27) *Gopeng*

2979482   Pte Charles Brandon 23.12.41
(29) *Salak.
Grave at Taiping.*

2979958   Pte Thomas Brandon
7.1.42 (24) *Slim River*

2979786   L.Cpl Douglas Brodie
21.2.42 (24)

2979867   Pte George Brodie
13.1.42 (26) *in the jungle*

2979723   Pte David Brown
13.1.42 (25) *in the jungle.
Grave at Taiping*

3322737   Pte Joseph Brown
13.1.42 *in the jungle*

7009563   L.Sgt Thomas Brown
23.12.41 (37) *Salak.
Grave at Taiping*

3322739   Pte Robert Buckley
18.2.42 (27)

3324879   Pte Thomas Burke
13.1.42 (29) *in the jungle*

3132410   Pte Thomas Burns *Missing*
29.12.41 *Kuala Dipang*
Official date 6.1.42 (31)

3321661   L.Cpl Stanley Burrows
30.12.41 (25) *Bidor*

3132837   Pte Robert Caldwell
13.1.42 (23)

2980572   Pte Samuel Cameron
15.2.42 (26) *Singapore*

2979560   L.Cpl Duncan Campbell
13.1.42 (25)

2989050   Pte Robert Carlton
20.12.41 (27) *Lenggong*

3132838   Pte Richard Clark
15.2.42 (22) *Singapore*

3321669   Pte John Catling
7.1.42 (25) *Slim River*

2979837   L.Cpl John Child
Missing 29.12.41
Kuala Dipang.
Official date 6.1.42 (23)

2029585   Cpl James Conlon
15.2.42 (28) *Singapore*

3323221   Pte George Connolly
7.1.42 (27) *in the jungle*

2990948   Pte John Cronin
13.1.42 (32)

2979854   C.Sgt Frederick Crouth
1.2.42 (27)

2982047   Pte William Crozier
19.12.41 (22) *Sumpitan*

332272   Pte Thomas Curley
13.2.42 (27) *Singapore*

2989476   Pte Robert Currie
17.12.41(28)
Titi- Karangan

2979724   Pte William Daly
13.1.42 (24)

2979925   Pte Francis Davidson
11.2.42 (25) *Singapore*

2979629   Pte William Darby
27.1.42 (28)

2980642   Sgt. Albert Darroch DCM
29.12.41 (26)
Gopeng-Dipeng

2982027   Pte Neil Devlin
7.1.42 (23) *Slim River*

70257924   C.Sgt James Ditcham
10-15.2.42 (35) *Singapore*

2982044   Pte John Docherty
13.1.42 (23)

2979966   Cpl William Doherty
14.2.42 (20) *Alexandra Hospital
Singapore*

2979747   Pte Edward Donnelly
1.1.42 *died of wounds following
Kuala Dipang action.
Grave at Taiping.*

2975321   Cpl John Duff
13.1.42 (43) *in the jungle.
Grave at Taiping*

3322778   L.Cpl George Duffield
29.12.41(21) *Telok Anson
Grave at Taiping*

3322779   Pte Ronald Dunbar
13.1.42 (27) *in the jungle*

3322782   Pte Frederick Etherington
13.1.42 (27)

3323228   Pte Robert Edgar
14-15.2.42 (27) *Singapore*

6459446   Pte William Farrell
7.1.42 (22) *Slim River*

2982225   Pte Michael Feighan
13.1.42 (24)

2879883   Pte Thomas Ferry
12.3.42 (23) *in the jungle*

2982076   Pte William Fotheringham
1.42 (22)

2979638   Pte Donald Fraser
13.1.42 (27)

3322787   Pte Owen Gartland
29.12.41 (26)
Gopeng-Dipang

2979365   Cpl Charles Gentles
13.1.42 (27)

2985986   Pte David Gibson
11.2.42 (22) *Singapore*

3322788   Pte Gordon Gibson
7.1.42 (21) *Slim River*

2979705   L.Cpl Robert Gillies
2-11.2.42 (24)

2990009   Pte James Goldie
13.2.42 (27) *Singapore*

2979859   Pte John Graham
1.3.42 (25) *in the jungle*

2979856   Pte Christopher Gray
13.1.42 (24)

2979847   Cpl William Greenan
20.12.41 (23) *Lenggong*

3322704   L.Cpl John Gray
3.3.42 *at sea*

2979280   Pte Andrew Grewar
7.1.42 (30) *Slim River*

2989018   Pte. Stephen Hall
20.12.41 (28) *Lenggong*

3322796 Pte Thomas Halfpenny
21.3.42 (27) *in the jungle*
Grave at Taiping.

2979289 Sgt Andrew Hamilton
21.1.42 (28)

2979694 Sgt Robert Hamilton
2-3.3.42 *at sea*

3322799 Pte William Harbron
14-15.2.42 (26) *Singapore*

2979998 Pte John Harcourt 13.1.42 (22)

2979749 Sgt James Hardie 7.1.42 (24)
Slim River

2979976 Pte Albert Hardie 3.42 (24)
at sea

3325256 Pte Frederick Hardy
28-29.12.41 *Gopeng*

2989508 Pte James Harkins MM
7.1.42 (28) *Slim River*

3131443 Pte John Harrison
10.2.42 (22) *Singapore*

2979655 Pte Patrick Hartford
13.1.42 (25)

3322803 Pte John Hastings
10-11.2.42 (27) *Singapore*

3053016 Pte Ralph Henderson
21.12.41 (30) *Kota Tampan*

2978069 Pte Daniel Holmes
23.12.41 *Salak*
Grave at Taiping

2978675 Sgt Victor Hookey
17.12.41 *Titi Karangan*

2979462 Cpl Sydney Hylan
7.1.42 (26) *Slim River*

3322820 Pte Harold Jackson
14.1.42 (27)

4622902 Pte Walter James
8.2.42 (33) *Singapore*

2979802 Pte George Jamieson
22.12.41 (24) *Grave at Taiping*

2975608 Sgt Donald Johnson
15.2.42 (34) *Singapore*

3322823 Pte Lawrence Johnson 12.41
Grave at Taiping

2023032 C.Sgt James Johnstone
13.1.42 (31)

2985292 Pte Hugh Johnstone
3-7.2.42 (22)
Grave at Kranji

3312150 Pte Alexander Kane
27.3.42 (26) *Ampang*

2979968 Pte William Kinghorn
14-15.2.42 (26) *Singapore*

2981100 Pte John Laidler
29.12.41 (23)
Gopeng-Dipang Grave at Taiping

3322835 Pte John Lowes
21.12.41 (27) *Kota Tampan*

2979647 Pte John Lyons
13.1.42 (21)

2978565 Cpl James Marshall
1.6.42 (28) *in the jungle*

2990102 Pte David Marshall
1.1.42 (28)

2992064 Pte John Martin
13.1.42 (20)

3322716 Pte Archibald Martin
7.1.42 (27) *Slim River*

3322838 Pte George Maugham
18.3.42 (27)

2979914 Pte Alexander Milne
14.1.42 (28)

2984381 Pte William Montgomery
6.1.42 (21)

2986020 Pte J. Murray
13.1.42 (32)

3318447 Cpl Douglas Morris
13.2.42 (22) *Singapore*

2979781 L.Cpl Charles Munro
13.1.42 (30)

2980831 Pte Neil Munro
13.1.42 (22)

2974761 Pte James Murray
13.1.42 (32)

2979810 Pte Michael McArdle
12.4.42 (24) *Grave at Taiping*

2979951 Pte James McArthur
3.1.42 (25) *Grave at Taiping*

2974440 Pte Duncan McArthur
13.2.42 (34) *Singapore*

2982068 Pte Daniel McAuley
20.12.41 *Lenggong*
Grave at Taiping

2984610 Pte Philip McCafferty
1.1.42 (24)

2967356 Pipe Major John McCalman
16.2.42 (29)

2985938 Pte Richard McColl
7.1.42 (22) *Slim River*

2972296 CSM Archibald McDine
20.12.41 (34) *Lenggong*
Grave at Taiping

2979495 Sgt William McDonald
3.3.42 (30) *at sea*

845774 Cpl Thomas McDougall
(brother of Hugh and Alex M.)
21.12.41(25)
Kota Tampan

2980727 Pte James McDougall
20.12.41 (25) *Lenggong*

2974997 Pte Henry McEwan
31.12.41(33) *Bidor*

2979874 Pte Charles McEwan
13.1.42 (28)

2979377 L.Cpl Piper James McFadyen
6.1.42 (26)

3130595 Pte Joseph McGuire
21.12.41 (25)
Kota Tampan

2992171 Pte John McKay
25.2.42 (35) *Muntok,*
Grave at Jakarta

2980606 Pte James McKee
13.1.42 (25)

2978471 Sgt Donald McKinnon
13.1.42 (29)

2979756 Pte William McKnight
15.2.42(24) *Singapore*

2986112 Pte James McKnight
wounded 7.1.42   1.3.42 (22)
in the jungle

2979908 Pte William McLachlan
13.1.42 (24)

3326707 Pte Richard McLachlan
16.12.41 (30) *Grik*

3326708 Pte Francis McLauchlin
2.42 (30) *Singapore*

2982022 Pte John McLean
13.2.42 (22) *Singapore*

2985962 Pte John McLean
31.3.42 (23)

3318459 Pte James McLean
7.1.42 (22) *Slim River*
Grave at Cheras

2979693 Piper Charles McMenemy
1.2.42 (22)

2979732 Pte John McMurray
16.12.41 (21) *Grik Road*
Grave at Taiping

3324741 Pte Thomas McNairney
15.2.42 (27) *Singapore*

2979565 Pte John 'Big Jock' McNee
8.2.45 (26)
Grave at Jankerbos, War
Cemetry, Holland.
Escaped Singapore 2.42 but
killed-in-action in Europe

2982002 Pte Richard McNeil
10-11.2.42 (18) *Singapore*

3323250 Pte Mark McNeish
13.1.42 (26)

2977810 Pte Daniel McNicol
13.1.42 (30)

2979850 Pte Edward McParland
19.12.41 (22) *Sumpitan
Grave at Taiping*

3323251 Pte John MacPherson
15.2.42 (26) *Singapore*

2979579 Pte Robert McQueen
18.2.42 (26)

2987350 Pte William McVey
16.12.41(24) *Grik Road*

3322852 Pte Anthony Newton
11.2.42 (27) *Singapore*

2067567 Pte George O'Neill
7.1.42 (22) *Slim River*

3310709 Cpl Robert O'Neill
20.12.41 (27) *Lenggong*

2990126 Pte Hugh Orr
13.1.42 (27)

3322855 Pte Thomas Parkinson
13.2.42 (21) *Singapore*

2976637 Sgt Robert Parry
7.1.42 (28) *Slim River*

2987012 Pte William Pendreigh
2-3.3.42 (25) *at sea*

2979817 L.Cpl George Paterson
1.3.42 (27)

2146942 Pte James Pattison
20.12.41 (35) *Lenggong*

2979423 Pte James Peddie
14-15.2.42 (27) *Singapore*

2979845 Pte Walter Prow
22-27.12.41 (23) *Grik Road.
Grave at Taiping*

2974492 Sgt Thomas Purves MM
4.2.42 (36)

2985950 Pte James Robertson
11.2.42 (22) *Singapore*

3322869 L.Cpl Wilfred Renton
19.1.42 (26)

3322872 Pte William Richardson
13.1.42 *in the jungle*

2979989 Pte Peter Rodger
7.1.42 (23) *Slim River*

2978521 Pte George Rodgers
15.2.42 (28) *Singapore*

2992389 Pte John Rumbold
15.2.42 (27) *Singapore*

2979980 Pte Andrew Scott
13.1.42 (22)

2983577 Pte John Sheekey
missing 13.1.42
5.2.42 *in the jungle*

3322881 Pte Thomas Sheldon missing
16.12.41 *Grik*
17.12.41(27) *Perak River*

2568849 Pte Peter Smith
8.2.42 *Singapore*

2979459 L.Cpl John Smith
20.12.41 (26) *Lenggong*

2990167 Pte James Smith
13.1.42 (27)

2979261 Cpl William Somerville (real
surname: Pedder. He enlisted
using his mother's maiden name)
13.1.42 (27) *in the jungle*

2979263 Pte James Stewart
13.1.42 (23)

3322896 Pte Thomas Tennant
18.2.42 (27) *Singapore*

2977308 Piper Robert Thompson
29.12.41(30)
*Gopeng-Dipang.
Grave at Taiping*

2979555 Cpl Robert Thomson
2.1.42 (26) *Telok Anson
Grave at Taiping*

2979831 Pte James Thomson wounded
23.12.41 7.1.42 (24) *Slim River*

2978030 Pte John Todd 28.12.41 *Gopeng*

3322911 Pte J. 'Rocky" Wanless

	7.1.42 *Slim River*
2976557	Pte James Walker 9.2.42 (38) *in the jungle.* *Grave at Taiping.*
3327002	Pte Alexander Walker 13.1.42 (21)
3318945	L.Cpl Henry Wardle 13.1.42 (22)
2978966	Pte Joseph Warner 1.6.44 (33) *in the jungle*
2977566	Cpl James Watt 13.1.42 (27)
2979971	L.Cpl George Watt 13.12.42 (25) *Singapore*

2979166	L.Cpl James Williamson 15.2.42 (31) *Singapore*
2979166	Pte(Bandsman) David Wilson 11.2.42 (26) *Singapore* *General Hospital – mass grave.*
3322920	Pte Charles Wilson 13.1.42 (21)
2983032	Pte Albert Wynn 7.1.42 *Slim River*
2977548	L.Sgt James Young missing 13.1.42 (28). *Died in the jungle much later.*
2979919	Pte Edward Westhead missing in the jungle 17.12.41(23). *In fact died in the jungle late* *1.42.*

Those listed as died 13.1.42 were either killed at Slim River 7.1.42 or died shortly afterwards escaping Slim River. Most of those listed as *'died in Singapore'* 15.2.42 were killed between 9–11.2.42 in the Singapore fighting. The dates 13.1.42 and 15.2.42 are roll call dates.

Died in Japanese Captivity

OFFICERS

187155	2nd Lt John MacInnes 19.2.42 *Taiping gaol*
152972	Lt. Colonel James MacKellar MC 12.3.45 *Nakhon Nayok* (C.O 4 Btt. FMSVF)
	Lt WGS Morrison (from Army Officers Emergency Reserve) 18.11.43 *Chungkai*
177904	2nd Lt Robert Orr 9.7.42 (25) *Pudu gaol* *Grave at Cheras*
279794	2nd Lt George Taylor 3.3.42 (42) *Taiping gaol*

OTHER RANKS

3322720	Pte Raymond Airey 3.12.43 (23) *Thailand* *Grave at Kanchanaburi*

3130917	Pte John Allan 23.5.42 (22) *Pudu gaol* *Grave at Cheras*
2984051	Sgt James Alston 12.9.44 (27) *Maru victim*
3128682	Pte James Anderson 4.3.43 (27) *Japan* *Grave at Yokohama*
2982162	Pte William Ashcroft 9.4.45 (26) *Singapore*
3322726	Pte Edward Bain 8.6.43 (28) *Niki* *Grave at Thambyuzayat*
838872	Cpl James Balfour 11.10.43 (33) *Niki* *Grave at Thambyuzayat*
2982021	Pte Alex Baird 7.10.43 *Kanchanaburi*

3130487 Pte (Bandsman) Raymond
Bartley 20.1.45 (25) *Labuan*

13029025 Pte George Bellett
20.6.44 *at sea*

2989711 Pte Arthur Bennett
8.6.43 (28) *Thailand*
Grave at Kanchanaburi

2752163 Cpl Aubrey Bentley
3.3.42 (23) *Taiping gaol*
Grave at Taiping

2984349 Pte William Black
22.2.42 (28) *Pudu gaol*
Grave at Cheras

4981095 Pte Stanley Blatherwick
21.9.44 *Maru victim*

2978796 Cpl Edward Bonar
29.10.43 (29) *Thailand*
Grave at Kanchanaburi

2979909 Pte Alfred Booth
21.9.44 (23) *Maru victim*

13021189 Pte Henry Branson
10.1.42 (26) *Taiping gaol*

2977260 Pte Robert Brown
21.9.44 *Maru victim*

3324880 Pte James Burnett
23.8.43 *Thailand*

2989044 Pte Robert Cain
31.12.42 (28) *Japan*
Grave at Yokohama

2979504 Sgt James Calderwood
21.9.44 (31) *Maru victim*

3322843 Pte Jack Calland
21.9.44 (29) *Maru victim*

2976016 Pte John Campbell
22.8.43 *Chungkai*

3323216 Pte William Campbell
4.7.43 (26) *Thailand*
Grave at Kanchanaburi

2986248 Pte Henry Campbell
26.8.43 (25) *Thailand*
Grave at Kanchanaburi

2979195 Pte Harold Campbell
12.8.43 (28) *Thailand*
Grave at Kanchanaburi

2981967 Pte Thomas Cannon
5.7.43 (23) *Thailand*
Grave at Kanchanaburi

2979220 Pte William Carroll
1.6.43 (26) *Thailand*
Grave at Kanchanaburi

3323218 Pte James Carson
26.6.43 *Thailand*

3323405 Pte Peter Christie
27.8.42 (28) *Pudu gaol*
Grave at Cheras

2983517 L.Cpl Hector Clark
15.9.43 (25) *Hintok*
Grave at Kanchanaburi

3322698 L.Cpl Bernard Clark
28.9.43 (29) *Thailand*
Grave at Kanchanaburi

2979730 Pte Frederick Clarke
31.7.43 (31) *Thailand*
Grave at Kanchanaburi

3322763 Pte Henry Clasper
27.5.45 (31) *Japan*
Grave at Yokohama

2979739 Pte George Cochrane
21.9.44 (26) *Maru victim*

2979983 Pte William Cochrane

2979670 Pte Thomas Cornish
25.7.45 (31) *Kuching*
Grave at Labuan

225875 2nd Lt Walter Cole (formerly
MCS) 31.5.43 (36) *Thailand*
Grave at Kanchanaburi

3322766 Pte Arthur Connell
21.9.44 *Maru victim*

2982011 Pte Charles Cooper
8.6.42 (24) *Pudu gaol*

3323224 Pte Peter Corr
18.2.42 (27) *Pudu gaol*
Grave at Cheras

2031458 Pte John Crone
24.1.42 *Pudu gaol*
Grave at Taiping

3321547 Sgt Aidan Crooks (HQ 12
Indian Brigade) 6.7.44(26)
Palembang
Grave at Jakarta

2984527 Pte James Cruickshank
4.8.43 (23) *Thailand*

2979993 Pte Alexander Cunningham
21.9.44 *Maru victim*

2986637 Pte Duncan Davenport
11.4.42 (24) *Pudu gaol*
Grave at Cheras

3132101 Pte John Davidson
5.3.42 (23) *Taiping gaol*

2973393 Pte Alfred Day
21.7.42 (38) *Pudu gaol*
Grave at Cheras

3324609 Pte George Donald
10.6.43 (30) *Thailand*
Grave at Kanchanaburi

2979938 Pte James Dick
22.9.43 (24) *Thailand*
Grave at Kanchanaburi

2979294 Cpl John Dickie
21.9.44 *Maru victim*

2779587 Pte John Doran
21.9.44 *Maru victim*

2986095 Pte Joseph Duffy
21.9.44 *Maru victim*

3855072 Pte Robert Eastham
2.8.45 (28) *Singapore*

2982105 Pte William Eckford
16.9.43 (23) *Chungkai*

3053290 Pte Alexander Elliott
30.9.43 *Chungkai*

3321544 Pte William Elliott
14.4.42 (24) *Pudu gaol*
Grave at Cheras

3132866 Pte William Ewen
16.3.42 (23) *Pudu gaol*
Grave at Cheras

3322783 Pte Harry Evans
28.6.44 (30) *Thailand*
Grave at Kanchanaburi

2982014 Pte Walter Fairless
29.7.43 *Thailand*

2989492 Pte William Feenie
26.9.43 (31) *Thailand*

2191594 Pte James Ferguson
20.1.45 (27) *Brunei*

2979743 Pte John Fitzpatrick
25.6.43 (26) *Thailand*
Grave at Kanchanaburi

2979378 Pte Archibald Fletcher
31.10.42 (29) *Java*

2975265 Pte Michael Follan
9.10.43 *Thailand*

2989009 Pte Allan Forster
26.1.43 (28) *Japan*
Grave at Yokohama

2975232 Pte Alexander Fotheringham
21.6.44 (36) *Singapore*

2982090 Pte William Fraser
21.9.44 *Maru victim*

3320201 Pte Thomas Gee
21.8.43 (26) *Thailand*

2982987 Pte James Gibson
22.4.42 (28) *Pudu gaol*
Grave at Cheras

2979074 Pte Richard Gibson
21.9.44 (27) *Maru victim*

2979979 Pte Norman Gibson (brother of
Richard) 25.3.42 (18) *Pudu gaol*
Grave at Cheras

2979453 Pte. Ernest Gibson
29.6.44 (28) *Thailand*

3322789 Pte William 'Charlie' Gilbert
27.7.43 *Nong Pladuk*

2979907   Pte W.Gilchrist
30.7.43

2986406   Pte George Gilfillan
23.8.44 *Chungkai*

2979473   Pte Hamish Gordon
5.12.43 (29) *Thailand*
Grave at Kanchanaburi

2990015   Pte Robert Graham
26.12.43 (30) *Singapore*

2990343   Pte William Graham
27.9.44

4450370   L.Cpl Edward Green
15.10.45 *on the way home*
Grave at Ranchi, Bihar

2979680   Cpl James Greig
16.6.43 (26) *Thailand*
Grave at Kanchanaburi

3322792   Cpl Thomas Grieves
11.8.45

2979127   Pte John Grierson
circumstances unknown

2979769   Pte William Groom
1.3.42 (36) *Pudu gaol*
Grave at Cheras

2979264   Pte John Gwynne
8.3.42 (28) *Pudu gaol*
Grave at Cheras

2988091   L.Cpl Arthur Haddock
4.1.45 (29) *Labuan*

3322795   Pte Stanley Haddon
16.4.42 (26) *Pudu gaol*
Grave at Cheras

2979668   L.Cpl James Haggart
21.9.44 (28) *Maru victim*

3322804   Pte Hartford Hawthorn
6.6.43 *Thailand*
Grave at Kanchanaburi

4268688   Cpl George Hayes
14.5.42 (27) *Pudu gaol*
Grave at Cheras (R.C)

2979836   Pte Eric Hird
23.8.43 (29) *Thailand*
Grave at Kanchanaburi

2980883   Pte William Hislop
21.9.44 (26) *Maru victim*

2981610   Pte Peter Holmes
7.8.42 (26) *Pudu gaol*
Grave at Cheras

2819674   Pte William Hunter
15.6.42 (26) *Pudu gaol*
Grave at Cheras

2986059   Pte Alexander Innes
17.4.45 (25) *Labuan*

2979922   Cpl Albert Jackman
5.6.43 (25) *Thailand*
Grave at Kanchanaburi

2974394   Pte Michael Jardine
18.10.43 (36) *Burma*
Grave at Thambyuzayat

2974394   Pte David Johnston
12.9.43 (23) *Burma*
Grave at Thambyuzayat

2979825   Pte Charles Keenan
3.6.43 *Thailand*
Grave at Kanchanaburi

2979514   Pte David Kellock
14.10.43 (30) *Thailand*
Grave at Kanchanaburi

2979282   Pte Hector Kennedy
6.9.43 (32) *Burma*
Grave at Thambyuzayat

2984609   L.Cpl Thomas Kennedy
18.12.43 (25) *Thailand*
Grave at Kanchanaburi

2989869   Pte Dennis Kerr
25.1.42 (21) *Taiping gaol*
Grave at Taiping

3131219   L.Cpl Samuel Landsborough
(attached to CMP)
21.9.44 (23) *Maru victim*

2972823   Pte William Lawrence
2.2.42 (22) *Taiping gaol*
Grave at Taiping

3322831 Pte Charles Lee
6.11.43 (29) *Chungkai*

3324835 L.Cpl James Lees
5.6.43 (26) *Thailand*
Grave at Kanchanaburi

13021734 Pte John Lewis
3.11.43 *Chungkai*

2979221 Pte James Liddle
16.5.43 (29) *Thailand*
Grave at Kanchanaburi

2986052 Pte William Linn
19.8.43 *Thailand*
Grave at Kanchanaburi

2979352 PSM James Love
29.5.43 (32) *Chiang Rai*
Grave at Kanchanaburi

2987551 Pte John Lyon
12.9.44 (24) *Maru victim*

2989157 Pte Philip Lyon
8.9.43 (22)

2986501 Pte Alexander MacInnes
31.3.42 (24) *Pudu gaol*
Grave at Cheras

2978391 Pte Roderick MacDonald
21.9.44 (29) *Maru victim*

28224558 Pte James McCafferty
23.11.43 (27) *Burma*
Grave at Thambyuzayat

2985491 Cpl James McCall
26.1.44 *Thailand*
Grave at Kanchanaburi

2980481 Pte Gerald McCallum
11.6.43 (37) *Thailand*
Grave at Kanchanaburi

2982083 Pte James McCuaig
13.7.43 *Thailand*
Grave at Kanchanaburi

2979298 L.Cpl William McDermott
(Indep.Inf.Comp) 13.8.43 (26)
Burma. Grave at Thambyuzayat

2979872 Pte Hugh McDougall (brother,
Thomas kia) 21.9.44 (26)
Maru victim

2998076 Pte Robert McGhee
13.10.42 (24) *Pudu gaol Grave*
at Cheras

2978717 Cpl A. McGibbon
7.9.43 (21) *Thailand*
Grave at Kanchanaburi

2875111 Pte Alistair McGillivray
24.1.43 (27) *Thailand*
Grave at Kanchanaburi

3326907 Pte William McGowan
22.7.43 (23) *Thailand*
Grave at Kanchanaburi

3308928 Pte Daniel McGrath
26.9.43 (36) *Thailand*
Grave at Kanchanaburi

2987929 Pte William McHugh
10.7.43 *Thailand*
Grave at Kanchanaburi

2979722 L.Cpl Jonathan McKell
(no.2 British Casualty Depot)
6.2.44(26) *Chungkai*

2981666 L.Cpl Robert McLardie
20.1.45 (24) *Labuan*

2982017 Drummer Edward McLeod
8.2.45 (23) *Labuan*

2992030 Pte John McMillan
13.4.42 (30) *Pudu gaol*
Grave at Cheras (R.C)

2985819 Pte Alexander McMillan
3.4.42 (23) *Pudu gaol*
Grave at Cheras (R.C)

2985819 L.Cpl John McNiven
12.9.44 (29) *Maru victim*

2989540 Pte John McQueen
24.11.43 (27) *Burma*
Grave at Thambyuzayat

2981599 Pte Duncan McShane
12.9.43 (24) *Thailand*
Grave at Kanchanaburi

2989071	Pte Alfred Metcalfe 11.12.44 (30) *Labuan*
2979949	Pte Benjamin Miles 24.12.43 (25) *Thailand* *Grave at Chungkai*
3130864	Pte Thomas Mckernon 13.10.42 (24) *Pudu gaol* *Grave at Cheras*
2979852	Pte Patrick Monk 4.1.44 (26) *Chungkai*
2979965	Pte George Moreton 30.1.45 (23) *Labuan*
3321262	Pte Stephen Morrice 9.10.43 (27) *Thailand* *Grave at Chungkai*
2979632	Pte William Mowat 1.3.42 (29) *Pudu gaol* *Grave at Cheras*
2981025	C.Sgt.Archibald Moyes (from Movement Control) 13.1.45 (25) *Labuan*
2979712	Pte Joseph Muchan 31.7.43 (27) *Thailand* *Grave at Kanchanaburi*
3130745	Pte Patrick Murray 21.9.44 (27) *Maru victim*
2980559	Pte Allan Murray 18.3.44 *Chungkai*
2989074	Pte James Myers 25.11.43 (27) *Burma* *Grave at Thambyuzayat*
2974092	Pte William Neagle 1.6.43 *Thailand* *Grave at Kanchanaburi*
3324793	Pte Frank O' Brien 21.9.44 (32) *Maru victim*
3322856	Pte Charles Parry 21.9.44 (29) *Maru victim*
807088	Pte John Phillips 4.3.42 (28) *Pudu gaol* *Grave at Cheras*

2974400	CSM Alexander Porter 9.12.44(36) *Labuan*
2985536	Pte James Ralston 9.4.42 (23) *Pudu gaol Grave at Cheras*
2979990	Pte James Ramsay 18.12.42 (19) *Roberts Hospital,* *Changi, Grave at Kranji*
2979776	Pte George Rankin 1.5.45 (29) *Kuching* *Grave at Labuan*
3318432	Pte Malcolm Reardon 25.9.43 (24) *Burma* *Grave at Thambyuzayat*
2816681	Pte Robert Reid 25.6.44 *Chungkai*
2979984	Cpl Angus Rennie 29.11.44 (25) *Thailand* *Grave at Chungkai*
3322871	Cpl William Richardson 12.11.43 *Chungkai*
2979204	L.Cpl George Ritchie 22.9.44 (30) *Maru victim*
3326745	Pte Peter Robertson 1.12.43 (31) *Thailand* *Grave at Kanchanaburi*
3322876	Pte Norman Robson 21.9.44 (29) *Maru victim*
3319046	Pte George Robson 29.7.43 (24) *Thailand*
2983952	Cpl Alexander Ronald 1.1.42 (20) *Taiping gaol*
2978768	Cpl Arthur Ross 1.4.42 (24) *Pudu gaol* *Grave at Cheras*
801743	Pte David Russell 21.9.44 (33) *Maru victim*
2979806	Pte John Russell 4.3.44 (23) *Chungkai*
3322879	Pte Sydney Rutter 9.4.42 (27) *Changi*

2979681   L.Cpl Edward Scanlan
1.3.42 (30) *Pudu gaol*
Grave at Cheras

3323262   Pte Hugh Scott
10.4.42 (27) *Pudu gaol*
Grave at Cheras

2979896   Pte James Scott
27.6.43 (31) *Thailand*
Grave at Kanchanaburi

2979863   Pte William Shanks
11.12.44 (27) *Labuan*

3322882   Pte William Shields
30.5.43 (36) *Thailand*
Grave at Kanchanaburi

2990757   Pte Frank Shingler
5.3.42 (20) *Pudu Gaol*
Grave at Cheras

2979134   Pte Donald Simpson (Indep. Inf.
Company) 16.4.45 (31) *Japan*
Grave at Yokohama

2979692   PSM Hugh Sloan
11.3.42 (39) *Pudu gaol*
Grave at Cheras

2979771   Pte George Smith
1.6.42 (25) *Pudu Gaol*
Grave at Cheras

2982034   Pte William Smith
21.9.44 *Maru victim*

2979182   Sgt Norman Smith
(attached to Military Police)
16.7.45 (27) *Singapore*
Grave at Kranji

2982004   Pte John Sneddon
9.8.43 (23) *Thailand*
Grave at Kanchanaburi

2974437   Pte James Somerville
29.6.44 (36) *Thailand*
Grave at Kanchanaburi

4124675   C.Sgt Ronald Steele
1.4.42 (30) *Pudu gaol*
Grave at Cheras

2979853   Pte David Steven
17.6.43 (29) *Thailand*
Grave at Kanchanaburi

2987224   Pte William Stevenson
19.7.42 (26) *Pudu gaol*
Grave at Cheras

2979752   L.Cpl Patrick Stewart
13.9.42 (25) *Pudu gaol*
Grave at Cheras (R.C)

5567203   Sgt George Sutherland
6.3.43 (34) *Japan*
Grave at Yokohama

2966508   Bandsman Reginald Taylor MM
15.1.44 (42) *Singapore*

2926576   L.Cpl Joseph Thomson
21.4.42 (24) *Pudu gaol*
Grave at Cheras

2981450   Pte Samuel Thompson
11.2.42 (22) *Taiping gaol*

3322904   Pte Dennis Tindall
11.6.43 (28) *Thailand*

2979849   Pte George Trail
13.3.42 *Pudu gaol*
Grave at Cheras

3322905   Pte John Trench
13.2.45 (30) *Labuan*

175540   Captain Timothy Turner
(formerly SSVF) 7.6.43 (32)
Thailand
Grave at Kanchanburi

3322908   Pte Thomas Wakenshaw
1.8.42 (27) *Pudu gaol*
Grave at Cheras

3322909   Pte Walter Walford
29.3.44 (29) *Chungkai*

3322913   Pte Edward Watson
29.6.43 (28) *Thailand*
Grave at Kanchanburi

2982098   Cpl Harry White
(no.7 MRC) 10.8.45 (25)

2982154   L.Cpl Samuel Wilson
13.5.42 (23) *Singapore*

3055059   Pte Andrew Skeldon
8.9.45 (29) *in an air crash* near
Moulmein, Burma, during the
evacuation of POWs.

2977837   L.Sgt William Jack
*appears on Brigadier Stewart's
"died in captivity" list but his
grave is in Sydney, Australia;
date of death 12.12.42.*

PLYMOUTH ARGYLL ROYAL MARINES

Royal Marines who lost their lives on December 10th 1941 are not included in this list

HMS PRINCE OF WALES DETACHMENT

Killed-in-action, Died of wounds, Missing:

Marine Archibald Anderson
missing 2.42 (23) *Singapore*

Marine David Boyd
missing 13.2.42 (21)

Marine Cyril Brown
19.2.42 *Singapore General Hospital*

Marine Sidney Davis
missing 13.2.42 (20)

Sgt William Edmunds
2.3.42 (32) *at sea*

Marine Albert Fudge
2.3.42 (44) *at sea*

Marine Ernest Harry
missing 13.2.42 (21)

Marine Arnold Holland
16.2.42 (22)
Singapore General Hospital

Marine Norman Lightfoot
missing 2.42 *Singapore*

Marine Francis McNamara
14.2.42 (24) *HMS Grasshopper*

Marine Richard Morris
2.3.42 *at sea*

Marine George Passmore
13.2.42 (30) *Tyersall Park*

Marine Albert Rogers
missing 2.42 (28) *Sumatra*

Marine Peter Roy
missing 13.2.42 (23)

Sgt James Skinner
11.2.42 (24) *Bukit Timah*

Marine Victor Smart
10.2.42 (24) *Bukit Panjang*

Marine Raymond Stanford
missing 13.2.42 (21) *Singapore*

Sgt Henry Tranter
15.2.42 (33) *Tyersall Park*

Marine Thomas Wallace
missing 2.42 (25) *Singapore*

Marine George Western
13.2.42 (26)

Marine Stanley Williams
14.2.42 (18) *on the Elizabeth*

Died in captivity:

Marine Percy Back
   25.10.43 (38) *Chungkai*
   Grave at Chungkai

Marine James Benson
   9.44 *Maru victim*

Cpl John Brown
   8.7.43 Konue 11
   Grave at Kanchanaburi

Marine George Burrows
   9.44 *Maru victim*

Marine Clarence Corney
   11.3.45 *Palembang*
   Grave at Jakarta

Marine George Dalley
   13.5.43 (26) *Thailand*
   Grave at Chungkai

Marine John Davenport
   9.44 *Maru victim*

Marine Roy Davies
   30.11.42 (21) *Palembang,*

Marine John Dunn
   22.6.44 *Taiwan*

Cpl R. Fluck
   12.9.44 *Maru victim*

Marine Frederick Hannaford
   7.7.43 *Konue 111,*
   Grave at Kanchanaburi

Marine Douglas Higgins
   28.6.43 (23) *Chungkai*
   Grave at Chungkai

Marine Jack Hill
   9.8.45 *Palembang,*
   Grave at Jakarta

Marine Samuel Lomax
   4.3.45 *Palembang.*
   Grave in Jakarta

Marine David Mills
   23.9.42 (25) *Changi.*
   Grave at Kranji

Cpl Francis Murfin
   8.7.43 *Konue 1*
   Grave at Kanchanaburi

Sgt Leonard Jack Reynolds
   4.4.45 (33) *Ambon*

Marine Frederick Rossiter
   18.7.43 (23) *Thailand*
   no known grave

Cpl Edward Scantlebury
   12.9.44 (28)
   Maru victim

Marine A. Summers
   no known grave

Cpl Lionel Thompson
   7.12.43 *Thailand*
   Grave at Kanchanaburi

Marine Francis Tincknell
   17.12.43 (23) *Chungkai Grave at
   Chungkai*

Marine Richard Varty
   9.8.43 *Tarsao*
   Grave at Kanchanaburi

HMS REPULSE DETACHMENT

Killed-in-action, Died of wounds, Missing:

Marine Robert Blohm
10 .2. 42
Bukit Panjang

Marine R. Carter *missing*
13.2.42

Marine Thomas Gibbons
14.2.42 (25)
HMS Grasshopper

Marine M W Graney
28.2.42

Sgt Edward Hornby
31.3.42 (29) Tjebia island
Grave at Kranji

Bugler F.S Leavers
14.2.42 *HMS Grasshopper*

Cpl Robert McKillen
14.2.42 (23) on the *Elizabeth*

Marine S.T. Sully
31.3.42 (21) Tjebia island
Grave at Kranji

Marine J. Thomas
missing 13.2.42

Marine Cyril Tideswell
13.2.42 (19) *Tyersall Park*

Marine Robert Young
missing 13.2.42

Died in captivity:

Marine Kenneth Anthony
1.6.43 Thailand *Grave at Kanchanaburi*

Cpl Victor Buckley
29.7.43 Tamarkan, *Grave at Kanchanaburi*

Marine Samuel Duncan
19.7.43 Konue, Thailand
Grave at Kanchanaburi

Marine David Elliott
29.6.43 Tarsao *Grave at Kanchanaburi*

Marine Gordon Healey
27.5.45 Palembang
Grave at Jakarta

Marine Owen Locke
22.2.42 (28) *Muntok*
No known grave

Marine Keith Mill
26.6.43 *Thailand*
Grave at Chungkai

Cpl James Moore
11.6.44 *Palembang*
Grave at Jakarta

Marine Philip Nugus
29.10.43 *Ban Pong*
Grave at Kanchanaburi

Marine James Robinson
12.9.44 (28) *Maru victim*

The graves of these young men inevitably, grow lonelier. But wreath-laying can be arranged at anytime through the Overseas Wreath Laying Service, of the British Legion, RBL Village, Aylesford, Kent ME20 7NX, England. Or by telephoning this service at (UK) 01622 717172. This is arranged by them through the Commonwealth War Graves Commission, if necessary. A gardener and superviser (possibly with, on formal occasions, an Ambassador or Pro-consul) will lay the wreath with due ceremony. Grave plots can be traced, given some appropriate detail. A stock of wreaths is kept in each country. Present basic cost is £8.00. RBL is a charity however, so an additional donation is appropriate if possible. Photographs may be arranged.

BIBLIOGRAPHY

PUBLISHED BOOKS

Allen Louis *"Singapore 1941- 1942* Davis Poynter 1977

Alexander Stephen *Sweet Kwai Run Softly"* Merriott's Press 1995

Apthorpe D. *British Sumatra Battalion* The Book Guild 1980's

Bell Frank *Undercover University* Elizabeth Bell 1991

Boyle James *Railroad to Burma* Allen and Unwin 1990

Brooke Geoffrey *Singapore's Dunkirk* Leo Cooper, London 1989

Callahan Prof. Raymond *The Worst Disaster: Fall of Singapore* Associated University Press 1977

Chapman F. Spencer *The Jungle is Neutral* Chatto and Windus, London 1947

Chippington George *Singapore – the Inexcusable Betrayal* Hanley Swan 1992

Chye Kooi Loong *The History of the British Battalion – Malayan Campaign 1941- 42* (Richard Lane 1992)

Churchill Winston *The Second World War, Vol. IV.* Cassell 1951

Clisby M. *Guilty or Innocent?: the Gordon Bennett Case* Allen and Unwin 1992

Dunlop A.E *The War Diaries of Weary Dunlop* Nelson 1987

Elphick Peter *Singapore: the Pregnable Fortress* Hodder and Stoughton 1995

Gibbs Pancheri Paul *Volunteer!* (Self Published 1995)

Gibson Walter *The Boat* W.H. Allen, London 1974

Highland Laddie W.H. Allen, London 1954

Gordon Ernest *Miracle on the River Kwai* Collins 1963

Gough Richard *Escape from Singapore* Kimber 1987

Hayes Admiral Sir John *Face the Music* Pentland 1993

Holman Dennis *Noone of the Ulu* Oxford University Press 1984

Holmes Richard and Kemp Anthony *The Bitter End* Anthony Bird 1982

Howarth Harry *Where Fate Leads* Ross Anderson 1983

Ismay Lord *The Memoirs of Lord Ismay* Heinemann 1960

Iwaichi Fujiwara Lt. General *F. Kikan – Japanese Army Intelligence Operations in South-East Asia during WW2"* Heinemann 1983

Kinvig Clifford *Scapegoat: General Percival of Singapore* Brassey 1996

Kirby Major-General S. Woodburn *History of the Second World War Vol. 1. The War against Japan* HMSO London 1957

Lane Arthur *One God, Too Many Devils When You Go Home* A.Lane Publications 1993

Lee Kuan Yew *The Singapore Story* Times Publishing Group, Singapore 1998

Lee Cecil *Sunset of the Raj* Pentland Press 1994

Lewis T.P.M *Changi: the Lost Years* Malaysian Historical Society 1984

Lim Janet *Sold for Silver* Oxford University Press 1985

McCormack Charles *You'll Die in Singapore* Robert Hale 1954

Malcolm Lt Colonel G.I of Poltalloch *The History of the Argyll and Highlanders (Princess Louise's) 1794-1949*

Maxwell Sir George *The Civil Defence of Malaya* Hutchinson and Co.

Middlebrook Martin and Mahoney Patrick *Battleship* London 1977

Mitchell Keith *Forty-two Months in Durance Vile* Robert Hale 1997

Morrison Ian *Malayan Postscript* Faber and Faber 1942

Ong Chit Chung *Operation Matador* Times Academic Press, Singapore 1997

Patterson George *A Spoonful of Rice with Salt* Pentland 1993

Percival Lt.General A.E. CB DSO OBE MC *The War in Malaya* Eyre and Spottiswoode 1949

Operations of Malaya Command 1941-2: General Percival's Report (London Gazette 1948)

Pool Richard *Course for Disaster* London 1987

Poole Philippa *Of Love and War* (the letters and diaries of Captain Adrian Curlewis and his family 1939-1945) London 1983

Rose Angus *Who Dies Fighting* Jonathan Cape, London 1944

Simson Ivan *Singapore: Too Little too Late* Leo Cooper, London 1970

Stewart Brigadier I.M *The Thin Red Line: 2nd Argylls in Malaya* Nelson 1947

Stubbs Ray S. *Prisoner of Nippon* Square One Publications 1995

Titherington Arthur *One Day at a Time* Self Publishing Association 1993

Ward Ian and Modder Ralph *Battlefield Guide: the Japanese conquest of Malaya and Singapore* Media Masters, Singapore 1989

Wardrope Thomas *Sayonara Mine Enemy* Excaliber Press, London 1995

Wilson Duncan *Survival was for me* C.G. Books Ltd.Wigtown 1991

Wyett John *Staff Wallah at the Fall of Singapore* Allen and Unwin 1996

PUBLISHED ARTICLES, NEWSPAPERS ETC

A Tale of Two Regiments by **Captain R. Lang RM** 'Globe and Laurel' 1945

The Last of the Plymouth Argylls by QMSgt T. Webber 'Globe and Laurel' 1965

Memoirs of VJ Day by Major C.D.L. Aylwin 'Globe and Laurel' 1985

The Stirling Observer newspaper 1941–1946 – various articles.

The Thin Red Line (Regimental journal Argyll and Sutherland Highlanders) 1946-1997 – various articles, letters and obituaries including 1946 report on the 1st post-war Argylls reunion and Hayes' BBC radio broadcast)

The Times Newspaper: *Obituary to Brigadier I. McA. Stewart,* March 23rd 1987 and 1941–2, 1945–6.

The Straits Times (Singapore) 1939–1942, 1945–1946

840 Red Poppies by C.Sgt A. Webb 1986

When liberty came to the jungle by David Smiley (The Sunday Telegraph August 20th 1995)

More Plymouth Argylls by J.G.M. (an article in The Thin Red Line)

Scottish T.V. series *Scotland at War*

UNPUBLISHED SOURCES:

Record Book of the 2nd Argylls in Malaya by QMS George Aitken, and various documents and letters relating to the 2nd Argylls in Malaya (Argyll and Sutherland Highlanders archive/ museum, Stirling Castle)

The Causeway and Singapore Island by David Wilson (written at Dimapur Rest Camp 9.42).

The Bridge at Seremban by David Wilson (1995 recollections)

Report from Captain R.G.S. Lang RM 19.11.45 (RM Museum Archive)

The Papers of Major C.D.L. Aylwin RM (Imperial War Museum)

The Epic of Alexandra Military Hospital by Cpl R.T. Warn, and a similar account by Dick Lee RA (1997)

The Matter of a Massacre Alexandra Hospital Singapore 14th/15th February 1942 by Peter Bruton 1989.

HMS Prince of Wales RM Plymouth Division 1941-1945 and *HMS Repulse RM Plymouth Division 1941-1945* by Peter G. Dunstan 1990 and 1995.

The Forming of the Plymouth Argylls by Peter G. Dunstan 1989.

Jungle Journey, a manuscript deposited at Stirling Castle by Malaysian historian Chye Kooi Loong.

The Volunteer Forces: Private memoirs, correspondence, public documents, interviews with Colonial civilians and members of the Volunteer Forces of the former Straits Settlements and Malaya by Audrey Holmes McCormick

Correspondence with Argylls and Marines: Jon Moffatt.

Interviews and correspondence: Argyll and Sutherland Highlanders Audrey Holmes McCormick 1997-1999

The Old 93rd – Malayan Campaign, a manuscript deposited at Stirling Castle by an un-named author.

The Diary of Rev. Henry C. Babb (Padre, East Surreys) – a copy of the original in the possession of Dick Lee.

Adventures of a Royal Marine – the Evacuation by Peers Crompton.

War Diary of No.1 Independent Infantry Company by Major S.P. Fearon.

(PRO CAB 106/36)

Various papers donated by Major D. Montgomery-Campbell.

Reminiscences of the Malayan Campaign by R.H. Beattie and an account of his escape from Singapore written for the author 1998.

Lanchester Six Wheel Armoured Cars by Raymond Surlemont.
(Armoured Car Journal March 1992)

Memoirs of Guy Hutchinson, JVE Cambridge University Library, Royal Commonwealth Society Collection.

Diary of Harvey Ryves, Kuala Kangsar Police 1941 (Imperial War Museum).

Interview with Douglas Broadhurst (Singapore National Archives)

Diary of an unknown FMSVF officer (Singapore National Archives)

POW notes by C.R. McArthur (A&SH Archive, Stirling Castle)

INDEX

ACTION - 2ND BATTALION:

Bukit Timah, Singapore, 118-138, 153

Chemor, 54, 67, 68, 69

Gopeng-Dipang, 54, 69-74

Kampar, 75

Kroh/Grik Road, 45-47, 54-57

Lenggong & Kota Tampan, 62-68

Slim River/Trolak, 79-95

Sumpitan, 54, 61, 62

Telok Anson/Bidor, 74-76

Titi Karangan, 48, 49, 52, 53

Adamson, Sgt D., 40, 174

A & S H, 2nd Battalion (Old 93rd),
Regimental history, 1, 6, 11, 12, 20, 159

Aitken, QMS George R., 40, 180, 194

Alexander, Mne, 136

Alexander, Cmdr C. C. RN, 145, 156,
161

Alexandra Barracks, 3, 22

Alexandra Hospital, 72, 102, 120, 122,
126, 131, 147, 186, 191

Alexandra Hospital massacre, 128-130,
155, 199

Andes, 14

Ando, Col Tadao, 45, 65

Angus, 2nd Lt Stewart, MCS Argylls,
100, 101, 196

Anderson, Pte J., 69, 127, 128, 156, 158

Aquarius, 143

Argyll temporary commissions, 100

Armoured Cars, 23, 24, 32, 33, 35, 40,
41, 43, 44, 49, 52, 53, 57, 59, 61-63,
69, 71, 74, 75, 79-81, 83-86, 89, 97-
107, 111, 114, 116, 119-122, 126,
127, 132, 133, 174, 193

Armstrong, 2nd Lt R., 65

Asaka Maru formerly known as
Glasgow Belle, 177

Aylwin, Captain C. RM, 111, 114, 116,
119, 120, 134, 135, 139, 154, 160,
180, 181, 186, 187, 195, 196

Babb, Padre H., MBE, 158, 177

bagpipes, 3, 9, 12, 13, 17, 21, 22, 52, 94,
97, 101, 102, 106, 107, 118, 153,
154, 164, 192, 195, 200

Ban Tsan Chuan, Pte MM, 72, 91, 108

Banka Straits, 136, 143, 145, 146

Bannatyne, Pte W., 178

Bardwell, Capt M. E., 4, 17, 40, 53, 62,
73, 90, 115, 116, 120, 200

Barnardos/orphan boys, 4, 101, 157, 174

Barnes, Mne Tom, 136

Barron, E. A. 'Sonny', Frontier Patrol
FMSVF, 55, 58

Bartlett, Capt J. E. A. RAMC, 89, 100,
120, 129, 130

Batory, 14, 15

Batu Caves, 66, 87, 89, 93-95, 97

Baxter, Sgt R., 72, 74

Beattie, Padre R. H., 15, 17, 21, 27,
29, 63, 67, 72, 74, 80-82, 84, 89,
97, 99, 100, 102, 119, 137, 138,
144, 145, 191

Beckett, Capt R. H. C., 4, 22, 40, 48,
87-89

Belfast, 195

Bell, Lt F. E., 27, 65, 149

Bell, Pte Jockie, 4, 8, 11, 16, 24, 25, 28,
37, 47, 66, 68, 71, 82-86, 90-92, 153,
157, 158, 163, 165, 171, 179, 185,
192, 193, 200, 201

Bell, Pte John, 68, 190

Bennett, Lt Gen Gordon H, AIF, 98, 105,
117, 118, 145, 148, 150

Bennett, Pte J., 87, 95

Benny, Pte H., 58

Bentley, Cpl A, 25, 57, 58

bicycles, 46, 58, 89, 91, 137

Bing, CSM A., 16, 40, 69, 70, 131, 133, 143, 197

Biggarstaff, CSM A., 8, 40, 65

Blackwood, Capt F. M. P., 27, 37, 98, 104, 118, 122, 132, 134, 151, 152

Boon Pong Siri Vejjabhandu, 173

du Boulay, Noel, FMSVF Argylls, 100

boy soldiers, 3, 4, 8, 9, 28, 81, 94, 110, 122, 158, 190

Boyle, Capt J. D. L. , MC, 4, 7, 16, 17, 29, 38, 40, 49, 61, 66, 84, 86, 87, 89, 90, 91, 108, 157, 162, 163, 181-183, 189, 199

Bremner, Lt E. G., 122

Broadhurst, Capt D., Police Argylls, 47, 63, 67, 75, 80, 81, 88, 89, 93, 94, 151, 153, 196

Brooks, Sgt T. RM BEM, 110, 120, 132, 138, 161, 179

Calderwood, 2nd Lt R. W., Police Argylls, 100, 101, 201

Cameron, Pte A. 'Civvie', 3, 9, 28, 62, 83, 153, 155, 159, 168, 184, 194

Campbell of Lochnell, 6

Campbell, Maj H. A., SOE, 151

Campbell, Pte R., 137, 148

Campbell, Sam, surgeon, 126

Canteen Singers, 28

Carroll, Pte H., MM, 108

Carruthers, Sgt A., 25, 27, 202

Carter, Pte J. 'Nick', 4, 18, 21, 28, 67, 129, 155, 171, 184, 191, 201

Catto, Sgt N., 24

the Causeway, 63, 64, 103-107, 111, 117, 195, 197, 199

cemeteries, 26, 74, 102, 157, 159, 177, 178, 199, 201

Chapman, F. Spencer, 34, 36, 46, 90, 95

Chapman, Pte F., 148

Christie, Pte J. 'Crasher', 158, 194

Chye Kooi Loong, 119, 136

cigarettes, 14, 29, 86, 93, 94, 123, 136, 155, 161, 167, 169, 173, 183, 186, 193

clubs , 10, 24-31, 37, 43, 82, 101, 116, 127, 131, 156, 174

Coffey, Mr, 47

Cole, 2nd Lt W., Dato, MCS Argylls, 100, 170

Colliston, 2nd Lt J. J., 88, 92

Colvin, PSM F., 40, 65, 90, 95, 108, 147, 148, 191

Connelly, Sgt A., 58, 191

cookhouse/cooking, 4, 67, 91, 92, 153, 155, 164, 169, 176, 182, 186

Crompton, Mne P., 120, 130, 135, 136, 146, 184

Dalley, Col J., 101

Darroch, Sgt A. D. DCM, 24, 71, 74, 108

Davis, Lt R. J. L. RM, 111, 112, 116, 120, 122, 133, 134, 161, 162, 195

Deakin, Lt Col C., 32, 80

Dillon, Col F. IASC, 151

Doherty, Capt J. S. 'Doc' QM MBE, 5, 8, 9, 40, 60, 67, 74, 85, 97, 100, 101, 108, 134, 164, 165, 183, 189, 194, 199

Doherty, Cpl W., 5, 121, 122, 128, 129, 199

Drummond Hay, Capt D., 80, 84, 88, 162

Duchess of Bedford, 10

Duckworth, Padre N., 158

Dunstan, Mne Peter G., 110, 114, 116, 121, 127, 155, 156, 161, 179, 183, 184, 189, 196, 200

Eckford, Pte W., 25, 67, 154, 171

Edwards, Mne Maurice, 114, 115, 118-120, 123, 127, 131, 134, 154, 156, 161, 162, 173, 175, 182, 184, 189, 196

Edwards, Pte S., 178

Egra, 3

Electra, 110

Elliot, Maj 'Scruff', 17

Elliott, Col C. M. L. AIF, 145

Erskine Hospital, 198, 200

escape route, Sumatra, 144, 145, 151

Esprit de corps, 6, 11, 16, 115, 130, 164, 202

Evans, Sgt P., 7, 8, 22, 40, 66, 67, 127, 131, 151, 154, 155, 178

Express, 110

families, 4, 16, 22, 93, 100, 115, 137, 138, 145, 189, 190, 191, 194, 196, 200, 201, 202

family regiment, 5, 91

Farquhar, Cpl H., 137

Farquhar, Maj N. P., 191

Fearon, Maj, 1st Independent Coy, 60, 75

Ferguson, Pt D., 8, 11, 13, 14, 16, 17, 19, 21, 22, 24, 25, 27, 28, 37, 55, 62, 66, 67, 75, 81, 102, 104, 114, 121, 126, 137, 154, 155, 167-169, 171, 172, 174-176, 180, 183, 185, 186, 192, 193

fifth column, 22, 24, 35, 43, 52, 70, 71, 84, 106, 111

Fitzpatrick, Pte S. J., 165, 174

Fleming, RQMS J., 8, 40, 101

Flynn, Cpl J., 178. 179, 191

food, 7, 9, 25, 55, 69, 74, 80, 90-95, 119, 131, 134, 135, 144, 146, 149, 155, 156, 158, 163, 166-168, 170, 172, 174-178, 182, 183, 185, 186

Fuller, Maj-Gen J. F. C., 2

Gairdner, Maj K. D. 'Mali', 28, 40, 49, 54, 63, 67, 72, 75, 81, 82, 153, 157, 190, 199

Garner, Mne J., 136, 137

'Geordie' Argylls, 1, 16, 148, 174

Germans, 49, 52, 59, 64, 89

Giang Bee, 143, 145

Gibbs Pancheri, 26, 102

Gibson, Cpl W. G. 'Hoot', 37, 87, 88, 91, 92, 94, 151-153

Gilfillan, Pte G., 18

Gispert, Lt A. S., FMSVF Argylls, 100, 101, 105, 106

Glasgow, 20

Gordon, Capt E., 4, 8, 9, 17, 27, 40, 48, 52, 53, 102, 107 108, 115, 145, 151, 160, 165, 169, 170, 175, 176, 180, 183, 189, 190, 191, 197

Gordon, 2nd Lt I., 89

Graham, Lt Col W. J., 10

Grasshopper, 135, 136

Gray, L/Cpl J., 93, 94, 151-153

Gray, L/Cpl W., 52, 53

Green, L/Cpl E. 'Dodger', 174, 189

Green, Walter RAF, 115, 144

Greenfield, Lt Col H., 4, 10, 101

Greig, Cpl J., 30

Grey, L/Cpl J., 158

Hall, Bon AIF, 174

Hall, Chief of Police CWD 'Bill', 46, 47

Harcourt, Pte J., 24

Hardie, Drummer Pte A., 48, 52, 53, 107, 134, 152, 198

Harkins, Pte J. MM, 108

Hayes, Lt J. RN, 103, 105-107, 198

Heath, Lt Gen Sir Lewis, 45, 46, 79, 98, 105, 149

Hedley, Lt J. JVE, 153

Heeps, Pte D., 21, 63

Hendry, Capt G. B. 'Bal', 14, 15, 21, 26, 34, 52, 62, 69, 73, 75, 108, 146, 158, 197

highland dancing, 28, 164

Hobart, 145

Hoggan, Pte A. MM, 71

Holmes, Lt Col E. B. MC, 10

Holmes, Pte Peter, 158
Howarth, Fusil H., 164
Hulton, Lt G. RM, 110, 116, 132, 195
Hunter, Pte J., see photographs
Hyslop, Maj J., 67, 160, 183, 189

illnesses, *see also treating disease*, 17, 58,
  89, 91, 92, 94, 95, 120, 145, 155-158,
  160, 161, 166, 170-173, 175, 177, 189,
  191, 193, 194, 200
Indomitable, 109
Indragiri River, 136, 144
Ipoh, 44-46, 58, 67, 68, 72, 79, 101

Japanese army units, 43, 45, 65, 66, 68,
  69, 75, 107, 129
Java, 28, 133, 135, 144-146, 148, 149,
  152, 153, 171, 183, 185
Jennings, Cpl J. 'Big' MM, 101, 108
Joan, 147
Johnstone, CQSM J., 40, 87, 115
Johnstone, Mrs. Jessie, 115
Jupiter, 199

Karagola, 3
Kedah, 143, 151
Kennard, Maj R. W. MC, 17, 20, 40, 46,
  47, 54-56, 63-65, 108, 147, 199
Kerr, Sgt Rab, 94, 150, 175, 185
kilts, 12, 14, 19, 20, 104, 114, 169,
  170, 190
King, Sgt J. RM, 118, 135, 145, 147, 189
King, Cpl R., DCM, 24, 52, 57, 59,
  64, 83, 108, 147, 148, 174, 178, 185,
  189, 193
Kirk, Pte J., 148
Kirkwood, Capt P. IAMC, 138, 144
Krohcol, 45, 46
Kuala Lumpur, 23, 25, 38, 44, 74, 79,
  80, 87, 92-94, 97, 100, 101, 112, 157
Kuala, 143
Kudat, 112

Lang, Capt R. G. RM, 110, 111, 113,
  114, 116, 119, 123, 132, 133, 134,
  139, 154, 161, 176, 177, 180, 189, 195
Lapsley, Capt I. 'John', 5, 31, 75, 81, 88,
  89, 91, 92
Lavender Street, 25, 26, 28
Layton, Vice-Adm Sir G., 110
Leadbetter, Mne H., 135
Leadbetter, Joe, 171, 191
Leach, Capt John, see photograph
Leahy, 2nd Lt J. B., Police Argylls, 100,
  123
Lee, Sgt Cecil, 105, 106
Lee Kuan Yew, 154
Lee, R. Don-R RA, 128, 171-173
Lees, Maj R., 165
Locklin, Sgt T. RM, 118, 179
Lonsdale, L/Cpl J. L., 5, 16, 52, 64, 118,
  127, 131, 148, 165, 179
Love, Lt J., MCS Argylls, 100, 127, 196
Love, PSM J. 'Jimmy', 22, 55, 58, 80
Lyon, Capt Ivan, 151

MacDonald, Maj A., 4, 10, 89, 122, 132,
  134, 135, 151, 152
MacDonald, Tom, 84, 86, 90
MacDonald, Sgt W., 71, 134, 151, 152
MacKellar, Lt Col James 'Gertie' FMSVF
  Argylls, 11, 32, 113, 182
Mackie, Capt J. B., 150
MacLean, 2nd Lt K., 64, 73
MacMillan, Lt Gen Gordon 'Babe', 194

MALAYA COMMAND:
Australian Imperial Force (AIF), 75, 76,
  98, 103, 106, 112, 117, 132, 144,
  150, 161, 184
British Battalion, 69, 74, 75, 133, 158
Dalforce, 117, 119, 150
East Surreys, 36, 69, 74, 75, 129, 158,
  173, 181

135th Field Regiment RA, 162, 163

137th Field Regiment RA, 69, 75, 85

155th Field Regiment RA (formerly Lanarkshire Yeomanry), 85, 87

FMSVF, 32, 34, 55-58, 69, 74, 98, 102, 104-106, 123-129

Gordon Highlanders, 10, 24, 38, 103, 149, 151, 165

Gurkhas, 62, 69, 74, 81, 85, 87

Hyderabads, 19, 21, 32, 35, 44, 47, 57, 69-71, 75, 80, 81, 85, 86, 89

1st Independent Company, 36, 57, 61, 62, 65, 75, 111, 113

Johore Volunteer Engineers, 32, 118, 130, 153, 167

Kedah Volunteer Force, 86, 87, 100

Leicesters, 54, 58, 69, 74, 75, 167

Malay Regiment, 17, 27, 137, 196

Malayan Volunteer Field Ambulance Corps, 108

Manchesters, 10, 27, 29, 102, 154

Punjabs, 32, 34, 35, 44, 45, 47, 48, 57, 63-65, 70, 72, 75, 80, 81, 85, 88, 89, 117

SSVF, 23, 26, 35, 102, 137

Malaysian National Anthem, 29

Malcolm, Lt Col G. I., 6

Malcolm, Sgt W., 108

Mata Hari, 135, 136

Matsui, Lt Gen Takuro, 43

McArthur, 2nd Lt C. R., FMSVF Argylls, 100, 101, 120, 150, 156

McCuaig, Pte J., 27, 171

McCutcheon, Pte J. 'Big', 38, 87, 165, 191

McDine, CSM A., 21, 27, 40, 56, 65, 108

McDougall, Sgt A., 5, 6, 10, 18, 25, 27, 29, 31, 49, 65, 68, 70, 71, 82, 94, 158, 168, 174, 175, 178, 190, 191

McDougall, Pte H., 5, 178

McDougall, Pte J., 5

McDougall, Cpl T., 5, 65

McDougall, Pte Wm., 5, 22

McFadyen, Pte J., 25, 114, 158, 174

McGregor, Pte T. 'Skin', 27, 65, 83, 92, 107, 166

McLachlan, Pte F., 83, 107, 159, 160, 190, 191

McLean, 2nd Lt J., 5, 16, 26, 70, 73, 170, 171, 199, 200

McLean, Piper, 106, 195

McLean, Lt W., Police Argylls, 4, 100, 101, 195

McLeod, Lt K. I., 8, 13-15, 17, 20, 21, 34, 52, 80, 81, 84, 88, 89, 92, 162, 163, 171, 173, 183, 189, 194, 200

McNaught, CSM H. 'Hoostie', 22, 27, 28, 36, 40, 86, 90, 114, 158, 191, 192, 200, 202

McPhee, Sgt A. L. 'Sandy', 5, 65

McPhee, Cpl Duncan, 5, 65

McPhee, Sgt M. M. 'Malkie', 5, 62, 71, 108

McPherson, Mne J. DSM, 116, 136, 137, 196

McRitchie Reservoir, 127

McTavish, CSM A., 7, 13, 29, 40, 81-83, 90, 158, 169, 181, 183, 184, 189, 200, 201

McTavish, Rose, 22, 115

McVey, Pte T., 5, 18

Meldrum, Capt RAMC, 155, 171, 191

Miller, Cpl C. T. RM, 110, 123, 127, 134, 154, 156, 159, 177, 178, 183, 195, 196

Moir, Brig R. 'Bobby' DSO MC FMSVF Argylls, 32, 98, 112

Montgomery-Campbell, Lt D. G., 5, 16, 18, 23, 24, 33, 34, 40, 43, 54, 59, 79-82, 86, 87, 89, 91, 95, 147-150, 166, 185, 190, 191, 200

Montgomery, Field Marshal, 198

Moon Over Malaya, 29, 158

Moorhead, Lt Col Henry 3/16th Punjabs, 45-47, 70

Morrisson, Lt W. G. A., ex Officers Reserve, 100

Moss, Capt Eric 'No Socks', 6, 9, 10, 13, 17, 19-22, 24, 27, 28, 30, 36, 37, 44, 45, 52, 76, 99, 101, 102, 121, 137, 138, 154, 155, 159-161, 164, 166, 167, 169, 171, 181-183, 194, 197, 200, 202

Mowat, Pte G. SSVF, 137, 158

Mundie, Lt R. H., 100, 133

Munnoch, RSM A. R. 'Sandy', 6, 10, 40, 48, 53, 72, 74, 107, 108, 127, 131, 171, 174, 177, 190, 194, 199

Murray, Pte F., 18, 137

Murray, Pte J., 147

Murray, Pte G. M. 'Schnozzle', 175

Murray-Lyon, Maj Gen D., 45, 67

Napier, Lt D. J., 80, 84, 87, 89, 97, 100, 127

Nishimura, Lt Gen, 66

Noone, Lt Pat, FMSVF Frontier Patrol, 34, 35, 47, 57, 58

Noone, Lt Richard, FMSVF Frontier Patrol brother to Pat, 34, 47, 56

Noor Mohammed, 13

Nunn, Sgt R. RM, 119, 134

nurses, 27, 102, 116, 129, 138, 143, 144

Nuttall, Sgt H. W. 'Harry', 24, 85, 86, 98, 99, 101, 102, 107, 108, 122, 200

O'Callaghan, 2nd Lt J., Kedah VF Argylls, 100, 101, 123

Orion, 16

Overington, Cpl N., RM, 121, 155, 161, 180, 195

Padang, 137, 144, 145, 147, 150-153, 156

Pangkor, 144

Paris, Brig A. MC, 32, 36, 47, 53, 67, 79, 97, 100, 114, 117, 121-123, 127, 132, 134, 147, 151, 152

pay, 3, 4, 14, 22, 25, 26, 91, 168

Pekan Baroe airfield, 147

Penang, 31, 48, 113, 126, 160, 199

People's Journal, 95

Percival, Lt Gen Arthur MC DSO, 19, 35-37, 43, 45, 79, 105, 112, 113, 117, 138, 149, 150, 160

pets, 17, 18, 21, 32, 170

phantom bugler, 26, 28

Phillips, Admiral Sir T. KCB, 109, 110

Plymouth Argylls, history, 113

Pool, Lt R. RN, 150, 161

Port Dickson, 37, 38, 43, 44, 90, 93, 95

Porter, CSM A. 'Sonny', 37, 149

Porter, Pte D., 24

Porter, Mne, 136

POW CAMPS/PRISONS

Ban Pong, 161, 162, 168, 174, 177

Changi, 3, 37, 84, 94, 127-129, 149-151, 154-156, 160-162, 164, 183, 184

Chungkai, 161, 164, 174-178, 194

Glugor, 153

Kanchanaburi, 160, 161, 165, 181

Kinsaiyok, 164

Konyu, 162, 173

Kranji, 159

Kuching, 149, 150, 166, 184, 185, 190

Nakhon Pathom, 182, 185

Outram Road, 94

Padang, 150, 153

Palinbang, 135, 143, 147, 189

Pudu Jail, 87, 92-94, 137, 157-159, 162, 181, 200

Pasir Panjang, 137

River Valley, 159

Songkrai, 163

Tamarkan, 162-165, 175, 179, 180, 181, 184

Tamuang, 163, 182

Tanjong Priok, 148, 149, 152

Tarsao, 161, 162

Tha Muang, 179

Thambyuzayat, 162, 165

Tonchan Springs, 171

Wampo, 59

Waterfall, 171, 191

Wood Camp, 171

Port Dickson army camp, 37, 38

prahu, 147, 151

Presbyterian Church, Orchard Road, 29

Primrose, 2nd Lt I. M., 22, 27, 54, 64, 82, 85, 86, 108, 159, 163, 170, 200

Prince of Wales, 43, 45, 102, 109-111, 114-116, 132-136, 143, 145, 156, 160, 178, 179, 195, 196, 201

Purves, Sgt T. MM, 101, 108

Puteh Bin Awang, 57, 58

rations, 7, 18, 23, 33, 34, 67, 127, 166, 167, 175, 182, 191

regimental silver, 6, 20, 115, 159, 160, 194, 195

Repulse, 43, 45, 102, 103, 109, 110, 112, 113, 115, 116, 134-136, 143, 150, 162, 177, 184, 185, 195, 196, 201

Reynolds, Sgt J. RM,135

Roberts, Pte S., 64, 66, 70, 81, 89, 92, 158, 179

Robertson, Cpl, 86, 90, 91, 95, 148

Robertson, Lt Col L. B. 'Uncle', 37, 80, 87, 89, 91, 95, 152, 165

Robertson, Pte J., 126, 127

Robertson, Sgt R. MM, 108

Roberts Hospital, 3, 129, 155, 161

Rose, Maj A. J. C., 6, 10, 21, 30, 35, 37, 38, 45, 58, 64, 69, 88, 100, 103, 104, 106, 108, 112, 113, 115-118, 123, 132, 133, 143, 144, 197

Roseforce, 111-113

Ross, Pte A. 'Lanny', 27, 28, 171

Roy, Capt A. RAMC, 74, 173

Russell, Pte Joe, 107, 122, 126, 155, 165, 172, 192, 201

sampan, 38, 63, 69, 90, 105, 137, 148

Schiach, 2nd Lt D. G., 14, 15, 63, 71-73, 83, 102

Scout, 136, 145

Searcher, 187

Setia Berganti, 151

Sheffield, 195

Sheridan, Lt G. RM, 116, 118, 126, 161

Simpson, Drum Maj Jack 'Busty', 164, 179

Simson, Brig Ivan, 79

Singh, Lt Col Garbuk 'Gearbox', 119

Siow Ah Kiew, 93, 94

Skinner, Sgt A., 55, 58, 178

Skinner, Sgt J. RM, 123

Skinner, Capt C. G., 162

Slessor, Capt Tam, 9, 40, 60, 74, 83, 97, 107, 114, 133, 138, 154, 160, 180-182, 184, 199

Smart, Mne V., 120

Smith, Davy 'Smudger', 26, 28, 126, 158, 193
  Possibly 2 diff. men

Smith, Lt J. G. 'Nipper', 86

Smith, Lt J. H., 63, 115, 178

Spooner, Vice Admiral E. J. 'Jackie' DSO, 103, 116, 135, 145, 150

sport, 7, 9, 14, 15, 27, 28, 36, 113, 114

Stewart, Ian family history, 1-3

Stewart, Lt Col Ian MacAlister OBE MC, 1-4, 8-11, 16-19, 21, 28, 32-36, 40, 44, 47-49, 52-54, 60, 61, 63, 65, 67, 69, 73, 76, 79, 80, 85, 87, 89, 93, 94, 97-101, 103-108, 114, 116-121, 123, 126, 127, 131-134, 137, 143-145, 148, 154, 164, 173, 194-200

Stewart, 2nd Lt Neil, Police Argylls, 100, 101, 130

Stewart, L/Cpl P. 'Sophie', 27, 64, 157

Stewart, 2nd Lt Sandy, 5, 14, 15, 73, 74

Stewart, Ursula wife of Ian, 2, 145, 194, 196

Strathairn, 2nd Lt H. W., Police Argylls 100, 127, 155, 195, 201

streetfights/rivalry, 24-26, 28, 114, 163

Stuart, Piper C. 'Boy', 81, 102, 104, 106, 118, 154, 174, 195, 201

Stirling Observer, 130, 189

Stitt, Lt Col J. MC, 10, 103

Stonor, Lt I. G., 36, 37, 138, 150, 160

Sumatra POWs, 148, 150, 152, 165, 174, 184, 189, 197

tactics, Allied, 4, 8, 10, 23, 33, 34, 44, 45, 56, 61, 62, 64, 69, 98, 114, 144

tactics, Japanese, 45, 46, 58, 62, 71, 75, 87

Taiping, 34, 48, 58, 74, 86, 94, 159

Tanglin, 19, 26, 28, 30, 114, 134

Tapah, 135, 136, 145-147

Taylor, Bandsman Reg, 30

Telfer, Douglas FMSVF Don-R, 104

Tenedos, 110, 145

Tengah, 24, 115, 117-121

Tennant, Capt RN, 113

Thomas, Sir Shenton, 19, 119, 185

Thomas, Sgt W. R. RM,111, 127, 180

Thompson, Pte 'Spud', 8, 148, 154, 165, 170, 190

Possibly 2 diff. men

Thompson, Cpl L., 177

Tiddy, Mne C., 133, 134

Tiger patrols, 33, 34, 55, 61, 68, 101, 116, 123, 126

Titherington, A., 178, 179

tobacco, 149,168, 171, 176

Toosey, Lt Col P. 'Champagne', 162, 163, 165, 181, 183

training, 2-5, 9-11, 13, 15, 16, 18, 19, 23, 26, 28, 32-38, 44, 53, 68, 97, 98, 100, 102, 111, 114, 116, 117, 121, 129, 150, 173, 193, 197, 200, 202

treating disease, 92, 156, 157, 166, 170, 173-175

Truculent, 152

Turner, Capt T., 23, 24, 40, 80, 83, 88, 93, 94

Tyersall, 12, 18-22, 26, 88, 97, 99, 100, 102, 104, 107, 113, 114, 117, 123, 126, 127, 131-134, 138, 151, 153-155, 158, 170

uniform, see also kilts, 11-14, 24, 26, 32, 44, 52, 54, 80, 100, 109, 110

uniform, Japanese, 46

Vampire, 110

Verdon, Lt C. RM, 111. 116, 187, 195, 196

Wailes, Sgt J., 27, 137, 157

Walker, Pte W. 'Hooky', 28, 86, 87, 90, 114

Wallace, Sgt C. 'Bluff', 127, 137, 191

Wanless, Pte J. 'Rocky', 48

Wardrope, Pte T., 3, 38, 63, 135, 145, 147, 186, 189, 191, 192

Warn, Cpl R. T. RM, 119, 120, 160

Warren, Col A. F. RM DSC, 112, 113, 151, 156, 161

Warspite, 137

Watson, Pte D., 178, 199

Wavell, Gen Sir A., 97, 98, 132, 144,
    145, 149, 150, 194
Webber, Lt R. H., 40, 83, 86, 87, 90,
    91, 181, 191, 196
Webber, Mne T. 'Jan', 114, 121, 123,
    132, 138, 144, 160, 184
Weir, 2nd Lt D. A., Police Argylls, 100,
    101, 123, 126, 127, 155, 170, 201
Wemyss, Maj Gen W., 6
Wickens, 2nd Lt P. O., MCS Argylls, 100
Wilkie, Lt A. D., 97
Wilson, Cpl A., 24, 89
Wilson, Capt, later Brig D., 5, 7, 37,
    97-100, 103, 104, 106, 114, 117,
    119, 120, 122, 131-133, 143, 144,
    197, 198
Wyatt, John, 129, 173

Yamagida, 168, 184
Yamashita, Lt Gen Tomoyuki, 43, 66,
    121, 138, 161